WORDS OF LOVE

GARLAND REFERENCE LIBRARY
OF THE HUMANITIES
(VOL. 382)

WORDS OF LOVE
A Complete Guide to Romance Fiction

Eileen Fallon

GARLAND PUBLISHING, INC. · NEW YORK & LONDON
1984

Library of Congress Cataloging in Publication Data

Fallon, Eileen.
  Words of love.

  (Garland reference library of the humanities; vol. 382)
  Bibliography: p.
  1. Love stories—History and criticism—Addresses, essays,
lectures. 2. Love stories—Bibliography. I. Title. II. Series: Garland
reference library of the humanities; v. 382.
PN3448.L67F35   1984   809.3'85   82-49132
ISBN 0-8240-9204-X

Cover design by Laurence Walczak

Printed on acid-free, 250-year-life paper
Manufactured in the United States of America

CONTENTS

For
Godelieve Mercken-Spaas

AUTHOR'S NOTE

A book of this scope naturally requires the collaboration of a great number of people, and I was particularly fortunate in my dealings with the staff of Garland Publishing, with the members of publicity departments and editorial staffs of the publishing houses contacted for information, and with the romance writers themselves. I would like to specially thank Mary Mills, who brought my interests and background to the attention of Jeff Conrad of Garland, who initiated this project and guided it with insight and expertise. Pam Chergotis of Garland also provided vital enthusiasm and support. When I was first gathering information for the book, the aid and advice of Diane O'Connor Glynn, then Director of Advertising, Promotion, Publicity and Public Relations at Berkley/Jove, was invaluable, as was that of Anne Maitland, the Director of Publicity and Public Relations of Pocket Books, and of Joan Schulhafer, Publicity Manager of Pocket Books. Special thanks are due to my contributors, Annette Townend and Florence Stevenson, and to librarian Susan Scott of Raleigh, N.C., whose research on the historically important writers was both thorough and prompt. Kay Mussell, the author of *Women's Gothic and Romantic Fiction*, a groundbreaking scholarly investigation of the topic, not only wrote the foreword to this book but also prepared the bibliography of critical works.

Finally, the general support and comments of a number of people was crucial, and I'd most like to thank Margaret Arculus, Anne Badger, Lillian Brennan, Maureen Brennan, Maripat Dienst, Marion Chesney Gibbons, Karen Gerdetz, Vicki Heland, Susan Laity, Denise Marcil, Frank Pike and François Strauss for their contributions.

FOREWORD

Kay Mussell

In 1965, armed with a brand-new degree in English, I began teaching high school students in an Iowa small town. Although I had taken a course in adolescent literature and was prepared to be tolerant of the reading tastes of my students, my mission—I thought at the time—was to instill in them the same love of literature I had absorbed during my college years. I wanted my students to laugh at Mark Twain, to empathize with Holden Caulfield, to discover the joy of words. In short, my ideals were lofty—and entirely unrealistic.

Nevertheless, for two years I persisted by setting aside several weeks of each semester for individualized reading. "Choose your own books," I told them, "and when you have finished reading, come to me for a private conference. But you'll have to give me your book the night before so I can look it over before we meet."

Every night, I lugged home heavy shopping bags and thanked the paperback industry. Seventy-five high school juniors, even slow readers, can read at least a book a week when it's their only assignment, and I remember few individual titles after all this time. But during those two years, I caught my first glimpse of what I later came to call the "gothic underground."

Many of the teenaged girls in my class were not reading the books I remembered from my own youth, nor did they make selections from the long reading lists I passed out in class. Instead, they brought me paperback gothic and Regency romances recommended by their mothers and older sisters. Like many women, these sixteen-year-olds were enthralled by Mary Stewart, Victoria Holt, Georgette Heyer, and the other romance writers whose books were then in print in the United States.

Two years later, when I returned to full-time graduate work, my curiosity about romances led me to study popular fiction, and I began to see connections between the modern paperbacks I had read with my students and some of the novels colleges assign for class. Jane Austen, the Brontës, Henry James, Edith Wharton—all these writers and others wrote books that derived from romance conventions and that led me to examine gothic novels of the eighteenth and nineteenth centuries as sources for contemporary romance fiction for women.

During my graduate school years, I also discovered the forgotten sentimental romances of the nineteenth century, written by women for women and outselling by far the novels of Hawthorne and Melville. As literature, the works of Mrs. E.D.E.N. Southworth, Maria Susanna Cummins, and Lydia Maria Child now seem dated, but reading them today provides insight into the value system of the women who read them a century ago.

I began to see similarities between contemporary romances and the reading I had done as a teenager. Nancy Drew was as spunky and upright a heroine as any in a Mary Stewart book. The mysteries she solved were as complex as the dire plots against Victoria Holt's heroines. The teen romances of Rosamund DuJardin had many of the same qualities of appeal as category romances, and historical novels by Gladys Malvern made the past live for young girls much as those of Georgette Heyer and Anya Seton did for adults.

And yet, almost no one I knew had noticed this phenomenon of fiction for women. The bibliography of criticism for those few romances that had entered the canon of literature—*Pride and Prejudice, Jane Eyre, Pamela*—was long and complex, but only rarely did scholars relate those novels to the more ephemeral romances that women had been reading for two centuries. Popular romances of the past were virtually ignored. I located books and articles about detective stories, Westerns, spy stories, and science fiction, but I could find very little scholarly criticism of romance—or of any form of women's popular culture.

I knew that romances were exceptionally popular and that their readers were devoted. I learned that romances had been more popular in some periods of history than in others. And I noted by the early 1970s that the United States was in a phase of increased attention to the issues of contemporary women's lives that coincided with increased success of romance fiction among the public. It made little sense that women, who were now offered expanded opportunities to participate in the world at large, would choose stories about heroines whose most meaningful reward was the love of a superior man and a life of domesticity.

I began to wonder why the most popular genres of fiction for men—thrillers, hard-boiled detective stories—featured heroes who recurred from book to book, while protagonists of women's fiction, once married, were no longer interesting enough to sustain another book about their lives. As I observed demographic changes in the world around me—increases in cohabitation, earlier sexual initiation and use of contraceptives, later average ages for marriage—the heroines of the most popular books for women remained virginal and pure.

That final paradox, however, was temporary. By mid-decade, gothic romances had been replaced in the public taste by the longer, sexually explicit, and adventurous historical romances of Kathleen Woodiwiss and Rosemary Rogers. A few years later, category romances became more sophisticated to compete with the more sensual "bodice-rippers," and Harlequin began to lose its market monopoly to Silhouette, Candlelight Ecstasy, and Second Chance at Love. Despite the successes of the women's movement, the number of romance readers continued to grow.

And finally, romances were no longer an underground—and disreputable—phenomenon. Newspapers, magazines, and television caught on to the trend, and, although most media reports were condescending, at least some women no longer had to hide their reading matter in plain brown bags on the bus or sneak books into their purses.

Romances may not be great literature, but very few novels ever reach the high school or college classroom. Nevertheless, scholarship on other formulas of popular fiction—Westerns, detective stories, thrillers—exists and critical controversies abound. I can only assume that it must be more respectable to analyze and evaluate those popular formulas that appeal primarily to men, just as it is more respectable to confront male issues in virtually all disciplines. But as women's issues make inroads into the traditional curriculum, those literary expressions that are dominated by female authors and readers also deserve serious attention. Although feminist scholars have diligently recovered the work of many women writers whose works have undeservedly languished in obscurity, they have often seemed reluctant to evaluate the more commercial forms of entertainment that appeal to women. Perhaps this is true because the message of romance, on the surface, seems to threaten the new and still tenuous sense of the female self that contemporary feminism espouses. Perhaps it is merely because so many areas of female experience remain unexplored and few scholars have found time to turn to the evaluation of romances.

And that is unfortunate, because romances have been a significant aspect of female experience for more than two centuries, and generations of women have found pleasure and delight in the one literary genre that belongs especially to them. It is futile and self-defeating to try to make a case for the literary excellence of paperback romances, but that, of course, is not the issue. For a literary scholar, condescension toward mass-produced novels is appropriate, but too often that condescension spills over onto the audience for genre fiction, and the fantasy experience of women is dismissed as though it were of no importance, not even important enough to bother reading a few of the novels to find out what their secret may be.

Now that public curiosity has turned to the contemporary romance phenomenon, media reports regularly ask why romances are so popular. Over the past year, I have been interviewed by several reporters, each of whom has told me apologetically, "Of course, I don't know much about romances. I've never read one. What can you tell me?" I told one of them that he could not hope to do justice to romances unless he had read a few, and I sent him home with two books which he returned with no comment. But his report was, at least, fair to romance readers.

Other reporters express surprise when I comment that there are clear distinctions in quality among romance writers and series. But anyone who follows the field is aware that not all romances are alike. Now that it is virtually impossible for any one individual to purchase—much less read—each month's output of category romances, booksellers report that customers are choosing more selectively than ever before. Readers may try a new series for several months, but if the novels are less satisfying than old favorites, the series will not succeed—as Bantam Books learned in 1982 when it launched Circle of Love.

Perhaps the contemporary romance phenomenon will collapse of its own weight as competition and saturation winnow out all but the very best romance novels and series. Historically, romance fiction, like other popular formulas, appeals to a wide audience for a time and then declines, to emerge later in a different version. Seduction stories and gothic novels dominated fiction for several decades before and after 1800, and then romances faded for a few years before the genre was revitalized in the historical romances of Catharine Maria Sedgwick and the sentimental novels of Maria Susanne Cummins, Anna Warner, and others. Popular fiction is always ephemeral. Who today has read Mrs. E.D.E.N. Southworth's *The Hidden Hand*, or Susanna Rowson's *Charlotte Temple*, a book that was in print for more than a century?

Mary Roberts Rinehart and Edith M. Hull attracted millions of readers in the early twentieth century, as did their successors Daphne du Maurier and Mignon Eberhart, long before publishers issued romances in numbered series every month. In our own time, we have seen romances go through several distinct phases: from the gothics of the 1960s through Regency and erotic romances of the 1970s to the category romances of the 1980s.

And yet all these books however distinct from each other, are still romances, for they focus on the exquisite torture of courtship, structuring the story from the meeting of the lovers to their commitment to each other for all time. All romances tell their tales with a heroine at the center—even when part of the story is narrated from a male point of view. All romances provide models of heroines who confront those female aspects of culture—love, emotion, commitment—that are so rarely explored in mainstream fiction. Systematic analysis of this neglected genre can provide us with valuable information about the experience of women in our culture.

Until recently, those of us who sought to understand the romance phenomenon could find few sources to consult. The bibliography in this volume lists some of the most useful. *Words of Love* adds a valuable resource to that body of criticism, in its historical essays tracing romances back to their roots in Greek and medieval literature, in its careful delineation of romance formulas, and in its biographical and critical essays on many of the neglected writers who have specialized in the romance genre.

Romances may be unrealistic, but they do not devalue human emotion nor do they treat love and domesticity as if they were insignificant adjuncts to the universal issues of human life. In a culture where only male experience is a fully acceptable subject for public discussion, women's experience exists on the periphery: in soap operas during daylight hours despite rapidly increasing numbers of working women, in mainstream novels that are reviewed as "women's books" or not at all, in women's magazines that "ghettoize" female experience as if it were all cooking, and cleaning, and child care.

Romances provide an alternative entertainment for the powerless and forgotten by dramatizing and heightening experiences about which many women may be ambivalent. The cultural message to women in an age of liberation implies a classic double bind: "Have a career, live fully in the world, but don't forget your femininity. You can do it all."

And yet the culture provides few models for how these competing, complex imperatives might be carried out by individual women. Romances do not have the answer—but does any formula of popular fiction aspire to realism? I think not. Instead, romances offer women readers a model for a portion of their dilemma and an attractive fantasy about love, adventure, and sexuality with heroes who are both strong and tender.

Is the romance phenomenon really more difficult to understand or less authentic than the appeal of James Bond and "Magnum P.I.?" Or is it merely that our patriarchal culture so rarely defines female experience and female fantasy as fully relevant to the human dilemma?

I sometimes wonder about those teenagers who introduced me to Mary Stewart, Anya Seton, and Georgette Heyer. They are in their mid-thirties now, the age when romance reading approaches its highest frequency among readers. I wonder if any of them slip paperbacks by Charlotte Lamb, Brooke Hastings, and LaVyrle Spencer to their own daughters and if those teenagers share their favorite books with a much younger English teacher.

If they do, I hope she understands.

Introduction

When I was first approached by Garland Publishing about the possibility of doing a book dealing with the current romance boom, I had no idea of how little information was available for the reader of romance. As an editor in a paperback publishing house for over two years, one who had come to work more and more in the romance field, I was aware of the popularity of the genre and just assumed that there were a number of books about it, similar to the ones that dealt with mysteries and science fiction, those two other popular fiction genres. I was wrong.

To get the best idea of what could be added to an existing collection of texts, I spoke with the head reference librarian of The New York Public Library. I was informed that *nothing* was available and advised to see the library's extensive collection of books dealing with mysteries and the somewhat smaller one of science fiction references. To my surprise, I discovered that The New York Public Library owned over forty books about mysteries and that over seventy-five percent of these were copyrighted after 1970. I also learned that 1981 saw the publication of both a critical guide to horror literature and a dictionary of literary biography featuring twentieth-century American science fiction writers.

Obviously, mysteries and science fiction had attained a certain level of respectability; it was acceptable for serious people to treat them seriously. Two of the mystery references were even edited by Jacques Barzun, for heaven's sake! Keeping in mind the copyright dates of the mystery texts, I realized that a great deal of this acceptability was achieved in the wake of changes that took place in the sixties. The decade which began with the civil rights movement and ended with the women's movement, the sixties produced a mentality which questioned traditional assumptions about our cultural history. The campuses began to react to this new way of thinking; both individual courses, and in some cases, whole departments, were created to study the contributions of blacks and women to American society. Popular culture in general came to be seen more and more as worthy of critical attention. In literature, the new perspective was revealed in the offering of courses featuring science fiction and crime fiction. During this time, the critical and reference books in these fields began to appear in number.

Paradoxically, the major popular movement of American publishing from the mid-seventies to the present, the publication of a wide variety of romances, was first ignored; when it finally grew large enough that it *had* to be mentioned, it was most often in gushing or patronizing prose, in formats abounding in pink curlicues. Feminist scholars, while laudably resurrecting "lost" works of serious fiction and poetry, frequently reprinted by small, non-profit presses, emphatically shunned the popular commercial romance, seemingly denying the genre's deep roots in our literary tradition, and in the work of such fine writers as Jane Austen and Charlotte and Emily Brontë (writers who are considered to have sufficiently risen above their genre to be accepted in mainstream, i.e., male-approved, literature courses). In fact, due to an August 30, 1980 *New Republic* article critical of Harlequin romances, academic Ann Douglas became a spokeswoman of sorts for the naysayers of the currently popular "category" romances, even appearing opposite romance writer Janet Dailey on a broadcast of The Phil Donahue Show in the fall of 1981.

I don't want to sound as if I'm dismissing the opinions of those who have at least realized that romances are somehow important to our current culture and have commented on them. Yet many of them label everything produced in the genre as mediocre at best and a means of keeping women down at worst. I am sure that those who think that all romances are alike and even that all of them within a particular sub-genre are exactly the same have not read heavily in the genre. Those who are adamantly critical of the effects of romances on those who read them (an editorial in the October 1982 issue of *Mademoiselle* states that those girls who read teen romances "will not grow up to write—or to read—The Great American Novel"; one is made to speculate about the fate of those who read fashion magazines) are not aware of how much the category romance in particular has changed to meet women's new roles and demands. None of these critics, certainly, realizes just how much skill it takes to produce one of the shorter romances.

Yet if I had not worked as an editor in this field, I know that I would be among the most vocal of those critics. After all, like so many of us interested in books, I had earned a degree in literature at a university which included few women writers in the curriculum (and even fewer on the faculty); I, too, had assumed the attitude of the English department. If my job hadn't required it, I certainly would not have read even one romance, be it historical, a longer contemporary, or a category book. I'd read at least one Harlequin years ago as a teenager; similar to other critics, I'd just have assumed that nothing had changed.

But my experience in-house as an editor and my current work as a literary agent have made me realize that the above assumptions are just that—assumptions rooted in attitudes prevalent in our culture. I learned to respect the romance writer, from having worked with fine writers who had a respect for their readers and the ability to use the limitations of their particular sub-genre to advantage, making each book seem fresh—and from having tried to get publishable books from many professional writers who were absolutely incapable of producing one category book as American publishers made an effort to compete with Canadian-based, British-flavored Harlequin in a time in which the status of women in America was changing. Women no longer saw an executive secretarial position as their highest career aspiration; they were moving into new, formerly all-male fields. The American category books reflected this change—and the changing role of men. No longer silent, brooding, and arrogant, heroes in the books had to be willing to talk and to listen—and to join their lives with those of women who had definite interests, opinions, and often careers of their own.

As I witnessed these changes, the media witnessed the phenomenal growth of this field. An estimated one fourth of all books sold in the United States are romances, and *Life*, *Time*, and the *New York Times,* among other publications, have featured articles on the boom. Romance writers and fans themselves followed the lead of their science fiction and mystery counterparts and in 1981 organized the Romance Writers of America (RWA). Their first conference attracted 700 writers and would-be writers, and chapters now exist throughout the United States. Still, however, the genre is not taken seriously, the writers not respected.

Obviously, the time has come to study romance, both as a popular literary genre and as a phenomenon that says something about the culture in which it flourishes. The field is large, and the questions to be raised cannot be answered easily. I hope to break the ground for the study of this field as well as meet a growing reference need. Primarily designed for the reference librarian, this book will also be a useful tool for those with an academic interest in the field, and makes for enjoyable, informative reading or browsing on the part of the romance fan, and would-be romance writer.

It is the writers, both past and present, who are highlighted in this book. We are all familiar with the best-known of those who have written romance, authors such as Jane Austen, the Brontës, and more contemporary writers such as Georgette Heyer. More obscure is the fact that authors known for writing other kinds of books—writers such as George Eliot and Mrs. Gaskell—successfully tried their hands at romance, and the very existence of certain excellent writers—the recently rediscovered Emily Eden most readily comes to mind—is not widely known. Yet all these writers and the traditions they built upon, the sub-genres they developed, have influenced the development of the genre.

These writers important to the romance tradition and the writers working today are the major concerns of this volume. Reference librarians currently have no one source to consult when seeking information about both the "classic," acknowledged romance writers and lesser-known today but very influential writers such as Jeffery Farnol, to whom the current Regency genre owes a tremendous debt because of his influence on Georgette Heyer, or E.M. Hull, whose *The Sheik* inspired countless romances as well as some steamy silent films. Certainly no source is available to help reference librarians deal with questions about the writers of paperback romance fiction, who range from such strong historical writers as Roberta Gellis to the phenomenal Janet Dailey, a writer of contemporary romance. First published by Harlequin in 1976 (and the first American taken on by that firm), she has since sold over ninety million copies of her books, over the years moving to Pocket Books and becoming the spokeswoman for Simon & Schuster's Silhouette line of category romance—in addition to becoming one of the world's top five best-selling living writers.

After three opening chapters which deal with the place of romance in our literary tradition, the Regency romance, and the current romance boom, a guide to the romance sub-genres is provided. A writer's resource listing follows this guide, detailing information about romance writers' associations, publications, and conferences. This section is followed by a brief bibliography of recent critical works examining romance prepared by Kay Mussell of American University. Authors no longer living are then discussed in a section featuring biographic and bibliographic information. Finally, current writers, whether published in hardback or paperback, are listed. In addition to biographic and bibliographic information, these writers have answered some questions that both romance fans and those generally interested in writing will find of interest: which books and authors have influenced them, what is their philosophy of writing and of writing romance specifically, and how did they first become published and/or find an agent. The writers provide a wealth of information and entertaining, often provocative, reading. For the further convenience of the reference librarian frequently asked to suggest books in a particular sub-genre, a separate guide to authors organized by genre follows the author entries, as does a guide to the authors based on pseudonyms.

In addition to meeting a basic reference need, this book explores the important questions that the current romance boom raises about our society. It does so in the first chapter, which actually traces the development of romance in our literary tradition from the third century A.D. through the middle ages and the Renaissance, a span of time when romance was at the very center of literature, to the period in the late Renaissance and beyond when the word "romance" became more and more associated with love stories written for women—a time when romance began to move to the periphery of literature. We discover that romance has always been popular as a genre in times when the identity of the individual is in doubt, that it offers the reader comfort by underscoring the relationship that most strongly makes the individual aware of her or his worth and uniqueness. We also learn that the popular fiction genres—the mystery, the western, science fiction and romance as we now know it—are offshoots of the medieval romance. We see as well that romance is considered the poor sister of the other three and read some interesting, informed speculation as to why this attitude exists. The investigation continues in the chapter, "The Romance Boom."

In short, we're breaking ground here as well as filling a too-long-neglected reference need. Perhaps by the end of this decade, enough other volumes will have appeared so that the collections on romance will rival those on mystery, and our understanding of this genre will approach its importance throughout our literary history and its significance in our culture today.

WORDS OF LOVE

Historical Overview

Annette Townend

I. Early Romances

First a quotation. Guess where it's from:

> Chariclea followed close . . . The eye of a lover is quick as
> lightning in recognising the object of its passion—a single
> gesture, the fold of a garment, seen behind, or at a distance,
> is sufficient to confirm its conjectures. When she knew
> Theagenes afar off, transported at the long-wished-for
> sight, she ran frantickly towards him, and, falling on his
> neck, embraced him closely, breathing out her passion in in-
> articulate murmurs.[1]

"Lover," "passion," "inarticulate murmurs"—it could be
from the latest love story on sale in the supermarket—but then
there are the names: Chariclea, Theagenes. No, this is no modern romance, but one dating from the fourth century A.D.:
Heliodorus's *Aethiopica*. Things haven't changed; the emotions
depicted here and the way they are depicted have remained constant for sixteen centuries. But paradoxically the word "romance," the term that springs most readily to mind now for this
experience, has only recently come to be directly associated with
love. I used "modern" to define the romance of today; strictly
speaking, the term as we use it needs no such extra definition.
But "romance" meaning "love story" is an essentially modern
word; until the twentieth century a "romance" was a narrative
that included love but which also dealt with many other experiences.

Originally the term was a technical one and referred strictly
to the language in which the narrative was written. English critic

3

Gillian Beer summarizes the history of the term:

> . . . "romance" in the early Middle Ages meant the new vernacular languages derived from Latin, in contradistinction to the learned language, Latin itself. *Enromancier, romancar, romanz,* meant to translate or compose books in the vernacular. The book itself was then called *romanz, roman,* romance, *romanzo.* Then the meaning of the word extended to include the qualities of the literature in these tongues, in contrast to Latin literature or works composed in Latin. Thus, in old French, *romant, roman,* means "courtly romance in verse" but literally "popular book." The characteristics associated with the vernacular literature of the time were a preoccupation with love and adventure . . .[2]

Even now, the literary genre "romance" refers not to the love story but to narratives of love *and* war: "bold bawdry" and "open manslaughter" as Roger Ascham, an outraged sixteenth-century teacher, put it,[3] "sex and violence" in the more succinct modern idiom of a twentieth-century critic, Northrop Frye.[4] Dr. Johnson, the great eighteenth-century scholar, in his monumental dictionary defined "romance" as "a military fable of the *middle ages:* A tale of wild adventure of war and love." Romance has always been associated with the strange, the marvellous (in its root sense of something which causes wonder, astonishment and surprise), the mysterious. These are the qualities of the three greatest works of one of the greatest of that group of poets who wrote at the turn of the eighteenth and nineteenth centuries, a group now known as the Romantic poets. Coleridge's "Ancient Mariner," "Kubla Khan," and "Christabel," the first a tale of mysterious doom at sea, the second a dreamlike account of a rich and rare palace, the third dealing with a girl threatened by strange powers, together provide a sense of the atmosphere of traditional romance—and of why poets who on the whole wrote about anything but love are called "romantic." Are we then misguided in calling our love stories romances? Does this use limit the term too narrowly?

It does not seem so to me. The definition even of the literary genre always includes love and love is the common factor in romances from the first to the eighteenth century. Love is an individualizing emotion; to be in love is to be more fully aware of oneself and of the beloved than ever before. It is for this reason perhaps that in each of its early periods of development an upsurge of the romance coincided with a development of awareness of the importance of the individual; in fact the rise of romance is in direct response to the rise of the individual. Other fictional genres, the epic, the realistic novel, obviously deal with individuals, but where the epic—the *Iliad*, the *Aeneid*, *Beowulf*, the *Chanson de Roland*—deals with the individual as a representative of his nation and the realistic novel deals with the individual as a part of society, the romance presents the individual in isolation. The romance focuses on two people who are important to one another above all else and so give each other full identity. So our use of the term "romance" to mean "love" emphasizes an element which has been essential to the genre, has provided its primary impulse from the beginning.

There are two lines of descent for the romance: the Greek and the Medieval. The Greek romances are unique in the history of romance in that they seem to be an independent, spontaneous genre, to have no literary predecessors. It is this characteristic, of self-generation, that makes the Greek version of romance the most helpful in perceiving the origins of the genre; a literary historian is forced to look beyond the texts to the world which gave rise to them.[5] Some claims have been made for what are termed "love monologues" or "love elegies" as precursors to the romances but in fact the two genres are contemporaneous—around the first century B.C. The love monologues present lovers speaking about love—they could be incorporated into the romances as speeches by the characters—and this new emphasis on love is parallel to that displayed in the romances. Both genres are part of the same development: the concentration on the individual and her or his feelings.

To explain this development it is necessary to make a brief excursion into history, or rather socio-history. Although the Greek romances are habitually called "Greek," that is slightly misleading; they are written in Greek but are, in fact, Egyptian. Like the Alexandrian love-monologues, they are products of the Empire created by Alexander the Great before his death in 323 B.C., not literature of Greece itself, and this distinction is important. The literature of what we think of as ancient Greece, the

Greek ruins we go to visit as tourists to the Parthenon, to Delphi, was created in a country composed of small city states. The inhabitants of Athens or Sparta thought of themselves as "Athenians" or "Spartans" rather than as "Greeks." One lived in a community that was comparatively small in population— think of a town the size of Dixon, Illinois, where everyone knows or knows of everyone else—and this community operated as a unit. One's identity was bound up in that of the community. Yet when Alexander completed the work his father had begun, that of unifying Greece, and struck out across the Middle East and Asia, these communities lost their autonomy; they became part of a large whole, the Empire, with a shifting population. Instead of a stable, limited community within which one was known, by which one could measure oneself, there was now a vast anonymous sea of peoples. The individual was thrown back upon her or his own resources, forced to rely upon the self for a sense of identity. (The experience of going from a small home-town to a big city like New York or Los Angeles repeats this development in miniature.) And, in addition to the self, one was forced to rely upon love, upon one particular other. With the loss of the community to provide identity, the lover, the person who inspires a particular awareness of oneself as a special individual, becomes all the more important. It is this experience that is recreated in the Greek romances of the first few centuries of our era.

Unlike the Greek—and Roman—epics, the romances are in prose, and this fact is significant; it shows that the authors were aiming at a less lofty, more intimate atmosphere in their narratives. Typically, these depict a hero and heroine isolated in an alien world—either because they have been abandoned at birth, or because they have had to leave their families owing to a dispute of some kind—and surviving on a sea of troubles, surviving because of their faith in each other, and in their love. (The sea is usually literally a sea—the characters of the Greek romances spend a good deal of their time sailing around the Mediterranean.) They are separated by shipwreck, or pirates, or other misfortunes, and are reunited finally, both with each other and with the families that rejected them.

The Greek comedies of a slightly earlier date, and of which only fragments or, at best, near-complete copies survive, have somewhat similar plots: children lost at birth, young lovers frustrated in their love because of problems in class created by this loss of identity, revelation of the truth in one great reunion.[6] The difference is that they show a group, a community interacting; the problems the lovers experience are not due to chances of fate but to their communities' standards of who may marry whom. The emphasis is not so much on the lovers and the way they maintain their love, as on the group and the way the group brings the truth to light. So the Greek romances are a new development in literature, marking a new awareness of the individual, and what it means to be an individual, to have feelings which make one more aware of oneself and of others.

The work with which I began, Heliodorus's *Aethiopica*, is the most famous, and probably deservedly so, of these romances. It is organized in an extremely complex way, beginning in the middle of the story—a method which follows the pattern of the epics—with the earlier events recounted by various characters, in a series of backward loops, until there comes a point where the narrative catches up with itself, as it were, and proceeds straightforwardly—and this sense of each character having an individual experience to contribute is very different from the ethos of the epics. The events narrated are also extremely complicated, involving a series of characters, each with her or his own history, as I said, but the focus of the narrative is Chariclea and her lover, Theagenes. Chariclea is the white daughter of the King and Queen of Ethiopia, and is abandoned on the bare ground at birth by her mother, who fears being accused of adultery (exposing infants in this manner was the standard method of "birth control" among the Greeks).

In the course of two "adoptions" Chariclea arrives at Delphi and becomes a priestess of Diana, and vows herself to chastity. There she falls in love at first sight with Theagenes, a handsome descendant of Achilles, and the narrative traces their adventures following their flight from Chariclea's foster father, Charicles, who wants her to marry his nephew. They are aided by Calasiris, an Egyptian priest who, largely guided by oracular dreams, is intent on uniting them and reuniting Chariclea with her parents, a desire he imparts to Chariclea. So her falling in love becomes intertwined with a desire to return to her origins, to discover her full identity; indeed she and Theagenes vow chastity until their union can be fittingly celebrated—until she finds her parents. The couple go through a series of tribulations, involving pirates and robbers—whose leaders fall for Chariclea—a long separation, a lascivious queen who falls for Theagenes and tortures both him and Chariclea (they pose throughout as sister and brother), culminating in their being taken as tribute, destined for sacrifice, to Ethiopia. Even though Chariclea could now tell her father whom he has taken captive, she insists on waiting till her mother can witness this revelation.

The final scene, where the couple are confronting the King and Queen of Ethiopia in the public procession, is quite extraordinary. The revelation, which one can see coming, is drawn out, with each of Chariclea's foster fathers arriving on the scene and her relationship with Theagenes remaining secret until the young hero has proved his prowess by killing a sacrificial bull maddened by fright at the sight of a camelopard (a mythical wild beast), and overcoming the champion wrestler presented by the King's nephew, who has been betrothed to Chariclea on the revelation of her identity. It is the arrival of Charicles to demand justice against Theagenes for abducting Chariclea that catalyzes the Queen's favor to the young couple. With her realization that they are devoted to one another the union becomes sanctioned.

Obviously, these narratives are action packed, to say the least. They are very much on the lines of "with one bound he leapt out of the pit." At one point Theagenes thinks he's found Chariclea's body in the mouth of a cave where she has been left for safekeeping during a battle. His laments are interrupted by her voice coming from far back in the cave—the body is not hers but that of another woman left in the cave. Samuel Lee Wolff, an early twentieth-century critic who was the first writer to demonstrate a consistent connection between these romances and the development of English fiction, sums up this tendency: "The paradoxical, the bizarre, the inconsistent, the self-contradictory—these were stock in trade with the writers of Greek Romance."[7] The extraordinariness of such moments, typical of the Greek romances, is taken to the extreme by Achilles Tatius, whose *Cleitophon and Leucippe* is now thought to be parody rather than a serious representative of the genre. His heroine,

Leucippe, is murdered in full sight of her lover, and not just murdered: she is disembowelled, and her entrails are roasted on an altar and distributed among her captors, who eat them! Perhaps I should add that Cleitophon is watching this from a distance, and yes—you might guess—Leucippe is alive and well. Her "entrails" are a sheep's stomach that has been strapped to her body by friends intent on saving her definitively from her captors, who presumably will leave her alone once she is in her coffin.

In the serious romances these blows of fate seem designed to bring out the full range of the characters' emotions—horror, grief, joy. This impulse, the desire to heighten our consciousness of such feelings, is possibly behind what is an exception to the usual pattern. Longus's *Daphnis and Chloe* is an idyllic narrative; it recounts the development of love between its two title characters, but, instead of depending on extraordinary events to bring out the full force of their emotions, Longus shows that love has its own force and its own excitement. Daphnis and Chloe, like Chariclea, are exposed at birth, but unlike her they grow up in the peaceful seclusion of the countryside, fostered by shepherd families, and their love develops gradually. Longus shows how its apparently uneventful beginnings—with Daphnis chasing a mischievous goat—are intensely important for Chloe, who is suddenly struck with admiration for Daphnis when she is helping him to clean himself up after the chase:

> She looked at him when in the bath, and while looking at him, touched his skin: after which, as she returned home, she mentally admired him, and this admiration was the beginning of love. She knew not the meaning of her feelings, young as she was, and brought up in the country, and never having heard from any one, so much as the name of love. She felt an oppression at her heart, she could not restrain her eyes from gazing upon him, nor her mouth from often pronouncing his name.[8]

The peace *is* disturbed—by pirates and young rioters from the nearby town (a third-century yacht party, no less), but the distress caused in the young lovers by their inability to consummate their love is as strong as any caused by these disruptions. The inability is due to lack of knowledge; the frustrated wife of one of the shepherds kindly shows Daphnis what he has to do, but when he learns that, unlike the experienced woman, Chloe will be hurt by his lovemaking, he postpones the consummation until they are married. The narrative ends with this consummation, after the children—for Daphnis and Chloe are little more— have been discovered by their parents and taken to the town to be married. But the couple need neither parents nor town; they return to the countryside where they grew up and discovered themselves through discovering each other, through discovering love.

FOOTNOTES TO PART I

1. Heliodorus, *Aethiopica*, trans. Rowland Smith in *The Greek Romances of Heliodorus, Longus, and Achilles Tatius* (London: George Bell & Sons, 1889), p. 155.
2. Gillian Beer, *The Romance*, *The Critical Idiom* series no. 10 (London: Methuen, 1970), p. 4.
3. Roger Ascham, *The Schoolmaster*, ed. Lawrence V. Ryan (Ithaca, N.Y.: Cornell U.P., 1967), p. 68.
4. Northrop Frye, *The Secular Scripture: A Study of the Structure of Romance* (Cambridge, Mass.: Harvard U.P., 1976), p. 26.
5. For further reading on the Greek romances, theories about their origins, development, structure, etc., see Arthur Heiserman's *The Novel Before the Novel: Essays and Discussions About the Beginnings of Prose Fiction in the West* (Chicago: University of Chicago Press, 1977), Ben E. Perry's *The Ancient Romances: A Literary Historical Account of their Origins* (Berkeley: University of California Press, 1967), or, for a shorter account and if you have access to a college library, Bryan Reardon's article "Aspects of the Greek Novel," in *Greece and Rome*, second series, #24 (1977), pp. 118-31. Heiserman's work is easily the most lively and speculative, and is available in paperback.
6. Ben Perry, in *The Ancient Romances*, puts forward the theory that the Greek comedies were connected with the romances; see pp. 72-83.
7. Samuel Lee Wolff, *The Greek Romances in Elizabethan Prose Fiction* (1912; rpt. New York: Burt Franklin, 1961), p. 5.
8. Longus, *Daghnis and Chloe*, trans. Rowland Smith in *The Greek Romances*, p. 271.

II. The Medieval Romances

There is nothing in medieval romance which explores the growth of love in quite the way that *Daphnis and Chloe* does. The closest match might be *Floire et Blanchefleur*, a twelfth-century "idyll," but rather than tracing the development of emotion, *Floire et Blanchefleur* shows its strength. The love between two young people who have grown up together, Floire, the son of a pagan king of Spain, and Blanchefleur, the daughter of a trusted Christian slave of the queen's, is taken for granted. The focus of the story is Floire's devotion to Blanchefleur as he follows her across the Mediterranean after she has been sold to traders by his parents in an effort to end the relationship. Chretien de Troyes, one of the greatest and earliest of medieval romancers, does portray, through long interior monologues, the feelings of two lovers falling in love, but this is only a small part of his romance *Cligès*, in which the lovers involved are the parents of the hero, and are shown at only one stage in the progress of their love, rather than followed through its full development.

Medieval romance, in general, differs from the Greek romances in its emphasis. Instead of following two lovers in their emotional or physical progress, medieval romance concentrates on the hero, and on his adventures which are a response to love, rather than on love itself. In addition, the heroine is generally off-stage, unlike the Greek romances in which she is an active participant in the story. And this focus on the hero occurs despite the fact that medieval romance seems to have developed precisely from the addition of love and ladies to the epic *chansons de geste*, literally "songs of deeds." For the medieval romances are not descended from the Greek. There is possibly a tenuous connection through the "saints' lives," narratives of the marvellous, miraculous even, events surrounding holy individuals, which developed nearly at the same time as the Greek romances, and survived through to the medieval period. But on the whole it seems that the medieval romances are an independent generation, although unlike the Greek romances they *do* have a literary precursor, the *chansons de geste*.

The *Chanson de Roland* is probably the best known now of the narratives of the early middle ages, of the three centuries or so before 1100. It is the story of a heroic rearguard action in the Pyrenees, Franks against Moors, of the misplaced "valor" of the commander of the rearguard, Roland (he refuses to summon help until too late), and of his king's (Charlemagne's) vengeance on the Moors for breaking the pledge of safe-conduct they had given. The title names an individual, Roland, who is certainly clearly characterized in the poem, but his death comes halfway through, and its significance is not so much that the individual, Roland, has died, as that the last member of a group of defenders of Western Christianity, of Charlemagne's men, is gone. The emphasis of the *chanson de geste* is on the community, the group, the loyalty of man to man—Roland dying with his friend Oliver—and above all of a man to his lord. Women, romantic love, hardly enter the picture. As R. W. Southern, the author of *the* account of the development of the middle ages, points out, although we do see Roland's betrothed fainting at the news of his death, Roland's dying words aren't for her at all—he speaks only of his country.[1]

Then in the twelfth century something happened and the stories of heroic group actions on behalf of country, lord, or belief, began to give way to stories of individual knights falling in love and going out to perform heroic deeds inspired by that love. Arthur's knights belong to the Round Table, and though being part of this group is their highest honor, they go on quests as individuals, and can even end up fighting each other. W. P. Ker, writing at the end of the nineteenth century, pinpointed the difference between *chanson de geste* and romance by contrasting the favorite encounter of the *chanson*, "the defence of a narrow place against odds," with that of romance:

> A knight riding alone through a forest; another knight; a shock of lances; a fight on foot with swords; "racing, tracing, and foining like two wild boars;" then, perhaps, recognition—the two knights belong to the same household and are engaged in the same quest.[2]

So what happened? Why this quite dramatic change in emphasis from group to individual? The answer is not as clear cut as it is for the Greek romances and the civilisation that gave rise to them. There is no great event like Alexander's conquests to point to and say, "This changed Europe." There is, rather, a slow development of stability, dating from an insignificant battle—just another in the long line of efforts to keep the Norsemen at bay—the battle of the Lech, 922.[3] From then on, although no one was aware of it at the time, the struggle to preserve Western Christian Europe against the incursions of Norsemen to the northeast, and the Moslems, the Moors of Spain, to the southwest, ceased to be a struggle and the preservation became an established fact. With the new stability, Europe developed; trade, government and learning increased in volume and sophistication. And with these, so did the freedom of individuals to choose their role in life. From a world where the paths one could follow were defined from the start, in a hierarchically, rigidly ordered society, whether religious or secular, Europe moved into a world where one could choose (to some extent) one's own path, and with that freedom the individual, the unit, rather than the structure, became the emotional center.

I called the change in emphasis from group to individual "quite dramatic." Its most dramatic manifestation is in Christianity itself; Christ ceased to be seen as a conqueror, Christians triumphant as a band—the vision necessary for a war that looked outward, to enemy attacks—and became Christ the man, the human individual who suffered to save each individual human. You can see this evolution in the changing portrayals of the crucifixtion; from a triumphant figure on the cross, unaware of the nails in his hands and feet—and certainly without the crown of thorns—Christ becomes a figure wracked in suffering, his eyes closed, dying. The emphasis turned inward: "Know thyself" was *the* injunction reiterated by churchmen in the twelfth century, and the individual self became so important that we find St. Bernard of Clairvaux, one of the greatest of that era's monastic thinkers, writing to a friend:

> You could reach me if you but considered what I am; and you can reach me still whenever you wish, if you are content to find me as I am and not as you wish me to be. I cannot think what else you see in me besides what I am, what it is you are chasing which is not me.[4]

Parallel to this development in spiritual faith was the development of romantic love. As occurred in the society which gave rise to the Greek romances, the realization of the importance of the individual self gave rise to an awareness of the importance of one particular other. Suddenly the relationship of individual man to individual woman became worthy of celebration in songs and narratives. "Sudden" is the word; the rise of romantic love presents a striking change in sentiment, and R. W. Southern, when trying to summarize the change from the tenth to the twelfth centuries, chooses the literary development as most expressive of this revolution in feeling: his last chapter is called "From Epic to Romance." The love that arose in the twelfth century has been given a special name, "fin' amors" in French, the usual English translation being "courtly love." It is a love less focused on physical desire than on respect, worship almost, of the lady from afar—and seen more from the man's than the woman's point of view. (One of the standard plot lines of medieval romance is that of the lowly squire who loves his lord's daughter.) The physical is certainly not excluded, and there is a standard type of medieval beauty: fair hair, grey eyes, red lips, but it is almost more important that love brings one to a full consciousness of oneself than to a union with the beloved. The beloved is frequently envisioned as a mirror in the courtly love poetry of the troubadours. So the knights in romance come into their *own* in terms of prowess when the fall in love; the valor, the display of arms is to prove one's worth to the lady, but she is very much on the sidelines. The pattern of medieval romance is love, quest—and this takes up much of the narrative—then return to the lady.

Guy of Warwick, one of the most popular of medieval romances, displays both these elements: the worship from afar and the long demonstration of worth. (Don't rush to the library though; even to me, and I am a sucker for these stories, *Guy* is excruciatingly long winded.) Guy's lady, Felice, is herself responsible for his long absence. She is the daughter of the Earl of Warwick; he is the son of her father's steward, and a squire. And, of course, he is in love with her, so in love that he falls ill. Eventually he reveals his love to her and she responds by saying he must become a knight, which he does, by asking the Earl to knight him. This is not enough for Felice; Guy must prove his right to knighthood. So he goes to Europe and amongst other adventures wins a tournament in Almayne against all comers. This still is not enough for Felice; now she says she wants Guy to prove himself the best knight in the world. He does this (at great length), returns to her and this time she says yes. They marry, have a son, and—to serve Felice right—Guy now realizes how much violence he has committed at her behest and leaves her, for life, to do penance.

Guy's departure in penitence makes an unexpected twist on the conflict between love and honor that is inherent to medieval romance. Love may be the inspiration for knightly prowess, but in proving his worthiness of his chosen lady the knight has to be absent from her, and once he has won her, what happens to his knighthood? If he stays at home his knightly worth diminishes; if he continues to practice deeds of arms, his love, the goal he strove for, becomes pointless. Most medieval romancers leave the love/honor conflict implicit (little is made of Guy's abandonment of Felice, for instance) but Chretien de Troyes and Malory, the writers who could be said to mark the beginning and the end of medieval romance, are more conscious of the conflict—Chretien especially. Several of his "Arthurian romances" turn on it. *Erec et Enide* is the story of a husband and wife whose blissful marriage is disrupted by the criticisms of Erec for letting love absorb him at the expense of his sword; Erec overhears Enide lamenting her guilt in this, and sets out to prove his critics wrong—taking Enide with him, unusually enough. *Yvain* falls in love with a lady he encounters as a result of a quest; with her permission, once they are married, he rejoins Arthur's court, to continue to prove his prowess, but in his absorption he forgets the deadline she has set—a year—for his return, and spends much of the narrative in exile from his beloved. *Lancelot* pursues Queen Guinevere's captors and goes through pain and ignominy to rescue her. After various turns of the plot he comes to a tournament in disguise. She discovers his identity by testing his devotion; on the first day commanding him to do his "worst," with the result that he willingly shames himself before an audience; the next day she commands him to do his best and, of course, he carries the prize. This is the knight who has ridden in the condemned criminals' cart in

order to learn the way to his captive lady. Love and knightly hon-
or are pitted against each other throughout *Lancelot* and love
wins. Chretien narrates *episodes* from the Arthurian legend;
Malory narrates the story of Arthur from his birth to his death,
with the adventures of his knights in the middle, and Arthur's
death dramatizes the conflict between love and honor, love and
knighthood. It is because of the love between Lancelot and Guinevere that the Round Table is finally disrupted. The enemies of
the lovers steadily close in until their adultery is brought out into
the open and the knightly fellowship is split in two. But even in
the *Morte d'Arthur*, where we see some of the most famous lovers
of medieval romance, we see comparatively little of the women.
The Lancelot/Guinevere relationship only comes into the fore-
ground in the last part of Malory's work; Lancelot, like Tristram
in the middle section of the *Morte d'Arthur*, spends more time ab-
sented from his lady than with her. Medieval romance is born
from the union of love and war, but on the whole the love remains an inspiration, an idea, rather than a shared experience.

FOOTNOTES TO PART II

1. R. W. Southern, *The Making of the Middle Ages* (New Haven: Yale University
   Press, 1959), p. 242.
2. W. P. Ker, *Epic and Romance* (London: Macmillan and Co., 1897), pp. 5-6.
3. This "turning-point" is Southern's perception; I have followed his analysis of
   the change in Europe in the early middle ages throughout.
4. Quoted in Colin Morris's *The Discovery of the Individual*, Church History
   Outlines No. 5 (London: S.P.C.K., 1972), p. 103. Although it is published as
   "church history,"Morris's work is far more a general investigation of the phenomenon of the individual in the twelfth century; Chapters 4 and 5, "The
   Search for the Self" and "The Self and Other Selves," are well worth reading,
   as well as Southern's work, to get a sense of the period.

III. The Renaissance Romances

With Malory the story of romance comes finally to England. Medieval romance is a continental, and mainly French, creation; even the *Morte d'Arthur*, like previous romances in English, is in a way a translation from the French, as its title suggests. It is, however, a significant reworking of the Arthurian legend, and romance itself was to develop significantly in England in the Elizabethan period, the English Renaissance of the second half of the sixteenth century. During this period the two lines of romance, the Greek and the Medieval, come together, and again the emphasis shifts: from hero to heroine. And romance itself begins its slide from the center to the periphery of fiction.

This slide was caused by the combination of the recovery of classical texts, the literary rebirth which is one part of the Renaissance—and which included the revival of the Greek romances—and the development of literary criticism. Throughout the sixteenth century critics in Italy and France, and at the end of the century in England, debated the merits of medieval, chivalric romance, as opposed to those of the classical epics: Virgil's and Homer's. And romance lost. It was too diverse, too rambling, too unserious. The debate centered on *Orlando Furioso*, the work of the greatest Italian romancer: Ludovico Ariosto. During the first quarter of the century (he worked on the romance for twenty-five years) he wrote an elaborate, brilliant narrative, full of knights questing and falling in love and abandoning their duty of defending France against the heathen. One knight even makes an excursion to the moon. Both the critics and supporters of romance took the *Orlando Furioso* as their touchstone, as it was the most popular romance of its time, and as the debate continued the writing of romance—in place of an epic tracing the career of one hero who can be seen as representing his country—became more and more a questionable enterprise.[1]

Meanwhile the status of women was changing somewhat in England. There was by no means a liberation of women, or any

17

notion of their equality to men—man was still the supreme being—but the humanist scholars had begun to advocate educating girls along the same lines as boys; Sir Thomas More, Henry VIII's chancellor, taught his daughters Latin. This movement in education faded considerably as the sixteenth century went on (greater learning made them less marriageable),[2] but with the brilliant and supremely educated Elizabeth on the throne there was still a realization that women were capable of learning as well as men. And yet women were considered inferior. Women were now a viable readership and yet not a readership that would be held in esteem. It may be that this is why romance became "their" genre: the inferior or weaker fiction for the weaker sex.

This is sheer speculation, and it is jumping the gun to some extent; during this period, men still read romances for pleasure and instruction, as is shown by Sir Philip Sidney's comments on assorted narratives in his *Defence of Poesie*:

> Truly I have knowne men, that even with reading *Amadis de gaule*, which God knoweth, wanteth much of a perfect *Poesie*, have found their hearts moved to the exercise of courtesie, liberalitie, and especially courage . . . *Poetrie* is the Companion of Camps. I dare undertake, *Orlando Furioso*, or honest king *Arthure*, will never displease a souldier.[3]

These comments were written by a man who was expected by many to be the glory of Elizabethan England, a respected scholar and soldier, so they carry some weight. But the same man also wrote a romance exclusively for ladies, for his sister, in fact. The first version of his romance the *Arcadia* (this version, written probably between 1578 and 1580, is commonly called the *Old Arcadia*) is dedicated "To my dear Lady and Sister the Countess of Pembroke . . . you desired me to do it, and your desire to my heart is an absolute commandment." Throughout the first three books of the five-book romance Sidney addresses his audience as "fair ladies," "worthy ladies."

Sidney suppressed this version of the *Arcadia*; later, perhaps to make his work closer to the more respected epic form, he went back to the beginning and began to revise it completely, introducing heroic, knightly, *epic* material, and although the revision was never finished, it was the version that was published in 1590, by his sister and his friend, after his premature death in 1586. It remained the most popular work of fiction in England until the mid-eighteenth century. So this period, the end of the sixteenth century in England, marks the beginning of the transition, rather than the transition itself, in the status of romance, from a well-regarded form of fiction to one that was directed specifically at women, so that Clara Reeve, in her late eighteenth-century account of *The Progress of Romance* could take the single-sex readership as an accepted fact.

Even though the published version of Sidney's *Arcadia* was not directed at women, however, it gave them importance. Sidney's heroines are fully developed, fully realized characters—the sort of characters we're used to encountering in novels, rather than the two-dimensional figures of medieval romance—and they have plenty of spunk. His heroes, on the other hand, are less than impressive, and, by the time the narrative breaks off, are reduced to virtual ineffectiveness. This inadequacy is partly due to the plot; left over from the first version, it places them in a ludicrous situation. The two heroes, Pyrocles and Musiforus (the influence of Greek romance shows clearly in the names and the setting—Arcadia itself was a mountain district in Peloponesia, and the word came to mean an ideal, rustic paradise), disguise themselves in order to approach the princesses they have fallen in love with. The young women have been taken into strict seclusion by their father, in response to an ominous oracle. Well, fine—the problem lies in the disguise they choose. Musidorus becomes a shepherd, which doesn't sound too terrible, except that this severely lowers his status and he is reduced to wooing his chosen princess, Pamela, via her clodhopping attendant, Mopsa; he expounds his love in such grandiose terms that they are ridiculous applied to Mopsa, and Pamela begins to take note. Even though the ruse succeeds it does render the wooing somewhat ludicrous. Pyrocles is in even worse condition; he disguises himself as an amazon, with the result that the princesses' father falls for him, their mother falls for the man she perceives under the disguise, and Philoclea, whom he wants to get close to, is completely bewildered. Sidney describes her emotions in a long passage, which includes the various ways Philoclea dreams of to solve the intensity of her feeling for Zelmane (Pyrocles): that they should be chaste nymphs together, that they should be sisters,

> Then grown bolder, she would wish either herself or Zelmane a man, that there might succeed a blessed marriage betwixt them. But when that wish had once displayed his ensign in her mind, then followed whole squadrons of longings that so it might be, with a main battle of mislikings and repinings against their creation, that so it was not. Then dreams by night began to bring more unto her than she durst wish by day, whereout waking did make her know herself by the image of those fancies.

The third, and unfinished, book of the revised *Arcadia* shows the princesses kidnapped by their wicked aunt, and displaying extraordinary courage, while Pyrocles and Musidorus have very little to do.

The sensitive portrayals of the princesses, and even of their distressed mother, bring us closer to the spirit of Greek than of medieval romance, but the *Arcadia* is something more than either. Sidney shows love in full force, an individual experience. It is a cliche to describe Renaissance thought as centered on man, as opposed to medieval thought being centered on God, but there is some truth to the observation. The awareness of the self that had begun in the twelfth century continued and came to full flowering in the Renaissance. The individual human being became the clear focus of attention, as a creature of free potential for rising to the level of the angels or plunging to below the level of the beasts.[6] This development of interest in the individual's capacity for infinite variety perhaps lies behind the sharp, individual portraits of women in Sidney's *Arcadia*, and behind Shakespeare's creation of characters whom we seem to know so well that we can imagine full life histories for them.

Similar to Sidney, when Shakespeare presents romantic love, it is his heroines who shine, who win the audience's heart. The heroes of Shakespeare's comedies are notorious wimps— there is no other word for them—with the exception perhaps of Benedict, Beatrice's sharp-witted match in *Much Ado About Nothing*. Otherwise it is not the "heroes" we remember, but Rosalind, disguising herself as a man to escape her wicked uncle, and teaching her beloved how to woo in *As You Like It*; Viola, disguised as a page, and wooing her master's chosen lady with more wit than he ever displays, in *Twelfth Night*; Portia, saving her mercenary husband's friend with a ruse that a whole courtful of men have failed to come up with, in *The Merchant of Venice.* Why this shift from the emphasis on the man's role in the medieval vision of love, to showing women as coming into their own under the influence of this emotion? There was little in the society, apparently, to encourage such a development. As in the middle ages, marriages were usually arranged by parents—with the consent of the young couple, since the parents had to be sure the husband and wife-to-be could get on together—marriage for love was generally out of the question. Love itself was considered as a destructive emotion, "this inordinate and cruel effection"as the Spanish moralist Vives described it,[7] "this bastard Love . . . engendered betwixt lust and idleness," in Sidney's words.

Spenser's *Faerie Queene* presents love as almost a doomed emotion. This vast, late sixteenth-century narrative in verse (and therefore aiming at epic status), imbued with the elements of medieval romance, knights questing, Arthur himself seeking for the Faerie Queene he has seen once in a dream, contains only one relationship that comes to the consummation of marriage; otherwise the knights are perpetually leaving their ladies behind, restoring them to the bosoms of their families and travelling on in search of knightly deeds. Even though Spenser, like Ariosto, who is clearly one of his models, has a heroine in armor—she disguises herself as a knight and goes out to seek her beloved whom she has seen in a magic mirror—he doesn't allow this to be a solution to the conflict of love and knightly duty. Britomart, the warrior maid, and Artegall, her hero, only spend a short time together once she finds him, before they have to separate again for Artegall to pursue his quest of liberating a captive lady. Spenser almost arbitrarily keeps Britomart out of this quest, and we never see her in secure happiness with her beloved. The grimmest vision of love in the *Faerie Queene* is that symbolized by the torture of Amoret, seized by the magician Busyrane in the middle of the celebrations of her union with Scudamor; Busyrane imprisons her in a near-impenetrable castle and keeps her alive with her heart torn out of her body, palpitating in a silver dish. She is paraded through the rooms of the castle, the dish being born by two attendants, in a pageant presided over by Cupid. During this period, there was, however, another line of theorizing on love, and that was in the Puritan discussions of marriage; they advocated not passionate, irrational love as a basis for marriage, but rather a companionable love, a full appreciation of one's partner and working for a stability of emotion that would create a stable and Godly family.[8] This concept focussed as much on the man's role as the woman's, but the conflict displayed in medieval romance did not readily disappear. That is, the conflict between love, keeping the hero at home, and knightly duty, whereby he must go out and seek to exercise his prowess. This conflict still informs Sidney's *Arcadia*; the heroes feel guilty about their abandonment of knightly action to pursue their ladies. Love is the woman's domain, not the man's. So the emphasis on love and the heroine displayed by the Greek romances (particularly Heliodorus's account of Chariclea and Theagenes, much admired in the Elizabethan period) combines with the conflict between love and knightly duty displayed by the medieval romances to put the emphasis on women and their role in love in the Renaissance. It is a development that still affects our perception of romantic fiction to this day.

FOOTNOTES TO PART III

1. For examples of the Renaissance Romance Debate see *Literary Criticism: Plato to Dryden*, ed. Allan H. Gilbert (1940; rpt. Detroit: Wayne State University Press, 1962), especially the excerpts from Giraldi Cinthio's *On the Composition of Romances* (1549) and Antonio Minturno's *L'Arte Poetica* (1564).
2. Alison Plowden provides a very readable account of the status of women's learning in the sixteenth century in her *Tudor Women: Queens and Commoners* (London: Weidenfeld and Nicolson, 1979), Chapter Six, "When Women Become Such Clerks," pp. 105-124, and see also p. 168.
3. Sir Philip Sidney, *The Defence of Poesie*, in *The Prose Works of Sir Philip Sidney*, ed. Albert Feuillerat (1912; rpt. Cambridge University Press, 1968), III. 20 and 32.
4. Sir Philip Sidney, *The Countess of Pembroke's "Arcadia"* (*The Old Arcadia*, ed. Jean Robertson (Oxford: Oxford University Press, 1973). p. 3.
5. Sidney, *The Countess of Pembroke's Arcadia*, ed. Maurice Evans, (Harmondsworth, Middlesex: Penguin Books Ltd., 1977), pp. 239-240.
6. See Paul Oskar Kristeller's essay, "The Dignity of Man," in *Renaissance Concepts of Man and other Essays* (New York: Harper and Row, 1972), pp. 1-21, for an analysis of Renaissance thought on the individual.
7. Lu Emily Pearson summarizes Vives' *The Instruction of a Christian Woman*

(1523), and his invective against love, in *Elizabethans at Home* (Stanford: Stanford University Press, 1957), pp. 248-252.

8. See Lawrence Stone, *The Family, Sex and Marriage in England 1500-1800* (Harmondsworth, Middlesex: Penguin Books Ltd., 1979), pp. 101-105, and William and Mandeville Haller, "The Puritan Art of Love," *Huntington Library Quarterly* 5 (1941-1942), pp. 235-272.

IV. The Eighteenth-Century Romances

I have spent so much time on Sidney and his *Arcadia* because it was, as I've said, *the* romance from the late sixteenth to the mid-eighteenth century in England, so the traits it displays are likely to be the clearest indicator of the direction in which romance was moving. It also provides a link with the great eighteenth century development in fiction: the realistic novel. As Sidney commentators never seem to be tired of noting, Samuel Richardson named the heroine of his innovative narrative, *Pamela*, after the elder of Sidney's princesses.

The seventeenth century represents a lull in the development of romance; it was not till the eighteenth century, when a marked change in social conditions had taken place, that something other than *Arcadia* imitations began to be produced. "Something other" being the novel that deals with ordinary people in ordinary settings, the novel as we think of it today. By the end of the eighteenth century England had become an urbanized and commercial country, centered on London, as opposed to the predominantly rural and agricultural society of the seventeenth and preceding centuries. Not that the majority of people did not still live in the country, but the cities, and London especially, had come to dominate the way life was lived, and this development resulted in a clear increase in the number of women with time on their hands. In the earlier agricultural society both upper and lower class women had been as essential to the upkeep of the family as the men: running the house, spinning, weaving, taking care of the dairy and the poultry, helping in the fields. The com-

24

mercial and industrial development of the eighteenth century produced an urban middle class, whose women had households of servants to oversee, but little else to do. Their enforced leisure was due partly to their role as status symbols for their husbands, whose wealth was thus clearly demonstrated. They were educated enough to be a viable readership; printing was now a truly mass-production industry. In other words both the demand and the supply were there to create a fiction market something like the one we still know. All these elements were present in the sixteenth century but to a much slighter degree; you can see the first stirrings, but it is the eighteenth century that marks the real revolution in reading: a mass female market.

The eighteenth century also marks another development— in awareness. This is how Ian Watt, in the best-known and probably the best account of *The Rise of the Novel*, describes the development of individualism at the start of the period. The aspects he pinpoints should be familiar by now, from my accounts of the development of the individual in the Greek and medieval periods:

> Capitalism brought a great increase of economic specialisation; and this, combined with a less rigid and homogeneous social structure, and a less absolutist and more democratic political system, enormously increased the individual's freedom of choice. For those fully exposed to the new economic order, the effective entity on which social arrangements were now based was no longer the family, nor the church, nor the guild, nor the township, nor any other collective unit, but the individual: he alone was primarily responsible for determining his own economic, social, political and religious rules.[1]

Samuel Richardson's heroine, Pamela, exemplifies the capacity of the individual to break free of society's structures because of her innate qualities. She starts off as a servant, and ends the wife of her master, and would-be seducer, the rich Mr. B. It is in fact the Cinderella story, poor girl makes good through love, although Richardson would have resisted any such association with romance. He thought he was writing a novel about ordinary people; one of his main purposes in writing *Pamela* was to get away from the totally escapist fantasies of Arcadia-type romances. He probably didn't see that *Pamela* provided an even clearer wish-fulfillment fantasy—clearer because it was possible, as he had shown, here and now in England.

Pamela is written in the first person, in the form of letters, so that there is no barrier between individual character and individual reader. *Clarissa*, Richardson's next work, is also written in the first person, but this time a whole group of first persons, including the main male character; the importance of the individual becomes very clear in this desire to show how each person involved in a particular event perceives and responds to it. The event is a rape. At the start of the novel Clarissa is being emotionally bludgeoned by her family into marrying the repulsive Mr. Solmes for the financial advantages and the safe social status he can provide. She, however, accepts the services of her aristocratic and very unsafe wooer, Lovelace, to escape from her family; once in his power, though, there she stays. He tries various ways of seducing her, and finally drugs her and takes her while she is unconscious. Although she denies she has been violated because her mind was untouched, she goes into a decline and dies surrounded by mourning family and friends—her death takes approximately one third of the nearly 1,000,000-word novel. Gillian Beer explains how Richardson keeps the romance, escapist tendencies of his novels under control:

> In *Pamela* by devoting the second volume to the duties of his heroine's married life; in *Clarissa* by refusing the 'happy ending' of marrying his heroine to her loved seducer and driving the novel on into religious tragedy.[2]

Both *Pamela* and *Clarissa* are extraordinarily lascivious, in the face of Richardson's proclaimed purity of mind and desire to instill virtue in his readers. They do, however, illustrate the prime characteristic of romances from here on: they are about women for women. *Pamela* and *Clarissa* appeared in the 1730s and 40s (published volume by volume); by 1785, Clara Reeve, one of the first critics to trace the history of romance, could generalize: "The learned men of our own country, have in general affected a contempt for this kind of writing, and looked upon Romances, as proper furniture for a lady's Library."[3] They also show the individual overcoming the structures of society, actively in Pamela's case, passively in Clarissa's, who sees Lovelace for what he is, not for what his class proclaims him to be, ignoble rather than noble. Northrop Frye has described romance as having an "inherently revolutionary quality"[4] because of its impulse to wish-fulfillment, to break through the constraints of reality and because of its inherently popular—"for the people"—nature.[5] In the latter part of the eighteenth century, the period which coincided with the French revolution of 1759, the genre known as the Gothic novel was created, and it marks a rebirth of romance divorced from realism.

It was a genre virtually invented by a mid-eighteenth century dilettante, Horace Walpole, who disliked the tediously realistic novels of Richardson, Fielding, Sterne; to supply the lack of romance, he wrote, half in fun, *The Castle of Otranto*. The action is set in some ill-defined medieval period, and involves a middle-aged prince who, having lost the opportunity to ally himself with a neighboring marquis and preserve his family line by marrying his son to the marquis's daughter—a giant helmet falls out of the sky and crushes the young man—determines to marry her himself, holding her captive till she will agree. Walpole's little—literally, it is short and makes quick reading—fantasy set off a whole vogue, the most popular examples of which are probably Mrs. Radcliffe's *The Mysteries of Udolpho* (1794) and Matthew "Monk" Lewis's *The Monk* (1796). *Udolpho* depends on a knowledge of the genre for much of its effects; nothing much happens in the first 200 pages except for the occasional creaking door, which turns out to have a perfectly normal explanation. It also deals with a young girl being held captive to force her to marry against her will, this time in a sixteenth century castle in the Italian Apennines. *The Monk* includes a rape of a virgin by a monk underground in a church vault (the victim faints beforehand, so that, like Clarissa, she is unconscious at the actual moment of penetration: the only good woman is a dead woman) and the burying alive of a pregnant nun, who cradles her soon-dead infant till it is "a mass of putridity" and she comes to have her "fingers ringed with the long worms which bred in its corrupted flesh."[6]

It seems odd to describe as "revolutionary" a genre which

shows women as completely oppressed, held helpless in grim castles by powerful men—the theme of captivity which runs through *Pamela* and dominates *Clarissa* emerges in nightmare force—but these narratives represent in a phantasmagoric way the revolutions developing in Europe at the same time: the oppressed individual resists the powerful forces of evil and eventually overturns them.

They also represent the first "specialized" romance. The earlier romances include all the elements of romance: love, adventure, the supernatural, violence (the revised *Arcadia* is a good example of this). The realistic novel took over that all-inclusive role, but although it was inclusive, it was, as Walpole felt, too restrained, the imagination had to be held in check. Richardson's novels include elements of romance, and so do those of his nineteenth-century successors; Jane Austen's turn-of-the-century *Pride and Prejudice*, Charlotte Brontë's *Jane Eyre* are also structured on the Cinderella theme, Emily Brontë's *Wuthering Heights* has strong affinities to the Gothic novel, Dickens' work includes near-supernatural moments, and his plots are often pure romance, full of coincidences and long-lost children being discovered, but they all hold back from the full romance escapism, keeping it under control by an emphasis on presenting society as it actually was. The romance imagination, though, refuses to be completely suppressed, but the way it emerges now is in specialized forms; it can't be all-inclusive so it goes in one direction or another: horror, mystery, love.

This specialization of romance is something that affects our reading today. We are so used to the genres which developed in the nineteenth and early twentieth century: the detective novel, the western, science fiction, the historical novel, the love story, that we tend to think of them as essentially separate, not offshoots of the same creative impulse. But trace romance back to its origins and their common ancestry becomes clear. Two questions have arisen for me as a result of tracing this development: (1) Why should the "generalization" have taken place? (I have tried to answer this question *very* briefly in my account of the Gothic novel.) And (2) Why is the branch of romance we are concerned with here, "women's fiction," considered the poor relation of all these descendant genres? Why, when the detective novel, the western and science fiction have become legitimate fields of inquiry in academic circles, are love stories dismissed as merely "sub-literature . . . lightweight commercial fiction deliberately written to flatter day dreams," as Gillian Beer does at the beginning of her study of the progress of romance? The answer is perhaps too obvious: the love story is women's fiction, romance for women as opposed to the other romance genres, and therefore dismissable. Perhaps, though, we can use this question to think constructively about the modern love story and how it operates in our society, using our knowledge of its origins to provide a context for our reading of romance now.

FOOTNOTES TO PART IV

1. Ian Watt, *The Rise of the Novel: Studies in Defoe, Richardson and Fielding* (1957; rpt. Berkeley: University of California Press, 1974), p. 61.
2. Gillian Beer, *The Romance*, p. 54.
3. Clara Reeve, *The Progress of Romance through Times, Countries, and* Manners (New York: Garland Publishing, Inc., 1970), p. xi.
4. Northrop Frye, *The Secular Scripture: A Study of the Structure of* Romance (Cambridge, Mass.: Harvard University Press, 1976), p. 178.
5. Frye, pp. 23-26.
6. Matthew G. Lewis, *The Monk* (1952; rpt. New York: Grove Press, Inc., 1978), pp. 393 and 396.

The Regency Romance

Florence Stevenson

In recent years, many historical novelists have become intrigued with the Regency period. Various names spring to mind. First, of course, is that of Georgette Heyer, the doyenne of this particular demesne. She is the Pied Piper who led such ladies as Barbara Cartland, Caroline Courtenay, Barbara Paul, Marion Chesney, Joan Aiken, Jane Aiken Hodge, Constance Heaven . . . the list is lengthy, to board the stagecoach up the road to romance and royalties.

The Regency novel is pure escapism. It wafts its readers to a world peopled by handsome noblemen in well-fitting coats, high-starched cravats, muslin shirts, colored vests, skintight pantaloons, gold fobs, Hessian boots polished to a high shine and adorned with sparkling gold tassels. These gentlemen wear curly brimmed beaver hats and many-caped driving coats as they tool along in their curricles. They have fast horses, country estates, townhouses and fortunes. They are wildly ruthless until subdued by the love of a beautiful heiress or a poor but proud governess or an indigent orphan (who turns out to be Lady X) or a clergyman's daughter, provided, of course, that she is beautiful, witty, charming, dresses to the nines in see-through, form hugging muslins, bonnets adorned with cock feathers or flowers, shows a well-turned ankle and a tiny foot. Naturally, the road to their romance is never smooth. The heiress is promised to Another. The governess is ineligible because she is Poor. The nobleman believes himself in love with some beautiful but cruel female and only recognizes the heroine's true worth or she only recognizes his after some vicissitude. One hopes these will include the Regency equivalent of a car chase—as a stagecoach or

31

curricle or phaeton or post-chaise drawn by fleet horses (two or four) goes bouncing over the indifferent roads with an out-and-out villain, an irate father, a furious brother, or an impassioned suitor in hot pursuit. Naturally, the right people win, tangled webs are untangled and everyone, except those who shouldn't, lives happily ever after.

This sort of a plot has blossomed in other romantic climes but it is never so appealing as when it goes clad in muslin gowns and coats of superfine. There is a fascination about the genre which is irresistible. Before mentioning the writers who have helped in the flowering of the Regency rose, it is of value to consider why this period is so fertile a pasture for novelists and so felicitious a playground for their readers.

* * *

The Regency lasted for nine years. It began in 1811 when George III succumbed to a violent attack of a hereditary blood disease called porphyria. Its symptoms were much akin to madness and his physicians did not scruple to call it by its improper name; they diagnosed his malady as madness and put the unfortunate monarch in irons and a straightjacket. Consequently, at the end of January 1811, his Royal Highness, Prince of Wales, affectionately called "Prinny" by his close associates, became Prince Regent. He remained in this capacity until 1820, when the old king died. In 1821, the prince became George IV.

> "Georgie-Porgie, puddin' an' pie,
> Kissed the girls and made 'em cry."

That old nursery rhyme was only one of the many jibes directed at the prince. He was forty-nine when he became Regent and he had made several mistresses, a morganatic and an official wife very unhappy.

The morganatic wife was Mrs. Maria Fitzherbert, a beautiful and pious Catholic widow, some years older than the prince, who both loved and mothered him. (His childhood had been without parental affection and he nearly always sought older women for his paramours.) The prince secretly married Mrs.

Fitzherbert in 1785 and proceeded to be flagrantly unfaithful to her, even though he loved her dearly. The legal wife was his first cousin, Caroline of Brunswick, whom he agreed to wed very reluctantly and only upon the receipt of a million pounds, promised by William Pitt, the prime minister, but never delivered.

The royal bride and groom were not enthralled with each other. She found him fat. He found her foolish and also unclean in her personal habits. His wedding night was not a success; not only was he revolted by such close contact with his frowsy bride, she was embarrassingly ill, having been given a powerful emetic by his latest mistress, the jealous and conniving Lady Jersey. Soon after that debacle, the couple agreed to live apart.

Unlike Mrs. Fitzherbert, who had retired quietly, Princess Caroline took a lover for herself and lived riotously abroad. The public did not know about Caroline's far-from-public life or her near madness. Egged on by vicious lampoonists and cartoonists, who satirized the prince's habits and increasing girth, his subjects took up the cudgel for Caroline, who had been "cruelly" separated from the daughter (Princess Charlotte) she had borne the prince. Unaware of such escapades as appearing naked to the waist at a ball, they loved the princess and despised her husband. Fortunately, London society, known as the "ton,"knew the truth.

His marital problems were dormant when the prince assumed his Regency. Unfortunately, equally dormant was his popularity and gone was the appearance that had once gained him the nickname of "Prince Charming." As a young man, the fair-haired, blue-eyed heir to the throne had been a trifle plump; at forty-nine, he was obese. He looked even heavier in the skin-tight pantaloons of the period; he was heavily laced into corsets which creaked when he walked. He loved fine clothes and had a passion for dressing up in ornate uniforms that emphasized rather than diminished his bulk but withall he was horridly conscious of not looking his best.

Yet, personal problems and vices not withstanding, the prince was a man of elegance and exquisite taste. He was a connoisseur of fine paintings. Under his guidance, the Wallace Art Collection was obtained for the nation. Carlton House, his royal residence, had grown from a modest two-storey stucco building into a pillared "temple" of beauty. If it was a trifle ostentatious inside, running to mammoth marble columns and masses of floor-to-ceiling mirrors, it was still filled with magnificent paintings and other priceless treasures. Though that famous wit, the Reverend Sidney Smith, seeing the onion-shaped towers of the royal pavillion at Brighton, said that it looked as if St. Paul's Cathedral had come down from London and pupped, the interior of the pavillion was replete with wonderful Chinese art. The prince refurbished moldering Windsor Castle, where he spent a great part of his unhappy boyhood under a strict, penurious father and cruel tutors, turning it into a gracious and beautiful habitation. He did the same for the King's House at Pimlico, transforming it into Buckingham Palace. He cleared out slums and with his architect, John Nash, was responsible for an extensive face-lifting of London—including the laying out of Regent Street and the building of Carlton House Terrace.

He admired Sir Walter Scott and Jane Austen; one of the prince's physicians attended Miss Austen's father. He told the novelist that the prince had a set of her novels in every one of his residences. Later, she was bidden to Carlton House and one of the prince's aides gave her a guided tour of the palace, with an emphasis on the royal library. It was mentioned to her that his Royal Highness would appreciate it if she dedicated one of her books to him. She obliged with *Emma*.

The prince typified the Regency. He was the well-educated eighteenth-century man; he was well read in the classics. In addition to his native English, he could speak and write with equal ease in French, German, Greek and Italian. He could play the violincello and he could also sing reasonably well. His zeal in transforming as much of London as he could, his support of the Royal Society for Scientific Distinction, the Royal Society of Literature, the Royal Academy and the British Museum proved him to be a forward-looking man of the nineteenth century as well. As for his much-disputed character? After his death, the Duke of Wellington described the prince as "the most extraordinary compound of wit, talent, buffoonery, obstinacy and good feeling—in short a medley of opposing qualities with a great preponderance of good." In his way, the prince was rather eccentric. However, his eccentricities counted for little in a society studded with far more fabulous individuals, each vying for attention in his own unique way and dedicated to the pursuit of pleasures or, rather, what pleased them. It is possible that all the young men of the period were haunted by the French Revolution and determined to burn their candles at both ends—even if they went up in smoke with them.

A famous candle burner was the Second Baron of Alvanley, who one chronicler of the age characterized as the wittiest man in England. Lord Alvanley belonged to the race of dandies—but unlike these conceited and often sour individuals, he had great good humor. It was he who described the much-lionized dandy Beau Brummel as a "dandelion." Once when Gunter, a pastry cook, was mounted on a runaway horse with the king's hounds, he excused himself for riding against Alvanley by saying, "O, my lord, I can't hold him. He's so hot.""Ice him, Gunter, ice him," was Alvanley's reply.

As for those candles. Alvanley had what was described as a "delightful recklessness." He always read in bed and he extinguished his candle either by throwing it into the middle of the floor or taking a shot at it with a pillow or putting it, still lighted, under the bolster. Anxious hosts, aware of his habits, used to station a servant in a hallway, probably so that they could sniff smoke.

Beau Brummel could also qualify as an eccentric. He was of plebeian birth. His grandfather had been a valet and his father, starting out as a government clerk, became Private Secretary to Lord North. He managed to send his young son to Eton. Becoming friends of several young nobles, Brummel met the prince. Charmed by his handsome appearance and evident intelligence, the prince gave Brummel a commission in his Tenth Light Dragoons.

Brummel's combination of dry wit, cool impudence, sharp intelligence and the patronage of the prince brought him into the very best circles. He soon became a dictator of fashion and the most famous dandy in history. He decided what the well-dressed man should wear, remodeled the dress coat, insisted that cravats must be starched and brought pantaloons into fashion. He was the first man to wear black for evening and was extremely fastidious, taking as many as three baths per day. Some of his cronies did not take that many in a month!

The Beau insisted upon sartorial perfection. As advisor to the prince, he sent the heir to the throne into the dismals by inveighing against the cut of his coat and his passion for ostentatious clothes. During the time Brummel was president of Watier's Club, he reigned supreme over the world of fashion. However, he was also deeply in debt. He won and lost fortunes at cards and eventually he had a falling out with the prince. When his former patron cut him at a ball, the Beau inquired loudly of Lord Alvanley, "Who is your fat friend?" It was beautifully impudent; it was repeated all over London and it marked his downfall. In 1816, Brummel left England to escape his creditors.

More eccentric and less gifted were Robert Coates and Henry Cope. Coates hailed from the West Indies. He was wealthy and passionately fond of the theater. He was about thirty-six when he arrived in England but appeared older because of his yellow, wrinkled complexion. An amateur thespian, he longed to shine in the theater. He already shone outside the theater. He had a passion for diamonds and furs. He wore furs summer and winter; as for the diamonds, they glittered as buttons, studded the buckles of knee-breeches and shoes and gleamed from his sword handle.

His curricle resembled a scallop-shell. It was deep blue and emblazoned on its panels was his coat of arms, a crowing cock and the motto, "Whilst I live, I'll crow." Little boys used to pursue his marvelous equipage crying out "Cock-adoodle-doooo." It was a cry that would also echo from the galleries of several English theaters.

Coates started his remarkable career in Bath, where he met the beautiful heiress Catherine Tylney-Long, whose fortune was estimated at a million pounds sterling. Naturally, Coates was much attracted to the lady. Once, when he was escorting her to a *fête-champetre*, he and Miss Tylney-Long stopped to admire fish swimming in a pond. The heiress expressed a wish to feed the darling little gold-fishes. She handed him her reticule, asking him to hold it, while she performed this act of kindness. Accidently, he let the reticule drop into the water.

"Jump in and get it," Miss Tylney-Long ordered tersely.

Coates loved the lady (or her money) but he could not swim,

a fact he explained in loud and carrying tones, which attracted a large, amused audience. His explanation was lengthy, and he ended it with an offer to make good the rich Miss Tylney-Long's losses, which made his hearers more amused than ever. The lady felt that he had made her appear ridiculous. Consequently, she with other wags, begged Coates to turn his talents to the professional stage.

Coates, who thought himself far better than Edmund Kean, agreed readily. He made his professional debut as Romeo at the Theatre Royal in Bath—with hilarious results. His acting ability was non-existent, he had a dreadful speaking voice and his postures were invariably ridiculous. His costumes, however, were magnificent, being stitched with diamonds and trimmed with fur. He brought some unique stage-business to the evening. He took snuff during the balcony scene and before breathing his last in the death scene, mindful of his diamonds and silks, he brushed off the place where he would lie.

Evidently unaware that he was more spectacle then spectacular, Coates, now christened "Romeo" Coates, was persuaded to bring his talents to the Haymarket and Lyceum Theatres in London; he also appeared in Cheltenham, Richmond and Brighton.

When he finally retired and pressed his suit to the hand of Miss Tylney-Long, he received a reply that read in part:

> I have compelled you to be far more of a fool than you made me at the *fête-champetre* and I decided you should show yourself a fool before many people. But such Folly does not commend your hand to mine. Therefore, desist your attentions and, if need be, begone from Bath. I have punished you and would save my eyes the trouble to turn away from your person. I pray you regard this epistle as privileged and private.

Miss Tylney-Long, who was known as the "pocket Venus," eventually married Wellesley Pole, who in her honor changed his name to Wellesley Long Pole. He wasted her inheritance and broke her heart.

Henry Cope of Brighton longed to be different, but he had neither Alvanley's wit nor Coates' theatrical aspirations. Consequently, he decided to become green. He wore green coats, green cravats and green boots. He had green rooms in his house and green furniture. He dined off green dishes filled with nothing but green food—peas, celery, spinach, etc. His coach was green and his coachman and footmen also wore green livery. Eventually, poor Mr. Cope could no longer cope and leaped off Brighton's cliffs into the ocean—one hopes on a day when the water was green.

Probably the motivation behind "Romeo" Coates' excesses, Cope's deliberate eccentricities and Lord Alvanley's candle tossing was a desire to alleviate the boredom which was always waiting in the wings for a moneyed aristocracy with nothing to do but enjoy itself. The world it inhabited was small, select and circumscribed. It ranged from the great country houses to a very narrow quarter of London between Grosvenor Square and St. James, Bond Street and Park Lane. Mayfair was its center. The City was peopled by business men and the law. The mob and the crooks were to be found east of Charing Cross.

In his *Age of Elegance*, Arthur Bryant has described Regency London as follows:

> . . . There were no palaces and few large buildings, but street after street of unpretentious, uniform, exquisitely proportioned three-and-four storied houses of brown and grey brick, their skylines of parapet, tile and chimney stack broken only by trees and the white stone of Wren's belfries. The roadways were mostly straight, and, in relation to their height, wide with flagstoned pavements guarded from the traffic by posts and with wrought iron railings before the houses. Every house had the same sober unadorned face of free-stone bordered sash, the same stone steps over the area crowned by a lamp-post, the same neat white pillars on either side of the pedimented door. Only in the beautifully moulded doors and brightly polished knockers with their lion masks, wreaths and urns, did the English instinct for individuality break through that all-pervading, almost monotonous framework. There and in the narrow winding lanes and courts behind the Georgian facade, glimpsed through archways from which came whiffs of laystall and stable and where ragged children swarmed in darkness and cobblers sat at hutches with low open doors.

If those ordered houses could appear monotonous to the chance observer, those who dwelt behind the moulded doors, were, as has been noted, dedicated to relieving the monotony and boredom of their idle existence.

Their search for excitement was incessant. Magnificent dinner parties, balls and routs were constantly being given. There were art exhibitions, the opera, concerts and museums to attend or visit. Gambling, racing, prize-fights, dog-fights, bear-baiting or driving a stagecoach were some of the amusements open to gentlemen. Of these, gambling was the most popular, and the most elegant way to lose money was to join such exclusive clubs as White's, Watier's, Boodles or Brooks. There were numerous smaller gaming "hells" and at all of these, fortunes were lost, careers wrecked, lives blighted and families left destitute. Often the reason for such tremendous losses could be traced to the drink with which the players refreshed themselves. Play whist, piquet or faro from five in the morning until a comparable time the next morning and a man grows thirsty! Fine wines were served, and though bottles were smaller in those days, many players were known as four or five or even six-bottle men. One canny nobleman never ordered anything but water when he gambled. He won fortunes at cards.

In addition to cards, these youthful sprigs of the ton loved to bet. They laid some very strange wages. In the eighteenth century, two noblemen bet on a walking race from Norwich to London. If that sounds reasonably sensible, the participants in that race were five turkeys and five geese. Similar bets were inscribed in White's betting book during the Regency. Gentlemen would wager as to whether a certain Duchess would drop a boy or a girl at her next lying-in. Bets were also laid as to when an expiring peer might meet his maker.

More commonly, men bet on curricle races, on horse racing, and on prize-fighting. Though the latter was illegal (proscribed by the courts since 1750), it was immensely popular. Prize fights called "mills" enjoyed the patronage of the prince and his brothers, the royal dukes. It was a rough and unruly sport. Fists were bare, and there was kicking and eye-gouging. During one notable match, a fighter's eye was gouged out and left hanging on his cheek. With admirable sang-froid, he replaced it in the socket and went on with the match. Mills might last twenty or thirty rounds. There were no technical knockouts and death often occurred in the course of a fight. Champion prize fighters were called "pets of the fancy." One of the most famous of these was Thomas Cribb, who later opened Cribb's Parlor to teach the manly art of fisticuffs to young members of the ton.

Though the sword was beginning to be replaced by the pistol, men learned to fence and also to shoot. Though duels were outlawed, they took place. Sometimes they were over a fancied insult. Men died for jesting at the cut of a suit or the fit of a hat. They also fought for the honor of the ladies but probably only if they were beautiful.

The Prince Regent's taste might be for motherly mistresses but generally, the females who charmed the hearts and warmed the beds of the Regency and Corinthians were beautiful, witty, charming, sexy and expensive. Emma Hart, later Lady Hamilton, was one of these women, and Harriette Wilson (author of a dangerous, for some, autobiography) was another. Her book (quoted in *The Game of Hearts*, Leslie Blanche, ed.: Simon and Schuster, 1955) was full of such tender passages as the following:

> One night (I am sure he will recollect that night, when he thought me mad), one night, I say, I could not endure the thought of Lady W——. That night we slept in Argyle House and he really seemed most passionately fond of me. The idea suddenly crossed my mind, that all the tenderness and passion he seemed to feel for me, was shared between myself and Lady W——.
>
> I could not bear it.
>
> "I shall go home," said I, suddenly jumping out of bed, and beginning to dress myself, at three o'clock on a cold morning in December.
>
> "Going home!" said the duke. "Why, my dear little Harriette, you are walking in your sleep": and he threw on his dressing gown and took hold of my hand . . .

Reading this in later years, the duke may have gnashed his noble teeth but evidently he was not one who paid through the nose to avoid being mentioned. Many did and Harriette, who had been lean in pocket, grew rich on those who shunned publicity. She did not, however, live happily ever after on the wages of sin, but few Cyprians did. Still these ladies enjoyed a freedom of movement that their more virtuous sisters did not.

Despite certain restrictions, though, the Regency was a notable time for women. The winds of change had blown across the English channel from revolutionary France. They had toppled the mammoth head-dresses favored in the eighteenth century (as well as some of the heads they encased), and slimmed the skirts. There was a brief and rather horrid moment when it became the fashion in England to wear what was called "the victim's coiffure," which meant the hair was cut short and left tousled like that of those about to be guillotined. Some more daring ladies even wore thin red velvet ribbons around their necks depicting that final, fatal slash. Fortunately, that morbid fashion passed swiftly but the short curly hair remained and thin muslins caressed shapely figures or forms shaped by the light Circassian corset advocated by Mrs. Bell, wife of the publisher of that famous fashion journal, *La Belle Assemblee*.

Yet, if garments clung, so did custom and the woman's world was still dominated by her father, husband or brother. Her time for enjoying her youth was short. She remained in the schoolroom until she was about seventeen or eighteen. At that point, she was introduced to Society via a ball and hoped to be granted vouchers to the Wednesday Night Subscription Balls at Almack's Assembly Rooms.

Almack's was the Seventh Heaven of the Fashionable World. As Captain Gronow (*The Reminicences and Recollections of Captain Gronow, Being Anecdotes of the Camp, Court, Clubs and Society, 1810-1860*, reprinted New York: The Viking Press, 1964) said, "Good Society . . . was wonderfully select." There was nothing more select than Almack's. Of the three hundred officers of the Foot Guard, not more than half a dozen were honored with vouchers of admission to this exclusive temple of the beau monde, the gate of which was guarded by lady patronesses, whose smiles or frowns consigned men and women to happiness or despair. These lady patronesses were the Ladies Castlereagh, Jersey, Cowper and Sefton, Mrs. Drummond Burrel, the Princess Esterhazy and the Countess Lieven.

"The most popular amongst these grand dames was unquestionably Lady Cowper. Lady Jersey's bearing . . . was that of a theatrical tragedy queen, and whilst attempting the sublime, she frequently made herself ridiculous, being inconceivably rude and, in her manner, often ill-bred. Lady Sefton was kind and amiable, Princess Esterhazy was a *bon enfant*, Lady Castlereagh and Mrs. Drummond Burrel were *très grand dames".*—or, at least, that's how they appeared to Capt. Gronow, a first-hand observer.

The feminine government of Almack's was extremely despotic and subject to all the caprices of tyrannical rule. The ladies often refused to grant vouchers merely because they didn't like the family, the looks or the manners of some hopeful debutante. They might also be jealous of her. If a girl was fortunate enough to storm the barriers, if she was pretty and rich, she could be assured of a great success and in her first season, she might attract an eligible bachelor and receive an offer. Then, because no one save the Fashionable Impures like Miss Wilson seemed to understand anything about birth control, the newly married lass would become pregnant and begin to furnish new pupils for the schoolroom she herself had so recently vacated.

Married women, especially if they were peeresses, enjoyed more freedom than their single sisters, who must always be chaperoned by a mother, aunt or one of the many poor relations who seemed to exist solely to be companions since they were too aristocratic to earn their bread. Those who were a pinch less well connected generally became governesses or paid companions.

Though matrons were usually accompanied by females from the above-mentioned contingent, they could slip the leading strings. Madcap Caroline Lamb, wed to Sir William Lamb but wildly in love with the lame but enduringly glamorous young poet, Lord Byron, was an example of this ilk. Charming, unhappy and a little mad, Caroline Lamb was a victim of her own flagrant indiscretions. There were, however, numerous married ladies who discreetly played the field with the result that it was sometimes a very wise father who knew his own child.

Of course, there were other females who earned their living by their prowess with a pen. Many of these damsels wrote the novels published by William Lane's famous Minerva Press and ultimately destined for his fabulously successful string of circulating libraries.

Though these effusions were castigated by the critics of the day, Mr. Lane, the son of a poulterer and, at an early age, accepted into the profession (which he soon left) and often sneeringly called "the scribbling poulterer" or "the poulterer printer," made a fortune out of his press and his libraries. Some of his authors were equally successful. One Agnes Maria Bennett, who wrote *The Beggar Girl and her Benefactors*, which, incidently, ran into seven volumes (!) was compared to Jane Austen in popularity. Furthermore, in 1806 when her *Vicissitudes Abroad, or: The Ghost of My Father* was published, it sold 2000 copies on the first day of publication.

It was at the Minerva Press that the so-called Regency romance with its innocent heroine and manly hero, its cruel father and conniving villain, was born. The prince himself read Mrs. Bennett's works—and as for the others, their titles often hint at their stories.

Husband Hunters !!! was the name of one such novel; it ran to four volumes. In 1818, *An Angel's Face and a Devil's Heart*, in four volumes, appeared. One of the titles for 1819 was *Redmond the Rebel: They Met at Waterloo*, released four years after that unhappy battle.

To mention Waterloo is to remember one other factor that made the Regency period unique—a final end to conflict. During the first three years of the Regency, Wellington was in Spain fighting the French. In 1812, the same year that Napoleon declared war on Russia and the United States opened hostilities with Britain, the Duke of Wellington entered Madrid. In 1813, he defeated the French at Vittoria, seized San Sebastian and entered France. In 1814, Napoleon, who had stormed into Russia with an army 550,000 troops strong, retreated from burning Moscow. In the course of the Russian campaign, he had lost 530,000 men. He abdicated from the throne of France that same year and was exiled to the Island of Elba. In 1815, Napoleon left Elba and landed in France. On June 18, the Battle of Waterloo saw his defeat. He was banished to St. Helena, never to spread his eagle's wings over Europe again. From 1815-20 there was relative peace in England—though in 1819, there was the Peterloo massacre when soldiers fired on a crowd of unruly agitators, but still the young men were home from the wars and the fear of a French invasion of the Island was vanquished. It was time to trip the light fantastic, a time to relax, enjoy and read . . . the Regency romance.

* * *

Most people believe that the Regency romances written to-day have one root and that twined about the person of Jane Austen (1775-1817). However, in the world of the writer roots often have roots. It is quite possible that Miss Austen might have been inspired by Frances Burney (1752-1840). Miss Burney, too, must have found inspiration in the rather turgid prose of Samuel Richardson's *Pamela* and *Clarissa Harlowe* when, at the age of twenty-five, she wrote the epistolary novel, *Evelina, or: The History of a Young Lady's Entrance into the World*. Full of charm, wit, worldliness and just a touch of irony, this work, published anonymously, was an instant best-seller. In 1815, one of many subsequent editions was published by the Minerva Press. It has gone on being published and presents a malicious picture of the woman in eighteenth century society. It is definitely a comedy of manners and the picture it gives of London could easily lap over into Regency times even as Miss Burney herself did, surviving, indeed, until the second year of Victoria's reign.

In addition to its wit, it is full of the stratagems dear to the romantic novel. It abounds in deceived fathers, mistaken identities, unlikely coincidences, lovers' quarrels and, of course, a happy ending—when all devices are exposed and Evelina is restored to her rightful place in Society and wins as well the love of a noble, upright, ardent aristocrat. There is also, alas, a strong streak of snobbism in the novel when Evelina falls among her middle-class relatives. Her position is not unlike that of Fanny Price, the so-called heroine of Jane Austen's *Mansfield Park*, when after residing in the house of rich relations, she visits her old home again and is grievously upset. This particular theme has carried over into modern Regency romances. Taking a cue from the attitudes of the period, many a novelist has lifted the quizzing glass of scorn at the humble "cit"or middle-class member of society. Note Evelina's reaction to her grandmother, a French lady of plebeian origins named Madame Duval, on first recognizing her as such:

I heard no more: amazed, frightened and unspeakably shocked, an involuntary exclamation of *Gracious Heaven!* escaped me, and more dead than alive, I sunk into Mrs. Mirvan's arms. But let me draw a veil over a scene too cruel for a heart so compassionately tender as yours; it is sufficient that you know that this supposed foreigner turned out to be Madame Duval, the grandmother of your Evelina.

This sort of snobbism is not the only romantic convention upheld in Burney's novel. Like many another romance heroine, Evelina fell in love at first sight. Here is her description of the gentleman (Lord Orville):

His conversation was sensible and spirited; his air and address were open and noble; his manners gentle, attentive and infinitely engaging; his person is all elegance and his countenance the most animated and expressive I have ever seen.

The course of true love did not run smoothly, but finally an almost too grateful Evelina, her sense of humor abolished by love, was united with Orville. She writes to her guardian:

All is over my dearest Sir; and the fate of your Evelina is decided. This morning with fearful joy and trembling gratitude, she united herself forever with the object of her dearest, her eternal affection.

One hopes that Evelina regained a sense of self and went on with the pithy observations of people that call to mind Miss Austen. Forthwith dialogue between a rough sea captain, two fops, and a flirtatious young lady:

"The truth is that in all this huge town, so full as it is of folks of all sorts, there i'n't so much as one public place, beside the playhouse, where a man, that's to say, a man who *is* a man, ought not to be ashamed to shew his face. T'other day they got me to a ridotto: but I believe it will be long enough before they get me to another. I know no more what to do with myself, than if my ship's company had been metamorphosed into Frenchmen. Then, again, there's your famous Ranelagh (a famous pleasure garden) that you make such a fuss about; why what a dull place is that. It is the worst of all.
"Ranelagh, dull, Ranelagh, dull!" was echoed from

mouth to mouth; and all the ladies, as if one accord, regarded the Captain with looks of the most ironical contempt.

"As to Ranelagh," said Mr. Lovel, "most indubitably,
though the place is plebeian, it is by no means adapted to
the plebeian taste. It requires a certain acquaintance with
high life, and . . . and . . . and something of . . . of something *d' un vrai gout* to be really sensible of its merit. Those
whose—connections, and so forth, are not among *les gens
comme il faut,* can feel nothing but *ennui* at such a place as
Ranelagh." "Ranelagh," cried Lord—"O, 'tis the divinest
place under heaven,—or indeed,—for aught I know—."

"O you creature!" cried a pretty, but affected, young
lady, patting him with her fan, "you sha'n't talk so; I know
what you are going to say; but positively, I won't sit by you,
if you're so wicked."

"And how can one sit by you, and be good?" said he,
"when only to look at you is enough to make one wicked—
or wish to be so?"

* * *

Miss Jane Austen's dry wit and satirical eye was even
brighter than that of Miss Burney, though her world was smaller
and largely confined to the countryside or to such fashionable
watering places as Bath. Though they certainly provide inspiration for the modern Regency novelist, detailing the customs and
conversation of the time, they do not have the alarums and ex-
cursions prevalent in *Evelina* nor do they go in for pulsating romance. From a romantic point of view, the most satisfying of her
books is *Persuasion*.

Gentle Anne Eliot, the heroine of *Persuasion*, was too shy and
sensitive at nineteen to dare disagree with the worldly advice
given her by a family friend, Lady Russell. Consequently, she
broke off her engagement to the young naval officer she loved,
deluding herself that it was for his own good. The young man,
Captain Frederick Wentworth, did not agree. There is real pain
when Anne and her cast-off lover meet again. Anne, who still
loved him, found that eight years of separation were as nothing
to her. It was not the same with him. All seems lost when her sis-

ter says, "Captain Wentworth is not very gallant by you, Anne, though he was so attentive to me. Henrietta asked him what he thought of you, when they went away: and he said you were so altered that he would not have known you."

How pleasant it is to an anxious reader when, at the end of the story, the Captain and loving Anne are reunited.

* * *

The Regency romances that have bloomed in the twentieth century are even more satisfying since they have the virtue of distance and, consequently, an even headier combination of romance and love. Of the many novelists who have contributed to the present popularity of the form, Jeffrey Farnol must be mentioned first. Farnol (1878-1952) wrote his first novel, *The Broad Highway*, while still in his twenties. It had a Regency background and it was an instant best-seller. In 1912, he wrote what many people believe to be his magnum opus, *The Amateur Gentleman*. In addition to being a rousing good story, it is a fund of useful information about the period and introduces a canny Bow Street Runner (detective) named Jasper Shrig. This eccentric and down-to-earth custodian of the law was used in several other of Farnol's novels but never to such good advantage as in *Gentleman*.

The story of the Amateur Gentleman is as follows:

Barnabas Barty, son of an unlikely union between a noblewoman and a prize-fighter turned publican, inherits a large sum of money and decides to crash London Society. With his background, however, he would not be accepted. He changes his name, calling himself Barnabas Beverly. He is handsome, brave and intelligent. He is also very strong and has been taught the art of scientific fighting by his father. Eventually, he gets his wish and enters society. He is, however, foiled at every turn by a sneering member of the ton known as Mr. Chichester. Chichester is the so-called friend of Ronald Barrymaine, brother of Cleone, the woman Barnabas loves. Also involved in the story is the villainous moneylender Jasper Gaunt and Sir Mortimer Carnaby, an equally villainous type. Barnabas makes some good friends. Among them are a bewigged Duchess and a Viscount who has a small tiger named Milo of Crotona, a character used in many a Regency novel (not excluding Miss Heyer's). There are complications upon complications in the 625 pages of the novel. Chichester manages to expose Barnabas' plebeian background; he is shunned by his former acquaintances and expelled from his club. Only his true friends stand by this "amateur gentleman." Eventually, he confronts Chichester and demands that they duel with pistols. Chichester pretends to agree but shoots before the signal is given, seriously wounding Barnabas. He does the same to Ronald Barrymaine, who subsequently kills him and dies. All ends happily for Barnabas, once he recovers his health. He marries Cleone, the woman he loves.

The Amateur Gentlemen is woven of a rich Regency fabric. Some of the writing is old-fashioned but many of the scenes are extremely exciting, particularly those in a chapter called "The Gentlemen's Steeplechase." Descriptions in Farnol's novel also set the style for those in other modern Regencies. Here is Mr. Chichester:

> . . . Mr. Chichester's thin, curving nostrils began to twitch all at once, while his eyes gleamed beneath their narrowed lids . . . Barnabas shifted his gaze to Mr. Chichester's right hand, a white beringed hand, whose long slender fingers toyed with the seals that dangled at his fob . . .Now having opened the gate, Mr. Chichester passed through into the high road, and then, for one moment he looked at Barnabas, a long, burning look that took in face, form and features, and so, still without uttering a word, he went upon his way, walking neither fast nor slow, and swinging his tasselled cane as he went . . .

And how many readers are familiar with the following description of the typical Regency buck?

> Barnabas stood before a cheval mirror in the dressingroom of his new house, surveying his reflection with a certain complacent satisfaction.
>
> His silver buttoned blue coat, high-waisted and cunningly rolled of collar, was a sartorial triumph; his black stockinette pantaloons, close-fitting from hip to ankle and there looped and buttoned, accentuated muscled calf and

virile thigh in a manner somewhat disconcerting; his snowy waistcoat was of an original fashion and cut, and his cravat, folded and caressed into being by Peterby's fingers, was an elaborate masterpiece, a matchless creation never before seen upon the town. Barnabas had become a dandy from the crown of his curly head to his silk stockings and polished shoes, and, upon the whole was not ill-pleased with himself.

It is safe to say that Jeffrey Farnol set the style for the Regency novel for years to come. Characters such as the supercilious Messrs. Carnaby and Chichester have sneered themselves through many a contemporary Regency. The diminutive duchess has also pleased other authors, who have done Mr. Farnol the honor of kidnapping her for their own works. His heroines, however, are a little too full-blooded for the current style. It is here that Miss Heyer excells.

Georgette Heyer (1902-74) steers a course between the delicate ironies of Jane Austen and the shoals of Farnol, brushing up against one or another of these authors in her delightful and witty romances. With a few exceptions, she concentrates mainly on the distaff side with a strong emphasis on the ton. Only plain down-to-earth Jenny Chawleigh of *A Civil Contract* has her feet in the middle-class. An heiress, the daughter of a rich tradesman, she marries a penniless aristocrat and spends most of the book trying to atone for her background. Of course, Mary of *The Devil's Cub*, an eighteenth century romp, is half-middle-class, but her father was a nobleman, and eventually she is reclaimed by marriage to a peer. However, meeting her children in *The Infamous Army*, when she is now a grandmother, one learns that blood will tell and that her son is horridly middle-class. Miss Heyer herself came from a good family. Yet, if there is a touch of the same snobbism that characterized some of Miss Burney's and Miss Austen's work, it is not out of place in the Regency novel which, by its very nature, is at its best when roaming through castles, country estates and townhouses, introducing us to more aristocrats than ever lived in England or anywhere else. And Miss Heyer has a delicious knack for doing just that—as witness the charm of *Friday's Child*, *Cotillion*, *The Corinthian*, *Spring Muslin*, etc. *The Talisman Ring*, one of her earlier novels, has a foot in the

1790s and touches very lightly upon the French Revolution, but its antecedents are plainly Regency.

Another author who contributed to the Regency style circa the same period as Heyer was Baroness Emma Magdalena Rosalia Mona Josepha Barbara Orczy (1865-1947), who wrote under the name of Baroness Orczy and invented one of the most fascinating heroes of light historical fiction. His name: Sir Percy Blakely. His occupation: Rescuing hapless French aristocrats from the jaws of the guillotine. His nickname: The Scarlet Pimpernel.

There were nine books in the series, but the first, entitled *The Scarlet Pimpernel,* was easily the best of the lot, and appeared in 1905. Probably most people are familiar with the tale of the British baronet who, married to a beautiful French actress, learns to his sorrow that she has betrayed an aristocratic family to the guillotine and sets out to atone for what he mistakenly believes to be her guilt by organizing a band of intrepid Englishmen who set about their daring rescue work with zest and skill. Blakely is a master of disguise, and also seems to have a dual character, much emulated in other novels. His is both a simpering coxcomb and a bold adventurer. He is the very stuff of romance, as witness this description of his driving his wife home after a ball:

> Tonight, he seemed to have a very devil in his fingers, and the coach seemed to fly along the road, beside the river. As usual, he did not speak to her, but stared straight in front of him, the ribbons seeming to lie quite loosely in his slender white hands. Marguerite looked at him tentatively once or twice; she could see his handsome profile and one lazy eye, with its straight fine brow and drooping heavy lid.

Surely this enduring tale of court intrigue, adventure, romance, and mistaken identities, as well as of wit and elegance, qualifies as a Regency, and the Baroness as one of the genre's most beloved writers. The Regency is a great tradition. Long may it wave.

The Romance Boom

There has been a great deal of confusion about the popular publishing phenomenon known as the "romance boom," confusion about when and how it began, about the types of novels included in it, about the readers of the novels, and about the effects of the novels on their primarily female readership. There's reason for the confusion. First of all, the boom received little public attention in the 1970s, when it was getting underway, and when the novels comprising it were mainly historical romances of varying types (a definition of the sub-genres of romance novels appears at the end of this chapter). Better coverage came in 1981, the year that the newly formed Romance Writers of America held their first annual conference. That conference, in June of 1981, drew the media as well as almost 700 writers and fans to Houston, Texas; the following November, *Life* magazine featured a photo essay on top romance writers and a discussion of the tremendous sales in the genre, and the November 13th issue of *Publishers Weekly*, the publishing industry's trade journal, ran a forty-page special report on romance fiction.

Despite the increased attention, however, much of the misconceptions about romance fiction remain, to an extent because many of the articles which discuss it do not offer accurate information. A glaring example of this lack of respect for the genre (and the people interested in it) appeared, of all places, in the *New York Times* of February 14th, 1982; in an entry in the Editorial Notebook entitled "First Love and Candlelight," Karl Meyer, in addition to unknowingly grouping several teen romance lines with an adult line, wrote "Be it stressed, these books are not erotic or in any way pornographic. Quite the opposite: they offer

51

hard-core chastity and often end with nothing more carnal than a kiss." While the question of pornography, similar to that of beauty, it seems is best left to the eyes of the individual beholder, there is no doubt that adult category romances *are* erotic and were so at the time Meyer's piece was printed. It appeared, in fact, when two major adult romance series, Dell Candlelight Ecstasy and Second Chance at Love, were publishing six *very* erotic novels a month each, when Silhouette was about to introduce its extremely sexy Desire series, and just one month before Bantam launched its doomed Circle of Love category romance series. This last line of romances failed instantly, mainly because it offered "hard-core chastity," an element requiring characters and situations that the market had outgrown.

Why are such inaccuracies not only permitted but generally unchallenged after the articles appear? Obviously, there is a deepseated prejudice against, and, I think, a fear of, romance fiction and what it says about the desire of women—and about the true nature of their place in a supposedly egalitarian society. The prejudice against it—claims that the novels are poorly written, that they're all the same, that readers would buy any romance if it were packaged properly (again, the failure of the heavily promoted Circle of Love proves this concept wrong), that the readership is composed mainly of women of little education and equally limited expectations of life—combined with the difficulties of creating a feminist-oriented criticism in the face of the long-dominant male-oriented criticism, have prevented a useful and accurate analysis of romantic fiction, and in so doing have served the purpose of those who rail against it. If we do not examine the romance as dispassionately as we examine other types of art, be they "high" or popular, we never have to make legitimate a cultural activity that has women as its primary focus, as well as its creators and main audience. And, perhaps more importantly, we never then have to face what romance fiction tells us about the place of women in our society, and about women's desires. In this chapter we will attempt to rethink the meaning of romance and its popularity as it has evolved over the past twelve years or so—alongside, it might be pointed out, the women's movement. What we discover will lead, one hopes, to a new perception of the value of studying this popular fiction to an understanding of women in current American society, and will create a starting off point for feminist scholars who wish to study romance fiction as both a popular literary genre and as a vital indicator of women's view of themselves in a changing social context.

In order to intelligently discuss the meaning of the popularity of romance, it is important to be aware of the development of the romance boom, and of the sub-genres of romance that have enjoyed popularity at different stages of the boom. We must, as well, know how the boom actually got started and dispell some of the myths concerning this beginning. The tale of then-Avon editor Nancy Coffey taking home a long manuscript one sultry August weekend in 1970, and the ensuing battles between her and Peter Meyer, then the firm's editor-in-chief, to publish that manuscript, have become the stuff of publishing legend. As in the case of most legends, the story has been embellished over the years. The manuscript was, of course, Kathleen E. Woodiwiss's *The Flame and the Flower*, which finally achieved publication in April of 1972. This novel, and further ones by Woodiwiss, combined with others published by Avon to lead the romance boom through the middle years of the 1970s. Exactly how calculating was Avon in establishing itself in the vanguard of what was to be the major movement in mass-market publishing in the 1970s, a time of tremendous change throughout the publishing industry?

Not very calculating, it seems. In the late 1960s, when, as a matter of fact, one of the most popular forms of paperback fiction was the Gothic romance, the editorial directors of Avon decided to publish lead paperback originals, a decision made mainly because the firm could not at that time compete with wealthier paperback houses to buy the reprint rights to hardcover bestsellers. Instead, Avon would create its own bestsellers, and the name of Avon "Spectaculars" was coined to indicate these original novels. The first to be published was Burt Hirschfeld's sexy, commercial contemporary novel, *Fire Island*, in 1970. It worked, in the words of Nancy Coffey, "incredibly well," and the search was on for more original fiction. That very summer, Coffey read *The Flame and the Flower*, and saw its potential. And while convincing Peter Meyer of that potential was another matter entirely, his objections were not founded so much on the fact that the

Woodiwiss novel was a "woman's book" as they were on its being an historical novel. In the publishing business, which is nothing if not imitative, the last historical romance success that anyone could recall was Kathleen Winsor's *Forever Amber*—and that
had come out in 1944, nearly thirty years before. Yet Nancy
Coffey did eventually manage to convince Peter Meyer of the
wisdom of publishing the Woodiwiss novel as an Avon Spectacular, and Meyer even came to write part of the cover copy.

　　The romance boom was starting, though no one was quite
aware of it yet. It was not so much *The Flame and the Flower*'s constant returns to press that showed Avon that this historical romance had struck a very profitable nerve, as it was the amount of
fan mail that poured into the firm. Nor was anyone yet aware
that, in writing the novel that launched the romance boom,
Woodiwiss also created a sub-genre of romance known as the
"sensual historical." As pointed out in *Publishers Weekly*'s November 13, 1981 Special Report on romance fiction, two of the elements that distinguish this sub-genre are the "unfailing fidelity
of the heroine for the hero—and exclusive sex between
them." Yet the sensual historical was not the only innovative sub-
genre of romance to achieve popularity in the 1970s. Published in
1974 by Avon, Rosemary Rogers' *Sweet Savage Love* established
another—the "bodice-ripper" (originally referred to as the
"sweet/savage" novel). Also according to the November 13, 1981
Publishers Weekly, this type of historical romance depicts "explicit
sex with the hero and additional male characters; graphic sexual
variations; abuse and/or rape; and no guarantee that the heroine
will end up with the first man with whom she has had sexual relations." A third sub-genre of the historical romance co-existed
with the above-described two in the 1970s, the "romantic-
historical" (described by *Publishers Weekly* as "far more scrupu-
lously researched [than the other two sub-genres], these novels
for the most part exhibit a literary prose style and considerable
historical accuracy"), though the other two were by far more
popular. It is important to note that, during this time, any "Gothic" elements in a manuscript were an automatic kiss of death in
terms of the manuscript's being accepted for publication. So
popular before the romance boom, the Gothic was, in effect,
dead. Curiously enough, the newly tapped interest in sexy his-

toricals was not blamed for the decline of the Gothic novels by editors as much as the weakened qualities of the Gothics themselves were. It was claimed that the Gothic market had become over-saturated, that too many inferior novels were placed behind well-designed Gothic covers, causing the readers to become leery of this sub-genre. The important question of the change in taste in the romance market, of whether preferences alter in response to what's on the market alone, will be discussed shortly.

By 1976, the historical romance boom was in full swing. *Time* magazine could report the publication of over 150 paperback historical romances yearly, and by the end of the decade, both the press and trade reports estimated that at least one quarter of all books sold were romances, and that the readership of these novels numbered over twenty million. By 1978, paperback houses were so heavily inventoried in historical romances that they could take on very few new titles and found themselves rejecting novels which would have been bought even a year or two before. Conversely, some writers had been signed on for multiple-book contracts in the early years of the boom on the basis of a proposal for only one book. It seemed that what one assumed had happened to the Gothic had happened to the historical romance as well—a glut of bad but still beautifully packaged novels drove out the good. Presumably, the romance reader had to move on to fresher fields to find the quality that had once existed in the historical romance genre.

While this explanation of the decline of first, the Gothic, and then the historical romance is open to discussion (and will, in fact, be discussed below), there is no doubt about the kind of romance that became popular toward the end of the 1970s and has continued to grow in the early years of the 1980s. To anyone who's ever walked into a chain bookstore such as Dalton or Walden, or into the book section of any retail store that carries mass market paperbacks, or to anyone who's sat on a bus or subway and watched what other people are reading, the answer is obvious—the "category" romance is now the most popular. (The term "category" denotes "formula" books of a distinct type. Other types of category fiction are the mystery, the Western and the science fiction.) Most commonly around 55,000 words long, the category romances are of the kind pioneered by Harlequin

and now Americanized by a number of publishing firms,
including Dell Ecstasy, Second Chance at Love, Silhouette and
Silhouette Desire.

It is on the category romance that a great deal of attention has
been focused. Much of this attention is due to the fact that the
category novels were the most popular when the romance boom
began to receive a sizable measure of media coverage. Yet it also
seems that the category romance excites more passion in its critics than do either the historical romance or the Gothic. Why is the
category romance so misunderstood? Mentioned in the beginning of this chapter was the idea that fear of what an investigation not weighed down with preconceptions about the category
romance would reveal is one motivation for the type of criticism
the novels have received. The domination of the male point-of-
view in both cultural and literary criticism has also precluded a
feminist-oriented examination of the novels, and perhaps the
current reticence to develop innovative theories about the significance of romance can also be traced to the fear of rocking the boat
in a tight market for academics. In addition to these two factors,
fear and the male-dominated academy, must be added a third,
which is a general disrespect for category romance which enables
people who would never discuss any other topic without ade-
quate research to discourse about the novels without having fully
investigated them. Many of us read at least one older-style Harlequin romance as teens, or know someone who did; unfortunately, that kind of romance is what we assume the category romance
still to be like, much as Karl Meyer erroneously did in his *Times*
editorial. It seems that the topic discussed—category romance—
did not merit the checking of facts mentioned in the article. Yet
the category romance has received in-depth, unbiased, if somewhat outdated, treatment at the hands of one academic, Tania
Modleski, an assistant professor of film and literature at the University of Wisconsin, Milwaukee. In her book *Loving With a
Vengeance: Mass-produced Fantasies for Women* (Hamden,
Connecticut: Archon Books, 1982), Modleski breaks critical
ground in considering the significance of the Harlequin romance, the Gothic (both the more "high" art Gothic of writers
such as Mary Wollstonecraft and popular Gothics), and the soap
opera. Acknowledging the discomfort and defensiveness that

most women have felt in attempting to deal with these narratives, Modleski pinpoints the three general attitudes women critics have taken toward these popular forms: "dismissiveness; hostility—tending unfortunately to be aimed at the consumers of the narratives; or, most frequently, a flippant kind of mockery" (p. 14). Just as importantly, she points out that female power is the real concern of the forms, which for the purposes of our discussion will be limited to the Harlequin and the Gothic.

Since the popularity of the Gothic romance preceded that of the other sub-genres in the romance boom, it is best to consider Modleski's conclusions about this type of novel before discussing the category romance. By tracing the development of the Gothic, and considering the elements in it, Modleski concludes that ". . . Gothics in part serve to convince women that they will not be victimized the way their mothers were . . ." (p. 83). She points out that "avowed feminists," including Mary Wollstonecraft, have written Gothics (in a further reflection on the way female power is dealt with in Gothics, it is interesting to note that Wollstonecraft's daughter, Mary Shelley, wrote *Frankenstein*, the horror story about just what happens when men try to subvert the ultimate female power, that of creating life), and that, significantly, the longest section of Wollstonecraft's *Maria, or the Wrongs of Woman* is a letter written by the title character to her own daughter to explain her imprisonment in a mental institution by her own husband. Modleski believes that the act of explanation is an attempt to break the chain of victimization, definitely a feminist act. She further points out that the main difference between mass-produced popular Gothics and a militantly feminist Gothic such as *Maria* is that "the latter explores on a conscious level conflicts which popular Gothics exploit, yet keep at an unconscious level." (p. 84). Further, I think that a great deal of the appeal of the Gothics is that they show that the victimization of women is external, that it is not self-induced. And at the end of the 1960s, in a time when feminist assertions about American institutions were not yet articulated but most definitely were felt, what could better depict the American woman's determination not to be victimized than that inevitable Gothic cover, a painting of her fleeing a *house*, the very symbol which has traditionally defined a woman's "proper"—and limited—sphere?

Unfortunately, Modleski's analysis of the category romance deals only with the Harlequin, and does not take into account the very important changes in this sub-genre that have taken place since the appearance—and tremendous success—of the Dell Ecstasy novels in December of 1980. These novels introduced older, more sophisticated heroines, and a more up-dated female attitude toward sex in the age of "nice girls do"; the heroine no longer had to be semi-conscious or forced against her will to show the hero even the smallest sexual response. When discussing books in the Harlequin mode (and, of course, her complete analysis must be read for her conclusion to be fully understood), Modleski concludes that the novels not only reflect the "hysterical" state, but actually induce it to some extent. The novels become a type of narcotic by alternately describing and assuaging the anxiety produced by the novel's presentation of the heroine's psychic conflicts (p. 57). Yet the elements that lead Modleski to her conclusion, elements including the young, unworldly woman who totally wins without effort the love of an arrogant, enigmatic hero (in fact, does so without even being aware that she should seek it), the bitchy, sophisticated, older (but not by too much) "other woman," who both shows the evil of striving consciously for the hero's love and highlights the uniqueness of the heroine, are elements that no longer work in the American category romance. These books now feature older (i.e., twenty-five through forty-five) women as the heroine, and feature communicative heroes often willing to discuss the problems of the love relationship. Yet the main question of female power, of the focus of the books on a relationship in which the male is obsessed by a female, in which his waking hours are preoccupied by thoughts of her, is an element which remains even as the books evolve; in fact, it is one of the few basic elements retained. (The nature of the hero in these novels is a subject that could bear critical scrutiny; in discussing the hero, Ecstasy founder Vivian Stevens said in the November 13, 1981 *Publishers Weekly* Special Report on romance that the "popularity of the books says a lot about what women aren't getting in real life." It probably also has a lot to do with male reticence to fully examine the books.) Obviously, as women's perception of their sexuality and of their role in society evolved as the women's movement developed, the category romance evolved to reflect those new perceptions. (Even the much-beleaguered Harlequin introduced its more sensual Harlequin Presents line in 1973, just after the debut of the Woodiwiss-inspired sensual historical, and just before the Rogers-inspired sweet/savage historical sub-genre.)

Definitely, the popularity of romance from the late sixties through the present, the early eighties, is not an isolated phenomenon, but one that arises from the social and cultural climate and responds to the needs, desires, and perceptions of its audience. The Gothic romance was inevitably popular in a time when women were still widely condemned for dissatisfaction with a domestic role. Consequently, the decline in popularity of the Gothic might not have been due so much to saturation in the market, as to the changing psychic needs of American women. In the early seventies, in the beginnings of the women's movement, women were challenging the traditional view of female sexuality, and for a time experienced the desire to imitate what was perceived as a male attitude toward sexuality, a desire made possible by the changing social climate and by reliable birth control; is it really surprising that overtly sexy novels for women appeared and struck such a responsive cord throughout the country? Being set in the past, the novels were distanced enough from the reader's everyday experience to relieve any remaining guilt about the desire to be freer sexually. And, almost representing a need to "stick a toe in first," to become acquainted with the idea of greater sexual freedom, the first popular sexy historical romances, the sensual historicals, still featured commitment to one man, the man who had initiated the heroine into sexual experience. A few years later, the American woman was ready for the fantasy represented by the "bodice-ripper," sexual experience with more than one partner. Finally, the subsequent popularity of the category romance also arose from the social climate in general and the status of women in particular. By the end of the seventies, women's lives had undergone tremendous change but rather than being sure of what course they wished to chart in their lives, woman found themselves confused about the paths they wished to follow. Raised by women whose lives were much more circumscribed, they had a range of options, from full-time motherhood to demanding careers, to be decided on in the shadow of the mythic "Superwoman" who did it all. It is no wonder, then, that women turned to the category romance at this time, to romance novels more intense in their emphasis on the love relationship—and therefore on the individualizing quality of love for the significant other, a quality discussed by Annette Townend in the first chapter of this book. After all, set in the present and featuring characters the reader could more readily recognize and identify with than the ones featured in historical romances, the category contemporaries could respond to the deeper need for emphasis on the self felt by American women at the end of the decade (interestingly, bestselling category romance novelist Janet Dailey is almost a cult figure in Japan, a nation in which recent social changes have challenged women's traditional role).

While this discussion of the relationship between popular romance and the society that produces and devours it has necessarily been brief, I think that it shows that we must bring all our skills of scholarship to bear on the study of this phenomenon. The books are important in the lives of over twenty million readers, and we owe it to ourselves to explore their full significance. Until we do, we remain blind to the import of an extremely popular art form, and we conspire against the development of a truly feminist aesthetic.

The Romance Sub-Genres

As pointed out in the discussion of the romance boom, there are several varieties, or sub-genres, of novels grouped together under the general heading of romance. While certain sub-genres are more closely related to others, each has unique qualities which separate it from the others. For the last section of this book, almost two hundred writers working today have given information about themselves and their careers. In so doing, they've noted a total of ten romance subgenres in which they write. The sub-genres are defined below.

1. Category romance: The beginning of the 1980s saw the dominant popularity of the "category" romance, a term which comes from publishing. It indicates novels of a fixed length (so the page counts of a particular series are uniform), generally written to a publisher's specific guidelines, that can be grouped into one of the popular literary genres or "categories": the mystery, the romance, the science fiction and the western. As the category romance evolved in the early 80s to respond to the demands of its readership, three types have become distinct in the adult field, and teen category romances have also been developed. The types of category romance are:

> The sweet category romance: Epitomized by the original Harlequin line and the lavender-covered, original Silhouette romance, these novels feature a virginal heroine whose first real love involvement is with the hero, and whose age ranges from the late teens through the early twenties. The level of sensuality throughout is fairly restrained. Length is 50-55 thousand words.
>
> The sensual category romance: While the full-blown sensual romance appeared on the scene with the introduction of Dell Candlelight's Ecstasy romances in December of 1980,

the brainchild of senior editor Vivien Stevens, this type of sexier category romance was foreshadowed by the more sensual Harlequin Presents line, which premiered in 1973. The sensual category romances feature sexually experienced heroines ranging in age from the mid-twenties to the late thirties. The relationship with the hero is consummated well before the end of the novel, and a high level of sensuality is emphasized. As in the sweet romances, length is 50-55 thousand words.

The longer category romance: Pioneered by Silhouette's Special Edition line, these novels keep their focus on the developing love relationship between the heroine and hero, while incorporating more secondary characters and more realistic elements than those in the shorter category romances. Again, the heroines are more mature and sophisticated than those in the sweet romances, and a high level of sensuality is featured. Length is generally 70-75 thousand words; new lines introduced in 1983 and 1984 may exceed this length.

The teen category romance: Closest in tone to the sweet romances, these novels have as their heroine a teen-age girl becoming involved with a boy for the first time. Approximately 40 to 45 thousand words in length, this type of novel was pioneered by Scholastic's Wildfire series in 1980, and further popularized by Bantam's Sweet Dreams and Silhouette's First Love teen romance series.

2. Longer contemporary romance: As pointed out by Kathryn Falk and Elene Kolb in the *Publishers Weekly* November 13, 1981 Special Report on romance, this type of romance novel would have simply been called a love story forty years ago, before the advent of the category romance. In their words, these novels "feature contemporary settings, more sexually experienced heroines and unpredictable endings." Top practioners in recent years are Janet Dailey, Danielle Steel and the late Helen Van Slyke.

3. Edwardian romance: A light romance in the tradition of the Regency, set during the reign of Edward VII (1901-1910).

4. Family saga: An intergenerational novel following the lives of various members of several generations of a family, often one that immigrates to the United States in poverty and rises to a

high social standing. An emphasis is placed on the romances of the characters.

5. Georgian romance: A light romance in the tradition of the Regency, set in the years 1910-1920 of the reign of George V.

6. Gothic romance: Gothic romances trace their origin to the eighteenth-century novels of Horace Walpole and Mrs. Radcliffe, specifically to Walpole's 1764 *The Castle of Otranto*. They always feature a gloomy castle (or, in more modern times, a large, forbidding mansion), supernatural and/or horrifying elements, and a threatened heroine. Settings are both historical and contemporary.

7. Historical romance: Historical romances are set in past historical periods and, again as pointed out by Kathryn Falk and Elene Kolb in *Publishers Weekly*, are distinct from historical novels in that "the central focus . . . is *always* the emotional involvement of the heroine." They define three distinct types of modern historical romance:

> The sensual historical: Established by Kathleen E. Woodiwiss's 1972 *The Flame and the Flower*, these are romance novels in which "the passion of the hero and heroine propels the story." Usual elements are "the unfailing fidelity of the heroine for the hero—and exclusive sex between them; a lush historical background (but with limited historical details); and a happy ending depicting the loving couple together." The sweet/savage romance, or bodice-ripper: Rosemary Rogers's *Sweet Savage Love*, published in 1974, was the first of this type of historical romance. According to Falk and Kolb, these romance novels "contain explicit sex with the hero and additional male characters; graphic sexual variations; abuse and/or rape; and no guarantee that the heroine will end up with the first man with whom she has had sexual relations . . . 'certain liberties' are taken with historical details, but by and large these authors conscientiously research the historical background for their novels."
>
> The romantic-historical: According to Falk and Kolb, this type of historical romance is epitomized by the "Roselynde Chronicles" of Roberta Gellis. "Far more scrupulously researched [than the other two types], these novels for the most part exhibit a literary prose style and considerable historical accuracy."

8. Regency romance: These light romances can be traced to the novels of Fanny Burney and Jane Austen, and are set during the English Regency of 1811-1822. The most notable—and influential—recent practitioner of this type of romance was Georgette Heyer, whose attention to period detail and the slang and sparkling dialogue of the time has made her a favorite among romance writers and readers.

9. Romantic suspense: Romantic novels with contemporary settings and an emphasis on intrigue. While the term "romantic suspense" is often incorrectly used interchangeably with the term "modern Gothic,"the subgenres actually have only one element in common—a threatened heroine.

10. Victorian romance: A light romance in the tradition of the Regency, set during the reign of Victoria (1837-1901).

A Romance Writer's Resource List:
A Guide to Writers' Associations,
Publications and Conferences

While romance writers have been around for a long time, it was only in the early 1980s that American writers began to organize conferences and writers' associations specifically for authors in the genre. In addition, conferences of long standing started to offer special panels and seminars on the writing and publication of romance at this time. Below are listed the major association for romance writers in this country, Romance Writers of America (RWA), the International Women's Writing Guild, which has a number of romance writers among its membership and which offers a special week-long romance seminar at its yearly summer conference, the romance publications and the major conferences dealing specifically with romance. Further, the addresses of *The Writer* and *Writer's Digest* are given, since the May issues of both these magazines feature a list of the year's upcoming writers' conferences.

1. Writers' associations:

Romance Writers of America: The RWA was founded in 1980, and held its first annual conference in Houston in 1981. In addition to holding a national conference in a different location yearly, the RWA publishes a monthly newsletter, awards prizes in a romance fiction competition (the "Golden Heart" awards, with categories for both published and unpublished authors), and maintains chapters throughout the United States, which often sponsor regional conferences. Contact the RWA regarding all its activities at:
Romance Writers of America
5206 FM 1960 W., Suite 207
Houston, TX 77069

The International Women's Writing Guild: The IWWG publishes a bi-monthly newsletter which features items of interest to its membership, women writing all kinds of fiction
and non-fiction. It does focus on the needs of women writers, who make up the majority of romance writers. Also, its
yearly conference features a week-long seminar on romance
writing. Contact the IWWG at:

> International Women's Writing Guild
> Box 810, Gracie Station
> N.Y., N.Y. 10028

2. Romance publications:

Affaire de Coeur: This monthly, magazine-format publication
features reviews, articles, and news items. For subscription
information write:

> *Affaire de Coeur*
> 5660 Roosevelt Pl.
> Fremont, CA 94538

Barbra Critiques: Reviews of romance novels, published by
Barbra Wren, who works in a Missouri B. Dalton store
which boasts that chain's largest volume of romance sales as
a percentage of total sales. For subscription information
write:

> *Barbra Critiques*
> 2710 R.D. Mize Rd.
> Independence, MO 64057

Boy Meets Girl: A weekly newsletter published by Vivien
Jennings, the owner of several Mid-West bookstores. It features items on writers, upcoming novels, new romance
lines, etc. For subscription information write:

> *Boy Meets Girl*
> 2812 W. 53rd
> Fairway, Kansas 66205

Romantic Times: A tabloid-style newspaper published
monthly by Kathryn Falk, the author of *Love's Leading Ladies*,
a trade paperback that spotlighted top romance writers, and
the hardcover *How To Write a Romance and Get It Published*. It
features critiques, articles by and about romance authors,
and lots of news regarding upcoming conferences, what editors are looking for, etc. For subscription information write:

Romantic Times
163 Joralemon St., Suite 1234
Brooklyn Heights, N.Y. 11201

3. Conferences:

There are currently four national conferences specifically devoted to romance. These are:

Romance Writers of America national conference: First held in 1981, this conference holds seminars on achieving publication, the author/agent relationship, word processors, etc., and has top editors, agents and writers leading discussions on various romance publishing topics. For information write:
RWA—Conference information
5206 FM 1960 W., Suite 207
Houston, TX 77069

Romantic Book Lovers' Conference: Begun by *Romantic Times* publisher Kathryn Falk in 1982, this April New York conference features seminars similar to those at the above described RWA national conference. Top writers make guest appearances, and awards are given both for career achievement, and for individual titles. For information write:
Romantic Book Lovers' Conference
163 Joralemon St., Suite 1234
Brooklyn Heights, N.Y. 11201

Rom/Con (Romantic Readers, Riters Rendezvous): Begun by *Affaire de Coeur* publisher Barbara Keenan in 1982, this February California conference takes its somewhat unusual name from the science fiction/fantasy conference style of naming conventions, and, again similar to certain of the conferences for those genres, emphasizes the media promotion of authors and permits fans to meet favorite writers. For information write:
Affaire de Coeur—Rom/Con information
5660 Roosevelt Pl.
Fremont, CA 94538

University of California San Diego Extension Romance Writers Conference. First held in February of 1983, this confer-

ence features seminars led by top authors and editors. For
information write:
USCD Extension
University of California San Diego
La Jolla, CA 92093

The yearly conference of the International Women's Writing
Guild (IWWG), held in July or August at the campus of Skidmore
College in Saratoga, N.Y., features a week-long seminar on romance writing (see Elaine Raco Chase's author entry in the last
section of this book for her account of how this conference
helped launch her career as a top category romance writer). It is
not purely a romance conference, however, and attracts writers
working in all fields, in both fiction and non-fiction. For information write:
IWWG—Conference information
Box 810, Gracie Station
N.Y., N.Y. 10028

Due to the current popularity of romance, many other writers' conferences now feature seminars and panels on romance
writing. Excellent sources for each year's upcoming conferences
are the May issues of The *Writer* and *Writer's Digest*. Available on
newstands and in most libraries, these publications can be contacted at the addresses below:
The Writer
Writer, Inc.
8 Arlington St.
Boston, MA 02116

Writer's Digest
9933 Alliance Rd.
Cincinnati, OH 45242

Bibliography

Prepared by Kay Mussel

The sources listed include both scholarly criticism and journalistic analysis. Romances are, like all popular formulas, emphemeral; and the most useful information may be found in popular or professional sources, such as *Publishers Weekly*. The list is divided into three sections: works about romances before 1900, works about twentieth century romances, and reference or bibliographical works.

A. Romances Before 1900

Allen, Richard O., "If You Have Tears: Sentimentalism as Soft Romanticism," *Genre*, June 1975: 199-245.

Baym, Nina, *Woman's Fiction: A Guide to Novels by and About Women in America, 1820-1870*. Ithaca, N.Y.: Cornell Univ. Press, 1978.

Beer, Gillian, *The Romance*. London: Metheun, 1970.

Bell, Michael Davitt. *Hawthorne and the Historical Romance of New England*. Princeton, N.J.: Princeton Univ. Press, 1971.

Brown, Herbert Ross, *The Sentimental Novel in America, 1789-1860*. Durham, N.C.: Duke Univ. Press, 1940.

Kelley, Mary, "The Sentimentalists: Promise and Betrayal in the Home," *Signs*, 4 (Spring 1979): 434-46.

Moers, Ellen, *Literary Women*. Garden City, N.Y.: Doubleday, 1977.

Papashvily, Helen Waite, *All the Happy Endings*. New York: Harper, 1956.

Thompson, G. Richard, "Introduction: Gothic Fiction in the Romantic Age: Context and Mode," in *Romantic Gothic Tales*,

1790-1840. New York: Harper and Row, Perennial Library, 1979, pp. 1-54.

Welter, Barbara, "The Cult of True Womanhood," *American Quarterly*, 18 (Summer 1966): 151-74.

Varma, Devendra P., *The Gothic Flame*. 1957. Reprint, New York: Russell and Russell, 1966.

B. Romances of the Twentieth Century

Abartis, Caesarea, "The Ugly-Pretty, Dull-Bright, Weak-Strong Girl in the Gothic Mansion," *Journal of Popular Culture*, Fall 1979: 257-63.

Andgrson, Rachel, *The Purple Heart Throbs: The Sub-Literature of Love*. London: Hodder and Stoughton, 1974.

Berman, Phyllis, "They Call Us Illegitimate," *Forbes*, 6 March 1978: 37-38.

Britton, Anne, and Marion Collin, *Romantic Fiction*. London: Boardman, 1960.

Cawelti, John G., *Adventure, Mystery, and Romance: Formula Stories as Art and Popular Culture*. Chicago: Univ. of Chicago Press, 1976.

Douglas, Ann, "Soft-Porn Culture," *New Republic* 183, 30 August 1980: 25-29.

Greenfeld, Beth, and Juliann E. Fleenor, eds., *The Female Gothic*. St. Albans, Vt.: Eden Press, 1983.

Harlequin 30th Anniversary, 1949-1979: The First 30 Years of the World's Best Romance Fiction. Toronto: Harlequin, 1979.

Harvey, Brett, "Boy Crazy," *Village Voice*, 10 February 1982.

Mann, Peter H., *The Romantic Novel: A Survey of Reading Habits*. London: Mills and Boon, 1969.

Mann, Peter H., *A New Survey: The Facts About Romantic Fiction*. London: Mills and Boon, 1974.

Modleski, Tania, *Loving With a Vengeance*. Hamden, Ct.: Archon, 1982.

Mussell, Kay, "Beautiful and Damned: The Sexual Woman in Modern Gothic Fiction,"*Journal of Popular Culture*, 9 (Summer 1975): 84-89.

O'Toole, Patricia, "Paperback Virgins," *Human Behavior*, February 1979: 62-67.

Radway, Janice, "The Utopian Impulse in Popular Literature: Gothic Romances and 'Feminist' Protest," *American Quarterly*, Summer 1981: 140-62.

Ritchie, Claire, *Writing the Romance Novel*. London: Bond Street, 1962.

Robinson, Lillian S., "On Reading Trash," in *Sex, Class, and Culture*. Bloomington: Indiana Univ. Press, 1978, pp. 200-22.

"Romance Fiction: A PW Special Report," edited by Daisy Maryles and Robert Dahlin, *Publishers Weekly*, 13 November 1981: 25-64.

Ruggiero, Josephine A., and Louise C. Weston, "Pulp Feminists," *Human Behavior*, February 1978: 20.

Russ, Joanna, "Somebody's Trying to Kill Me and I Think It's My Husband," *Journal of Popular Culture*, Spring 1973: 666-91.

Thurston, Carol M., and Barbara Doscher, "Supermarket Erotica: Bodice-Busters Put Romantic Myths to Bed," *The Progressive* 46, April 1982: 49-51.

Weibel, Kathryn, *Mirror, Mirror: Images of Women Reflected in Popular Culture*. Garden City, N.Y.: Doubleday Anchor, 1977.

C. Reference and Bibliography

Mussell, Kay, "Gothic Novels," in M. Thomas Inge, ed., *Handbook of American Popular Culture*, vol. 1, pp. 151-69. Westport, Ct.: Greenwood, 1979.

Mussell, Kay, "Romantic Fiction," in M. Thomas Inge, ed., *Handbook of Popular American Culture*, vol. 2, pp. 317 43. Westport, Ct.: Greenwood, 1980.

Radcliffe, Elsa J., *Gothic Novels of the Twentieth Century: An Annotated Bibliography*. Metuchen, N.J.: Scarecrow, 1979.

Vinson, James, ed., *Twentieth Century Romance and Gothic Writers*. Detroit: Gale, 1983.

Yankelovich, Skelly, and White, *Consumer Research Survey on Reading and Book Purchasing*. The Book Industry Study Group, Inc. October 1978.

Historically Important Writers

As difficult as it is to believe, writers important to the romance genre in the English-language tradition, be they prolific writers in the genre, or not strictly romance writers who have nevertheless contributed to or been influenced by the development of romance, have not to this time been profiled in a single reference source. Obviously, vital insights to understanding romance fiction today are to be found in the lives and works of earlier writers. Why were the writers included chosen? Basically, because their work has touched upon, or been touched by, elements crucial to the development of the genre. It's a very long distance, both in time and style, from Tobias Smollett to Dorothy Eden, but certain works of the former helped lay the groundwork for those of the latter.

The sixty-six authors featured show a wide range of personal backgrounds and styles. We find writers who turned to their trade solely for money, others for solace, others still who wrote simply because they couldn't stop themselves from writing. We see that many writers—Louisa May Alcott, Maria Edgeworth and Charlotte Yonge, among others—felt a strong paternal influence, one that was not always positive, and that a large number wrote as children, while some began only after they'd had children of their own. Several first wrote and published mysteries. In fact, it was through a mystery, the 1935 *Merely Murder*, that Georgette Heyer first became known to American readers. And we discover as well that writers working in the field today are not the first to experience a prejudice against romance writers. Nathaniel Hawthorne felt contempt for the woman writers whose genre heavily influenced *The Scarlet Letter*; hostile and cynical reactions to the genre drove the extremely popular Frances Parkinson Keyes to write *The Cost of a Best-Seller* in 1950, in which she defended the skill of the popular novelist.

A number of sources were consulted by researcher Susan Scott as she gathered material for the entries. While information on the larger number of writers could be readily found in well-known sources, some writers very popular in their time seem to have written, lived and died with almost nary a trace left about their lives. On authors such as Charlotte Dacre, Eliza Parsons and Eleanor Sleath, critical material by Ann B. Tracy and, especially, Devendra P. Varma, was invaluable. Each entry on an author includes her/his bibliography, as complete as possible, in which the year of original publication of each title is noted. *Books in Print* should be consulted to determine if a book is currently available.

LOUISA MAY ALCOTT (November 29, 1832 - March 6, 1888)

Similar to countless other authors, Louisa May Alcott turned a child's interest in telling stories and keeping journals into an adult job when it became apparent that she would be the main support of her family. And, as was the case with many who wrote both "popular" and critically acceptable fiction, her more sensational works were hidden behind a pseudonym. In Alcott's case, that pseudonym was not discovered until 1943, over fifty years after her death.

Though born in Germantown, Pennsylvania, where her father was teaching, Alcott spent most of her life in Boston and Concord, Massachusetts. As a child Alcott enjoyed the presence of her father's intellectual friends; he was the teacher and transcendentalist philosopher, Bronson Alcott. Her own earliest friends were Ralph Waldo Emerson and Henry Thoreau; among her neighbors was Nathaniel Hawthorne; those in her father's circle included Margaret Fuller, Oliver Wendell Holmes, William Ellery Channing and Henry James, Sr. Alcott and her three sisters were educated by their father, whom they adored. He advocated women's rights, was an abolitionist and vegetarian and in 1843 even founded a short-lived utopian community, Fruitlands, in Harvard, Massachusetts. Yet Bronson Alcott was a much more intellectual than practical man, and Fruitlands failed after six months.

It was after this failure that Alcott's lifelong efforts to help provide for her family began. Before she turned to writing, she had made some money in other ways—even as a child she had made and sold doll's clothes. Growing older, she turned to other sewing, school teaching (a job she despised), and even worked briefly in domestic service, which she found to be particularly humiliating.

Alcott's first published book was FLOWER FABLES (1855), a collection of fairy tales originally told to Emerson's daughter, Ellen. Yet the author's first taste of fame came a little later, with the publication of HOSPITAL SKETCHES (1863). An ardent abolitionist like her father, she had volunteered as a nurse when the war broke out, though she quickly contracted typhoid from the unsanitary hospital conditions. HOSPITAL SKETCHES was a collection of her war reminiscences. MOODS, her first full-length novel, was a sentimental romance in which some modern readers have found undertones of cynicism about marriage. It did quite well.

But Alcott's major success came whan a Boston publisher suggested that she try her hand at the same kind of book that her fellow Massachusetts writer William T. Adams was turning out with profitable results. Adams, of the Presidental Adamses, published under at least eight *noms de plume*, the best known being "Oliver Optic." He wrote adventure books for boys; Alcott was urged to write something similar, but for an audience of girls. LITTLE WOMEN made her an immediate success and is, of course, still read by girls today. Alcott followed it with similar books for children.

As any reader of LITTLE WOMEN knows, the character of Jo is based on the author. In addition to her temperamental similarities to her creator, Jo, in order to help support her family, turned out potboilers, sensational stories for the papers of the day. And like Jo, Alcott was ashamed of these "blood-and-thunder" tales written for money. She kept their authorship secret, even going over her diaries and letters before she died to ensure that no reference was made to them. And remain a secret they did—until

1943, when two future owners of a rare-book firm, Dr. Leona Rostenberg and Madeleine Stern, went through the Alcott papers at Harvard's Houghton Library. In the course of painstaking work, they discovered Alcott's pseudonym, "A.M. Barnard,"in a letter from a magazine editor. The clue enabled them to find many of the stories, and in the mid-1970s Madeleine Stern brought out four of the tales in a book entitled BEHIND A MASK: THE UNKNOWN THRILLERS OF LOUISA MAY ALCOTT. The title novella, BEHIND A MASK, OR, A WOMAN'S POWER, was the featured fiction in the 1975 Christmas issue of REDBOOK magazine, and it is a fast-paced and fascinating tale of a governess who was not quite what she appeared to be. As Stern points out in the introduction to her collection of the Alcott tales, in BEHIND A MASK the reader can find an "intensely if obliquely feminist" insight.

Alcott's later years were shadowed by the deaths of her two remaining sisters (the model for Beth in LITTLE WOMEN had died much earlier) and that of her mother. Alcott died in the home of her physician, Rhoda Lawrence, on March 6, 1888, at the age of fifty-five. She was buried in Concord's Sleepy Hollow cemetary on Authors' Hill, near the graves of Emerson, Thoreau and Hawthorne.

Principal works of fiction for adults:
HOSPITAL SKETCHES (1863)
MOODS (1865)
WORK (1873)
A MODERN MEPHISTOPHELES (1877)
The best of Alcott's "blood-and-thunder" tales can be found today in: Madeleine B. Stern, ed., BEHIND A MASK: THE UNKNOWN THRILLERS OF LOUISA MAY ALCOTT (New York: William Morrow & Company, Inc., 1975).

JANE AUSTEN (1775 - 1817)

Of all the writers cherished by readers of romance, Jane Austen probably claims the greatest respect of literary critics— and the greatest number of fans among her fellow romance authors. And in addition to the overall quality of her books, there are two aspects of Austen's writing that are of particular value to today's writer of romance. First, she uses coincidence sparingly and discreetly. Second, it is only rarely that outside incidents stand between her characters and love; most often it's temperament and overall circumstances.

Jane Austen was born at Steventon, Hampshire on December 16, 1775, the second daughter and seventh child of Reverend George Austen and his wife Cassandra Leigh—a niece of the famous Reverend Theophilus Leigh, master of Balliol College. The Austen family was a lively, cheerful one, though their social life in the country was quiet. Like many young girls who grow up to be writers, Jane wrote sketches and stories from an early age, often imitating her favorite writers. Among the best of Austen's *juvenalia* is LOVE AND FRIENDSHIP.

Like that of many other writers, the first book that Austen submitted to a publisher was rejected; unlike most, however, Cadell, the publisher who refused Austen's first book, has gained a kind of immortality. The book was called FIRST IMPRESSIONS, and later retitled PRIDE AND PREJUDICE. Though Austen had completed three manuscripts between 1795 and 1798, it was not until 1802 that she sold her first book. Yet even this sale did not mean publication. Crosbie of London bought SUSAN for ten pounds, then did not publish it. (The book was a parody of the Gothic novel in general, and Walpole's THE CASTLE OF OTRANTO in particular; the popularity of the genre at this time may have affected Crosbie's decision not to publish.) Austen's brother Henry bought the book back for ten pounds fourteen years later, in 1816, and it did not come out until after Austen's death, as NORTHANGER ABBEY, in 1818.

In 1801, George Austen moved with his wife and two daughters from the parsonage at Steventon to the town of Bath, possibly in the hope of securing husbands for Jane, then twenty-six, and Cassandra, then twenty-nine. If so, the hope was in vain, as neither daughter married. George Austen died in 1805, leaving only a small income for his wife and daughters. They lived with the new wife of Francis Austen, a naval officer, in Southhampton. Just three years later, however, another brother, the wealthy Edward, became a widower. He offered his mother and sisters the use of a house on his estate at Chawton near Alton.

Jane Austen was finally settled and could turn her attention to her writing. She revised ELINOR AND MARIANNE, selling it as SENSE AND SENSIBILITY. It met with immediate success on its publication in 1811. Finally published in 1813, PRIDE AND PREJUDICE met with a similar success, and Austen then wrote MANSFIELD PARK, EMMA, and PERSUASION in rapid succession. In 1817, however, her health began to decline. Cassandra took her to Winchester, where a friend of the family practiced medicine, but her illness was never properly diagnosed. She died in her sister's arms and was buried in Winchester Cathedral.

Principal works:
SENSE AND SENSIBILITY (1811)
PRIDE AND PREJUDICE (1813)
MANSFIELD PARK (1814)
EMMA (1814)
NORTHANGER ABBEY (1818)
PERSUASION (1818)

FAITH BALDWIN (October 1, 1893 - March 19, 1978)

Many of the current writers featured in the next section of this book believe that the escapist qualities of their works are among their chief appeals. As a writer who achieved the height of her literary success during the Depression, Faith Baldwin was aware of the public's need for what she described as an "escape hatch, some way to get out of themselves." Nine of the twelve films based on Baldwin novels or short stories were produced during the thirties, and the *New York Times* claimed that "the key to her popularity was that she enabled lonely working people, young and old, to identify with her glamorous and wealthy characters,"characters who, despite their riches, shared the same problems of love and loneliness as the many who devoured Baldwin's books.

She was born in New Rochelle, New York, to Stephen C. Baldwin, a well-known trial lawyer, and Edith Finch Baldwin. Stephen Baldwin had been born in China, the son of missionaries who lived there for twenty-six years. Faith Baldwin also traveled a great deal in her life, both throughout the United States (she'd been in almost every state, as well as visiting Hawaii several times before its admittance to the Union) and the world, from Germany to Australia and New Zealand. In 1920 she married Hugh Cuthrell, president of the Brooklyn Union Gas Company, and eventually had two boys and two girls, including a set of mixed twins. The family lived in rural Connecticut.

Though Baldwin once claimed that she "would rather be a biologist, an obscure scientist, an actress, a doctor, an explorer," than a novelist, she was the founder and director of the Famous Writers School, located in Westport, Connecticut, and a member of the National League of Penwomen and Pen and Brush. She once confessed that she would rather "read than eat or sleep . . . much rather read books than write them." She was, however, a consummate pro as a writer, generally turning out two books a year (she could write a chapter in a day), and she was working on a book when she died at the age of eighty-four. In addition to the works listed below, Faith Baldwin wrote two books under the pseudonym "Amber Lee,"and ghosted three books.

Principal works:
    MAVIS OF GREEN HILL (1921)
    LAUREL OF STONEY STREAM (1923)
    SIGN POSTS (1924; poetry)
    MAGIC AND MARY ROSE (1924)
    THRESHOLDS (1925)
    THOSE DIFFICULT YEARS (1925)
    THREE WOMEN (1926)
    DEPARTING WINGS (1927)
    ALIMONY (1928)
    GARDEN OATS (1929)
    BROADWAY INTERLUDE (1929; with A. Abdullah)
    THE OFFICE WIFE (1930)
    MAKE-BELIEVE (1930)
    SKYSCRAPER (1931)
    TODAY'S VIRTUE (1931)
    JUDY (1931)
    BABS AND MARY LOU (1931)
    MYRA (1932)
    WEEK-END MARRIAGE (1932)
    DISTRICT NURSE (1932)
    SELF-MADE WOMAN (1932)
    GIRL-ON-THE-MAKE (1932; with A. Abdullah)
    WHITE-COLLAR GIRL (1933)
    BEAUTY (1933)

LOVE'S A PUZZLE (1933)
HONOR BOUND (1934)
INNOCENT BYSTANDER (1934)
AMERICAN FAMILY (1935)
THE PURITAN STRAIN (1935)
THE MOON'S OUR HOME (1935)
PRIVATE DUTY (1936)
MEN ARE SUCH FOOLS! (1936)
THIS MAN IS MINE (1936)
THE HEART HAS WINGS (1937)
TWENTY-FOUR HOURS A DAY (1937)
MANHATTAN NIGHTS (1937)
THE HIGH ROAD (1937)
ENCHANTED OASIS (1938)
RICH GIRL, POOR GIRL (1938)
HOTEL HOSTESS (1938)
CAREER BY PROXY (1939)
WHITE MAGIC (1939)
STATION WAGON SET (1939)
REHEARSAL FOR LOVE (1940)
"SOMETHING SPECIAL" (1940)
MEDICAL CENTER (1940)
AND NEW STARS BURN (1941)
TWO DIFFERENT PEOPLE (1941)
TEMPORARY ADDRESS: RENO (1941)
THE HEART REMEMBERS (1941)
BLUE HORIZONS (1942)
BREATH OF LIFE (1942)

VICKI BAUM (January 24, 1888 - August 29, 1960)

Austrian born and raised, and later naturalized as a U.S. citizen, Vicki Baum wrote her first novels in German, then switched successfully to English originals in the early 1940s. A talented dramatist, novelist, and screenplay writer, Baum was so prolific, and her popularity and publications so international, that she had a problem most authors would envy—she could never quite keep track of the number of works she'd produced. In the early 1950s she told an interviewer: "Sometimes when I'm trying to get to sleep I go over them. Did this book come after the baby or before? What was the name of the one following? Sometimes I get thirty-one, sometimes twenty-five. But it's an agreeable way to put yourself to sleep." Indeed.

Baum was the only child of Herman and Mathilde Donat

Baum, and grew up in Vienna in what she termed "very bour-
geois surroundings." Her parents thought that a strict education
would be the best way to curb her dreamy, romantic nature. She
began to study the harp at the age of eight, and though devoted
to music, she secretly read and wrote at night. Yet her nocturnal
rebellion was more profitable than that of most girls her age—the
first of her short stories appeared in print when she was only
fourteen.

Baum first married at the age of eighteen, to a fellow dreamer
(a writer) whom she once described as being as impractical as she
was. They divorced amicably after a brief marriage. She left
Austria for Germany after her divorce working as a professor in
the musical high school in Darmstadt, and playing harp in the orchestra there. A childhood friend, Richard Lert, just happened to
be the conductor of that orchestra, and the two married in 1916.

Despite her publication as a teenager, Baum owed her start
as a novelist to an actor friend's discovery of the stories and novels she'd written for fun. The friend happened to be the brother
of Jakob Wassermann; he sent one of the novels to a publisher
who, much to Baum's surprise, printed it. Yet after the publication of another book, Baum had two sons, and also spent a great
deal of energy in the moves required by her husband's con-
ducting career. She gave up writing for six years, but did begin to
edit magazines, however, for the German publisher Ullstein.
Again luck—and a friend's belief in her talent—put her back on
her writing career. Dr. Erdei, a young writer, suggested she
dramatize her novel GRAND HOTEL. The effort was extremely
successful, and eventually led to Baum's being invited to
America to see the play's New York production. She liked
America very much, and soon brought her whole family over.
Unlike other political refugees of that period (Baum and her husband were Jewish), they truly liked America, and remained in
this country after the war, having settled in Los Angeles. Lert became the conductor of the Pasadena Symphony; Baum continued to write, screenplays now as well as novels and plays, and
she traveled extensively while researching her novels.

GRAND HOTEL was Baum's first influential book; a "group
novel," it followed happenings in the lives of characters all
staying in a large hotel in post-World War I Germany. The tech-

nique she used became a popular literary convention. Yet her other books are also marked by the skill and psychological insight she displayed in GRAND HOTEL.

Vicki Baum died in Hollywood on August, 29, 1960.

Principal works: (English-language titles and dates of publication)
GRAND HOTEL (1931)
AND LIFE GOES ON (1931)
MARTIN'S SUMMER (1931)
SECRET SENTENCE (1932)
HELENE (1933)
FALLING STAR (1934)
MEN NEVER KNOW (1935)
SING, SISTER, SING (1936)
SHANGHAI '37 (1939)
TALE OF BALI (1937)
THE SHIP AND THE SHORE (1941)
THE CHRISTMAS CARP (1941)
MARION ALIVE (1942)
ONCE IN VIENNA (1943)
THE WEEPING WOOD (1943)—short story collection
HOTEL BERLIN '43 (1944)
MORTGAGE ON LIFE (1946)
HEADLESS ANGEL (1948)
DANGER FROM DEER (1951)
THE MUSTARD SEED (1953)
WRITTEN ON WATER (1956)
THEME FOR BALLET (1958)
IT WAS ALL QUITE DIFFERENT (1964)—memoirs

WILLIAM BECKFORD (October 1, 1760 - May 2, 1844)

William Beckford's fame rests on two creations, the Oriental tale VATHEK, a classic among Gothic novels, and his fantastic Fonthill Abbey, the most sensational building of the English Gothic revival (the actual architect was James Wyatt, but Beckford, who as a youth had studied architecture under Sir William Chambers, supervised the planning and building of the house).

Beckford was born in Wiltshire to a former Lord Mayor of London (who was, despite his worldly accomplishments, descended from a shoemaker) and his wife Maria, who was of the titled Hamilton family. The Earl of Chatham (William Pitt the Elder) served as his godfather, and Beckford wanted for nothing in his childhood. In addition to his architectural training from Chambers, Beckford received instruction from other prominent teachers, including piano lessons given by the eight-year-old Mozart (Beckford was five at the time). He never went to a formal school, or to a university, but he did travel a great deal on the continent, and eventually wrote accounts of his journeys as well.

Yet Beckford was intrigued by the Orient, and although he never went there, he was inspired by a suggestion of the Reverend Samuel Henley to write a novel set there. He began writing VATHEK in French in January of 1782, and finished it abroad several months later. A biographer invented the story that the entire book was written in one sitting of three days and two nights, a more than slight exaggeration. Henley was to translate the book for English publication, and though told not to publish it until after the French edition had appeared, he did so anyway in July of 1786—and even presented it as a translation from the Arabic, leaving Beckford's name off entirely. Beckford himself then issued two French versions the very next year. The book is considered a Gothic masterpiece, full of incredible happenings, and it features amazing descriptions of the East, descriptions which seem even more remarkable when one remembers that Beckford had never been there.

Beckford's expenses were as extravagent as his imagination, and in 1822 he had to vacate his beloved Fonthill and sell part of his collection of curios. He spent his remaining twenty-two years in Bath, still attempting periodically to obtain a title for himself (he'd succeeded in making one of his daughters the Duchess of Hamilton; the other eloped with an untitled young army officer, becoming permanently estranged from her father). Beckford's efforts were in vain, however, and he died a commoner at the age of eighty-four.

Principal works of fiction:
VATHEK (1786)
THE STORY OF AL RAOUI: A TALE FROM THE ARABIAN (1799)

GWEN BRISTOW (September 16, 1903 - August 16, 1980)

Though she achieved her greatest popularity in the field of

historical fiction/family saga, Gwen Bristow began her writing career collaborating with her husband, Bruce Manning, on three mysteries. And THE INVISIBLE HOST, the novel which started their careers as published writers, grew out of their schemes to dispatch a neighbor who had what they termed a "raucous radio." If only all of us with noisy neighbors could turn our annoyance to such productive ends!

Yet after writing three successful mysteries, Bristow turned her talents to the historical novel. Her plantation trilogy featured two families, one wealthy, one poor, and their progress in Louisiana from pre-Revolutionary days through the first World War. The NEW YORK TIMES described the last volume of the three as "a vigorous and thoughtful piece of work . . . very honest and well-written." Throughout her career, Bristow's skill as a storyteller was her strongest point, overcoming characterizations that were at times shallow.

Three of Bristow's novels were filmed, one each in the thirties, forties, and fifties, and they were translated into ten languages. The author died in New Orleans in 1980.

Principal works:
> THE INVISIBLE HOST (1930)—with husband Bruce Manning
> GUTENBERG MURDERS (1931)—with husband Bruce Manning
> TWO AND TWO MAKE TWENTY-TWO (1932)—with husband Bruce Manning
> DEEP SUMMER (1937)
> THE HANDSOME ROAD (1938)
> THIS SIDE OF GLORY (1940)
> TOMORROW IS FOREVER (1943)
> JUBILEE TRAIL (1950)—Literary Guild selection
> CELIA GARTH (1959)—Literary Guild selection
> PLANTATION TRILOGY (1962)—includes DEEP SUMMER, THE HANDSOME ROAD, and THIS SIDE OF GLORY
> CALICO PALACE (1970)

THE BRONTËS
> ANNE (January 17, 1820 - May 28, 1849)
> CHARLOTTE (April 21, 1816 - March 31, 1855)
> EMILY (July 30, 1818 - December 19, 1848)

The Brontës are among those romance authors whose lives are almost as fascinating as their works themselves. And since their lives were so closely intertwined, it is impossible to give each a separate, brief biographical sketch.

Anne, Charlotte, and Emily were three of the five daughters born to Patrick Brontë and Maria Branwell Brontë, who also had a son, named Patrick Branwell, but always known as Branwell. The father had been born Patrick Branty or Brunty in County Down, Ireland, in 1777; the name "Brontë" was later inspired by Lord Nelson's Sicilian dukedom. Though born into poverty, he was able to attend Cambridge due to the aid of the Wesleyan Methodists. In 1812, he married Maria Branwell, five years his junior. She was from Cornwall. Patrick became rector of Haworth, near Bradford, Yorkshire, in 1820, and moved there with his wife and six children. Mrs. Brontë died of cancer the following year.

Three years after their mother's death, the four eldest Brontë sisters, Maria, Elizabeth, Charlotte, and Emily were sent to board at the recently opened Clergy Daughters' School at Cowan Bridge in Lancashire (later immortalized as Lowood by Charlotte in JANE EYRE). Here, the conditions were harsh; Maria took ill and died, and was soon followed by Elizabeth. Charlotte and Emily were withdrawn from the school, returning home in the early summer of 1825.

At home together, Charlotte, Emily, Anne and Branwell played elaborate games of imagination, creating the Kingdom of Angria. They recorded the adventures of Angria in tiny books. Some six years after this game began, Emily and Anne created their own Kindgom of Gondal, abandoning Angria to the care of Charlotte and Branwell. About this time (1831), Charlotte was sent off to Miss Wooler's school at Roe Head. The romantic fantasies of Angria and Gondal were kept up by the sisters well into their twenties, and indeed the more mature works of Charlotte and Emily are quite imaginative, though Anne's first novel, AGNES GREY, is realistic. Branwell remained a dreamer for most of his short life.

Charlotte remained at Roe Head for a year, there forming a friendship with Ellen Nussy which lasted until Charlotte's death. It is from the Nussy/Brontë correspondence that much of the knowledge about Charlotte comes. For the next three years the family lived together at Haworth, until Charlotte returned to Roe Head as a teacher in 1835. Both Emily and Anne spent some time at the school as pupils before Charlotte resigned her position in 1838. The next year, Charlotte turned down offers of marriage from two young churchmen (one, Reverend Henry Nussy, was the brother of her friend Ellen). She and Anne found governess positions; Charlotte, with her independent nature, did not last long in the position, but Anne managed to establish herself with a family in Yorkshire, and remained with them until 1845. Meanwhile, in 1842, Charlotte and Emily went to Brussels to improve their French and learn some German. Here they came to the attention of Constantin Héger, a teacher. Though Emily stayed on in England after the death of their mother's sister brought both young Brontë women home in the fall of 1842, Charlotte returned to Brussels, becoming increasingly attached to M. Héger. At the same time, Branwell joined Anne as a tutor for the Robinson family in Yorkshire. Charlotte left Brussels in 1843, chased off to an extent by the jealousy of Mme. Héger. Charlotte had become devoted to Héger during her time in Brussels, and wrote affectionate letters to him after her departure until he told her that they could be misinterpreted. She abruptly ended the correspondence.

Back in England Charlotte tried to establish a school in her father's parsonage in 1844, yet no pupils could be enticed to distant Haworth. The following year Anne left the Robinsons, and Branwell was dismissed in scandal shortly thereafter, accused of making love to Mrs. Robinson. Indebtedness and drunken bouts marked the last three years of his life, spent at home at Haworth. His behavior particularly affected Anne, who made use of it in the description of the main character in her second novel, TENANT OF WILDFELL HALL.

Her school project having failed, Charlotte persuaded Emily and Anne to join in a self-publication of a book of their poems. POEMS BY CURRER, ELLIS AND ACTON BELL appeared in 1846 ("Currer" was, of course, Charlotte, "Ellis" Emily and "Acton" Anne). Though it only sold two copies, the book spurred the sisters on to seek publication of their novels. Charlotte's first novel, THE PROFESSOR, received nary a nibble from publishing houses, but both Anne's AGNES GREY and Emily's WUTHERING HEIGHTS were accepted by T.C. Newby. Charlotte, meanwhile, was hard at work on JANE EYRE, which was immediately accepted by Smith, Elder and Company, a firm that had turned down THE PROFESSOR. JANE EYRE was published on October 16, 1847, and met with instant success; Anne's and Emily's books appeared that December. All the women published under the various Bell pseudonyms they'd used for their book of poems, yet problems with these names soon cropped up. Some reviewers felt that WUTHERING HEIGHTS was actually by Currer Bell (Charlotte's pseudonym), and Newby, trying to sell the American rights to THE TENANT OF WILDFELL HALL, claimed that it, too, was by the author of the successful JANE EYRE. Anne and Charlotte were finally forced to go to London in the summer of 1848 to reveal the real women behind the pseudonyms.

Yet just as the Brontës' future as professional writers began, tragedy struck. After three years of dissolute living, Branwell collapsed on September 24th. Emily caught a chill at his funeral, and died of acute tuberculosis on December 19th. Anne as well started to decline from the same disease, and despite Charlotte's devoted attention, she died on May 28, 1849, at Scarborough, where she'd been taken to view the sea for one last time. Charlotte then resumed the writing of SHIRLEY, abandoned when Anne was taken ill, and this novel was published in October. In 1850, Smith, Elder and Company, Charlotte's publishers, reprinted both WUTHERING HEIGHTS and AGNES GREY, both with biographical notes by Charlotte. In the five years left to her, Charlotte paid several visits to London, staying with her publisher and meeting other literary men and women of the time, as well as traveling to other parts of England and Scotland. She declined a third offer of marriage, this one from James Taylor of Smith, Elder and Company, in 1851, and saw VILLETTE, her fourth novel, come out early in 1853. She finally married in 1854, accepting the proposal of the Irishman Arthur Bell Nichols, her father's curate, and began a fifth book, EMMA. Her married life did not last long, however, and she died on March 31, 1855, from pregnancy toxemia. Her husband saw that her first, unpublished novel, THE PROFESSOR, was published in 1857, and he remained at Haworth until Patrick Brontë's death. He then returned to Ireland. The story of the Brontës was first revealed to the world in the LIFE OF CHARLOTTE BRONTË (1857) by the novelist Mrs. Gaskell, a friend of Charlotte's. The Brontës have, of course, been the subject of other books and even films (in a recent French version, the stunning actresses Isabelle Huppert, Isabelle Adjani, and Marie-France Pisier portray the plain-looking sisters), and their lives have been of interest to many of the romantically inclined. A portrait of Anne, Charlotte and Emily, painted by the failed artist Branwell in 1835, hangs in London's National Portrait Gallery.

Principal works:
Anne Brontë:
AGNES GREY (1847)
THE TENANT OF WILDFELL HALL (1848)

Charlotte Brontë:
JANE EYRE: AN AUTOBIOGRAPHY (1847)
SHIRLEY: A TALE (1849)
VILLETTE (1853)
THE PROFESSOR: A TALE (1857)
EMMA (1860)—uncompleted

Emily Brontë:
WUTHERING HEIGHTS (1847)

CHARLES BROCKDEN BROWN (January 17, 1771 - February 22, 1810)

C.B. Brown was the first major American novelist, and the first American to support himself by his writing—or at least to do so for a few years. The youngest son in a prosperous Philadelphia Quaker family, he received a fine education and was viewed as a prodigy when his frail constitution lead to both voracious reading and several literary attempts while he was still at school.

As a young man, he was apprenticed to a lawyer, but made desperate by the thought of such a dull career, he threw it over and declared himself a literary man. Constantly seeking intellectual companionship in an America without longstanding cultural institutions, he founded the Belles Lettres Club in his native city. Yet its few members could not satisfy his needs, and he spent more and more time in New York, living in the home of Dr. Elihu Hubbard (a writer as well as a physician) from 1798 to 1801. Here he edited a journal and hastily wrote almost all his novels. Inspired by William Godwin, he also wrote a feminist dialogue, ALCUIN, during this period. He returned to Philadelphia in 1801 when both Dr. Smith and a yellow fever patient who had been moved into the house died of the disease.

In 1804, his marriage to Elizabeth Linn, a Presbyterian, led to his being read out of the Quaker church. Two years later, he fathered the first of their four children and was forced to earn enough of a living for himself and his family. Though he could count Scott, Godwin and Shelley among the wide readership of his novels (Shelley even named one of his poems after Constantia, the heroine of Brown's novel ORMOND), these books brought him no money. So, after a business partnership with his brothers failed, he earned a modest living as an independent trader and as an editor of journals. In addition, he wrote political pamphlets and had written the prospectus for a SYSTEM OF GENERAL GEOGRAPHY. He never finished that work, however, as he died of tuberculosis at the age of thirty-nine.

Driven and intense when it came to literary matters, Brown Americanized the popular Gothic horror novel of his time, setting his books in the towns and countryside of his new, untamed nation. He proved himself to be a master of danger, terror and suspense. His novels were as complex as he himself was; suspense was held at a high level throughout them, and his swiftly moving action, shifting narrative point-of-view, and the extremes in character he presented showed the skills he possessed and made his books among the most readable of his time. A pioneer in an America that had yet to establish a literary tradition, Brown paved the way for the later masterpieces of Poe, Hawthorne and Melville.

Principal works of fiction:
ALCUIN: A DIALOGUE (1798)
WIELAND: OR, THE TRANSFORMATION (1798)
ORMOND: OR, THE SECRET WITNESS (1799)
EDGAR HUNTLEY: OR, MEMOIRS OF A SLEEP-WALKER (1799)
ARTHUR MERVYN: OR, MEMOIRS OF THE YEAR 1793 (1799-1800)
CLARA HOWARD (1801)
JANE TALBOT (1804)
CARWIN; THE BILOQUIST AND OTHER AMERICAN TALES AND PIECES (1822)

EDWARD GEORGE BULWER-LYTTON (May 25, 1803 - June 18, 1873)

Born into comfortable circumstances in London, the third son of General William Earle Bulwer and Elizabeth Lytton Bulwer, the young Bulwer (he added Lytton to his name after his mother's death) was forced to the inkstand after marrying the beautiful but penniless Rosina Doyle Wheeler in 1827. Outraged by her son's flouting her wishes, the widowed, wealthy Elizabeth cut off his allowance, an action from which her son, and the reading public, came to profit.

Fortunately, among Bulwer's talents lay the ability to both anticipate and satisfy the public's taste. Though FALKLAND, his first novel, appeared to little success in 1827, the next year's PELHAM, a Gothic romance in a society setting, established him as a popular writer. THE DISOWNED came out the next year, and Bulwer followed these two successes with one or two novels a year for quite a while thereafter. His health weakened through overwork, however, so he won a seat in Parliament on the reform ticket, and took a year-long magazine editing post. The position led to associations, then friendships, with Disraeli and Dickens.

The marriage that had been the cause of his literary career weakened as well, and he separated from his wife in 1836, keeping custody of the children. Made the first Baron Lytton in 1838, he added this name to his own five years later. Before he returned to Parliament in 1852, he traveled heavily, gathering background for his historical novels. Made a Peer in 1866, he died in the resort town of Torquay seven years later.

Best remembered now for his historical novel THE LAST DAYS OF POMPEII (1834), Bulwer-Lytton was also one of the most successful playwrights of his time, and the libretto for the William Fry opera LEONORA was based on one of his plays. The first novel of Wilkie Collins, one of the fathers of the modern detective story, was an historical fiction ANTONIA, OR THE FALL OF ROME (1850), a work heavily influenced by the novels of Bulwer-Lytton. Despite his popularity, however, Bulwer-Lytton was attacked by contemporary critics, one of the fiercest of whom was Thackeray.

Principal works of fiction:
FALKLAND (1827)
PELHAM (1828)
THE DISOWNED (1828)
DEVEREUX (1829)
PAUL CLIFFORD (1830)
EUGENE ARAM (1832)
GODOLPHIN (1833)
THE LAST DAYS OF POMPEII (1834)
RIENZI (1835)
ALICE: OR, THE MYSTERIES (1838)
LEILA: OR, THE SIEGE OF GRANADA (1838)
CALDERON THE COURTIER (1838)
NIGHT AND MORNING (1841)
ZANONI (1842)
EVA, THE ILL-OMENED MARRIAGE AND OTHER TALES (1842)
THE LAST OF THE BARONS (1843)
CONFESSIONS OF A WATER PATIENT (1845)
LUCRETIA: OR, THE CHILDREN OF NIGHT (1846)
A WORD TO THE PUBLIC (1847)
HAROLD: OR, THE LAST OF THE SAXON KINGS (1848)
THE CAXTONS (1850)
THE COMING RACE (1871)
KENELM CHILLINGLY (1873)

FRANCES HODGSON BURNETT (November 24, 1849 - October 29, 1924)

Frances Hodgson Burnett was one of the last of the "lady novelists" (until recent times, that is). Her frilly clothing and opulent titian wigs were her hallmarks, just as fancy clothes and curly hair were the things we remember about her most famous character, the lead in her children's story LITTLE LORD FAUNTLEROY. Her most famous work, it won her the eternal enmity of little boys whose mothers curled their hair (the style was inspired by the locks of Burnett's own son Vivian) and forced them into lace-collared velvet suits (Burnett's model in this case was Oscar Wilde).

Yet while FAUNTLEROY is the story of an American who finds his fortune in England, Burnett's own story was the reverse. Born in Manchester, England, she was the daughter of a hardware store owner and his wife. When the father died,

Burnett's mother tried to run the business. But that area of England had become crippled by the American Civil War, and by 1865 the family was poverty-stricken. They emigrated to the Tennessee home of Mrs. Hodgson's brother.

An industrious young woman, "Fanny" at seventeen wrote the first story she submitted to a magazine. Her material sold well from the start (she later said that she had never written an unaccepted manuscript), though she first became widely known through the publication of a novel about English coal miners, THAT LASS O'LOWRIE'S (1877). Four years earlier she'd married Dr. Swan M. Burnett in Knoxville, though the couple had relocated to Washington D.C. by the time of her first major success. Here she had two sons, but her marriage, probably one of the first in which two careers collided, weakened, and she and her husband were divorced in 1898. She made a bad, impulsive marriage with a young actor named Stephen Townsend, and temporarily took his last name. This marriage also ended in divorce (in 1901), and Burnett resumed her first husband's name. She traveled extensively for years, then finally settled on Long Island, where she died in 1924 at the age of seventy-four.

While Burnett wrote both novels for adults and children's books (in addition to FAUNTLEROY, she also wrote SARA CREWE and THE SECRET GARDEN), she enjoyed success as a playwright as well, two of her most popular works being the stage adaptation of LITTLE LORD FAUNTLEROY and SARA CREWE (called THE LITTLE PRINCESS as a play).

Principal works:
THAT LASS O'LOWRIE'S (1877)
SURLY TIM AND OTHER STORIES (1877)
HAWORTH'S (1879)
LOUISIANA (1880)
A FAIR BARBARIAN (1881)
THROUGH ONE ADMINISTRATION (1883)
LITTLE LORD FAUNTLEROY (1886)
EDITHA'S BURGLAR (1886)
SARA CREWE (1888)
LITTLE SAINT ELIZABETH (1889)
THE ONE I KNEW BEST OF ALL (1893)
A LADY OF QUALITY (1896)
IN CONNECTION WITH THE DE WILLOUGHBY CLAIM (1899)
THE MAKING OF A MARCHIONESS (1901)

IN THE CLOSED ROOM (1904)
MISS CRESPIGNY (1907)
THE SECRET GARDEN (1909)
T. TEMBARON (1913)
THE HEAD OF THE HOUSE OF COOMBE (1922)
ROBIN (1922)

FANNY BURNEY (June 13, 1752 - January 6, 1840)

Fanny Burney was the fourth child and second daughter of Dr. Charles Burney, a musician and musical historian, and Esther Sleepe, a woman of Huguenot descent. After bearing two more children, Mrs. Burney died, and the family moved to London from Norfolk. Dr. Burney's unusual wit and charm made him welcome in London society, just as his daughter's would make her a pet of many after the publication of her first book.

But as a girl, Fanny did not show much promise of the talented, ebullient woman she would eventually become. In fact, shy and myopic, she was overshadowed by her bright, lively siblings, and was practically considered a dunce. She did not learn her letters til the age of eight, but at ten she started to write almost constantly. Yet her stepmother later had her burn her first manuscripts and early journals; her earliest work available to us is the diary she began in 1778 and continued for the rest of her life.

Fanny's anonymity was forever abandoned shortly after the psuedoanonymous publication of her first novel, EVELINA: OR, A YOUNG LADY'S ENTRANCE INTO THE WORLD, in 1778. The renowned Dr. Johnson made her a special favorite, and society itself embraced her whole-heartedly. In fact, her social life became such that her father practically had to lock her away to enable her to finish her second book, CECILIA, in 1782. While lacking the unpolished charm of her first book, CECILIA gave a fine account of society's "ton parties," and it was well received.

In 1786 Fanny accepted a position at the court of George III, only to resign five years later, unhappy with her position. She did receive a much-welcomed pension of one hundred pounds, and she and her father moved to Chelsea in London. Here they met a number of exiles from revolutionary France, among them the statesman Talleyrand and the critic and novelist Madame de Staël. Yet among these luminaries, it was General Alexandre D'Arblay who caught Burney's attention, and they were married on July 31, 1793. She was known thereafter as Madame D'Arblay.

Marriage to General D'Arblay made Burney's creative impulses return in full force, and she quickly wrote a pamphlet on emigrant French clergy, and an unsuccessful blank verse tragedy. She also bore a son. Her third novel, CAMILLA: OR, A PICTURE OF YOUTH, was published in 1796. Like her second book, it, too, lacked the charm of EVELINA, but it made Burney two thousand pounds.

In 1802, the D'Arblay family was caught in France when hostilities began anew between that country and England, and remained there for ten years. Burney published her fourth novel THE WANDERER: OR, FEMALE DIFFICULTIES, in 1814. Hereafter followed the most exciting period in a life that was far from pedestrian. Louis XVIII gave her the title of Countess. Then, leery of her position in an English society at war with France, she lived in Brussels during Waterloo, working among the injured. She wrote a lively account of this time.

After the war she and her husband received permission to settle in England. General D'Arblay died in 1818, leaving Burney disconsolate. She wrote a biography of her father, which was published in 1832. Five years later, her son died of influenza, and Burney herself died three years later, in January of 1840. She was eighty-eight.

Principal works of fiction:
EVELINA, OR, A YOUNG LADY'S ENTRANCE INTO THE WORLD (1778)
CECILIA: OR, MEMOIRS OF AN HEIRESS (1782)
CAMILLA; OR, A PICTURE OF YOUTH (1796)
THE WANDERER; OR, FEMALE DIFFICULTIES (1814)
Note: Fanny Burney's diary and letters would be of interest as well.

GEORGE GORDON, LORD BYRON (January 22, 1788 - April 19, 1824)

Pale of skin, dark of hair, brooding and alone, a man of action, and a poet—these are the qualities of the Byronic hero. Add to them wanderlust, early fame, a seemingly insatiable sexual appetite capable of shocking even London high society, a waistline requiring constant vigilance, and a club foot, and we have Lord Byron himself.

Byron inherited his title on the death of a granduncle in 1798, after having spent an impoverished boyhood with his widowed mother. He was schooled mainly at Harrow and Trinity College, Cambridge. HOURS OF IDLENESS, the first collection of his poetry, appeared in 1807; the first example of the poet's gift for satire and wicked wit appeared shortly thereafter, in response to an unfavorable critique in the EDINBURGH REVIEW. Byron then traveled to the Mediterranean, in the course of his two-year trip gathering information for the first two cantos of CHILDE HAROLD'S PILGRIMAGE. Published in 1812, they established his instant celebrity while introducing the Byronic hero.

Byron reveled in flouting society's conventions as much as he reveled in his fame. Affairs with Lady Caroline Lamb, Lady Oxford, and his own half-sister Augusta made him the talk of the ton. He married Anna Isabella Milbanks on the first day of 1815, but they soon separated, a turn of events used against Byron by the Tories, who'd been enraged by one of his satires mocking the Prince Regent. He left England forever in 1816.

Byron spent time in Switzerland with Shelley and wrote a third canto to CHILDE HAROLD (eventually followed by a fourth), as well as a novel and other poems. The greatest achievement of his later years was DON JUAN, which his early death fighting to free the Greeks from Turkish oppression prevented him from finishing. His life and writing affected countless people, from young men in the English Regency (and Regency writers of all ages) to the novelists Victor Hugo and Heinrich Heine.

Principal works:
   HOURS OF IDLENESS: A SERIES OF POEMS, ORIGINAL AND TRANS-
      LATED (1807)
   ENGLISH BARDS AND SCOTCH REVIEWERS: A SATIRE (1809)
   CHILDE HAROLD'S PILGRIMAGE: A ROMAUNT—cantos i and ii (1812);
      canto iii (1816); canto iv (1818)
   THE GIAOUR: A FRAGMENT OF A TURKISH TALE (1813)
   THE BRIDE OF ABYDOS: A TURKISH TALE (1813)
   THE CORSAIR: A TALE (1814)
   LARA: A TALE (1814)

THE SIEGE OF CORINTH: A POEM (1816)
PARISINA: A POEM (1816)
POEMS (1816)
THE PRISONER OF CHILLON, AND OTHER POEMS (1816)
THE LAMENT OF TASSO (1817)
MANFRED: A DRAMATIC POEM (1817)
BEPPO: A VENETIAN STORY (1818)
MAZEPPA: A POEM (1819)
DON JUAN—cantos i and ii (1819); cantos iii-v (1821); cantos vi-viii, ix-xi, and xii-xiv (1823); cantos xv-xvi (1824)
MARINO FALIERO: DOGE OF VENICE (1821)
THE PROPHECY OF DANTE: A POEM (1821)
SARDANAPALUS: A TRAGEDY (1821)
THE TWO FOSCARI: A TRAGEDY (1821)
CAIN: A MYSTERY (1821)
THE VISION OF JUDGEMENT (1822)

CHARLOTTE DACRE (1782 - ?)

To create a romantic pseudonym that would appear on well-received *and* fairly influential novels would be bliss to many writers of romance. To have that name lauded in lofty, Shelleyan-style verse in an important newspaper, and to influence the work of Shelley himself, would be beyond most writers' wildest dreams. Charlotte Dacre, writing as Rosa Mathilde, achieved both during the height of the Romantic period in England. Yet little is known about the life of this writer of Gothic romances; the only readily available information for the general reader appears in Devendra P. Varma's thorough introductory notes to a recent Arno edition of ZOFLOYA.

We do know the year of her birth, and that she was as esteemed for her poetry and personal beauty as for her novels. We know as well that she was betrothed to William Pit Byrne, editor of THE MORNING POST. Her books show the influence of Mrs. Radcliffe and M.G. "Monk" Lewis. In fact, her first book is dedicated to the latter.

Similar to Lewis, Dacre wrote her first Gothic novel while in her late teens, and also achieved popular success with this effort, THE CONFESSIONS OF THE NUN OF ST. OMER. The book was reprinted one year after its publication. Dacre's skillful turn of phrase was one reason for the book's success; doubtless, the theme of the fallen angel added to its appeal, as did the monastic setting. For all its sensational value, however, it contained some moral instruction, a quality in all her works. Critics cited it as having a redeeming value that most such novels lacked. Her second Gothic, ZOFLOYA; OR, THE MOOR, came out in 1806. In this book Dacre more consciously imitated Lewis' THE MONK in a book filled with action. Needless to say, this blood-and-thunder tale of the misadventures of the stunningly beautiful daughter of a Venetian marquis was quite popular. It, too, was a favorite of critics, ever impressed by Dacre's moral message. ZAFLOYA influenced Shelley's writing of two romances, ZASTROZZI and ST. IRVYNE; OR THE ROSICRUCIAN. (Though the teenaged Shelley's works did not meet with the critical approbation accorded Dacre's efforts—one referred to the earlier book as "fit only for the inmates of a brothel.")

Despite her popularity, Charlotte Dacre left this life quietly; all scholars can ascertain is that she must have died before 1842, the year her husband remarried.

Principal works:
   HOURS OF SOLITUDE (1805)—poetry
   THE CONFESSIONS OF THE NUN OF ST. OMER (1805)
   ZOFLOYA; OR THE MOOR (1806)

MAZO DE LA ROCHE (January 15, 1879 - July 12, 1961)

Mazo de la Roche wrote to remind herself of happier days spent in a happier place. The days were her childhood on a farm in Ontario, the place a lake deep in the Ontario woods. For de la Roche was forced to adjust to city life in Toronto when her father died and the family had to give up the farm, and though she, her mother, and a cousin lived for the summers they spent in a small lakeside cottage, that too had to be abandoned on the mother's death.

It was at this cottage that Mazo de la Roche first wrote, starting with plays, then also working on novels. After her mother died, she and her cousin lived on the strictest economy in Toronto, the cousin working in the city, and de la Roche writing at home, determined to succeed in her chosen field. Though two novels and a short story collection were published (the latter with a foreword by Christopher Morley, no less), and her plays won two prizes in competition, real success—and financial remuneration—were nowhere in sight.

This state of affairs changed suddenly in 1927, with the appearance of JALNA, which took ATLANTIC MONTHLY's $10,000 prize. It was the first of fifteen successful books (the last one came out in 1960) chronicling the Whiteoak family, and it is on these books that de la Roche's fame rests. Often compared to G.B. Stern's "Matriarch" novels, and even to GONE WITH THE WIND, the books were dramatized by their author as "Whiteoaks," and Ethel Barrymore once portrayed the centenarian grandmother, Adeline.

Principal works of fiction:
EXPLORERS OF THE DAWN (1922)—short story collection
POSSESSION (1923)
DELIGHT (1926)
LARK ASCENDING (1932)
BESIDE A NORMAN TOWER (1934)
THE VERY HOUSE (1937)
GROWTH OF A MAN (1938)
THE SACRED BULLOCK AND OTHER STORIES (1939)—short story collection
THE TWO SAPLINGS (1942)
A BOY IN THE HOUSE, AND OTHER STORIES (1952)—short story collection
THE "JALNA" SERIES:
JALNA (1927)
WHITEOAKS OF JALNA (1929)
FINCH'S FORTUNE (1931)
THE MASTER OF JALNA (1933)
YOUNG RENNY (1935)
WHITEOAK HARVEST (1936)
WHITEOAK HERITAGE (1940)
WAKEFIELD'S COURSE (1941)
THE BUILDING OF JALNA (1944)
RETURN TO JALNA (1946)
MARY WAKEFIELD (1949)
RENNY'S DAUGHTER (1951)
VARIABLE WINDS AT JALNA (1954)
CENTENARY AT JALNA (1958)
MORNING AT JALNA (1960)

E.M. DELL (August 2, 1881 - September 17, 1939)

Vickie Baum was forced to write her earliest works under the covers at night; that is how many of her loyal fans had to read the scandalous-seeming novels of E.M. Dell.

Born into a notable English family that could be traced back to the fourteenth century, Ethel Mary Dell achieved her first success with the publication of THE WAY OF AN EAGLE in 1912. Her books brought her tremendous wealth; by the time of her 1922 marriage to R.A.S.C. Colonel Gerald Savage, she was earning thirty thousand pounds a year. In the face of such immense popularity, nothing meant more to her than her privacy. More than content to have her sister Ella thought to be the novelist E.M. Dell, she even turned down an American publisher's offer of $50,000 for a portrait. It has been ventured that some of her reticence before press and public was due to personal plainness, a definite lack of color, and the fact that she had never actually been to India, though many of her most stirring books are set there (much of her "research" came from reading Kipling and the novels of now-forgotten authors Flora Anne Steele, Maud Diver, Alice Perrin, and F.E. Penney).

Dell wrote with her audience in mind, and she was aware that a great deal of that audience was composed of women with tiring, monotonous, often thankless jobs—governesses, domestic servants and the like. Yet her stories of valiant (though, at times, sadistic) heroes and unredeemable villains had a wide appeal—the young Nancy Mitford was one of those who read her on the sly. All in all, Dell wrote thirty-four novels, though her books enjoyed their greatest success during World War I.

Selected works of fiction:
THE WAY OF AN EAGLE (1912)
THE KNAVE OF DIAMONDS (1913)
THE ROCKS OF VALPRE (1914)
THE KEEPER OF THE DOOR (1915)
THE HUNDREDTH CHANCE (1917)
CHARLES REX (1922)
THE BLACK KNIGHT (1926)
STORM DRIFT (1930)
THE SERPENT IN THE GARDEN (1938)

DOROTHY EDEN (April 3, 1912 - March 4, 1982)

Dorothy Eden credited her lonely childhood on an isolated New Zealand farm with developing her imagination. So well developed did it become that, many years later, the WASHINGTON POST included her name along with those of Daphne du Maurier, Georgette Heyer, Victoria Holt, Mary Stewart and Norah Lofts when citing the best known of contemporary Gothic novelists. Yet Eden wrote more than Gothics, being renowned for the meticulous research that went into her historical fiction, both that which sprang totally from her imagination (such as the popular THE VINES OF YARRABEE), and that which was based to a great extent on real happenings, notably NEVER CALL IT LOVING. In this novel, Eden explored the relationship between Irish leader Charles Stewart Parnell and Katherine O'Shea, an affair which supposedly lead to the politician's early death.

Eden was educated in public schools in New Zealand, and it was while working as a legal secretary that she started writing—and sending her work out to publishers. Once a few of them had been accepted, she left New Zealand for London, and a career as a novelist. This move took place in 1954; Eden continued working for almost thirty more years. Shortly after her 1982 death, her last novel, AN IMPORTANT FAMILY was published. Most of its action takes place in New Zealand.

Principal works:
SINGING SHADOWS (1940)
THE LAUGHING GHOST (1943)
WE ARE FOR THE DARK (1944)
SUMMER SUNDAY (1946)
WALK INTO MY PARLOUR (1947)
THE SCHOOLMASTER'S DAUGHTERS (1948)
CROW HOLLOW (1950)
VOICE OF THE DOLLS (1950)
CAT'S PREY (1952)
BRIDE BY CANDLELIGHT (1954)
DARLING CLEMENTINE (1955)
DEATH IS A RED ROSE (1956)
THE PRETTY ONES (1957)
LISTEN TO DANGER (1958)
DEADLY TRAVELLERS (1959)

THE SLEEPING BRIDE (1959)
SAMANTHA (1960)—LADY OF MALLOW in US
SLEEP IN THE WOODS (1960)
AFTERNOON FOR LIZARDS (1961)
WHISTLE FOR THE CROWS (1962)
THE BIRD IN THE CHIMNEY (1963)
BELLA (1964)
DARKWATER (1964)
THE MARRIAGE CHEST (1965)
RAVENSCROFT (1965)
NEVER CALL IT LOVING: A BIOGRAPHICAL NOVEL OF KATHERINE
    O'SHEA AND CHARLES STEWART PARNELL (1966)
SIEGE IN THE SUN (1967)
WINTERWOOD, (1967)
THE SHADOW WIFE (1968)
YELLOW IS FOR FEAR, AND OTHER STORIES (1968)—short story
    collection
THE VINES OF YARRABEE (1969)
MELBURY SQUARE (1970)
WAITING FOR WILLA (1970)
AN AFTERNOON WALK (1971)
BRIDGE OF FEAR (1972)
THE BROODING LAKE (1972)
SHADOW OF A WITCH (1972)
SPEAK TO ME OF LOVE (1972)
THE MILLIONAIRE'S DAUGHTER (1974)
NIGHT OF THE LETTER (1976)
THE TIME OF THE DRAGON (1975)
THE DAUGHTERS OF ARDMORE HALL (1976)
FACE OF AN ANGEL (1376)
THE HOUSE ON HAY HILL AND OTHER ROMANTIC FICTION (1976)
THE SALAMANCA DRUM (1977)
THE STORRINGTON PAPERS (1978)
AN IMPORTANT FAMILY (1982)

EMILY EDEN (March 3, 1797 - 1869)

Phyllis Rose wrote in her April 25, 1982 NEW YORK TIMES
BOOK REVIEW critique of Emily Eden's two books, "The only
thing more gratifying to find than a good book is a good book
which has been neglected. THE SEMI-ATTACHED COUPLE,
written in 1829, published in 1860, popular for years, then largely
forgotten, is a comic gem about how difficult it can be to get used
to being married, even if you are young and beautiful and your

husband is rich and titled." She then notes that some readers will find THE SEMI-ATTACHED HOUSE "even more delightful." Eden's books are marked by wit and keen perception; she is often compared to Jane Austen, but writes about a social class higher than that known by the earlier writer. Never married, she accompanied her brother, the second Lord Auckland, to India in 1835 when he was appointed Governor-General. In addition to her novels, she wrote two books about her experiences in India, PORTRAITS OF THE PEOPLE AND PRINCES OF INDIA (1844) and UP THE COUNTRY (1866).

Eden anonymously published her second novel, THE SEMI-DETACHED HOUSE, in 1859. Its enthusiastic reception by the public encouraged her to bring out THE SEMI-ATTACHED COUPLE, which had been written in 1830. Both books are part of the Virago Modern Classics line published in paperback in the US by the Dial Press, and both are a must-read for Austen fans.

Works of fiction:
THE SEMI-DETACHED HOUSE (1859)
THE SEMI-ATTACHED COUPLE (1860)

MARIA EDGEWORTH (January 1, 1767 - May 22, 1849)

Like the American Louisa May Alcott, Maria Edgeworth was educated by a father she adored. Richard Edgeworth was a disciple of Rousseau, and a friend of the educational theorist Thomas Day. He firmly believed in education for women and particularly encouraged the writing ability of his second child. While in later years he unfortunately revised and "corrected" much of her writing, taking a lot of the life out of it (her letters retain her natural spontaneity), his enthusiasm was important to the writing career of his daughter, who is sometimes referred to as the "Irish Jane Austen."The Edgeworths were Irish gentry, and though Maria was born at Black Bourton in Oxfordshire to her father's second wife (married many times, he fathered twenty-one children in all), she moved to the family estate in Ireland at the age of fifteen, and it remained her home for the rest of her life. Here Maria was made her father's estate agent. His concern was for her to learn the business intricacies of such an operation, but she profited as much from the opportunity to observe the Irish peasants first-hand. The experience was vital to the success of her later work. But before Edgeworth produced the novels that would make her reputation, she worked on other projects. The first was a translation of Madame de Genlis' ADÈLE ET THÉODORE. Yet the appearance of Holcroft's translation prevented hers from being published. Her father's great friend, Thomas Day, applauded this turn of events, and in a letter congratulated Maria on her having escaped that unappealing category of humankind, the woman writer. Day's remark was partly responsible for Edgeworth's LETTERS TO LITERARY LADIES, a plea for education for women. She also worked on novels and stories during this period, but published nothing until after Day's death in 1789.

Many of Edgeworth's stories for children, originally told to her many younger siblings, were collected in 1796, and met with success and demands for subsequent volumes. The 1798 publication of PRACTICAL EDUCATION, written with her father, gave Edgeworth a second success. A landmark in the history of education, it was based on the Edgeworths' experience in educating members of their own family, and was the first text to take into account the workings of a child's mind.

Yet Edgeworth's real literary success came with the publication of her first novel, CASTLE RACKRENT, a book notable for its portraits of the Irish peasants Edgeworth had observed on her family estate. In the first edition of WAVERLY, Walter Scott even claimed that he hoped "in some distant degree to emulate the admirable Irish portraits of Miss Edgeworth." After the publication of BELINDA, Edgeworth both traveled on the continent and wrote a great deal. She published five more novels before her father's death in 1817; deeply affected by this loss, Edgeworth completed his memoirs, and wrote one last novel, HELEN, before her death at the age of eighty-eight.

Principal works of fiction:
THE PARENT'S ASSISTANT (1800)—short story collection
MORAL TALES FOR YOUNG PEOPLE (1801)—short story collection
EARLY LESSONS (1801)—short story collection
POPULAR TALES (1804)-short story collection
TALES OF FASHIONABLE LIFE (1809)—short story collection

CASTLE RACKRENT (1800)
BELINDA (1801)
THE MODERN GRISELDA (1804)
LEONORA (1806)
PATRONAGE (1814)
HARRINGTON (1817)
ORMOND (1817)
HELEN (1834)

GEORGE ELIOT (November 22, 1819 - December 22, 1880)

Unlike Charlotte Dacre and many of today's writers, an ultra-feminine pseudonym was the last thing Mary Ann Evans needed (and, of course, she wrote only one book in the romance genre in a career of novel writing). She took the pen name "George Eliot" in 1857, on the publication of her short story "Amos Barton," knowing that supposed male authorship would bring her books more serious attention. Yet her earlier literary efforts were hardly frivolous. In fact, her first published work was a translation of a book by David Strauss, THE LIFE OF JESUS CRITICALLY EXAMINED (1846). Appearing anonymously, it had a trememdous effect on English rationalism. Her novels, from ADAM BEDE, through MIDDLEMARCH, to DANIEL DERONDA, were for the most part innovative, serious mainstream literary achievements; MIDDLEMARCH is acknowledged as a masterpiece among English novels. Yet it is this very success in the world of mainstream books that has caused one of Eliot's novels to be much under-rated. Her novel, ROMOLA (1862), is an outstanding example of historical fiction.

Eliot was born at Chilvers Coton, Warwickshire, the daughter of an estate agent. Her education, concluded by study with the daughters of the Baptist minister at Coventry, developed in her a deep sense of religion. Yet this strong sense of traditional belief was challenged when she moved to Coventry with her widowed father. For here she came under the influence of the related Bray and Hennell families (Charles Hennell wrote the unorthodox AN INQUIRY CONCERNING THE ORIGIN OF CHRISTIANITY in 1938). It was her connection with these families that led to her translating the Strauss book in the early 1840s, an achievement that earned her reviewing work in THE WESTMIN-

STER REVIEW. This assignment gave her the confidence to move to London in 1851 to work as a writer. She became an editor of the review, and through it met one of the most important people in her life, the journalist George Henry Lewes. He was estranged from his wife, and though it was impossible for him to obtain a divorce, he and Eliot lived together as husband and wife from 1854 until his death in 1878.

Before writing ROMOLA, Eliot penned the novels ADAM BEDE (1859), THE MILL ON THE FLOSS (1860), and SILAS MARNER (1861), the last book being, of course, the one that everyone encounters in high school. Eliot originally planned ROMOLA as a serial for BLACKWOOD'S MAGAZINE, which had published the successful "Amos Barton" in 1857. Yet CORNHILL MAGAZINE's offer of ten thousand pounds lured her from her first publisher—though this sum was reduced by three thousand pounds when the author adamantly refused to divide the book into the sixteen installments desired by the editor.

Eliot first conceived of ROMOLA while living in Florence in 1860 and 1861, a time in which historical fiction was very much in vogue. The details of the book were exhaustively researched, both abroad and in the British musuem. Dealing with a young woman in the heady days of the Italian Renaissance and during the rise of Savonarola, the book has never received the same consideration as the other novels of the author.

Eliot's next novel, FELIX HOLT (1866), addressed social problems plaguing England, yet her masterpiece was MIDDLEMARCH (1871), which also spoke to those issues but on a much more comprehensive scale.

After the death of George Henry Lewes, Eliot married John Walter Cross, a close friend of Lewes, in 1880. She died in December of that year.

Principal works of fiction:
SCENES OF CLERICAL LIFE (1858)
ADAM BEDE (1859)
THE MILL ON THE FLOSS (1860)
SILAS MARNER: THE WEAVER OF RAVELOE (1861)
ROMOLA (1863)
FELIX HOLT, THE RADICAL (1866)
MIDDLEMARCH: A STUDY OF PROVINCIAL LIFE (1871-72)
DANIEL DERONDA (1876)

JEFFERY FARNOL (February 10, 1878 - August 9, 1952)

Though Georgette Heyer is generally credited with inspiring the modern Regency, she herself was heavily influenced by a countryman who wrote in the early years of this century. Somewhat picaresque himself at times (he penned his first Regency, THE BROAD HIGHWAY, while living in New York's Hell's Kitchen and earning a living painting scenery for the Astor Theatre), he spent over forty years writing popular romance.

After THE BROAD HIGHWAY was rejected by several American publishers as being "too British," Farnol sent the book to Britain, where it was published to immense popular success. He then returned to England, where he wrote THE AMATEUR GENTLEMAN, the story of a man of humble origins who becomes a dashing Regency buck after inheriting a fortune.

Farnol's later books were often hurried and inferior to his early works; it is the early books that should be read by anyone interested in the development of the Regency as a popular literary genre.

Selected works of fiction:
THE BROAD HIGHWAY (1910)
THE MONEY MOON (1911)
THE AMATEUR GENTLEMAN (1913)
THE CHRONICLES OF THE IMP (1915)
OUR ADMIRABLE BETTY (1918)
THE GESTE OF DUKE JOCELYN (1919)
BLACK BARTLEMY'S TREASURE (1920)
PEREGRINE'S PROGRESS (1922)

EDNA FERBER (August 15, 1887 - April 16, 1968)

Prolific, a sharp observer of society and individual psychology, and a celebrant of American life—these terms describe Edna Ferber, one of her nation's best-selling, and best-loved, authors. Despite her high output and high sales figures, Ferber was no lightweight as a writer; SO BIG, one of the first of her twelve novels, won the Pulitzer Prize in 1924.

Ferber used the wide variety of American life as the basic material of her work, highlighting the moneyed thoroughbred scene in SARATOGA TRUNK, the hustle of oil deals in GIANT, life on the Mississippi in SHOW BOAT, and our last frontier, Alaska, in ICE PALACE. Her talents were not confined to the novel, however; many of her works were turned into plays and films, and she herself collaborated with George S. Kaufman on a number of original plays, among them DINNER AT EIGHT (1932) and STAGE DOOR (1936).

Ferber was born in Kalamazoo, Michigan, and grew up there and in Appleton, Wisconsin. She did her earliest training in writing on newspapers, working as a journalist from her high school graduation in 1905 through the 1911 publication of her first novel, DAWN O'HARA. She remained indebted to her years as a journalist throughout her writing career, claiming that newspaper work developed her keen eye for human behavior. It was also in this field that she encountered the working-class Americans who would people her novels.

After 1911 Ferber worked solely as a writer, producing a high number of magazine stories that also sold well as story collections. Two of the best known of these collections are BUTTERED SIDE DOWN (1912) and MOTHER KNOWS BEST (1927). She first achieved best-sellerdom with 1924's award-winning SO BIG, and many of her later books followed that second novel's success.

The key to Ferber's popularity was her true interest in the people and places she wrote about, her ability to convey her own fascination with her characters to the reader. She gained in her lifetime the admiration of hundreds of thousands of unknown readers, as well as that of such luminaries as Theodore Roosevelt, J.M. Barrie, and Kipling.

Principal works of fiction:
DAWN O'HARA (1911)
BUTTERED SIDE DOWN (1912)—short story collection
ROAST BEEF MEDIUM (1913)—short story collection
EMMA McCHESNEY & CO. (1915)—short story collection
FANNY HERSELF (1917)—short story collection
CHEERFUL BY REQUEST (1918)—short story collection
GIGOLO (1922)—short story collection
SO BIG (1924)
MINICK (1925)—play; with Geo. S. Kaufman
SHOW BOAT (1926)

MOTHER KNOWS BEST (1927)—short story collection
THE ROYAL FAMILY (1927)—play; with Geo. S. Kaufman
CIMARRON (1930)
DINNER AT EIGHT (1932)—play; with Geo. S. Kaufman
STAGE DOOR (1936)—play; with Geo. S. Kaufman
THE LAND IS BRIGHT (1941)—play; with Geo. S. Kaufman
SARATOGA TRUNK (1941)
BRAVO! (1949)—play; with Geo. S. Kaufman
GIANT (1952)
ICE PALACE (1958)
Note: Edna Ferber wrote two autobiographies, A PECULIAR TREA-
SURE (1939) and A KIND OF MAGIC (1963).

PAUL LEICESTER FORD (March 23, 1865 - May 8, 1902)

Paul Leicester Ford was born into a distinguished, book-
loving family. His father's magnificent library, in which he
browsed freely as a boy, became part of the New York Public Library; his great-grandfather was Noah Webster. An injury to his
spine stunted his growth, so he was privately educated by tutors
and books were a focal point of his youth.

Always a bibliophile, he set up his own press with his brother Worthington. His works of history and his bibliographies were
of some importance, and one of his greatest achievements was
his ten volume edition of the works of Thomas Jefferson. Yet in
addition to these works and his biographies (two of his most
popular dealt with George Washington and Benjamin Franklin),
Ford published several popular novels. The success of the first,
THE HONORABLE PETER STIRLING (1894) was partially due to
the fact that the public mistakenly thought that its lead character
was based on Grover Cleveland. And his JANICE MEREDITH
was the first big American best-seller, 200,000 copies being sold
in three months.

How strong a novelist Ford would have grown to be will never be known. He was killed at the age of thirty-seven by a disin-
herited brother, Malcolm Webster Ford, who blamed him for his
financial problems.

Principal works of fiction:
THE HONORABLE PETER STIRLING AND WHAT PEOPLE THOUGHT
OF HIM (1894)

THE GREAT K. AND A. TRAIN ROBBERY (1897)
THE STORY OF AN UNTOLD LOVE (1897)
TATTLE TALES OF CUPID (1898)
JANICE MEREDITH: A STORY OF THE AMERICAN REVOLUTION (1899)
WANTED: A MATCH-MAKER (1900)
WANTED: A CHAPERONE (1902)

MRS. GASKELL (September 29, 1810 - November 12, 1865)

As many others have done before and after her, Elizabeth Gaskell started writing somewhat late in life. When she was thirty-five, her fifth child and only son died, and she began the novel MARY BARTON to ease her grief. A sociological work, it centered on a sensational murder but dealt seriously with the plight of workers, a problem which surrounded the novelist; her husband's parish (like her father, he was a Unitarian minister) was in industrial Manchester. Mrs. Gaskell worked on the novel between completing the household tasks required of a minister's wife with four children. It finally was published in the troubled, turbulent year of 1848, and brought its author immediate success, as well as the accolades of Dickens and Carlyle. Dickens also invited her to contribute to his magazine, HOUSEHOLD WORDS. It was in this magazine that the eight sketches later revised and combined into the novel CRANFORD first appeared. The novel described social life in the village of Knutsford in which Mrs. Gaskell spent her girlhood.

After the gentle CRANFORD, Mrs. Gaskell shocked the public with RUTH, a social novel dealing frankly with unwed motherhood. Though the young mother eventually comes to a tragic end, society was outraged at the novel's suggestion that such a fate might have been avoided. Then, at the request of Patrick Brontë, the author wrote THE LIFE OF CHARLOTTE BRONTE, the book which brought to public knowledge the story of this extraordinary family, about her late friend.

After this successful venture into non-fiction, Mrs. Gaskell returned to the novel, but instead of the social documents she so often produced, she penned instead a historical novel. SYLVIA'S LOVERS, appearing in 1863, chronicled the effect of the Napoleonic wars on the lives of simple people. Her last and most mature work, WIVES AND DAUGHTERS, was left unfinished at her death.

Principal works of fiction:
MARY BARTON (1848)
RUTH (1853)
CRANFORD (1853)
NORTH AND SOUTH (1855)
THE LIFE OF CHARLOTTE BRONTE (1857)
SYLVIA'S LOVERS (1863)
WIVES AND DAUGHTERS (1866)—uncompleted

NATHANIEL HAWTHORNE (July 4, 1804 - May 19, 1864)

One of the greatest writers in the American literary tradition, Nathaniel Hawthorne excelled in both longer works of fiction (works he referred to as "romances," but in modern terms would be called novels), and in the short story. The major details of his life are rather well known to American readers. Born into a Puritan-descended family in the Massachusetts port town of Salem, Hawthorne lost his father as a boy, and he and his mother and sisters lived with relatives. At Bowdoin College his strongest subject was composition (and one of his best friendships was with future President Franklin Pierce, a relationship that later led to his position in the Customs House discussed in the preface to *The Scarlet Letter*). His first novel, *Fanshawe*, was published at his own expense in 1824 and showed the difficulties of a first novel. After it appeared, Hawthorne developed the voice we know as his in a number of short stories, including the "My Kinsman, Major Molineux" and "Roger Malvin's Burial." It was not until the late 1840s, however, that he wrote his masterpiece, the novel *The Scarlet Letter*.

It is because of this book, and because of Hawthorne's reaction to its disappointing sales, that this author has been included in this section. For *The Scarlet Letter*, as Kay Mussel points out in her book, *Women's Gothic and Romantic Fiction* (Westport, Ct.: Greenwood, 1981), drew on a literary tradition established and practiced by women, that of the domestic sentimental novel. Mussell notes that "the output of women's romantic novels included a rather large number of historical fictions about women in Puritan New England, some of whom ran afoul of the religious and civil authorities of the colony, although for offenses more acceptable for nineteenth-century taste than was adultery." (p. 8) How did Hawthorne react to the fact that the reading public did not as readily embrace the story of Hester Prynne as it did these novels by women writers? He wrote to his publisher in 1855: "America is now wholly given over to a d——d mob of scribbling women, and I should have no chance of success while the public taste is occupied with their trash—and should be ashamed of myself if I did succeed." (p. 8)

Principal works:
FANSHAWE, A TALE (1828)
TWICE-TOLD TALES (1837)—short story collection
MOSSES FROM AN OLD MANSE (1846)—short story collection
THE SCARLET LETTER (1850)
THE HOUSE OF THE SEVEN GABLES (1851)
THE SNOW-IMAGE, AND OTHER TALES (1851)—short story collection
THE BLITHEDALE ROMANCE (1852)
THE MARBLE FAUN: OR, THE ROMANCE OF MONTE BENI (1860)

ELIZABETH HELME (published from 1787 -1813)

Heavily influenced by Mrs. Radcliffe, Lewis and Godwin in her Gothic novels, the attractive schoolmistress Elizabeth Helme was actually more of an original writer than most give her credit for. Though her historical/Gothic books were her most popular, she also tried her hand at adventure, travel, and history books, as well as translations from both French and German.

Unfortunately, Helme did not live to see the 1814 publication of Walter Scott's WAVERLY; a lover of Scottish laws and customs, as well as an accurate historical writer, she would have enjoyed Scott's well-constructed chronicle of the once-flourishing Highland civilization. In fact, critic Oliver Eaton once wrote that her first book, the tremendously popular LOUISA; OR, THE COTTAGE ON THE MOOR, "gives us a glimpse of what young ladies read in the years before WAVERLY."Mrs. Radcliffe's strengths were her ability to depict a Gothic landscape and her success at building suspense; Elizabeth Helme was a mistress of character development, as well as a maker of intricate plots often featuring cases of mistaken identity. Unlike Mrs. Radcliffe, Helme had an eye for historical detail, due to her familiarity with medieval English historical writing.

Principal works of fiction:
LOUISA; OR, THE COTTAGE ON THE MOOR (1786)
CLARA AND EMMELINE (1788)
DUNCAN AND PEGGY
THE FARMER OF INGLEWOOD FOREST (1797)
ALBERT; OR, THE WILDS OF STRATHNAVERN (1799)
ST. MARGARET'S CAVE; OR, THE NUN'S STORY (1801)
ST. CLAIR OF THE ISLES (1803)
PILGRIMS OF THE CROSS; OR, THE CHRONICLES OF CHRISTABELLE
   DE MOWBRAY (1805)
MAGDALEN; OR THE PENITENT OF GODSTOW (1812)
MODERN TIMES (1814)

GEORGETTE HEYER (August 16, 1890 - July 24, 1974)

When asked which one writer she would choose to read if marooned on a deserted island, Georgette Heyer had a quick reply—Jane Austen. And though her novels lack the depth and irony of those of Austen, Heyer does not do too bad a job herself. A writer frequently cited as a favorite by her colleagues working today, Heyer inspired the recent crop of Regencies, though her current following is generally unaware of her debt to Jeffrey Farnol.

Regency novels were not the only kind that Georgette Heyer wrote, though when confronted with the popularity of her historical books, we find it easy to forget that she, along with Ngaio Marsh and Agatha Christie, was considered a mistress of the mystery in the twenties and thirties, and that her popularity among Americans was first established by a mystery, MERELY MURDER (1935). Many delighted in her addition of humor to an often moribund genre; former NEW YORK TIMES mystery expert Isaac Anderson probably gave the most succinct view of her work in this field: "There are not so many shudders in Georgette Heyer's murder mysteries as there are in those of some other writers, but there is a lot more fun." Yet Regencies were her forte, and here as well did the reader encounter a refreshing wit.

Heyer's first novel, THE BLACK MOTH: A ROMANCE OF THE EIGHTEENTH CENTURY, was written to entertain her ailing brother when she was only seventeen. Her father encouraged her to work toward publication, and her efforts met with success at the age of nineteen. She was married, four years and three books later, to George Rougier, a barrister and author with whom she later co-wrote mysteries.

Despite considerable time spent in East Africa and Yugoslavia, the English Regency remained Heyer's most vividly portrayed setting. In fact, TIME magazine declared in 1964 that her books "will probably be consulted by future scholars as the most detailed and accurate portrait of Regency life anywhere." While her later books were criticized for having too much historical detail, her best books—VENETIA, FARO'S DAUGHTER, BATH TANGLE, SYLVESTER, OR, THE WICKED UNCLE—are wonderful, and the product of a writer with a finely honed skill.

Principal works:
    THE BLACK MOTH (1921)
    THE GREAT ROXHYTHE (1922)
    INSTEAD OF THE THORN (1923)—under the pseudonym "Stella Martin"
    THE TRANSFORMATION OF PHILIP JETTAN (1930)
    SIMON THE COLDHEART (1925)
    THESE OLD SHADES (1926)
    HELEN (1928)
    THE MASQUERADERS (1928)
    BEAUVALLET (1929)
    PASTEL (1929)
    THE BARREN CORN (1930)
    THE CONQUEROR (1931)
    FOOTSTEPS IN THE DARK (1932)—mystery
    WHY SHOOT A BUTLER? (1933)—mystery
    THE UNFINISHED CLUE (1934)—mystery
    THE CONVENIENT MARRIAGE (1934)
    DEVIL'S CUB (1934)
    MERELY MURDER (1935)—mystery
    REGENCY BUCK (1935)
    BEHOLD, HERE'S POISON! (1936)—mystery
    THE TALISMAN RING (1936)—mystery
    THEY FOUND HIM DEAD (1937)—mystery
    AN INFAMOUS ARMY (1937)—historical novel
    A BLUNT INSTRUMENT (1938)—mystery
    ROYAL ESCAPE (1938)
    NO WIND OF BLAME (1939)

THE SPANISH BRIDE (1940)
THE CORINTHIAN (1940)
ENVIOUS CASCA (1941)
FARO'S DAUGHTER (1941)
BEAU WYNDHAM (1941)
FRIDAY'S CHILD (1944)
THE RELUCTANT WIDOW (1946)
THE FOUNDLING (1948)
ARABELLA (1949)
THE GRAND SOPHY (1950)
DUPLICATE DEATH (1951)—mystery
THE QUIET GENTLEMAN (1951)
DETECTION UNLIMITED (1953)—mystery
COTILLION (1953)
THE TOLL-GATE (1954)
BATH TANGLE (1955)
SPRING MUSLIN (1956)
APRIL LADY (1957)
SYLVESTER; OR, THE WICKED UNCLE (1957)
VENETIA (1958)
THE UNKNOWN AJAX (1959)
PISTOLS FOR TWO AND OTHER STORIES (1962)
A CIVIL CONTRACT (1961)
THE NONESUCH (1962)
FALSE COLOURS (1963)
FREDERICA (1965)
BLACK SHEEP (1966)
COUSIN KATE (1968)
CHARITY GIRL (1970)
LADY OF QUALITY (1972)
MY LORD JOHN (1975)

GRACE LIVINGSTON HILL (April 16, 1865 - February 23, 1947)

Born into a family with seven Presbyterian ministers, to a mother who wrote stories for religious magazines, Grace Livingston Hill did the logical thing after the early death of her husband (also a Presbyterian minister) made her the sole support of herself and her two daughters—she started to write a weekly syndicated column that ran in religious papers. Then, following the example of her aunt, children's writer Isabella Auden, she also turned to fiction writing.

Her books have been described as "sugar-coated tracts," and though she claimed that she didn't write to a formula, the NEW

YORK TIMES once noted that she "used the same ingredients over and over again . . . romance, adventure, conflict and religion." She wrote up to three novels a year, and once switched publishers when asked to tone down her religious message. Active throughout her life, she had signed a new contract calling for two novels a year shortly before her death at the age of eighty-one. Her daughter completed the novel she was working on at that time.

Principal works of fiction:
 A CHATAUQUA IDYL (1887)
 A LITTLE SERVANT (1890)
 THE PARKERSTOWN DELEGATE (1892)
 KATHARINE'S YESTERDAY (1896)
 IN THE WAY (1897)
 LONE POINT (1898)
 A DAILY RATE (1899)
 AN UNWILLING GUEST (1901)
 THE ANGEL OF HIS PRESENCE (1902)
 THE STORY OF A WHIM (1902)
 ACCORDING TO THE PATTERN (1903)
 BECAUSE OF STEPHEN (1903)
 THE GIRL FROM MONTANA (1907)
 MARCIA SCHUYLER (1908)
 PHOEBE DEAN (1909)
 DAWN OF THE MORNING (1910)
 THE MYSTERY OF MARY (1911)
 AUNT CRETE'S EMANCIPATION (1911)
 LO, MICHAEL (1913)
 THE BEST MAN (1914)
 THE MAN OF THE DESERT (1914)
 MIRANDA (1915)
 THE OBSESSION OF VICTORIA GRACEN (1915)
 THE FINDING OF JASPER HOLT (1916)
 A VOICE IN THE WILDERNESS (1916)
 THE WITNESS (1917)
 THE RED SIGNAL (1918)
 THE SEARCH (1919)
 CLOUDY JEWEL (1920)
 EXIT BETTY (1920)
 THE TRYST (1921)
 THE CITY OF FIRE (1922)
 THE BIG BLUE SOLDIER (1923)
 TOMORROW ABOUT THIS TIME (1923)
 RECREATIONS (1924)

NOT UNDER THE LAW (1925)
ARIEL CUSTER (1925)
A NEW NAME (1926)
COMING THROUGH THE RYE (1926)
JOB'S NIECE (1927)
THE WHITE FLOWER (1927)
THE HONOR GIRL (1927)
CRIMSON ROSES (1928)
BLUE RUIN (1928)
FOUND TREASURE (1928)
DUSKIN (1929)
THE PRODIGAL GIRL (1929)
OUT OF THE STORM (1929)
LADYBIRD (1930)
THE GOLD SHOE (1930)
THE WHITE LADY (1930)
SILVER WINGS (1931)
THE CHANCE OF A LIFETIME (1931)
KERRY (1931)
HAPPINESS HILL (1932)
THE CHALLENGERS (1932)
THE PATCH OF BLUE (1932)
THE RANSOM (1933)
MATCHED PEARLS (1933)
THE BELOVED STRANGER (1933)
RAINBOW COTTAGE (1934)
AMORELLE (1934)
THE CHRISTMAS BRIDE (1934)
BEAUTY FOR ASHES (1935)
WHITE ORCHIDS (1935)
THE STRANGE PROPOSAL (1935)
APRIL GOLD (1936)
MYSTERY FLOWERS (1936)
THE SUBSTITUTE GUEST (1936)
SUNRISE (1937)
DAPHNE DEAN (1937)
BRENTWOOD (1937)
MARIGOLD (1938)
HOMING (1938)
MARIS (1938)
PATRICIA (1939)
THE SEVENTH HOUR (1939)
STRANGER WITHIN THE GATES (1939)
HEAD OF THE HOUSE (1940)
ROSE GALBRAITH (1940)
PARTNERS (1940)
BY WAY OF THE SILVERTHORNS (1941)

IN TUNE WITH WEDDING BELLS (1941)
ASTRA (1941)
GIRL OF THE WOODS (1942)

E.M. HULL (published in the twenties and thirties of the twentieth century)

Little is known about the Englishwoman Edith Maude Hull; one indisputable fact about her work, however, is that it stunned the public, and achieved a *succès de scandale* despite cries of woe issuing from established critics.

THE SHEIK (1921) was one of the most influential popular books of this century. It not only spawned two direct sequels by Hull, but inspired countless other romance authors (among them Barbara Cartland), and a memorable silent film starring Rudolph Valentino. Silhouette editor Alicia Condon calls it a "must-read" for today's younger romance writers. Though she wrote several "shockers" and a strong travel book, CAMPING IN THE SAHARA, Hull was even more tenacious in the preservation of her privacy than that other initialed Englishwoman who wrote in a similar vein, E.M. Dell.

Principal works of fiction:
    THE SHEIK (1921)
    THE SHADOW OF THE EAST (1921)
    THE DESERT HEALER (1923)
    SONS OF THE SHEIK (1925)
    THE LION TAMER (1928)
    CAPTIVE OF THE SAHARA (1931)
    THE FOREST OF TERRIBLE THINGS (1939)
    JUNGLE CAPTIVE (1939)

FANNIE HURST (October 18, 1889 - February 23, 1968)

Similar to the novels of Faith Baldwin, the works of Fannie Hurst achieved a great deal of their popularity during the Depression. Yet, while Baldwin's books featured the wealthy, Hurst's often dealt with the downtrodden, those whom happiness just seemed to avoid in a bittersweet (and commercially appealing) way.

Born in St. Louis, Hurst went to New York the year after her graduation from Washington University. Ostensibly while doing graduate work in English at Columbia, she lived in the slums and worked in sweatshops to gather information for her fiction. She published four collections of her short stories before her first novel, STARDUST, appeared in 1921. Yet two of her most memorable books came out in the early years of the Depression, BACK STREET in 1930 and IMITATION OF LIFE in 1933. The heroine of BACK STREET is Ray Schmidt, the mistress of a married man. Consigned to the "back streets" of his life, she comes to a sad end, dying poor and alone some years after her lover's death. In IMITATION OF LIFE, the widowed heroine achieves monetary success by selling maple syrup door to door. Despite the fact that she eventually becomes a prominent businesswoman, she never finds another man to love; thus hers is only an IMITATION OF LIFE.

In the face of the anti-feminist sentiment of her novels, it is interesting to consider Hurst's own domestic arrangement. Secretly married to immigrant Russian pianist Jacques S. Danielson in 1915, she did not announce the marriage until five years later; their union attracted attention due to their maintaining separate careers *and* domiciles. The marriage endured, however, until his death in 1952.

Principal works of fiction:
JUST AROUND THE CORNER (1914)—short story collection
EVERY SOUL HATH ITS SONG (1916)—short story collection
GASLIGHT SONATAS (1918)—short story collection
HUMORESQUE (1919)—short story collection
STARDUST (1921)
THE VERTICAL CITY (1922)—short story collection
LUMMOX (1923)
APPASSIONATA (1926)
SONG OF LIFE (1927)
A PRESIDENT IS BORN (1928)
FIVE AND TEN (1929)
PROCESSION (1929)—short story collection
BACK STREET (1930)
IMITATION OF LIFE (1933)
ANITRA'S DANCE (1934)
GREAT LAUGHTER (1936)
WE ARE TEN (1937)—short story collection
LONELY PARADE (1942)

HALLELUJAH (1944)
ANY WOMAN (1950)
THE MAN WITH ONE HEAD (1953)
ANATOMY OF ME (1958)
FAMILY! (1959)
GOD MUST BE SAD (1961)
FOOL—BE STILL (1964)

HELEN HUNT JACKSON (October 15, 1830 - August 12, 1885)

Some writers turn to the pen for money, others to conquer boredom. Still others, such as Helen Hunt Jackson, hope to ease their grief.

Jackson was educated at Massachusetts' Ipswich Female Academy, where she met and befriended Emily Dickinson. It has even been speculated that Edward Bissell Hunt, Jackson's first husband, was Dickinson's renounced love. Yet her marriage to the man who was the object of romantic inquiry did not last long; Major Hunt died in 1863 while testing one of his own military inventions. When the death of her second son was added to that of her husband and first son, Jackson felt her life was over. She was only thirty-five.

At the suggestion of Newport editor Thomas Wentworth Higginson, Jackson began to write, both poems and articles that were eventually published in national journals. She then met her second husband, banker William Sharpless Jackson, and moved to Colorado. Here she grew stronger in her opposition to the treatment accorded American Indians, and she researched and wrote the non-fiction A CENTURY OF DISHONOR, which she mailed to every member of Congress. It lead to her appointment as special commissioner to investigate the conditions of mission Indians. Their condition so appalled and outraged her that she knew she had to take extreme measures. In order to most effectively bring the problems of the Indians to the attention of white Americans, she wrote RAMONA (1884), a book which seized the public imagination; it remained popular enough to inspire three film versions in the early years of the twentieth century.

Principal works of fiction:
SAXE HOLM'S STORIES (1874-78)—short story collection

MERCY PHILBRICK'S CHOICE (1876)
HETTY'S STRANGE HISTORY (1877)
NELLY'S SILVER MINE (1878)
RAMONA (1884)
ZEPH (1885)

ELEANOR MERCEIN KELLY (August 30, 1880 - October 11, 1968)

Though Eleanor Kelly first gained the attention of the reading public with her trilogy of books set in Kentucky (the state in which she settled after her marriage), her most successful settings for her romantic fiction were the Basque country of Spain, Corfu, and Moorish Africa. Despite the appeal of her deft descriptions of the exotic locales she chose for her settings, it is generally agreed that her resilient, sympathetic heroines were the reason for her success. The Basque country trilogy that immediately followed the one set in Kentucky features in its first book her most appealing heroine, the flapper Emily Waldon. After a series of misadventures, Emily ends up with the man of her dreams, the Basque nobleman Esteban Urruty.

One of Kelly's most complicated heroines, however, was featured in her next-to-last book, RICHARD WALDEN'S WIFE. Aurora Fairmont becomes estranged from her husband during the Civil War; though they live in Wisconsin, her Southern background and his Northern one contribute to a damaging atmosphere of suspicion.

In addition to her novels, Kelly wrote travel sketches and short stories for the SATURDAY EVENING POST, the LADIES' HOME JOURNAL, and COLLIER'S.

Works of fiction:
TOYA THE UNLIKE (1913)
KILDARES OF THE STORM (1916)
WHY JOAN? (1918)
THE MANSION HOUSE (1923)
BASQUERIE (1927)
THE BOOK OF BETTE (1929)
ARABESQUE (1930)
SPANISH HOLIDAY (1930)
NACIO, HIS AFFAIRS (1931)

SEA CHANGE (1931)
SOUNDING HARBORS (1935)
MIXED COMPANY (1936)
RICHARD WALDEN'S WIFE (1950)
PROUD CASTLE (1951)

FRANCES PARKINSON KEYES (July 21, 1885 - July 3, 1970)

Remembered as the author of best-selling, popular romance, Keyes began her writing career as a regular contributor to GOOD HOUSEKEEPING magazine, where her monthly "Letters from a Senator's Wife" appeared for fourteen years. As a contributing editor, she also wrote about her world-wide travels. And though her first novel, THE OLD GRAY HOMESTEAD, appeared in 1919, she had to wait seventeen years for a best-seller. HONOR BRIGHT achieved this status, as did many of the novels that followed it.

Keyes favored the family saga, and though she set her first novels in New England, Washington, and Europe, the reception accorded 1942's CARNIVAL CRESCENT inspired her to winter yearly in Louisiana, and she came to alternate books set in this state with her others. One of her most popular books, with a definite New Orleans flavor, was DINNER AT ANTOINE'S.

Though Keyes' books followed the traditional romance formula of the innocent young heroine who breaks down the cynical defenses of an older hero, she was an extremely well-read woman who did not take kindly to the typical critical reaction to romance. Her feelings and experiences drove her to write THE COST OF A BEST-SELLER (1950), in which she stands up for the craft and skill of the popular novelist.

Keyes died in her beloved New Orleans in 1970. An unfinished autobiography, ALL FLAGS FLYING, appeared two years later.

Principal works of fiction:
THE OLD GRAY HOMESTEAD (1919)
THE CAREER OF DAVID NOBLE (1921)
QUEEN ANNE'S LACE (1930)
LADY BLANCHE FARM: SENATOR MARLOWE'S DAUGHTER (1933)
THE SAFE BRIDGE (1934)

THE HAPPY WANDERER (1935)
HONOR BRIGHT (1936)
FIELDING'S FOLLY (1940)
THE SUBLIME SHEPHERDESS (1940)
ALL THAT GLITTERS (1941)
CRESCENT CARNIVAL (1942)
ALSO THE HILLS (1943)
THE RIVER ROAD (1945)
CAME A CAVALIER (1947)
ONCE ON ESPLANADE (1947)
JOY STREET (1950)
STEAMBOAT GOTHIC (1952)
THE ROYAL BOX (1954)
THE BLUE CAMELLIA (1957)
VICTORINE (1958)
THE CHESS PLAYERS (1960)
ROSES IN DECEMBER (1960)
THE ROSE AND THE LILY (1961)
MADAME CASTEL'S LODGER (1962)
THREE WAYS OF LOVE (1963)
I, THE KING (1966)
TONGUES OF FIRE (1966)
THE HERITAGE (1968)

FRANCIS LATHOM (1777 - May 19, 1832)

A contemporary of the great English Romantic poets and of Sir Walter Scott, Lathom was as eccentric in his appearance and personality as he was prolific as a playwright and novelist. Theatrical in dress and gesture, he even entertained friends with songs of his own composition—he almost seems like an early version of Cole Porter. The wit of certain of his titles certainly reminds us of Porter's: THE WIFE OF A MILLION, A COMEDY; VERY STRANGE BUT VERY TRUE, A NOVEL; CURIOSITY, A COMEDY. Yet this Norwich-born writer, reputed to be the illegitimate son of a peer, also wrote in the blood-and-thunder mode (as Louisa May Alcott later did, though pseudonymously), producing such works as THE MYSTERIOUS FREEBOOTER, OR THE DAYS OF QUEEN BESS, A ROMANCE and THE FATAL VOW, OR ST. MICHAEL'S MONASTERY, A ROMANCE.

After 1801 Lathom retired to Bogdavie, a farmhouse in Aberdeenshire which belonged to Alexander Rennie. Known locally as "Mr. Francis" or "Boggie's Lord" (from the house name), he supposedly feared being kidnapped for his wealth. Toward the end of his life, he moved with Rennie to Monquhitter, where he died in 1832, five months before Walter Scott. He is buried in the Rennie family plot in Fyvie, Aberdeenshire.

Works:

ALL IN A BUSTLE, A COMEDY (1795)
THE MIDNIGHT BELL, A GERMAN STORY (1798)
THE CASTLE OF OLLADA (1799)
MEN AND MANNERS; A NOVEL (1799)
THE DASH OF THE DAY; A COMEDY (1800)
MYSTERY; A NOVEL (1800)
HOLIDAY TIME, OR THE SCHOOL BOY'S FROLIC; A FARCE (1800)
ORLANDO AND SERAPHINA, OR THE FUNERAL PILE; AN HEROIC DRAMA (1803)
THE WIFE OF A MILLION; A COMEDY (1802)
ASTONISHMENT!!! A ROMANCE OF A CENTURY AGO (1802)
THE CASTLE OF THE THUILLERIES, OR NARRATIVE OF ALL THE EVENTS WHICH HAVE TAKEN PLACE IN THE INTERIOR OF THAT PALACE (1806)
VERY STRANGE BUT VERY TRUE; A NOVEL (1803)
ERNESTINA; A TALE FROM THE FRENCH (1803)
THE IMPENETRABLE SECRET, FIND IT OUT (1805)
THE MYSTERIOUS FREEBOOTER, OR THE DAYS OF QUEEN BESS; A ROMANCE (1806)
HUMAN BEINGS, A NOVEL (1807)
THE FATAL VOW, OR ST. MICHAEL'S MONASTERY; A ROMANCE (1807)
THE UNKNOWN, OR THE NORTHERN GALLERY (1808)
LONDON, OR TRUTH WITHOUT TREASON (1809)
ROMANCE OF THE HEBRIDES, OR WONDERS NEVER CEASE (1809)
ITALIAN MYSTERIES, OR MORE SECRETS THAN ONE; A ROMANCE (1820)
THE ONE POUND NOTE AND OTHER TALES (1820)
PUZZLED AND PLEASED, OR THE TWO SOLDIERS, AND OTHER TALES (1822)
LIVE AND LEARN, OR THE FIRST JOHN BROWN, HIS FRIENDS, ENEMIES, AND ACQUAINTANCES, IN TOWN AND COUNTRY; A NOVEL (1823)
THE POLISH BANDIT, OR WHO IS MY BRIDE, AND OTHER STORIES (1824)
YOUNG JOHN BULL, OR BORN ABROAD AND BRED AT HOME (1828)
FASHIONABLE MYSTERIES, OR THE RIVAL DUCHESSES, AND OTHER TALES (1829)

MYSTIC EVENTS, OR THE VISION OF THE TAPESTRY. A ROMANTIC
LEGEND OF THE DAYS OF ANN BOLEYN (1830)

HARRIET LEE (1757 - August 1, 1851)
SOPHIA LEE (1750 - March 13, 1824)

Sisters, Harriet and Sophia Lee were both novelists, playwrights, and women of considerable wit. On their mother's
death, Sophia took over the running of their London home (their
father was an actor) but still managed to write two operas. The
second of these was critiqued by the manager of Covent Garden.
Not satisfied with his remarks, Sophia sent THE CHAPTER OF
ACCIDENTS to the manager of the Haymarket Theatre. On his
advice, she turned the work into a five-act comedy, and the play
was enthusiastically received in 1780.

The money Sophia earned from her play more than came in
handy. John Lee died the following year, and his daughters were
forced to fend for themselves. Sophia used her profits to found a
young ladies' seminary at Bath, and it is believed that the influential Gothic novelist Ann Radcliffe studied there. The school
was a success, as was Sophia's next literary effort. Browning considered THE RECESS, OR A TALE OF OTHER TIMES, one of the
first historical romances, and it was well received by the public
when it appeared in 1785.

Sophia and Harriet worked together on a story collection,
THE CANTERBURY TALES, one of which was dramatized by
Lord Byron as WERNER, OR THE INHERITANCE. Harriet's career as a dramatist was less successful than that of her sister,
though not for want of trying. Perhaps the sisters' most lasting
achievement was their influence on Ann Radcliffe, whose THE
CASTLES OF ATHLIN AND DUNBAYNE is believed to have
been inspired by Sophia's THE RECESS. A further point of interest about the sisters' lives is William Godwin's pursuit of Harriet
after the death of his wife, Mary Wollstonecraft (who died giving
birth to Mary Shelley, the author of FRANKENSTEIN). Harriet
refused his offer of marriage, and remained single until her death
at ninety-four.

Principal works:

Harriet Lee:
THE NEW PEERAGE, OR OUR EYES MAY DECEIVE US (1787)—play
THE MYSTERIOUS MARRIAGE, OR THE HEIRSHIP OF ROSALVA (1798)—play
THE THREE STRANGERS (1826)—play
THE ERRORS OF INNOCENCE (1786)
CLARA LENNOX (1797)
THE CANTERBURY TALES (1797-1805)—short stories; with Sophia Lee

Sophia Lee:
THE CHAPTER OF ACCIDENTS (1780)—play
THE RECESS, OR A TALE OF OTHER TIMES (1783-85)
ALMEYDA, QUEEN OF GRANADA (1796)—play
THE CANTERBURY TALES (1797-1805)—short stories; with Harriet Lee
THE LIFE OF A LOVER, IN A SERIES OF LETTERS (1804)
ORMOND, OR THE DEBAUCHEE (1810)

THOMAS LELAND (1722 - 1785)

In her foreword to the recent Arno edition of Thomas Leland's LONGWORTH, EARL OF SALISBURY, Devendra P. Varma succinctly sums up the book's importance—it "forms the top archway under which we enter the splendid portals of Gothic romance." Obviously, Leland's book was heavily influential in the development of the Gothic novel, appearing nine years after Tobias Smollett's FERDINAND, COUNT FATHOM (1753), the book which hinted at the Gothic trend to come. A fast-paced, tightly constructed tale, LONGWORTH, EARL OF SALISBURY came out two years before Walpole's THE CASTLE OF OTRANTO, and possibly influenced that book. Its influence on Clara Reeve, Harriet and Sophia Lee, and Walter Scott is more certain.

Thomas Leland was a fellow of Trinity College, Dublin, and while there has been some debate that the anonymously published LONGWORTH, EARL OF SALISBURY was actually written by a John Leland, most sources suggest Thomas. Leland brings his training in history and the classics to bear in the story of Longworth, and while it cannot be claimed along with Richardson's CLARISSA to be "one of the greatest of the unread novels," it is more spoken about for its historical importance in the development of the Gothic and historical novels than read—to the possible detriment of the would-be reader's enjoyment.

Principal work of fiction:
LONGWORTH, EARL OF SALISBURY (1762)

MATTHEW GREGORY "MONK" LEWIS (July 9, 1775 - May 14, 1818)

Many woman writers historically important to the romance genre were influenced by their fathers, notably Louisa May Alcott, Fanny Burney, Maria Edgeworth and, to a lesser extent, Georgette Heyer. "Monk" Lewis, one of the most important male writers, was extremely close to his mother, whose greatest wish was for him to become a professional writer.

The Lewises were quite wealthy; as the eldest and a son, Lewis was trained from an early age for the diplomatic service, and received his schooling at Westminster and Christ Church, Oxford. Yet he read heavily in the romantic novels favored by his mother. He also summered abroad in preparation for his future. Spending the fall and winter of 1772-73 in Germany, he learned the language fluently, and also met Goethe. The strong influence of German romanticism was later exhibited in his work.

A precocious writer, Lewis had produced several poems, a drama, and long portions of both a novel and a romance by the age of seventeen. In 1794 he was appointed attaché to the British embassy at the Hague. In ten weeks he wrote AMBROSIO; OR, THE MONK; he was not yet twenty. When the book which gave him his nickname was published the following year, Lewis's life was changed forever in the wake of an instant celebrity of the sort later experienced by Byron. The sensational book, filled with German-inspired horror elements previously unknown in the English tradition, brought its young author both fame and notoriety, however; some critics, notably Samuel Taylor Coleridge, even accused him of blasphemy and immorality.

Lewis then briefly pursued a career in Parliament, but writing and the theatre were his true loves, and he returned to both, soon becoming the leading popular playwright of his time. The first and most successful of his plays was THE CASTLE SPECTRE, a Gothic musical drama produced by Sheridan at the Drury Lane Theatre. Chaffing under Sheridan's restraining influence, in 1801 Lewis started to have his plays produced by Harris at Covent Garden. Here his Gothic romanticism was granted free reign, resulting in audiences full of hysterical, fainting spectators.

While he continued to write plays, Lewis also wrote two more romances, two collections of German and Spanish-inspired tales, and a collection of sixty poetic ballads of the supernatural. Contributors to TALES OF WONDER included Lewis himself and Walter Scott.

Lewis inherited property in Jamaica on his father's death, and first sailed out to see it in 1815 (and eventually wrote the non-fiction THE JOURNAL OF A WEST INDIA PROPRIETOR). Returning, he spent August of 1816 in Geneva with Shelley and Byron, translating Goethe's FAUST aloud to the latter. He died of yellow fever in 1817 while returning from a second voyage to Jamaica. Appropriately enough for this author of Gothic horror, his own coffin lost its weights once it hit the water, and floated back toward Jamaica.

Principal works of fiction:
AMBROSIO; OR, THE MONK (1795)
THE CASTLE SPECTRE (1796)—play
VILLAGE VIRTUES (1796)—play
THE MINISTER (1797)—play; translation of Schiller
ROLLA (1799)—play; translation of Kotzebue
THE EAST INDIAN (1799)—play
ADELMORN THE OUTLAW (1800)—play
ALPHONSO KING OF CASTILE (1801)—play
THE BROVO OF VENICE (1804)
RUGANTINO (1805)—play
FEUDAL TYRANTS (1806)
ADELGITHA (1806)—play
WOOD DEMON (1807)—play
VENONI (1809)—play
TIMOUR THE TARTAR (1812)—play
RICH AND POOR (1812)

ANNA MARIA MacKENZIE (published during the last years of the eighteenth century and the early years of the nineteenth)

A prolific writer, Anna Maria MacKenzie achieved her greatest success with MONMOUTH, an historical romance. While little is known about Mrs. MacKenzie's life, we do know that she was married three times, having outlived her first two husbands, and that she sometimes wrote under the pseudonym "Ellen of Exeter." We also have more than a slight inkling of her view of historical romances. She writes about the contemporary popularity of the genre in her sixth novel, MYSTERIES ELUCI-DATED, to an audience she addresses as "Readers of Modern Romance:" ". . . ladies are contented to be interested and improved [by reading historical romance], without being terrified" (an allusion to the Gothic novels also popular at this time).

Principal works of fiction:
BURTON WOOD (1785)
THE GAMESTERS (1786)
MONMOUTH (1790)
THE DANISH MASSACRE; AN HISTORICAL FACT (1791)
MYSTERIES ELUCIDATED (1795)
THE NEAPOLITAN, OR THE TEST OF INTEGRITY (1796)
FEUDAL EVENTS (1797)
DUSSELDORF, OR THE FRATRICIDE (1798)
MARTIN AND MANSFELDT, OR, THE ROMANCE OF FRANCONIA
(1802)
THE IRISH GUARDIAN; OR, ERRORS OF ECCENTRICITY (1809)

CHARLES ROBERT MATURIN (1780 - October 30, 1824)

Irish by birth, of Huguenot descent, Charles Robert Maturin was heavily influenced by the German-rooted Gothicism of "Monk" Lewis, as well as by Mrs. Radcliffe's THE ITALIAN. His first book, FATAL REVENGE, OR, THE FAMILY OF MONTORIO earned the writer a very left-handed compliment by Walter Scott, who called it "a remarkable instance of genius degraded by the labor in which it was engaged." Despite his view of the book, Scott was interested in fostering Maturin's talent, and his influence brought the author's BERTRAM to Drury Lane in 1816. Edmund Kean himself played the title role, and the Gothic play was a success.

Leaving London and his heady success, Maturin returned to Dublin where he was curate of St. Peter's, and promptly spent the money BERTRAM had earned him. Three of the novels written after his success in London are notable: THE WOMEN (1818), an early example of the psychological novel; MELMOTH, a Gothic novel with a Faustian theme; and THE ALBIGENSES.

Maturin died at the age of forty-four; some critics feel that, had he lived longer, his achievements in the Gothic novel would have matched those of Radcliffe and Lewis. Based on his actual output, however, he has to be ranked below those two masters of the genre.

Principal works of fiction:
FATAL REVENGE; OR, THE FAMILY OF MONTORIO (1807)
THE WILD IRISH BOY (1808)
THE MILESIAN CHIEF (1812)
BERTRAM; OR, THE CASTLE OF ST. ALDABRAND (1816)—play
MANUEL (1817)—play
WOMEN; OR, POUR ET CONTRE (1818)
FREDOLFO (1819)—play
MELMOTH; THE WANDERER (1820)

MARY MEEKE (? - October 1816)

Much of romance writing is formula writing, but the formula often begins and ends with "boy meets girl, boy loses girl, boy gets girl."The romance writers most popular today in the "category" books are those who bring creative elements to a confining form. Mary Meeke, one of the most popular writers of the years leading into the Regency, wrote to an unvarying formula: the rags-to-riches heroes, always the focal characters in her books, were by the end revealed to be members of the aristocracy, often identified by a birthmark. Unlike the vibrant heroines of her contemporary Mrs. Radcliffe, those of Meeke seem to exist solely to serve the hero.

While her books bore suitably commercial Gothic titles, Meeke was not a Gothic writer; no ghosts appear in her books, and about the closest we come to nightmares is hearing someone's dream recounted. Her success lay mainly in having developed a very appealing formula, and following it through with consistent writing—frequently; in one year she produced six books (though in the wake of Barbara Cartland's recent years of producing over twenty books, Meeke's output doesn't seem so impressive). A practical writer, she advised would-be authors to "consult the taste of [the] publisher" before writing to determine what would do best in the marketplace. Certainly a favorite among the leisured women of her day, Mrs. Meeke even claimed Macaulay as a fan. Married to the Reverend Francis Meeke, she died in Staffordshire in the fall of 1816.

Principal works of fiction:
COUNT ST. BLANCARD (1795)
ELLESMERE (1799)
MIDNIGHT WEDDINGS (1802)
ELLEN, HEIRESS OF THE CASTLE (1807)
MATRIMONY, THE HEIGHT OF BLISS OR EXTREME OF MISERY (1811)
CONSCIENCE (1814)

MARGARET MITCHELL (November 8, 1900 - August 16, 1949)

What single book is cited most frequently by authors writing today in the romance genre as their favorite? To anyone who's ever been a book-crazed teenager, the daughter of a woman who was a book-crazed teenager, or a Leslie Howard fan, only one answer is possible: GONE WITH THE WIND.

GWTW was ten years in the writing, and was begun when its author, who had been working as a journalist, badly sprained her ankle and was confined to the house. The sprain turned out to be a blessing in disguise; the author's only novel, GWTW set sales records, won the 1937 Pulitzer Prize, was adapted into an unforgettable, Oscar-winning motion picture, and earned its author tens of thousands of fan letters (Mitchell was ultimately forced to hire two secretaries to help her answer them).

Born into a prominent Atlanta family, Mitchell grew up hearing stories about the Civil War, especially from her mother and older brother. These tales were decidedly partisan; Mitchell did not learn that the South had lost the war until she was ten. It was a shocking discovery.

Graduated from Washington Seminary in Atlanta, Mitchell attended Smith College for a year. She had hoped to eventually become a doctor, but that dream was cut short when her mother died at the end of her freshman year, and she returned permanently to Atlanta. After the publication of GWTW, she did receive an honorary M.A. from Smith.

The sensation caused by the success of her book prevented its author from writing another. She died after being struck by a car on an Atlanta street when she was only forty-nine. Her book, a vibrant historical romance, continues to influence writers.

Only published work of fiction:
GONE WITH THE WIND (1936)

LUCY MAUDE MONTGOMERY (November 30, 1874 - April 24, 1942)

Similar to her countrywoman Mazo de la Roche, L.M. Montgomery's greatest setting for her books was a beloved part of Canada. Yet while de la Roche set her stories in the forests of Ontario, Montgomery placed all but one of her tales on "the only island that is"—Prince Edward Island.

A journalist and teacher, Montgomery had written since childhood, at twelve winning a short story contest sponsored by a newspaper. She claimed that she always hoped to write a novel but couldn't stand the thought of starting one. She then chanced upon a plot idea she'd scribbled in a notebook: "Elderly couple apply to orphan asylum for a boy. By mistake a girl is sent them." The novel produced was, of course, ANNE OF GREEN GABLES, and instead of just the audience of girls the author expected, Montgomery found herself the recipient of fan mail from people in all walks of life from all over the world.

Due to the popularity of the first book, six "Anne" sequels were written, though none achieved the same popularity as the first book. In addition to other children's books, Montgomery also wrote two adult novels, THE BLUE CASTLE and A TANGLED WEB, which were less successful than her books for younger readers.

Principal works of fiction:
ANNE OF GREEN GABLES (1908)
ANNE OF AVONLEA (1909)
KILMENY OF THE ORCHARD (1910)
THE STORY GIRL (1911)

CHRONICLES OF AVONLEA (1912)
THE GOLDEN ROAD (1913)
ANNE OF THE ISLAND (1915)
ANNE'S HOUSE OF DREAMS (1917)
RAINBOW VALLEY (1919)
RILLA OF INGLESIDE (1921)
EMILY OF NEW MOON (1923)
EMILY CLIMBS (1925)
THE BLUE CASTLE (1926)
EMILY'S QUEST (1927)
MAGIC FOR MARIGOLD (1930)
A TANGLED WEB (1931)
PAT OF SILVER BUSH (1933)
MISTRESS PAT (1935)
ANNE OF THE WINDY POPLARS (1936)
JANE OF LANTERN HILL (1938)

KATHLEEN NORRIS (July 16, 1880 - January 18, 1966)

When Kathleen Norris was nineteen years old and preparing to make her San Francisco debut, her mother unexpectedly died of pneumonia. Her banker father followed a month later, and she and her five siblings were left alone and penniless. Kathleen and the other two eldest children took an assortment of jobs and among them managed to bring in $95 a month. To provide entertainment for the struggling brood, Kathleen began to tell them stories, a pastime that eventually led to a writing career.

Norris soon sold a story to the San Francisco ARGONAUT; later she became society editor of the EVENING BULLETIN, an experience which gave her background for some of her novels. She was eventually discharged from the paper, then told by the Associated Press that writing was not her forte. Fortunately, she did not believe this pronouncement, and when she moved to New York with her editor husband, Charles Norris (the brother of Frank Norris), she started to sell short stories to magazines. When a short story for the AMERICAN grew larger than planned, it became her first novel.

Norris eventually wrote ninety books, many of them featuring California backgrounds. Her most ambitious book, CERTAIN PEOPLE OF IMPORTANCE, dealt with the descendants of a Forty-Niner. A realistic book, it was not well received, and

Norris never again attempted a work of its scope.

Principal works of fiction:
MOTHER (1911)
THE RICH MRS. BURGOYNE (1912)
POOR DEAR MARGARET KIRBY (1912)
SATURDAY'S CHILD (1914)
THE STORY OF JULIA PAGE (1915)
THE HEART OF RACHEL (1916)
MARTIE, THE UNCONQUERED (1917)
UNDERTOW (1917)
JOSSLYN'S WIFE (1918)
SISTERS (1922)
HARRIET AND THE PIPER (1920)
BELOVED WOMAN (1921)
CERTAIN PEOPLE OF IMPORTANCE (1922)
BUTTERFLY (1923)
THE CALLAHANS AND THE MURPHYS (1924)
LITTLE SHIPS (1925)
THE BLACK FLEMINGS (1926)
HILDEGARDE (1926)
THE BARBERRY BUSH (1928)
THE SEA GULL (1927)
BEAUTY AND THE BEAST (1928)
THE FOOLISH VIRGIN (1928)
STORM HOUSE (1929)
RED SILENCE (1929)
HOME (1929)
MOTHER AND SON (1929)
MARGARET YORKE (1930)
THE LUCKY LAWRENCES (1930)
THE LOVE OF JULIA BOREL (1931)
HANDS FULL OF LIVING (1931)
BELLE MERE (1931)
SECOND HAND WIFE (1932)
THE YOUNGER SISTER (1932)
TREEHAVEN (1932)
WALLS OF GOLD (1933)
WIFE FOR SALE (1933)
ANGEL IN THE HOUSE (1933)
MANHATTAN LOVE SONG (1934)
MAIDEN VOYAGE (1934)
THREE MEN AND DIANA (1934)
BEAUTY'S DAUGHTER (1935)
SHINING WINDOWS (1935)
WOMAN IN LOVE (1935)

THE AMERICAN FLAGGS (1936)
SECRET MARRIAGE (1936)
BREAD INTO ROSES (1937)
YOU CAN'T HAVE EVERYTHING (1937)
HEARTBROKEN MELODY (1938)
LOST SUNRISE (1939)
MYSTERY HOUSE (1939)
THE RUNAWAY (1939)
THE SECRET OF THE MARSHBANKS (1940)
THE WORLD IS LIKE THAT (1940)
THESE I LIKE BEST (1941)
THE VENABLES (1941)
AN APPLE FOR EVE (1942)
COME BACK TO ME, BELOVED (1942)
DINA CASHMAN (1942)
ONE NATION INDIVISIBLE (1942)
STAR-SPANGLED CHRISTMAS (1942)
CORNER OF HEAVEN (1943)
LOVE CALLS THE TUNE (1944)
BURNED FINGERS (1945)
MOTIONLESS SHADOWS (1945)
MINK COAT (1946)
OVER AT THE CROWLEYS' (1946)
THE SECRETS OF HILLYARD HOUSE (1947)
HIGH HOLIDAY (1949)
MORNING LIGHT (1950)
SHADOW MARRIAGE (1952)
MISS HARRIET TOWNSHEND (1955)
THROUGH A GLASS DARKLY (1957)
FAMILY GATHERING (1959)

BARONESS ORCZY (September 23, 1865 - November 12, 1947)

Writers faced with rejections slips can take heart from the experiences of Baroness Orczy; her second novel met with the disapprobation of at least twelve publishers. In fact, THE SCARLET PIMPERNEL was not published as a novel until after a dramatic version was successfully staged throughout England. Of course, many of us today first encounter the tale of the foppish-on-the-outside, gallant-on-the-inside Sir Percy Blakeney through the film adaptation starring Leslie Howard.

Born in Hungary, Emmuska Orczy was taken to England at the age of fifteen. Her family was musical, though she herself decidedly was not. She studied painting, and met the illustrator Montague Barstow, an illustrator; they married in 1894. It was by writing and illustrating children's stories that the baroness first published. Her first piece for adults, the short story "Juliette," appeared in 1899, as did her first novel, THE EMPEROR'S CANDLESTICKS. That novel was far from popular, but Orczy then achieved success with a series of crime stories in the ROYAL MAGAZINE.

The long struggle to have THE SCARLET PIMPERNEL published, and its later success, is not the only interesting part of that book's background; readers and writers alike are fascinated that the whole tale was inspired by Orczy's seconds-long sighting of a fascinating stranger in a train station. She never saw him again, but something about his look led her to create her most enduring character.

After the success of THE SCARLET PIMPERNEL, Orczy often wrote two, and sometimes three, books a year, most of them historical romances. She died in London in November of 1947.

Principal works of fiction:
THE EMPEROR'S CANDLESTICKS (1899)
THE SCARLET PIMPERNEL (1905)—numerous sequels also appeared
I WILL REPAY (1906)
FLOWER O' THE LILY (1918)
NICOLETTE (1922)
THE CELESTIAL CITY (1926)
SKIN O' MY TOOTH (1928)
BLUE EYES AND GREY (1929)
THE TURBULENT DUCHESS (1935)
NO GREATER LOVE (1938)
MAM'ZELLE GUILLOTINE (1940)
WILL-O'-THE-WISP (1946)

ELIZA PARSONS (1748 - February 5, 1811)

Doubtless, all the literary repercussions of what the British term the "American War" have not been chronicled. Yet the colonists' seizure of two goods-laden ships belonging to a certain Mr. Parsons of Plymouth led indirectly to his wife's career in letters. For in attempting to recoup his fortune by expanding his domestic turpentine trade, Parsons found himself totally destitute after a 1782 fire destroyed this business. Despite a lifesaving position in the Lord Chamberlain's office at St. James, a post secured by the Marchioness of Salisbury, his financial ruin, combined with the death of his eldest son, was too much to bear. On his death, Eliza Parsons and her seven surviving children, all born to a life of wealth, were on the verge of destitution. She had no choice but to take up the pen.

Her first novel, THE HISTORY OF MISS MEREDITH (1790), was epistolary. Dedicated to the Marchioness of Salisbury, it numbered among its subscribers the Prince of Wales and Horace Walpole. The books which followed it were highly moral in tone, condemning those mothers who dressed their daughters beyond their means in order to draw wealthy husbands (for what was such fortune hunting if not a form of prostitution?), and other behavior of which she disapproved. The influence of Richardson is shown in the epistolary first novel, and in the author's later LUCY (1794). She even penned two of the "Horrid Novels," showing a real flair for the Gothic romance a la Mrs. Radcliffe. Both THE CASTLE OF WOLFENBACH (1793) and THE MYSTERIOUS WARNING (1796) are outstanding examples of the genre.

While she knew that her books were not quite up to the caliber of those of the top writers of her day, Mrs. Parsons did achieve considerable popular success; many of her books were, after all, published by William Lane's Minerva Press. Pursued by misfortune throughout her life (the deaths of her husband and eldest son were followed by those of three more of her eight children), Mrs. Parsons nevertheless produced more than sixty full-length works. Financial pressures forbade the honing of any of these novels, and it was her outstanding talent as a storyteller that made her success.

Principal works:
THE HISTORY OF MISS MEREDITH (1790)
ERRORS OF EDUCATION (1791)
THE INTRIGUES OF A MORNING; OR AN HOUR IN PARIS (1792)—from
   Moliere's "Monsieur of Pourceaugnac"
ELLEN AND JULIA (1792)
THE CASTLE OF WOLFENBACH (1793)

WOMAN AS SHE SHOULD BE (1793)
LUCY (1794)
THE VOLUNTARY EXILE (1795)
THE MYSTERIOUS WARNING (1796)
WOMEN AS THEY ARE (1796)
ANECDOTES OF TWO WELL-KNOWN FAMILIES (1798)
LOVE AND GRATITUDE; OR, TRAITS OF THE HUMAN HEART
(1804)—translated from La Fontaine.

EDGAR ALLAN POE (January 19, 1809 - October 7, 1849)

The life of Edgar Allan Poe has been discussed as much as his
works of literature. From English classes in school, we are all familiar with his never-legalized adoption by a wealthy, Richmond, Va., family (and his incorporating their name, Allan, into
his own), his expulsion from West Point, his moving around constantly as an adult, taking editorial jobs in different cities on the
Eastern seaboard . . . and with his marriage to his sickly thirteen-
year-old cousin Virginia, the Annabel Lee of the poem, who died
eleven years later of a lingering illness. And we certainly remember the stories of his bouts with alcoholism, his undignified
death in Baltimore just before the flowering of American letters
witnessed by the early years of the 1850s, years which saw the
publication of major works by Whitman, Hawthorne and
Melville. Not so familiar are his involvements with wealthy
women of literary aspirations after Virginia's death, in what
some critics view as an attempt to marry the money that could
buy him his own magazine. Also not known to many readers is
his influence on the French poet Baudelaire, and, through him,
on the Symbolist movement in French poetry.

Yet no matter what we remember about his life, we all remember his rhythmic poems, and his tales of the supernatural.
But while Poe was heavily influenced by the Gothic tradition of
Walpole, one brought to the United States by Charles Brockden
Brown, he differed from previous writers in an important respect. The confrontation in his works is not between the main
character and an outside source of evil, but is one that takes place
within the main character—in essence, a confrontation with the
self. Even the house, the equivalent of the Gothic castle and ac-

knowledged as a character even in the traditional Gothic, was changed by Poe. He more clearly personified it, identifying it with the main character—see especially the short story THE FALL OF THE HOUSE OF USHER, in which Poe describes the dwelling's "vacant, eyelike windows"—and in which it represents the family in question, both being houses of Usher. Obviously, his work in the Gothic genre is a useful counterpoint to the Gothic tradition developed by women writers.

Principal works:
TAMERLANE AND OTHER POEMS (1827)
AL AARAAF, TAMERLANE, AND MINOR POEMS (1829)
POEMS (1831)
THE NARRATIVE OF ARTHUR GORDON PYM (1838)
THE CONCHOLOGIST'S FIRST BOOK (1839)
TALES OF THE GROTESQUE AND ARABESQUE (1840)
THE PROSE ROMANCES OF EDGAR ALLAN POE (1843)
THE RAVEN AND OTHER POEMS (1845)
EUREKA: A PROSE POEM (1848)

OLIVE HIGGINS PROUTY (January 10, 1882 - March 24, 1974)

The conflict between home and career is one currently felt by many women. It was, as well, one both featured in the popular novels of Olive Higgins Prouty and faced by her in her life. Unfortunately for Mrs. Prouty, it was a conflict much more easily dealt with in fiction.

At the age of twelve, Prouty suffered the first of two nervous breakdowns when a beloved nurse died; the breakdown lasted almost two years. She then went to Worcester Classical High in her Massachusetts hometown, doing miserably in athletics and mathematics, but managing to equal her peers in composition. She took a Bachelor of Literature degree from Smith in 1904.

Prouty was first published five years later when the AMERICAN MAGAZINE ran her short story, "When Elsie Came." At her editor's urging, she followed it with several more, all about the same family; she finally developed the stories into her first novel, BOBBIE, GENERAL MANAGER (1913). Prouty herself said that through this method she "drifted into writing [her] first novel." Her second novel as well was based on short stories; she once wrote that only with her third novel had she "acquired enough technique to attempt a novel without the preliminary short steps." Her second novel, entitled FIFTH WHEEL, dealt with the theme of career versus home and family, the latter option winning hands down. Prouty's personal battle was not so easily won, and in 1925, two years after the publication of STELLA DALLAS, she suffered her second breakdown.

STELLA DALLAS was one of Prouty's most popular works, and, adapted as a radio serial, ran for fifteen years. It was also adapted for the stage and as a motion picture.

Prouty then embarked on the series that produced one of the best-loved of the "women's pictures" of the thirties and early forties. The third of five novels about Boston's wealthy Vale family, NOW, VOYAGER (1941) dealt with Charlotte Vale's breaking away from the domination of her mother through spending time in a sanatorium and undertaking a voyage on which she meets—and falls in love with—an unhappily married man. Two unforgettable performances by Bette Davis and Paul Henreid, and one of the most poignant last lines in motion picture history, have made the film a favorite among film buffs—and romantics—of all ages.

Sanatoriums figured not only in Prouty's personal life and in her fiction, but also in the life of a talented young woman holding the Olive H. Prouty Scholarship at Smith in the early 50s. After Sylvia Plath's 1953 suicide attempt, Prouty paid for the younger woman's stay in a private sanatorium; Plath later unflatteringly caricatured her benefactor as Philomena Guinea in THE BELL JAR.

Though certain of her books were considered sentimental, Prouty's work sold in the millions, and through the radio, screen and stage adaptations touched the lives of countless more. Such influence was no mean accomplishment for a woman who tried to see her work merely as a hobby, and her home as her career— and repeatedly tried to resolve the conflict not in her life, but in her fiction.

Principal works of fiction:
BOBBIE, GENERAL MANAGER (1913)
THE FIFTH WHEEL (1916)
THE STAR IN THE WINDOW (1918)
GOOD SPORTS (1919)

STELLA DALLAS (1923)
CONFLICT (1927)
WHITE FAWN (1931)
LISA VALE (1938)
NOW, VOYAGER (1941)
HOME PORT (1947)
FABIA (1951)
PENCIL SHAVINGS (1961)

ANN RADCLIFFE (July 9, 1764 - February 7, 1823)

Unlike the many writers of popular fiction who are driven to pick up the pen in order to fill their coffers, the Gothic romantic novels of Ann Radcliffe were written to fill time—her own and that of her many fans who belonged to the leisure class. Dorothy Scarborough defined the impetus for her writing in this way: "Her journalist husband was away until late at night, so while sitting up for him she wrote frightful stories to keep herself from being scared."

No matter what the motivation for her work, Ann Radcliffe wrote books that enjoyed tremendous popularity as well as earned her the admiration of Byron, Coleridge, and Christina Rossetti. The latter even attempted a biography in 1883, but was forced to abandon the project due to a lack of information about the author. And while her own work was inspired by Horace Walpole's THE CASTLE OF OTRANTO (1764), Mrs. Radcliffe's books set the style of the Gothic romance; she alone had the ability to combine a romantic sensibility with scenes of terror and suspense, and her novels remain among the most distinguished of the genre. The villain of THE ITALIAN was particularly influential. The perpetrator of a horrible crime, he wins our sympahty by virtue of the tragic loneliness of his fate. The direct inspiration of the villains of "Monk" Lewis and Charles Robert Maturin, and of those of Walter Scott and Byron, the Radcliffe villain exerted a personal influence on Byron as well. One critic even claimed that "The man that Byron tried to be was the invention of Mrs. Radcliffe."

Though her first novel, THE CASTLES OF ATHLIN AND DUNBAYNE (1789) was not a success, her next four were heartily embraced by the public. Her many fans were seemingly undisturbed by the lack of accuracy exhibited; they were less concerned by the fact that Italian servants incorrectly addressed their masters as "maestro" (the word for teacher) as they were by their desires for the qualities they found in her work—a moody, romanticized view of nature, and good, old-fashioned suspense.

Mrs. Radcliffe died in 1823, and three years later GASTON DE BLONDEVILLE, an historical novel written in 1802, was published. Though not strong in itself, it is of interest in that Mrs. Radcliffe attempted in it to paint an accurate historical picture twelve years before the appearance of Scott's WAVERLY.

Principal works of fiction:
THE CASTLES OF ATHLIN AND DUMBAYNE (1789)
A SICILIAN ROMANCE (1790)
THE ROMANCE OF THE FOREST (1791)
THE MYSTERIES OF UDOLPHO (1794)
THE ITALIAN (1796)
GASTON DE BLONDEVILLE (1826)

CLARA REEVE (1729 - December 3, 1807)

Clara Reeve's first major work owes a considerable debt to Horace Walpole—the preface to THE CHAMPION OF VIRTUE, A GOTHIC STORY claims that the work is an edition of an ancient manuscript, the same false claim made by Walpole regarding THE CASTLE OF OTRANTO. Yet Reeve sought to lessen the supernatural effects, so favored by the earlier writer, and strengthen the principal characters. When her book appeared anonymously in 1777, it made no mark on the public; a year later, a title change (to THE OLD ENGLISH BARON) and the mention of Reeve as the author, for some reason had a drastic effect, and the book took off. Reprinted as late as 1883, it certainly helped inspire the novels of the highly influential Mrs. Radcliffe.

Reeve's other major work is not a novel at all, but a kind of literary criticism. THE PROGRESS OF ROMANCE, THROUGH TIMES, CENTURIES, AND MANNERS (1785) was a historical review presenting Reeve's view of what she thought the novel should accomplish—that it had to deal with everyday people and problems, and encourage moral improvement. These ideals are, of course, expressed in her own work, from her second novel, THE TWO MENTORS, through her last, DESTINATION, OR,

MEMOIRS OF A PRIVATE FAMILY. She was a firm believer in didactic fiction. As James Trainer points out, the "fear of excess which characterizes her work leaves the reader with a feeling of a benevolent writer almost afraid of herself and of the possibility of giving offense or of weakening the moral fibre of society."Sir Walter Scott himself wrote a brief memoir of her life and work for the 1823 edition of THE OLD ENGLISH BARON.

Principal works:
POEMS (1769)
THE PHOENIX (1772)—translation of a Latin romance
THE CHAMPION OF VIRTUE (THE OLD ENGLISH BARON)—(1777)
THE TWO MENTORS, A MODERN STORY (1783)
THE PROGRESS OF ROMANCE THROUGH TIMES, CENTURIES AND MANNERS (1785)
THE EXILES (1788)
THE SCHOOL FOR WIDOWS (1791)
THE MEMOIRS OF SIR ROGER DE CLARENDON (1793)
DESTINATION, OR MEMOIRS OF A PRIVATE FAMILY (1799)

SAMUEL RICHARDSON (August 19, 1689 - July 4, 1761)

Few have come to the task of writing fiction as late as Samuel Richardson, yet few have been as influential as this very successful printer who wrote PAMELA, OR VIRTUE REWARDED, in 1740, his fiftieth year. For it is this story of a young woman's attempted seduction by the master of the household in which she works that is considered the first true novel in the English language. Certainly novel-length works had appeared before PAMELA, notably GULLIVER'S TRAVELS and ROBINSON CRUSOE, but Richardson's work alone concentrates on a single action.

Richardson's first book was a guide to conduct, directed at apprentices (Richardson himself had been an apprentice to the printer John Wilde). THE APPRENTICE'S VADE MECUM; OR, YOUNG MAN'S POCKET COMPANION, appeared in 1733, and was followed by A SEASONABLE EXAMINATION two years later. It was a pamphlet in favor of a parliamentary bill to regulate the London theaters.

The idea for PAMELA, which is an epistolary novel, came to Richardson after he was approached by two booksellers who wanted him to write a book of model letters for social occasions. The letters in PAMELA describe her difficulties as a servant being pursued by the fairly young and very well-off master of the house, Squire B____. The two-volume novel met with instant and tremendous popular success on its publication late in 1740, though the book has always had its critics, many of whom claim that Pamela's recalcitrance in the face of Squire B____'s advances had more to do with calculation than virtue (Pamela does end up marrying him, an event that surely would not have come about if she'd given in to his demands). Henry Fielding lampooned Richardson in his novels, even giving the Squire the last name of Booby.

In response to a spurious sequal to PAMELA, Richardson wrote his own, which details the heroine's married life. Needless to say, it lacks the spark of the first book. And finally, after the outrageous success of PAMELA, Richardson did write LETTERS WRITTEN TO AND FOR PARTICULAR FRIENDS, DIRECTING THE REQUISITE STYLE AND FORMS . . . IN WRITING FAMILIAR LETTERS. He then wrote two more novels, the seven-volume CLARISSA HARLOWE (called by some "one of the greatest of the unread novels") important for its depiction of the rapidly changing society of mid-eighteenth-century England. In response to the criticism that greeted CLARISSA, that he had made the villain Lovelace too attractive a figure, Richardson wrote SIR CHARLES GRANDISON, his last novel. Though the character of Charles himself is too flawless and moral to be remotely likeable, the book was a particular favorite of Jane Austen's.

Works of fiction:
  PAMELA, OR VIRTUE REWARDED (1740)
  CLARISSA HARLOWE (1747-1748)
  SIR CHARLES GRANDISON (1753-1754)

AMY ROBERTA RUCK (August 2, 1878 - August 11, 1978)

Berta Ruck came to writing through a somewhat glamorous back door—having studied at London's Slade School of Art, and then in Paris, she was still living in that city when she found herself commissioned to illustrate a story for a London magazine. On reading it she knew immediately that she could do better. She wrote a sketch of Latin Quarter life, illustrated it herself, and sent it to the same magazine. It was accepted for the sum of four guineas. Imagining her fortune made (and so easily!), she plunged into writing—and did not sell again for over a year.

It was a fast/slow beginning to what eventually became one of the twentieth century's most successful and prolific literary careers. Ruck's first novel, HIS OFFICIAL FIANCEE (1914) met an enthusiastic reception, and was even made into a silent film. She married the English novelist George Oliver (his name at birth was Oliver Onions, and he published under that name), had two sons and a penchant for titles that expressed the verve found in her books themselves. Some of the most appealing are THE WRONG MR. RIGHT, OUT TO MARRY MONEY, SHOPPING FOR A HUSBAND, and MONEY ISN'T EVERYTHING.

Principal works (American titles and pub dates, unless never printed here):
HIS OFFICIAL FIANCEE (1914)
THE WOOING OF ROSAMOND FAYRE (1915)
KHAKI AND KISSES (1915)
THE BOY WITH WINGS (1915)
MISS MILLION'S MAID (1915)
GIRLS AT HIS BILLET (1916)
IN ANOTHER GIRL'S SHOES (1916)
THE THREE OF HEARTS (1917)
THE GREAT UNMET (1918)
RUFUS ON THE REBOUND (1918)
THE DISTURBING CHARM (1919)
A LAND-GIRL'S LOVE STORY (1919)
SWEETHEARTS UNMET (1919)
THE BRIDGE OF KISSES (1920)
AMERICAN SNAP-SHOTS (1920)
SWEET STRANGER (1921)
THE ARRANT ROVER (1921)
THE SUBCONSCIOUS COURTSHIP (1922)
THE WRONG MR. RIGHT (1922)
SON OR MADAM (1923)
THE DANCING STAR (1923)
THE CLOUDED PEARL (1924)
THE LEAP YEAR GIRL (1924)
LUCKY IN LOVE (1924)
KNEEL TO THE PRETTIEST (1925)

THE IMMORTAL GIRL (1925)
HER PIRATE PARTNER (1927)
THE PEARL THIEF (1926)
THE MIND OF A MINX (1927)
JOY RIDE! (1929)
THE YOUNGEST VENUS (1928)
MONEY FOR ONE (1928)
THE UNKISSED BRIDE (1929)
TODAY'S DAUGHTER (1930)
COURTSHIP OF ROSAMOND FAYRE (1930)
POST-WAR GIRL (1930)
WANTED ON THE VOYAGE (1930)—short stories
THE LOVE-HATER (1930)
OFFER OF MARRIAGE (1931)
FORCED LANDING (1931)
DANCE PARTNER (1931)
THIS YEAR, NEXT YEAR, SOMETIME (1932)
THE LAP OF LUXURY (1932)
SUDDEN SWEETHEART (1933)
UNDERSTUDY (1933)
ELEVENTH HOUR LOVER (1933)
CHANGE HERE FOR HAPPINESS (1933)
THE BEST TIME EVER (1934)
SUNBURST (1934)
SUNSHINE STEALER (1935)
A STAR IN LOVE (1935)
SPRING COMES (1936)
SLEEPING BEAUTY (1936)
A STORY-TELLER TELLS THE TRUTH: REMINISCENCES AND NOTES
    (1937)—autobiography
LOVE ON SECOND THOUGHTS (1937)
ROMANCE ROYAL (1937)
WEDDING MARCH (1938)
LOVE COMES AGAIN LATER (1938)
HANDMAID TO FAME (1939)
MOCK-HONEYMOON (1939)
ARBELLA ARRIVES (1939)
IT WAS LEFT TO PETER (1940)
HE LEARNED ABOUT WOMEN (1940)
MONEY ISN'T EVERYTHING (1940)
FIANCEES ARE RELATIVES (1941)
JADE EARRINGS (1941)
WALTZ CONTEST (1941)
SPINSTER'S PROGRESS (1942)
QUARREL AND KISS (1942)
FOOTLIGHT FEVER (1942)
BREAD AND GREASE PAINT (1943)

INTRUDER MARRIAGE (1944)
SHINING CHANCE (1944)
YOU ARE THE ONE (1945)
THE SURPRISE ENGAGEMENT (1946)
THROW AWAY YESTERDAY! (1946)
TOMBOY IN LACE (1947)
SHE DANCED IN THE BALLET (1948)
GENTLE TYRANT (1949)
JOYFUL JOURNEY (1950)
LOVE AT A FESTIVAL (1951)
THE RISING OF THE LARK (1951)
SPICE OF LIFE (1952)
HOPEFUL JOURNEY (1952)
FANTASTIC HOLIDAY (1953)
BLIND DATE (1953)
THE MEN IN HER LIFE (1954)
WE ALL HAVE OUR SECRETS (1955)
ROMANCE IN TWO KEYS (1955)
A WISH A DAY (1956)
ADMIRER UNKNOWN (1957)
LEAP YEAR ROMANCE (1957)
MYSTERY BOYFRIEND (1957)
THIRD TIME LUCKY (1958)
A SMILE FOR THE PAST (1959)—autobiography
ROMANTIC AFTERTHOUGHT (1959)
LOVE AND A RICH GIRL (1960)
SHERRY AND GHOSTS (1962)
DIAMOND ENGAGEMENT RING (1962)
RENDEZVOUS IN ZAGHARELLA (1963)
SHOPPING FOR A HUSBAND (1967)
A TRICKLE OF WELSH BLOOD (1967)
AN ASSET TO WALES (1970)
ANCESTRAL VOICES (1972)

RAFAEL SABATINI (April 29, 1875 - February 13, 1950)

The fathers of quite a few of the authors featured in this section were highly influential on their offsprings' writing careers, and such is the case of Rafael Sabatini, the Swiss-educated son of an Italian tenor and an English soprano. Yet the influence of Sabatini's father was less direct than that of most; rather than encouraging his son to write, he encouraged him to choose English as his primary language (he spoke six), and to settle in that country. He did so not because of the literary climate, but because he felt that here his son would find the best opportunities in commerce.

Sabatini settled in Liverpool, and wrote correspondence to foreign firms. He also started to write short stories, and read two excellent historical novels by the late-nineteenth-century writer Mary Johnston, PRISONERS OF HOPE and TO HAVE AND TO HOLD. Though his stories sold readily, he encountered difficulty in marketing his historical novels, a problem due to a glut of so-called historical novels that really were not worthy of the name (the same situation has occurred in recent years in the American market with the Gothic, the historical romance, and the Regency). Though his novel THE TAVERN KNIGHT appeared in 1904, his first real success came with SCARAMOUCHE in 1921. His other books include such classics as THE SEA HAWK and CAPTAIN BLOOD, and several were made into films. Sabatini is as well a favorite of the current best-selling author Rosemary Rogers.

Principal works of fiction:
    THE TAVERN KNIGHT (1904)
    BARDELYS THE MAGNIFICENT (1906)
    THE SEA HAWK (1915)
    THE SNARE (1917)
    SCARAMOUCHE (1921)
    CAPTAIN BLOOD (1922)
    THE CAROLINIAN (1925)
    BELLARION (1926)
    THE HOUNDS OF GOD (1928)
    THE CHRONICLES OF CAPTAIN BLOOD (1931)
    THE BLACK SWAN (1933)
    THE FORTUNES OF CAPTAIN BLOOD (1936)
    COLUMBUS (1942)

SIR WALTER SCOTT (August 15, 1771 - September 21, 1832)

The start of the romantic period in English literature is 1798, the year that Wordsworth and Coleridge published LYRICAL BALLADS; the end of it is 1832, the year which marks the death of Sir Walter Scott.

Scott's earliest publications were translations of German romantic poetry and fiction, but it was his narrative poems that brought him his first wide success. Works such as THE LAY OF THE LAST MINSTREL and THE LADY OF THE LAKE were devoured by the public, and Scott enjoyed quite a reputation as a romantic poet—until Lord Byron entered the scene. Scott, while pursuing both his legal career and his non-fiction writing, started to explore a new avenue, the novel. WAVERLY appeared in 1814; dealing with the 1745 Jacobite rebellion, the attempt to restore the Stuart line to the throne of England, it captured all the flavor and intrigues of an already vanished Highland civilization (see the entry on Maria Edgeworth for Scott's debt to this Irish writer for the technique of displaying national color). An immediate critical and popular success, WAVERLY established its author as an outstanding writer of historical fiction; it did not, however, establish him by name—Scott had published the book anonymously, and signed his subsequent novels (until 1827) "by the author of WAVERLY." A tremendous influence on British writers, the WAVERLY novels greatly affected writers on the continent.

Despite the success of both WAVERLY and the novels that followed it, Scott was not unmasked as their author for thirteen years. It is thought that the affable Scott immensely enjoyed public speculation that he was the "Great Unknown;" in fact, after the disclosure on February 23, 1827, he himself joked that he was now the "Small Known."

Scott wrote quickly, always with a tremendous expense of energy. WAVERLY was conceived and written practically in its entirety in the summer of 1814, and the next five years saw the publication of several of Scott's most important books, among them GUY MANNERING, ROB ROY, and the extremely influential IVANHOE (QUENTIN DURWARD, a book which exerted quite an influence on William Faulkner, appeared in 1823). In addition to twenty-seven novels, Scott penned a considerable amount of poetry, a number of plays, and some works of non-fiction. Always sociable, he would rise hours before his houseguests and do most of his writing at that time, leaving him free to be with them during the day. This habit, combined with the speed and intensity of his work, damaged his health.

In Naples in 1832, trying to recover his health, Scott suffered an attack of apoplexy. He returned home, where he died in September of that year. Befriended by both Wordsworth and Byron, no easy task, adored by critics and the public, Scott's death was met with "the signs of mourning usual on the demise of a king" according to biographer J.G. Lockhart.

Principal works of fiction:
WAVERLY (1814)
GUY MANNERING (1815)
THE ANTIQUARY (1816)
THE BLACK DWARF (1816)
OLD MORTALITY (1816)
ROB ROY (1818)
THE HEART OF MIDLOTHIAN (1818)
THE BRIDE OF LAMMERMOOR (1819)
A LEGEND OF MONTROSE (1819)
IVANHOE (1819)
THE MONASTERY (1820)
THE ABBOT (1820)
KENILWORTH (1821)
THE PIRATE (1822)
THE FORTUNES OF NIGEL (1822)
PEVERIL OF THE PEAK (1822)
QUENTIN DURWARD (1823)
ST. ROMAN'S WELL (1824)
REDGAUNTLET (1824)
THE BETROTHED (1825)
THE TALISMAN (1825)
WOODSTOCK (1826)
THE HIGHLAND WIDOW (1827)
THE TWO DROVERS (1827)
THE SURGEON'S DAUGHTER (1827)
ST. VALENTINE'S DAY; OR, THE FAR MAID OF PERTH (1828)
ANNE OF GEIERSTEIN (1829)
COUNT ROBERT OF PARIS (1832)
CASTLE DANGEROUS (1832)

ELEANOR SLEATH (? - 1815?)

Similar to Charlotte Dacre, Eleanor Sleath was a novelist who enjoyed considerable popularity in the early years of the nineteenth century, but about whom modern scholars know very little. Devendra P. Varma investigated this woman whom she calls an "elusive Gothic novelist" in her introductions to a 1967 Folio Press (London) edition of THE ORPHAN OF THE RHINE and to a 1972 Arno Press (New York) edition of THE NOCTURNAL MINSTREL, OR THE SPIRIT OF THE WOOD. This biographical entry is based on information given in those two introductions.

We have little factual knowledge of this writer, whom Varma feels might be the widow of a certain military doctor named Sleath, who died in September of 1794; the ensuing poverty of the widow, Varma speculates, could very well have driven her to write, since her first novel appears four years after the doctor's death. From the novels themselves, Varma has made a further guess about Mrs. Sleath, that she was a Roman Catholic. The reasoning behind this assumption is the unique treatment given Catholicism in the Gothic novels of Mrs. Sleath. While, as Varma points out, the traditional function of Catholicism in the Gothic was to evoke "monastic gloom," one finds in Sleath's work a more amiable attitude toward the religion. Instead of providing an appropriately foreign-seeming, shadow-filled setting for the action, as it does in most Gothics, Mrs. Sleath shows the landscape of the faith—cloisters, etc.—as one providing a place for respite. Further, in Varma's words, the "smell of incense wafts from the pages," as the author exercises her fondness for the rituals of the church.

Varma believes that, as a novelist, Mrs. Sleath is midway between Mrs. Regina Maria Roche and Mrs. Eliza Parsons, and that she shows a strong literary style and a gift for description. She was heavily influenced by and reminiscent of Mrs. Radcliffe. Similar to her noted predecessor, Mrs. Sleath employed a romantic use of nature, her works featuring, for example, appropriate fear-inspiring murmurs of the wind. Again as pointed out by Varma, it is interesting to note that Mrs. Sleath's THE ORPHAN OF THE RHINE, her first novel, was published the same year as Wordsworth's and Coleridge's LYRICAL BALLADS, the collection which established the credo of the romantic poets. (This first novel was, as well, one of the "Horrid Novels" noted in Jane Austen's mock of Gothics, NORTHANGER ABBEY.) Mrs. Sleath is also similar to Mrs. Radcliffe in this novel in the use of flashback and her attempts to explain supernatural goings-on. The novel was, in fact, criticized by early reviewers as being a weak imitation of the works of the earlier writer.

So little is known of Mrs. Sleath's life that we are not even sure if she died shortly after the publication of her last novel, GLENOVEN, OF THE FAIRY PALACE, in 1815. The publication of her novels covers a span of seventeen years, and it seems we will never know if, after such an amount of work, she was able to enjoy a lengthy retirement.

Principal works:
    THE ORPHAN OF THE RHINE, A ROMANCE (1798)
    WHO'S THE MURDERER? OR, THE MYSTERY OF THE FOREST (1802)
    THE BRISTOL HEIRESS OR, THE ERRORS OF EDUCATION (1809)
    THE NOCTURNAL MISTRESS OR, THE SPIRIT OF THE WOOD (1810)
    PYRENEAN BANDITTI (1811)
    GLENOVEN, OF THE FAIRY PALACE (1815)

CHARLOTTE SMITH (May 4, 1749 - October 28, 1806)

Charlotte Smith's poetry was praised by Wordsworth and Coleridge; a character in one of her novels (Mrs. Rayland of THE OLD MANOR HOUSE) was declared to be "without a rival" by Sir Walter Scott. These remarks make it difficult for us to remember that Mrs. Smith was among those driven to take up the pen to support a family, which in her case meant twelve children and a wastrel husband (who was, at one time, imprisoned for debt).

Mrs. Smith did not publish until after her separation from her husband. Curiously enough, despite her financial problems, she brought out a volume of poetry at her own expense. In ELEGAIC SONNETS AND OTHER ESSAYS, she expressed an attitude toward nature reminiscent of that of William Cowper as she extolled the joys of the ordinary English countryside. After the initial printing, paid for by the author, other editions came out by subscription.

Mrs. Smith then turned to the novel; though her primary goal was to make money, she also expressed her radical social and political ideas in novels (influenced by the French Revolution, she believed in equality between the classes). In fact, the theme of many of her novels was that of an unhappily married woman aided by a lover. Her romantic descriptions of landscape are the first in the English novel and heavily influenced Mrs.

Radcliffe, particularly in THE ROMANCE OF THE FOREST. THE OLD MANOR HOUSE is considered Mrs. Smith's best work. In a reversal of the careers of such writers as Maria Edgeworth and Louisa May Alcott, her later books are not novels at all, but instructive books for children.

Principal works:
ELEGIAC SONNETS, AND OTHER ESSAYS (1784)
EMMELINE, OR THE ORPHAN OF THE CASTLE (1788)
ETHELINDE, OR THE RECLUSE OF THE LAKE (1789)
CELESTINA, A NOVEL (1791)
DESMOND (1792)
THE OLD MANOR HOUSE (1793)
THE WANDERINGS OF WARWICK (1794)
THE BANISHED MAN (1794)
MONTALBERT (1795)
DARCY (1796)
MARCHMONT (1796)
THE YOUNG PHILOSOPHER (1798)
LETTERS OF A SOLITARY WANDERER (1798-1801)

LADY ELEANOR SMITH (1902 - 1945)

Born Eleanor Furneaux Smith in Birkenhead, England, this popular novelist of the first half of the twentieth century was the elder daughter of F.E. Smith, who was made the first earl of Birkenhead in 1922. In her girlhood the family moved to London, where several governesses and two London day schools failed to educate her. A French school did no better. She was finally placed in a household outside Brussels, and found happiness. Always interested in gypsies because of her father's gypsy blood, she was introduced in Brussels to the people of the fairground. She found them as compelling as her own gypsy ancestors and the flamenco artists of Spain, another of her romantic favorites.

Returning to England, she wrote three novels, none of which was ever published. Then, at seventeen, she started as a journalist (society reporter and film critic for the London *Dispatch*, *Sphere* and *Bystander*). Commissioned to write a series of articles about the Great Carmo Circus, she went on tour with them.

RED WAGON (1940), her first published novel, met instant success, and was followed by a number of popular novels. Yet

Words of Love

her two most famous and best known are THE MAN IN GREY (1941) and CARAVAN (1943). Never one to stay in England during its harsh winters, she was forced to do so during World War II. It is believed that this enforced stay contributed to her long illness and early death in 1945.

Principal works
RED WAGON (1930)
FLAMENCO (1931)
BALLERINA (1932)
SATAN'S CIRCUS AND OTHER STORIES (1932)
CHRISTMAS TREE (1933; reprinted as SEVEN TREES)
TZIGANE (1935; in America, ROMANY)
PORTRAIT OF A LADY (1936)
THE SPANISH HOUSE (1938)
LIFE'S A CIRCUS (1939; biography)
LOVERS' MEETING (1940)
THE MAN IN GREY (1941)
CARAVAN (1943)

TOBIAS SMOLLETT (March 1721 - September 17, 1771)

The modern-day reader knows of a certain type of writing "factory"—the Nancy Drew books loved by so many as girls were not written by "Caroline Keene,"but rather turned out by a stable of writers who received complete instructions from the Strathmeyer syndicate; the current trend toward the "packaging" of books was inspired partly by the success of Lyle Kenyon Engle's Book Creations, whose best-selling contribution to the 1970s and 1980s book scene was the American Bicentennial series written by John Jakes. Yet there were earlier such "factories," and Tobias Smollett set up the first of them in the Chelsea section of London in the middle of the eighteenth century. Yet his was not quite as well run as those of our day, and Smollett was constantly in need of money. He is also the first major writer to publish a novel serially (his fourth, THE ADVENTURES OF SIR LAUNCELOT GREAVES), and his FERDINAND, COUNT FATHOM, is considered the father of the "Gothic" novel. It came out in 1753.

Born in Dumbartonshire, Scotland, Smollett originally trained as a surgeon in Glasgow. Yet when he arrived in London after his training, it was not to practice surgery but to attempt to have a play (THE REGICIDE, a tragedy on the death of James I) produced. This play is generally considered one of Smollett's weakest works; he did not succeed in having it produced. Desperate for money, in 1740 he signed on as ship's surgeon under Admiral Vernon. This expedition to the West Indies proved unsuccessful, and when the fleet finally made port in Jamaica, Smollett left the navy for good. Here he met Anne Lascelles, the woman he later married.

Yet Smollett's experience in the navy provided him with more than the opportunity to meet his wife. In 1748, the publication of THE ADVENTURES OF RODERICK RANDOM in "two neat Pocket-Volumes" made the cantankerous writer/surgeon a literary celebrity. This bold, picaresque tale was influenced by Alain Rene Lesage's GIL BLAS (and Smollett published his own translation of this work in 1748 as well), but Smollett injected new life into this genre. In addition, he created a new type of character, the British sailor. Smollett's next novel, also picaresque, was PEREGRINE PICKLE.

Smollett went on to write further works of satire, book reviews, and translations. His health broke in 1763 from the double burden of the death of his beloved daughter at fifteen and overwork. He and his wife stayed in the south of France for two years, then returned for a time to England. Plagued again by bad health, despite time spent at Bath taking the waters, he went to Italy in 1769. He died in Leghorn in 1771, and was buried in the English Protestant Cemetery.

Principal works of fiction:
THE ADVENTURES OF RODERICK RANDOM (1748)
THE ADVENTURES OF PEREGRINE PICKLE (1751)
THE ADVENTURES OF FERDINAND COUNT FATHOM (1753)
THE ADVENTURES OF SIR LAUNCELOT GREAVES (1762)
THE HISTORY AND ADVENTURES OF AN ATOM (1769)
THE EXPEDITION OF HUMPHREY CLINKER (1771)

GLADYS BRONWYN (G.B.) STERN (June 17, 1890 - September 19, 1973)

The NEW YORK TIMES once claimed that the 1916 publication of TWOS AND THREES, one of her earliest novels, established G.B. Stern as a "witty and accomplished" writer. Those adjectives described not just the author and her books, but her friends as well, among whom was Noel Coward. And it was Coward who sent TWOS AND THREES off to the wounded, hospitalized journalist Geoffrey Lisle Holdsworth in 1919. Holdsworth wrote to Stern, expressing his objection to the way the man in the book was portrayed; Stern responded, and asked her correspondent to come see her. There were married shortly afterward. Coward writes briefly of the marriage (which ended in divorce) in PRESENT INDICATIVE.

During her London girlhood, Stern wanted to be an actress (she eventually attended the Royal Academy of Dramatic Art), and wrote her first play at the age of seven. A real literary breakthrough came ten years later, when the first poem she sent to an editor was published. At twenty, she wrote her first novel, PANTOMINE, and it appeared in 1914. In 1920, Stern began producing about a book a year, having settled down into regular work habits with established "office hours." While the fans of Barbara Cartland might believe that she was the first writer to dictate her books to others from a reclining position, Stern described her use of this technique in 1932, on her first American tour.

The family saga was a favorite form of G.B. Stern's, and her work was often likened to Galworthy's Forsythe Saga. While much of her work was autobiographical, MATRIARCH, which led to four other volumes, was especially so. The personality of the main character was based on that of one of the author's great-aunts. In 1929, the first two of the MATRIARCH books were dramatized on the London stage, with Mrs. Patrick Campbell in a leading role.

Stern also did free-lance journalism reviews, and wrote short stories. Her last novel, PROMISE NOT TO TELL, was published in 1964.

Selected works of fiction:
PANTOMINE (1914)
SEE-SAW (1914)
TWOS AND THREES (1916)
GRAND CHAIN (1917)

A MARRYING MAN (1918)
CHILDREN OF NO MAN'S LAND (1919)—Bk. 1, Trilogy on Jewish life;
   American edition, DEBATABLE GROUND
LARRY MUNRO (1920)—American edition, THE CHINA SHOP
THE ROOM (1922)
THE BACK SEAT (1923)
TENTS OF ISRAEL (1924)—Bk. 2, Trilogy on Jewish life; American edition,
THE MATRIARCH
THUNDERSTORM (1925)
A DEPUTY WAS KING (1926)—Bk. 3, Trilogy on Jewish life
BOUQUET (1927)
THE DARK GENTLEMAN (1927)
DEBONAIR (1928)
PETRUCHIO (1929)
MOSAIC (1930)
SHINING AND FREE (1935)
THE YOUNG MATRIARCH (1942)
DOGS IN AN OMNIBUS (1942)
TRUMPET VOLUNTARY (1944)
REASONABLE SHORES (1946)
NO SON OF MINE (1948)
BENEFITS FORGOT (1949)
A DUCK TO WATER (1949)
THE DONKEY SHOE (1952)
A NAME TO CONJURE WITH (1953)
TEN DAYS OF CHRISTMAS (c. 1955)
FOR ALL WE KNOW (1956)
THE WAY IT WORKED OUT (1957)
ONE IS ONLY HUMAN (1960)
PROMISE NOT TO TELL (1964)

Note: G.B. Stern also published several short story collections and three autobiographical novels, and wrote numerous plays.

HELEN VAN SLYKE (July 9, 1919 - July 3, 1979)

Many writers have to rely on research, imagination and their own daydreams in order to create the worlds of glamour featured in their books. While Helen Van Slyke was certainly no stranger to hard work, the worlds she created in her novels were not always so distant from a world of high-fashion and glamour that she knew quite well, for the position which she left in order to pursue her writing career full-time was that of vice-president of creative activities in the New York office of Helena Rubenstein.

The positions she'd held prior to this one also spoke of hard work and glamour—she began her newspaper career at age fourteen, and at nineteen became fashion editor of the WASHINGTON STAR. At the time, she was the youngest editor on a major American newspaper. Leaving journalism, she she was beauty editor at *GLAMOUR* magazine for ten years, then held various executive positions in women's wear, advertising, and perfume.

Van Slyke was over fifty when she met then-Doubleday editor Lawrence Ashmead at a party. She told him that some day she would write a book; he later sent her some novels to read. As do most aspiring novelists, she felt that she could do better. Unlike most, she was right, and her first book, written on weekends, appeared as THE RICH AND THE RIGHTEOUS in 1971. It was a best-seller, as were all the books that followed. On her death in 1979, the NEW YORK TIMES described her books as being "realistic yet romantic stories about middle-aged, uncertain and independent women . . . [who] successfully come to terms with their professional and personal doubts after a succession of intricately plotted confrontations with their husbands, lovers, friends or relatives."

While that description is succinct it certainly doesn't capture the appeal all the Van Slyke novels held for a large audience. Nor does it convey the fact that even today, several years after her death, editors and readers alike are still looking for "the new Helen Van Slyke."

Principal works:
    THE RICH AND THE RIGHTEOUS (1971)
    ALL VISITERS MUST BE ANNOUNCED (1972)—THE BEST PEOPLE in paperback
    THE HEART LISTENS (1973)
    THE MIXED BLESSING (1975)
    THE BEST PLACE TO BE (1976)
    ALWAYS IS NOT FOREVER (1977)
    SISTERS AND STRANGERS (1978)
    A NECESSARY WOMAN (1979)
    NO LOVE LOST (1980)
    THE SANTA ANA WIND (1981)
    PUBLIC SMILES, PRIVATE TEARS: THE LAST NOVEL (1982)—Helen Van Slyke and James Elward

HORACE WALPOLE (September 24, 1717 - March 2, 1797)

Similar to his countryman William Beckford, Horace Walpole was a Gothic novelist whose tastes in literature echoed his taste in architecture. Just as Beckford constructed the fabulous Fonthill Abbey, Walpole used his skill as an amateur architect to remodel his country house, Strawberry Hill, to resemble a Gothic castle. Unlike Beckford, however, Walpole entered the aristocracy when, on the death of his nephew, he became the fourth Earl of Orford.

Walpole is perhaps best known for starting the Gothic genre of novel with THE CASTLE OF OTRANTO, published in 1764. This tale of the struggle for an Italian kingdom featured violence, intrigue, and supernatural events, and heavily influenced such writers as Ann Radcliffe, "Monk" Lewis, and Charles Robert Maturin (in addition to giving Jane Austen's satiric wit a field day in being the alleged inspiration of her parody NORTHANGER ABBEY).

Though Walpole went on to write other books, his works of most interest today are his letters. An outstanding and prolific correspondent even in a time when letter writing was at its height as an art form, Walpole left a legacy of warmth, insight, and historical detail in his voluminous correspondence. In addition to THE CASTLE OF OTRANTO in the area of non-fiction, Walpole penned a play that attempted to treat incest as a tragic subject. Briefly an object of sensation, THE MYSTERIOUS MOTHER was forgotten soon after its publication; the play was described by Regency critic Anna Letitia Barbauld as "disgustingly repulsive."

Principal works of fiction:
THE CASTLE OF OTRANTO (1764)
THE MYSTERIOUS MOTHER (1768)—verse play

MARY GLADYS WEBB (March 25, 1881 - October 8, 1927)

Fame comes to some writers early in life, to others when they have few years left to enjoy it. Unfortunately for Mary Gladys Webb, the author of five novels and a good amount of poetry, it was achieved only after her death, and was initially due to the admiration a Prime Minister had for her depictions of Shropshire.

Born in that lush section of the English countryside to a schoolmaster and his wife (whose family was related to Walter Scott's), Webb spent two years at a school in Southport, though she was mostly educated at home. She married a schoolmaster in 1912, and her first novel, THE GOLDEN ARROW, appeared a few years later. All in all, she wrote five, the last (ARMOUR WHEREIN HE TRUSTED) being published unfinished and post-humously. A collection of poetry and essays also came out short-ly after her death, with a preface by Walter de la Mare. He stated that "all she wrote is suffused with poetry;" harsher critics of her novels might claim that she lacked a certain skill with characteri-zation and plot development. Yet her knowledge of the cruelties of life has lead to comparisons with Thomas Hardy, though a heavy influence on her prose style was the seventeenth-century writer Sir Thomas Browne.

Unacclaimed at their publication, all of Webb's four pub-lished books were reissued with critical introductions after Prime Minister Stanley Baldwin praised her work at a Royal Literary Fund dinner some months after her death. Baldwin himself wrote one of the introductions, and another was by Chesterton.

Principal works:
    THE GOLDEN ARROW (1916)
    GONE TO EARTH (1917)
    THE HOUSE IN DORMER FOREST (1920)
    SEVEN FOR A SECRET (1922)
    PRECIOUS BANE (1924)
    ARMOUR WHEREIN HE TRUSTED (1929)
    THE SPRING OF JOY (1929)—poems and essays
    FIFTY-ONE POEMS (1946)—poetry

MARGARET WIDDEMER (1890 - July 14, 1978)

Margaret Widdemer once wrote that she was "strongly against specialization in art or life," a philosophy certainly reflected in her eclectic literary career. Though she'd first seen her work published at the age of ten (poems appearing in the *St. Nicholas League*), she prepared for a career as a librarian at the Drexel Institute of Arts and Sciences. Yet she soon discovered she wasn't cut out for that particular connection to books; she was discharged from an early post at the University of Pennsylvania for inaccuracy in copying catalogue cards. Turning to writing full-time, she soon found herself earning more than she ever had as a librarian.

The author of more than thirty popular novels dealing with both historical and contemporary topics, Widdemer published numerous collections of poetry, both for adults and children, both serious and comic, and won many awards for her poetry. A tireless worker, she also belonged to many professional organizations, and lectured widely on fiction and poetry, notably for NBC radio (on a show entitled "Do You Want to Write?") and at the Middlebury Writers' Conference at Breadloaf. Her memoirs, GOLDEN FRIENDS I HAD, appeared in 1964.

Principal works of fiction:
THE ROSE GARDEN HUSBAND (1915)
WHY NOT? (1916)
THE WISHING-RING MAN (1917)
YOU'RE ONLY YOUNG ONCE (1918)
THE BOARDWALK (1919)
I'VE MARRIED MARJORIE (1920)
YEAR OF DELIGHT (1921)
A MINISTER OF GRACE (1922)
GRAVEN IMAGE (1923)
CHARIS SEES IT THROUGH (1924)
GALLANT LADY (1926)
MORE THAN WIFE (1927)
RHINESTONES (1929)
LOYAL LOVER (1930)
ALL THE KING'S HORSES (1931)
TRUTH ABOUT LOVERS (1932)
GOLDEN RAIN (1933)
BACK TO VIRTUE, BETTY (1934)
MARRIAGE IS POSSIBLE (1936)
THIS ISN'T THE END (1937)
HAND ON HER SHOULDER (1938)
SHE KNEW THREE BROTHERS (1939)
SOME DAY I'LL FIND YOU (1940)
LOVER'S ALIBI (1941)

LET ME HAVE WINGS (1941)
ANGELA COMES HOME (1942)
CONSTANCIA HERSELF (1944)
LANI (1948)
RED CLOAK FLYING (1950)
LADY OF THE MOHAWKS (1951)
THE GOLDEN WILDCAT (1954)
BUCKSKIN BARONET (1960)
RED CASTLE WOMEN (1968)

MARY WOLLSTONECRAFT (April 27, 1759 - September 10, 1797)

Early forced to support themselves because of the death of their mother and the remarriage of her father, Mary and her two sisters, Evelina and Eliza, experienced first-hand the difficulties of being an independent woman in a time when a woman's fate was generally bound to that of a man. She first went to Lisbon at the request of her close friend Fanny Blood, who had made an unhappy marriage and who wanted Mary to be with her at the birth of her first child. Yet even before the future author and women's rights advocate arrived, her friend was dead; it was a sad foretelling of Wollstonecraft's own death.

Her first post was as governess in the household of Lord Kingsborough, but she was dismissed from this job in a year due to her charges' fondness for her, which sparked the jealousy of their mother (interestingly enough, one of these youngsters, later Lady Mountcashel, became a friend of the Shelleys, Wollstonecraft's daughter and her famous poet husband, in Italy). The traditional female calling of governess having led to a bad experience, Wollstonecraft made her way to London and did literary work for the publisher James Johnson. It was while working here, in 1791, that she first met William Godwin, who she was to marry six years later, but theirs was hardly a case of love at first sight—it is said that he actually disliked her intensely on meeting her, since she was the only person who could out-talk Thomas Paine, who was also present.

While she later married Godwin, after more pleasant-encounters, Wollstonecraft first lost her heart to the American,

Captain Gilbert Imlay, a veteran of his own country's War of Independence. She left England with him to see Revolutionary France first-hand; she traveled as his wife, and in Le Havre in 1794 gave birth to their illegitimate daughter, Fanny. Deeply in love with the unscrupulous former soldier who had long since fallen out of love with her, if, indeed, he had ever been in it, Wollstonecraft followed him back to England in 1795, only to eventually discover his liaison with another woman—carried on in their home. After their break in 1796, she tried to drown herself. While accepting no money from him for her own support, she did make an arrangement for him to contribute to that of their daughter, which he reneged on. Wollstonecraft returned to writing for a living.

At this time, 1976, she again met up with Godwin, and he fell in love with her. They married in March of 1797, since she was three months pregnant. The marriage did not last long; Mary Wollstonecraft died eleven days after the birth of her second daughter, Mary.

Wollstonecraft was a passionate feminist with a strong belief in education, and her VINDICATION OF THE RIGHTS OF WOMAN caused a major scandal in its day. In it, Wollstonecraft advocated equality and companionship between men and women, and asked that women be educated, particularly to prepare them to make their own way in the world, as so many of them had to do. Her peceptions about the relationship between men and women carried over into her highly didactic Gothic novel, MARIA, OR THE WRONGS OF WOMAN, in which she complained that the lives of young girls were too often cramped and confined. Further, the heroine of the novel is confined against her will in an insane asylum—by her own husband. Following Wollstonecraft's faith in education, in the transmitting of knowledge, the longest section of the novel is a letter from the woman to her daughter, in which she explains what has happened to her and which acts as a warning to prevent the same thing from happening to her. And though Wollstonecraft's second daughter, Mary, knew her own mother only through her writings, she also wrote, being the author of the Gothic classic FRANKENSTEIN, a novel which explores the consequences of men usurping female power, and trying to create life.

Principal works:
THOUGHTS ON THE EDUCATION OF DAUGHTERS (1787)
MARY, A FICTION (1788)—dedicated to Fanny Blood
THE FEMALE READER (1789)—compiled by Wollstonecraft
AN HISTORICAL AND MORAL VIEW OF THE ORIGINS AND PROGRESS OF THE FRENCH REVOLUTION (1790)
ELEMENTS OF MORALITY FOR THE USE OF CHILDREN (1790)—translated from C.G. Salzmann
A VINDICATION OF THE RIGHTS OF WOMAN (1792)
A VINDICATION OF THE RIGHTS OF MAN (1793)—in a letter to Edmund Burke
LETTERS WRITTEN DURING A SHORT RESIDENCE IN SWEDEN, NORWAY, AND DENMARK (1796)
POSTHUMUS WORKS (1798)—edited by Wm. Godwin
MARIA, OR THE WRONGS OF WOMAN (1799)—posthumus fragment

CHARLOTTE MARY YONGE (August 11, 1823 - March 24, 1901)

The author of over one hundred and sixty books, including works of biography, history and fiction for both young people and adults, Charlotte Yonge enjoyed immense popularity in her lifetime—and never kept a cent of the money her writings earned. Her family came from a strict clerical tradition (though her father was a retired army officer who had been at Waterloo), and they permitted Charlotte to continue what they viewed as an "unsexing" profession only if all the proceeds from her work were donated to missionary activities.

While the influence of her family, and especially her father, was very strong, Yonge early came under the thrall of John Keble, the famous theologian who was assigned to Otterbourne, where Yonge spent most of her life. Because of him, she became a strong supporter of the Anglican revival led by Newman before his conversion to Catholicism. In the movement which divided the Anglican church into the Broad (Protestant-leaning) and the High (Catholic-leaning) schools, Yonge espoused the High Church faction. She taught Sunday school from the very early age of seven, and her first published articles appeared in the *Magazine for the Young*, in 1842. She continued to write a great deal for children, often under the name of "Aunt Charlotte."

Though rather didactic, Yonge's novels of contemporary life were devoured by readers of both sexes, from all walks of life. Sentimental works underlining the importance of sacrifice, particularly for the sake of one's family, and obedience to paternal authority (Keble and her father, in fact, edited and censored all her writing), they exerted a strong influence. THE HEIR OF REDCLYFFEE is notable for the impression it made on William Morris and other members of the Pre-Raphaelite poets and painters.

Far less didactic than her contemporary novels were Yonge's historical romances, which showed the results of fine historical research. They should have; educated at home, Yonge received a thorough grounding in ancient and modern languages, literature and history, and her years as a student lasted until she was twenty, quite unusual for a woman at the time. She also taught at the local school.

Yonge's novels are noted for the strength of their characterizations and dialogue. In fact, her dialogue is stronger than that in the novels of Anthony Trollope, with whom she can be compared. Yet Yonge's reputation is lesser than Trollope's, and for a good reason. She simply wrote too much, her writing being one of the few outlets for a strong personality early, continuously, and thoroughly stifled, and her early efforts are definitely superior to those produced later in her career.

Principal works of fiction:
ABBEY CHURCH (1844)
THE HEIR OF REDCLYFFE (1853)
THE LITTLE DUKE (1854)
HEARTSEASE (1854)
THE LANCES OF LYNWOOD (1855)
THE DAISY CHAIN (1856)
DYNEVOR TERRACE (1857)
THE PIGEON PIE (1860)
COUNTESS KATE (1862)
THE TRIAL (1864)
THE PRINCE AND THE PAGE (1865)
THE CLEVER WOMAN OF THE FAMILY (1865)
THE DOVE IN THE EAGLE'S NEST (1866)
THE CHAPLET OF PEARLS (1868)
THE CAGED LION (1870)
THE PILLARS OF THE HOUSE (1873)

STORIES FROM GREEK, ROMAN, AND GERMAN HISTORY FOR CHIL-
DREN (1873-78)
MAGNUM BONUM (1879)
MODERN BROODS (1900)

Current Romance Authors

The following section features biographic and bibliographic entries on over one hundred and fifty romance writers working today. While the authors represent a wide range in terms of years spent as a professional writer, their fame, and the types of romances they write, it is the incredible variety of their backgrounds that belies any stereotype about the sort of author who writes romance. The majors in which they've taken college degrees include sociology, journalism, music, chemistry, and even agriculture; the universities they've attended range from Oxford and Harvard to the top public universities in the United States.

Even more interesting than the authors' backgrounds, however, are their views on writing in the romance genre. Far from detracting from the importance of the escape element in the appeal of romance, most of the authors underline the ability of their novels to remove the reader from the world of cares, even if for just a while. Many have given serious consideration to the question of the place of romance in the world of popular literature, especially when compared to that occupied by the mystery. Victoria Heland, the author of several Regency novels and contemporary romances, responds to the often-voiced criticism that romances tend to confuse the reader's perception of reality and fantasy in this way: "It is highly unlikely that the scores of mystery readers will ever encounter a dead body, much less solve a crime. And I have never heard it charged that mysteries as a genre encourage such fantasies." Candace Camp, an author whose credits include both longer historical and contemporary romance novels, writes that she believes that "much of the criticism levelled at romance literature has a sexist origin, because romance literature is primarily written by and for women, which to many puts it in a lesser category of literature." Sondra Stanford, the author of numerous contemporary romances, likens a woman's escapism in reading romance to that enjoyed by a man watching a football game or a John Wayne movie, pointing out that "society never puts men down for their little pleasures." Amen.

In describing how they first became published and acquired an agent, the authors have been extremely generous to aspiring writers, giving advice and encouragement useful to writers of any kind of book, not just those in the romance genre. Not surprisingly, they emphasize the importance of reading heavily to determine current trends, of studying those novels the aspiring writer admires, of attending conferences to exchange information with other writers. In addition to direct technical remarks concerning writing itself, they dicuss the psychological requirements. As Nancy Morse notes, to succeed as a published author, one must develop a thick skin; rejection is a part of life in the business. Finally, the authors' lists of their own favorite novels and authors provide a pre-selected guide to top books for those who wish to study the genre. (Please note: While it can be seen from the copy of the questionnaire included that the names of *romance* authors and novels were specifically requested, many authors did not limit their responses to the romance field. It should not, therefore, be assumed that those authors who cited only romance novels and authors have a narrower range of reading than those who did not; they were answering the question as it was posed.)

The contacting of authors to be included in WORDS OF LOVE:

In the late spring of 1982, publicity directors in ten major paperback houses, as well as those in several hardcover houses known for their publication of romances, were contacted with information about this reference book, and with a copy of the author questionnaire (see pages immediately following for a copy of the questionnaire). Working with the romance editors in their firms, the publicity directors sent the questionnaires out to the majority of their romance authors. At the end of the summer of 1982, Garland Publishing sent out a second questionnaire to those writers who had not yet responded to the first. (Unfortunately, Harlequin/Mills and Boon did not wish to send questionnaires out to their English authors, and attempts to contact these writers were not successful; the Harlequin writers featured are among the few North American writers sent the questionnaire by Harlequin, and some were reached by virtue of having published with other romance series as well. Others saw the mention of this reference book in the romance press, and personally wrote to request questionnaires so they could be included.)

The following entries feature authors ranging from those first known in hardcover, to those who have established large followings through paperback original publication. All but three of the entries were taken directly from the questionnaire completed by the authors themselves; while Rosemary Rogers, Danielle Steel and Kathleen Woodiwiss did not return completed questionnaires, they were cited as favorite authors by so many of their colleagues, and have been so important in the recent publication of romances, that entries on them have been drawn up and included. In addition to biographic information, and the authors' responses to three longer questions about their work, the entries include bibliographies current through the fall of 1982, with a note mentioning future publications. In most cases, the romance sub-genre (category contemporary, historical romance, Regency, etc.) of each title has been noted, as well as the publisher, year of publication, and pseudonym. If no pseudonym is listed for a particular title, that novel appeared under the author's name. An index of authors according to pseudonym and to romance sub-genre follows the author entries.

Current Romance Author Questionnaire

1) Author's real name.
2) Pseudonyms.
3) Real name at birth, plus date and place of birth.
4) Name of spouse and date of marriage.
5) Names of children.
6) Education—date of degree (if any); name of college; major.
7) Professional associations.
8) Awards.
9) Genres.
10) Agent's name and address.
11) Author's current residence—town and state.

Longer responses:
1) Favorite romance authors and books—This section lets the fan know who her own favorite authors have read and enjoyed, both writers of years past and of the current romance boom.
2) Thoughts on writing—particularly on writing romance, since it's so often considered a step-child of publishing. Do you see these books as pure escapism? Were you a fan for years before becoming a writer? In a sense, what is your philosophy of writing?
3) How did you first become published/find an agent?

Bibliography—Please list your titles, the pseudonyms they appeared under, the publishing house and year of publication (can be checked on the copyright page), and the sub-genre of each book, noting those that have won awards. Finally, please list all your books, even those that aren't romances.

The Authors

JOAN AIKEN
B. Joan Aiken, Rye, Sussex, England, 9/4/24, married Ronald George Brown 7/7/45, widowed 1955; married Julius Goldstein

9/2/76. *Children*: John Sebastian, Elizabeth Delano. *Education*: Educated by her mother (who had Radcliffe, McGill Degrees) till age 12; private boarding school, Wychwood, Oxford, England till 17; no college education. *Professional associations*: Authors' Society, England; Writers' Guild, England; Mystery Writers of America. *Awards*: Guardian Award for children's literature for three books, THE WOLVES OF WILLOUGHBY CHASE, NIGHTBIRDS ON NANTUCKET, BLACK HEARTS IN BATTERSEA, 1969. Runner up for Carnegie Award, 1969. Lewis Carroll Award in USA for THE WOLVES OF WILLOUGHBY CHASE. Mystery Writers of America award for junior mystery, 1972, for NIGHTFALL. *Genres*: Contemporary mystery, historical romance, Regency, Victorian. *Agent*: Charles Schlessiger, Brandt & Brandt, 1501 Broadway, N.Y., N.Y. 10036. *Current residence*: Petworth, Sussex, England in summer, New York, Greenwich Village, in winter.

Favorite authors and books: Georgette Heyer (no imitations); Mary Stewart (pre-Authurian); Jane Austen; Ouida; Ethel M. Dell.

Thoughts on writing: Romances vary as much as any other category of fiction. Yes, some are pure escape, no more nutritious than candy. But there is a place for candy in life. And others may contain material of lasting value just as easily as any other kind of writing. I'm not a great romance fan but there are times (when I'm tired, ill, suffering from depression) when, like a pain-killer or soporific, it is exactly what one needs. I'm proud if any of my books have helped anyone in similar circumstances. Somebody once wrote me that a book of mine had whiled away a long, terribly dull train journey for her. I'm proud of that too.

Becoming published/finding an agent: I sent stories to magazines and a book of children's stories to a publisher. After I had a magazine story published (in *The New Statesman*), an English agent wrote, offering to take me on. The second publisher I sent my collection to took them, after I had followed some of their suggestions. I have now written approximately fifty books, both adult and juvenile.

Bibliography: (all adult books; paperback house in parens after hardcover information)

THE SILENCE OF HERONDALE, Gollancz 1964, Doubleday 1964, (Panther, Ace, Pocketbooks).
THE FORTUNE HUNTERS, Doubleday, 1965 (Bantam).
TROUBLE WITH PRODUCT X, Gollancz, 1966, Doubleday (as BEWARE OF THE BOUQUET), 1966.
HATE BEGINS AT HOME, Gollancz, 1967, Doubleday (as DARK INTERVAL), 1967, (Panther).
THE RIBS OF DEATH, Gollancz, 1967, Doubleday (as THE CRYSTAL CROW), 1968.
THE WINDSCREEN WEEPERS, Gollancz, 1969—stories.
THE ENBROIDERED SUNSET, Gollancz, 1970, Doubleday, 1970 (Sphere).
THE BUTTERFLY PICNIC, Gollancz, 1970, Doubleday (as A CLUSTER OF SEPARATE SPARKS) 1972 (Sphere)
DIED ON A RAINY SUNDAY, Gollancz, 1972, Holt, Rinehart, 1972.
VOICES IN AN EMPTY HOUSE, Gollancz, 1975, Doubleday, 1975.
CASTLE BAREBANE, Gollancz, 1976, Viking Press, 1976 (NEL).
LAST MOVEMENT, Gollancz, 1977, Doubleday, 1977 (Warner).
THE FIVE-MINUTE MARRIAGE, Gollancz, 1977, Doubleday, 1978 (NEL, Warner).
THE SMILE OF THE STRANGER, Gollancz, 1978, Doubleday, 1978 (NEL, Warner).
A TOUCH OF CHILL, Gollancz, 1979, Delacorte, 1980—horror stories.
THE WEEPING ASH, Gollancz, 1980, Doubleday, 1980.
THE YOUNG LADY FROM PARIS, Gollancz, 1982, Doubleday (as THE GIRL FROM PARIS), 1982.
FOUL MATTER, Gollancz, 1983, Doubleday, 1983.
Note: THE FIVE-MINUTE MARRIAGE was the first Regency featured by the Book-of-the-Month Club. Aiken is also the author of over thirty juvenile novels, several of them award-winners.

MARSHA ALEXANDER

B. Marsha Durchin, 11/2/40, N.Y., N.Y., married Al Alexander, 1957; married Robert Bourns, 1968. *Children:* Lauren, Kimberly, and Sage. *Education:* Scattered—attended a variety of schools. *Professional associations:* Mystery Writers of America, Romance Writers of America, Womens National Book Association. *Genres:* Contemporary, Category contemporary, gothics and mainstream occult. *Agent:* Steven J. Axelrod, The Sterling Lord Agency, Inc. 660 Madison Avenue, N.Y., N.Y. 10021. *Current residence:* L.A., California.

Favorite authors and books: I have problems with this question—I'm not so much a fan of authors and books that fall into this category as I am of writers and books of passion, of any kind. The essence of romance is passion. Poe, Melville, Steinbeck, to me, understood passion. Muriel Bradley is a current favorite for romance books.

Thoughts on writing: Writing romance books is writing books about life. However sophisticated, we all yearn for romance. I write books about people, so even my non-category books are romantic works to some degree. About escapism—most of us read to escape reality for a little while. Romance books are a delightful escape. Happy endings give the child in us a sweet moment of pleasure without risking a thing.

Becoming published/finding an agent: I wrote a book that was supposed to be a satire on love and lust, and it was bought as a romance! For years I simply wrote and submitted manuscripts. At an autograph session I met Steven Axelrod. He suggested I send him ALL MINE TO GIVE. I did, and he sent me a contract. I've been writing professionally for eighteen years, supporting my family exclusively as a writer all these years.

Bibliography:
Contemporary:
    ALL MINE TO GIVE, Gallen Books, 1981.
    ROYAL SUITE, Gallen Books, September 1982.

Gothic:
    BIRTHMARK OF FEAR, Major Books, 1968
    WHISPERS IN THE WIND, Major Books, 1968.
    THE CURTIS WIVES, Major Books, 1969. (THE CURTIS WIVES was also translated into German.)
    HOUSE OF SHADOWS, Major Books, 1969.

Non-Romance Books:
    DEMON FIRE, Pinnacle, 1982. (occult book).

BARBARA ANDREWS
B. Barbara L. Rock, 3/15/35. Kalamazoo, MI., married Warren C.

Andrews, 1957. *Children:* Pamela, Joan, Stephen, Mark. *Education:* B.A. Kalamazoo College, political science. *Genres:* Category contemporary. *Current residence:* Ames, Iowa.

Favorite authors and books: I first read WUTHERING HEIGHTS when in love myself. Heathcliff belongs in the nineteenth century; there are hopeful signs in the romance field that he is being laid to rest in favor of warm, fascinating, complex, modern heroes. An author in any field who can make me say, "Yes, that's a new way of saying it," has my enthusiasm and support. Of the romance writers publishing today, I'm expecting good work from Anne N. Reisser and Rachel Ryan.

Thoughts on writing: There's an element of escapism in all good entertainment. But it's a mistake to write romances off as pure fluff. The heroines are maturing, with character development no longer a romance writer's taboo, and heroes are appearing who are far more interesting than the dull macho stereotype. In this sense the romance genre is still in a pioneer stage, only beginning to realize its potential.

The major part of my published work in the last seventeen years has been nonfiction, but trying different types of writing is vital to me. I love writing, and what comes next is always more interesting than the work that's finished.

Becoming published/finding an agent: After the experience of publishing in a number of fields, I was prepared for the lumps and bumps of entering a new field, but not for the courtesy and enthusiasm of romance editors, beginning with Alicia Condon who bought my first book. Anne Gissony, senior editor of Candlelight Ecstasy romances, is a wonderfully acute judge of what works and what doesn't, and is a great source of encouragement. The suggestions of Carin Cohen, who edited my third Dell, have been so helpful I look forward to doing revision.

To date I've never sought or felt a need for an agent. In speaking to classes or other groups on free-lance writing, I advise beginners to write, write, write, and worry about an agent when their contracts become so complicated they need one. Romance editors read the submissions that come to them, and a great first chapter is much more important to the unsold writer than an army of agents.

Bibliography:
Category contemporary:
  LIMITED ENGAGEMENT, Gramercy Park Productions, 6/80.
  LOVE THY NEIGHBOR, Gramercy Park Productions, 9/80.
  LOVE TRAP, Dell Candlelight Ecstasy, 10/82.
  STOLEN PROMISES, Dell Candlelight Ecstasy, 1/83.
Note: Barbara Andrews currently has one book under contract with Dell under the "Candlelight Ecstasy" series.

ELEANOR R. AUFDEM-BRINKE
Pseudonyms: Nora Roberts, Jill March B. Eleanor Robertson, October 10, 1950, Washington D.C.. Married Ronald Aufdem-Brinke, August 17, 1968. *Children*: Daniel, Jason. *Education*: High school, Montgomery Blair. *Professional associations*: Romance Writers of America, Washington Romance Writers. *Genres*: Category contemporary. *Agent*: Amy Berkower, Writers House 21 W. 26th Street, N.Y., N.Y. *Current residence*: Keedysville, Maryland.

Favorite authors and books: Anything by Mary Stewart and Georgette Heyer. GONE WITH THE WIND for the all time romance novel.

Thoughts on writing: More than escapism, I like to think of romance novels as entertainment. The main purpose of a novel, in any genre, is to entertain. A romance should center on a relationship. I personally like to incorporate some humor in that relationship as life's full of it. Love should be fun.

Becoming published/finding an agent: I was fortunate enough to become published and find an agent almost simultaneously. SEARCH FOR LOVE, IRISH THOROUGHBRED and BLITHE IMAGES were all being considered by Silhouette. When the first manuscript sold, I was already in contact with my agent through a friend. There were revisions, and a great deal of learning on my part. Writing is a craft which takes constant practice. Nancy Jackson, my editor, saw something in those first manuscripts and worked with me. Bless her.

Bibliography:
Category contemporary:
IRISH THOROUGHBRED, Nora Roberts, Silhouette, 1981.
BLITHE IMAGES, Nora Roberts. Silhouette, 1982.
SONG OF THE WEST, Nora Roberts. Silhouette, 1982.
SEARCH FOR LOVE, Nora Roberts. Silhouette, 1982.
ISLAND OF FLOWERS, Nora Roberts. Silhouette, 1982.
MELODIES OF LOVE, Jill March, Rhapsody Romances, 1982.
Note: Eleanor R. Aufdem-Brinke currently has a book under contract with Silhouette.

CATHY JO LADAME BALDWIN
Pseudonyms: Cathryn LaDame, Cathryn Ladd. *B.* Cathy Jo LaDame, 9/21/47, Litchfield, Il., married Michael Jerome Baldwin, 3/2/68. *Children:* Sarah Rose. *Education:* B.A. 1970, Eastern Illinois University, English. *Professional associations:* Romance Writers of America, Authors Guild. *Genres:* Category contemporary. *Agent:* Henry Dunow, Scott Meredith Literary Agency, Inc., 845 Third Ave., NYC, 10022. *Current residence:* Benld, Illinois.

Favorite authors and books: Has there ever been a book like Kathleen Woodiwiss's SHANNA? It completely captivates me and always will—I reread it regularly! Of course, I love everything else she has written, too. I also read Rosemary Rogers' historical romances. As for contemporary romances—I try to read representatives of all the lines currently being published, but my reading time is limited. So, in addition to books of plays and essays, I pick and choose —but never miss Anne Mather or Charlotte Lamb. From the past—Jane Austen's PRIDE AND PREJUDICE for its marvelous heroine, and of course, Emily Bronte's WUTHERING HEIGHTS for its dark passion and achingly, moodily romantic aura.

Thoughts on writing: In college, as an English major, I was exposed to what is considered the best in prose and poetry. Needless to say, romances and other genres weren't included. I hadn't even read a romance until I was in my late twenties! Then I was hooked. I've had to fight feelings of inferiority, even guilt, for even reading them— imagine the struggle to be proud of writing them!

Like most writers I spent long hours as a child making up stories. Somewhere in the back of my mind, I always wanted to be a writer— although I wasn't at all sure if one could do that sort of magical thing for a living! But I loved it.

That's why I write romances: I love it. I love the incredible "high" when it's all so right, and I just can't stop writing all night long (I am not so enamoured of the weeks when I can't make myself work, but that's all part of it, I suppose.) I love putting myself in places I may never see, with the best bits, pieces and chunks of people I know or simply want to know. I love researching the locales, the food, the customs and the sensory realities of the mountains and islands of my dreams. I love being suprised by what my characters do—it's that childlike wonder everyone is always talking about. Well, writers experience that regularly, and I love it!

I read hundreds of romances for about three years before I began one of my own. When mine was published, I had the sense to listen to my husband (M.A. in English) and others I respected, including former professors, when they pointed out the differences between entertainment and "Art." Escapism? Absolutely—but what painting, drama, motion picture or great novel doesn't offer escape into another world? If that other world is not created, then the painter, author, etc., has failed.

Whether or not romances are "pure escapism" depends on how successfully and totally that world has been created and on how much effort the reader is willing to expend to escape, to make that marvelous leap into the author's landscape of dreams.

Becoming published/finding an agent: With vague notions of writing short stories, I subscribed to WRITER'S DIGEST magazine. For about a year I played with a story which grew and grew until it somehow became book-length. My husband helped me find the courage to submit it to the only romance publisher I knew—Harlequin. But when I took it to the post office, the clerk wasn't sure about return postage from Canada, so I took the manuscript home, certain that this was just an omen—I wasn't meant to be published!

The same day that month's WRITER'S DIGEST arrived, with an ad announcing Silhouette Books as a new publishing venture of Simon & Schuster. It requested manuscripts. Within hours a synopsis and sample chapters of WINTER'S HEART were on the way. I don't believe in omens, but there was another!

That was September. By November Silhouette had accepted the manuscript, and after some cutting by the editor there, it was published a little over a year later. On the strength of that book, I wrote to Scott Meredith at his literary agency— recommended to me by another writer—and was accepted as a client.

Bibliography:
Category contemporary:
> WINTER'S HEART, Cathryn LaDame, Silhouette, 1981.
> CENTENNIAL SUMMER, Cathryn Ladd, Signet-Adventures in Love, 1982.
> ISLAND AUTUMN, Cathryn Ladd. Signet-Adventures in Love, 1982
> TAPESTRY OF LOVE, Cathryn Ladd. Signet-Adventures in Love, Sept. 1982

Note: Cathy Jo LaDame Baldwin currently has a book under contract with Silhouette and two books under contract with NAL.

JANET BIEBER

Pseudonym: Janet Joyce (shared with co-writer Joyce Thies) *B.* Janet Lynn Parker 12/25/42, Catawba Island, Ohio, married James C. Bieber, August 28, 1965. *Children:* Bradley, Lynne, and Lorraine. *Education:* B.S. Education, The Ohio State University, June 1964. *Professional associations:* Romance Writers of America. *Genres:* Historical romance, Category contemporary. *Agent:* Irene Goodman, Irene Goodman Literary Agency, 134 West 81st Street, N.Y., N.Y. 10024. *Current residence:* Columbus, Ohio.

Favorite authors and books: Anything by Laurie McBain, Shirley Busbee and Kathleen Woodiwiss. I also enjoy Janet Dailey's category contemporaries, Day Taylor's THE BLACK SWAN, LaVyrle Spencer's THE ENDEARMENT, Kate Belmont's THAT CERTAIN SMILE, anything written by Jude Deveraux, Jayne Castle. Lastly, I can't forget Barbara Cartland who wrote the first category novel I ever read.

Thoughts on writing: I do believe that romance fiction provides an escape from much of today's pressures and sordid news. I probably never outgrew my Cinderella fantasy and have a strong belief that true love will conquer all. I most enjoy the historical romances as I have a great love for history and find that a well written and researched historical romance can provide the reader with a little more insight into a by gone time and also show that the relationship bewteen a man and a woman who love each other is timeless. I do enjoy, as well, the contemporary romances that show that modern day men can be just as exciting a hero as a swashbuckling pirate and that real romance is alive and well in the 1980's. I was a fan of genre fiction, romances—especially the historicals, for only a couple of years before I met my writing partner. I had just begun to think that I might want to write before being introduced to Joyce.

I would hope that every book that Joyce and I write brings some happiness to our readers. Escape for a few hours into a story that ends happily, get to know two people who fall in love, enjoy each other completely forever and ever. We always try to include some humor to show that falling in love is not deadly serious all the time and that two people can laugh together as well as love.

Becoming published/finding an agent: We (Joyce Thies and I) completed our first book and sent a query letter to Richard Gallen Books. It was rather tongue in cheek as we listed our credentials for writing a marketable manuscript. We humorously stated that since Columbus, Ohio was a national test center and we, ourselves, had tested many products, we knew what the public wanted and our book was it. Unbelievably, they responded and asked for a synopsis plus the usual first chapters. We complied, then they wanted the entire manuscript and again we complied. Less than a week after sending them the manuscript, they called with an offer. Eventually, our editor at Gallen, after reading some of our other works, suggested we get an agent and gave us a suggested list. We narrowed the list down, eventually, to Irene Goodman and were delighted when she agreed to represent us.

Bibliography
Historical romance:
    CONQUER THE MEMORIES, Janet Joyce. Richard Gallen Books, 1982.
Note: Janet Bieber and Joyce Thies currently have three books under contract, two for Silhouette Desire and one for Pocket Books' new Tapestry line.

DIANE GUEST BIONDI
Pseudonyms: Diane Guest. *B*. Diane Reidy Guest, 2/9/39, Hartford, CT, married Gerald S. Biondi, 1975. *Children*: Anne, Barry, Matthew, Allison. *Education*: B.A. College of New Rochelle, French. *Genres*: Romantic suspense. *Current residence*: Canton, CT.

Favorite authors and books: Jane Austen, Georgette Heyer, and the Brontës are unquestioningly the best. I read very little contemporary romance. REBECCA is one of my favorites.

Thoughts on writing: Romance is an important ingredient in my writing, but it is not the central theme. I think a strong storyline is essential and has to be developed before the characters are paired off. I don't write social commentary; I would rather be remembered for having written "a darn good story" than a boring philosophy of social customs.

Becoming published/finding an agent: I queried four publishers after I finished my first novel. Bernard Geis Associates bought it, and since they are co-publishers, they sold it to Ace Books. I am under contract for my next book, which I expect to finish in November. It is not a romance, per se, but it does have a strong love interest.

Bibliography:
Romantic suspense:
TWILIGHT'S BURNING, Diane Guest, Ace, 8/72.

KATRINKA BLICKLE

B. Katrinka Blickle, 2/1/49, Exeter, New Hampshire, married Michael Pellecchia, 12/1/79. *Children:* Adam. *Education:* Chatham College, Pittsburgh, PA; B.A. in fine arts, May 1970. *Genres:* Historical romance, gothic romance. *Agent:* Barney Karpfinger, John Schnaffner Assoc., 425 East 51st Street, N.Y., N.Y. 10022. *Current residence:* Fort Worth, Texas.

Favorite authors and books: All of Jane Austen. Among modern day writers: Mary Stewart, Catherine Gaskin, and Victoria Holt (her earlier works). My favorite books include WUTHERING HEIGHTS, JANE EYRE and GONE WITH THE WIND.

Thoughts on writing: I regard romance novels as entertainment. The best ones are those that teach me something—i.e., historical facts, descriptions of other countries, and also have believable plots and characters. I've tried to do this in my own books. The historical romance/gothic genre is one I've always enjoyed; I've read thousands (at least)—some good, mostly bad. Just because a book is a romance, there's no excuse for it not to be well written. That, in part, was the motivation for my own first book. I took the standard gothic formula, and applied it to modern day situations. It was a challenge, but fun.

Becoming published/finding an agent: After I had finished my first book, I contacted an editor I knew at Doubleday. She liked it enough to buy it and the others I had written. I found my agent through a fellow writer.

Bibliography:

Gothic:
NORTH SEA MISTRESS, Doubleday, 1977.
HEART OF THE HARBOR, Doubleday, 1979.

Historical romance:
DARK BEGINNINGS, Doubleday, 1978.
VAIN AND THE VAINGLORIOUS, Doubleday, 1981.
Note: Katrinka Blickle is currently under contract with Bantam books.

PATTI and CHARLES BOECKMAN
Pseudonyms: Patti Beckman B. Patricia Ellen Kennelly, Chicago, IL; and Charles Boeckman, San Antonio, TX, married 7/65. *Children.* Sharla. *Education:* Patti received her B.A. in English from North Texas State University and her M.A. in Educational Supervision from Texas A&I University. *Professional associations:* Romance Writers of America, American Society of Journalists and Authors. *Awards:* A short story by Charles was selected for the anthology, BEST DETECTIVE STORIES OF THE YEAR, 1976. *Genres:* Category contemporary. *Current residence:* Corpus Christi, TX.

Favorite authors and books: There are so many good ones, it would be hard to select favorites. Our favorite really is a type of book; we prefer novels in which the heroine has a personal problem to overcome in addition to the love problem. We like books that are strongly plotted with complications, and also with insights into human nature. The emotions of the heroine should be real.

Thoughts on writing: We see romances as different things to different people. They are escapism for some, and we all need a certain amount of escape. Others read for pleasure, for vicarious trips to places they cannot visit in person; for relaxation; in order to recapture the thrill of new love, etc. We became fans about four years ago. Our philosophy of writing is that everyone loves a good story, and we try to make our stories as well-written, entertaining, and convincing as we can. We like clean books that sizzle.

Becoming published/finding an agent: Patti wrote articles for two years before breaking into romance; Charles had been writing fiction all his adult life. We heard about Silhouette at a writer's conference and submitted a manuscript; the manuscript was accepted within a week. In fact, we were told ours was the first proposal they bought.

Bibliography:

Category contemporary: (All as Patti Beckman)
CAPTIVE HEART, Silhouette, 1980.
THE BEACHCOMBER, Silhouette, 1980.
ANGRY LOVER, Silhouette, 1980.
LOVE'S TREACHEROUS JOURNEY, Silhouette, 1981.
LOUISIANA LADY, Silhouette, 1981.
SPOTLIGHT TO FAME, Silhouette, 1981.
DARING ENCOUNTER, Silhouette, 1982.
BITTER VICTORY, Silhouette Special Edition, 1982.

Young adult: (All as Patti Beckman)
PLEASE LET ME IN, Silhouette First Love, 1981.
MERMAID'S TOUCH, Silhouette First Love, 1982.

PARRIS AFTON BONDS
B. Parris Afton Wilkes, married Ted Bonds. *Children*: Dean, Kirk, Brandon Jason and Ted. *Education*: New Mexico Junior College; English and history. *Professional associations*: Romance Writers of America (vice-president); Western Writers of America. *Awards*: DUST DEVIL—Best Novel of 1981 (Texas Press Women). *Genres*: Category contemporary, historical romance. *Agent*: Chuck Neighbors, 7600 Blanco, Apt. 2001, San Antonio, Tx. 78216. *Current residence*: San Antonio, Tx.

Favorite authors and books: Edna Ferber, Frank Yerby, Rafael Sabatini, Dale Van Every.

Thoughts on writing: I've always written (since I was six). But I have also always enjoyed an action/romance book. Romance novels are entertainment, as every fiction book should be.

Becoming published/finding an agent: Luck. I sent my novel over the transom to Kate Duffy at Popular Library.

Bibliography:

Category contemporary:
MADE FOR EACH OTHER, Silhouette, April 1981.

Historical romance:
SWEET GOLDEN SUN, Popular Library, June 1978.
FLASH OF THE FIREFLY, Popular Library, December 1979.
SAVAGE ENCHANTMENT, Popular Library, February 1979.
DUST DEVIL, Popular Library, August 1981.
LOVE TIDE, Popular Library, April 1980.
DEEP PURPLE, Fawcett Columbine, May 1982.
Note: Parris Afton Bonds has two historical romances under contract with Fawcett.

BARBARA BONHAM
Pseudonyms: Sara North. B. Barbara Lee Thomas, 9/27/26, Franklin, NE., married Max L. Bonham, 1950. *Education:* University of Nebraska. *Professional associations:* Author's Guild. *Genres:* Historical romance, romantic suspense. *Agent:* John K. Payne, Lenniger Literary Agency, 104 East 40th Street, New York, NY 10016. *Current residence:* Omaha, Nebraska.

Favorite authors and books: Daphne du Maurier, Norah Lofts, Victoria Holt, Mary Stewart, Joan Aiken, Marnie Ellingson, Katherine Court.

Thoughts on writing: Love stories are loved by me. I believe a strong love story can be told against any background, but, for me, an historical setting adds much to my enjoyment of a book. Frontier history, so uniquely American, is my favorite period. In such a setting, the beauty of love stands out against the harshness that so often was a factor of life on the frontier.

Becoming published/finding an agent: I began by writing short stories and, after a few years of developing my writing skills, I sent some of my manuscripts to an agent, and he accepted me as a client. Later I wrote nurse novels and children's books. Aware of my interest in history, my agent advised me to try historical romances when they burst onto the market.

Bibliiography:

Historical romance:
PROUD PASSION, Playboy Press, 1976.
PASSION'S PRICE, Playboy Press, 1977.
DANCE OF DESIRE, Playboy Press, 1978.
THE DARK SIDE OF PASSION, Playboy Press, 1980.
GREEN WILLOW, Playboy Press, 1982.

Romantic suspense:
SWEET AND BITTER FANCY, Popular Library, 1976.
JASMINE FOR MY GRAVE, as Sara North, Playboy Press, 1978.
Note: Barbara Bonham also has written juvenile books and nurse novels.

MURIEL BRADLEY
B. Muriel Demens, Los Angeles, 'CA., married John Bradley, 6/15/43. Children: Lucy Anne. *Education*: Chaffey College, business. *Genres*: Contemporary, historical romance. *Agent*: Pauline Fox, 2195 Roberto Drive, Palm Springs, Ca. *Current residence*: Encino, Ca.

Favorite authors and books: Norah Lofts, Victoria Holt, Marsha Alexander, Marilyn Granbeck.

Thoughts on writing: Unfortunately, I've had no contact with the buying public, so I don't know what the reader *thinks*. Fan letters on my historicals say, "What a beautiful romance."But, to me, the research is fascinating; it's like educating oneself continually. I also enjoy working at home.

Becoming published/finding an agent: When I married and stopped working at M.G.M. studios, I was restless and wrote a novel that turned out to be a mystery. An agent friend in Hollywood took it to New York and gave it to a big agency there, Curtis Brown, and Doubleday Crime Club published it, as well as six other titles. Then I stopped writing for years. By this time I had a daughter, and my husband and I were busy being transferred around the country. When we returned to Los Angeles, I started writing again, this time romances.

Bibliography:

Contemporary:
THE SUDDEN SUMMER, Gallen/Pocket, July, 1981.
FLOWERS IN WINTER, Gallen/Pocket, August 1982.

Historical romance:
TANYA, GallenJPocket, June 1980.
DESTINY'S STAR, Gallen/Pocket, March 1982.

MARY REBECCA WADSWORTH BRANDEWYNE
Pseudonym: Rebecca Brandewyne B. Mary Rebecca Wadsworth, 4/4/55, Knoxville, Tennessee. *Education:* B.A. Wichita State University, Wichita, Kansas, 1975 degree in journalism, M.A. Wichita State University, 1979, journalism. Graduated Cum Laude with departmental honors. *Professional associations*: Affaire de Coeur, The National Writers Club, Romance Writers of America, The Society of Professional Journalists, Women in Communications, Inc. *Awards*: Novel, FOREVER MY LOVE, number eleven on B. Dalton bestseller list, 1982, Novel, NO GENTLE LOVE, number one on MS News Co., Inc. bestseller list, 1980. Cover Girl for the WICHITAN magazine, 1978, the IBM Informal Award, 1977. *Genres*: Historical romance. *Agent:* Maxwell J. Lillienstein, Esq., Rich, Krinsly, Katz, & Lillienstein, P.C., Attorneys at Law, 99 Park Avenue, N.Y., N.Y. 10016. *Current residence:* Wichita, Kansas.

Favorite authors and books: Anything by Mary Stewart, but especially her NINE COACHES WAITING (my all time favorite). Margaret Mitchell's GONE WITH THE WIND. Anything by Georgette Heyer, but especially FRIDAY'S CHILD. Anything by Frank Yerby, but especially FLOODTIDE. Charlotte Bronter's JANE EYRE. Emily Brontë's WUTHERING HEIGHTS. Anything by Daphne du Maurier, but especially REBECCA. Anything by Susannah Leigh, but especially GLYNDA. Anything by Gimone Hall, but especially HIDE MY SAVAGE HEART.

Thoughts on writing: I write romance because I am a romantic at heart, and I love love stories. I don't see my books as pure escapism, since I work at putting a lot of the elements of interpersonal communication (which I taught for two years) theory in the relationships between my main characters. Also, my plots are extremely complex and involve a great deal of factual history as well. I have always read love stories, primarily gothics when I was growing up, so I was a fan of the genre for many years before beginning my writing. As far as my philosophy of writing goes— it's very simple: to write about what I know and love in the best way I know how.

Becoming published/finding an agent: I found my agent through the brother of my financial advisor. My agent subsequently took my first novel over to Warner, and they bought it about two months later.

Bibliography:

Historical romance:
    NO GENTLE LOVE, Rebecca Brandewyne. Warner Books, September 1980.
    FOREVER MY LOVE, Rebecca Brandewyne. Warner Books, 1982.
Note: Rebecca Brandewyne is currently under contract with Warner Books.

MARY BRINGLE
Pseudonyms: Kathleen Morris, Ian Kavanagh B. Mary Hanford Brannum, Racine, Wisconsin, married J.E. Bringle, 7/2/68. *Children:* Adam J. Bringle, Alexander H. Burton. *Education:* University of Colorado, New York University; no degree. *Professional associations:* P.E.N. *Genres:* Historical, Contemporary, family saga, children's Gothic, general fiction. *Current residence:* New York City.

Favorite authors and books: none.

Thoughts on writing: My philosophy for "writing romance" is the same as for writing any other fiction. I try to make my characters as full and complex as possible and I like to include many subplots. Most romantic fiction is too simply written and low-level to engage me.

Becoming published/finding an agent: Mystery novel sold to Doubleday by myself, 1975; before that I was a free-lancer for ten years.

Bibliography:

Contemporary:
AN ELEGANT AFFAIR, Kathleen Morris. Gallen Books, 1981.

Historical romance:
MARA, Kathleen Morris. Bryans Books, 1978.

Gothic (young adult):
DON'T WALK ALONE, Scholastic, 1981

Non-romance books:
FOOTPATH MURDER, Doubleday, 1975—mystery.
FORTUNES, Putnam, 1980—novel.
Note: Mary Bringle currently has one book under contract with Dell/Emerald and one with NAL.

SANDRA BROWN
Pseudonyms: Rachel Ryan, Erin St. Claire, Laura Jordan *B.* Sandra Lynn Cox, 3/12/48, Waco, TX., married Michael Brown, 1968 *Children:* Rachel, Ryan. *Education:* University of Texas at Arlington, English. *Professional associations:* Romance Writers of America. *Genres:* Category contemporary, historical romance. *Current residence:* Arlington, TX.

Favorite authors and books: I was initially inspired by Kathleen Woodiwiss—as I think almost all current writers of romance fiction were. I also enjoy reading Lisa Gregory, especially her RAINBOW SEASON. THE FULFILLMENT by LaVyrle Spencer remains one of my favorite books. Anne Mather is a genius at creating mood. Charlotte Lamb is spontaneous. Though she is not of the romance genre, I still study Taylor Caldwell for character development.

Thoughts on writing: Telling a good story is still the best reason for writing. One must have compelling characters that the reader truly cares about. I do feel that romance books are escapism, but the reader is intelligent and appreciates a provocative story. When I incorporated a deaf child into my book ELOQUENT SILENCE, I was gratified by the response the book received. The reader wants to know that romance can still exist in a world of problems. By not making the stories so outlandish, the reader can relate to the characters. One would like to believe that wonderful things can still happen between two people.

Becoming published/finding an agent: I was writing, but as yet unpublished when a friend of mine who owns a bookstore and is a real fan of romance fiction read one of my manuscripts. At the time, Dell Ecstasy was in the incubation stage, and manuscripts of a certain type were being sought. Fortunately, I was writing in a more sensuous style than previously allowed in category books. My friend called the editor and told her to watch for my manuscript when it came in. She liked it and bought it. That was my first sale, and I was elated. I still work without an agent, preferring at this point to work on a one-to-one basis with my editors.

Bibliography:

Category contemporary:
LOVE'S ENCORE, Rachel Ryan, Dell Candlelight Ecstasy, 1981.
LOVE BEYOND REASON, Rachel Ryan, Dell Candlelight Ecstasy, 1981.
ELOQUENT SILENCE, Rachel Ryan, Dell Candlelight Ecstasy, 1982.
A TREASURE WORTH SEEKING, Rachel Ryan, Dell Candlelight Ecstasy, 1982.
NOT EVEN FOR LOVE, Erin St. Claire, Silhouette Desire, 1982.
SEDUCTION BY DESIGN, Erin St. Claire, Silhouette Desire, 1982.

Historical romance: (All as Laura Jordan)
HIDDEN FIRES, Pocket, 1982.
THE SILKEN WEB, Pocket, 1982.

Note: Sandra Brown currently has three books under contract with the Jove line, "Second Chance At Love," and one book under contract with Harlequin. She has also written one of the first books in Bantam's new "Loveswept" series.

DIXIE BURRUS BROWNING
Pseudonyms: Zoe Dozier B. Dixie Stevens Burrus, 9/9/30, Elizabeth City, North Carolina, married Leonard Larkin Browning, 10/29/50. *Children*: Elizabeth Burrus Browning (Fox), Leonard Larkin Browning. *Education*: one year at Mary Washington College, one year at Virginia Commonwealth University, studied art, and one year studied nursing. *Professional associations*: Watercolor Society of North Carolina, Romance Writers of America.*Awards*: twenty-four art awards, none in writing. *Genres*: Category contemporary. *Agent*: Steven Axelrod, Sterling Lord Agency, 660 Madison Avenue, N.Y., N.Y. *Current residence*: Winston-Salem, North Carolina.

Favorite authors and books: Betty Neel, Elaine Raco Chase, Jayne Krentz, aka Jayne Castle/Stephanie James; Catherine Coulter; Sandra Brown, aka Rachel Ryan and Erin St. Claire.

Thoughts on writing: I began reading romance as a girl, went on to other types fiction and nonfiction, and came back to romance. I believe it's necessary to respect the genre to write it well. All fiction is an escape, in a sense; in another sense, it's merely expanding one's universe. I have a compulsion to create a world that's warm and exciting and fulfilling. I describe that world and its people and share it with others.

Becoming published/finding an agent: My first two books were published by the second publisher I sent them to. After four more had been published by Silhouette I sought an agent. At the first RWA conference I talked to several, made my choice and have been exceedingly pleased with the results.

Bibliography:

Category contemporary:
WARM SIDE OF THE ISLAND, Zoe Dozier. Thomas Bouregy, Inc. 1977.
HOME AGAIN, MY LOVE, Zoe Dozier. Thomas Bouregy, Inc. 1977.
UNREASONABLE SUMMER, Dixie Browning. Silhouette Romances, 1980.
TUMBLED WALL, Dixie Browning. Silhouette Romances, 1980.

JOURNEY TO QUIET WATERS, Dixie Browning. Silhouette Romances, 1980.
WREN OF PARADISE, Dixie Browning. Silhouette Romances, 1981.
CHANCE TOMORROW, Dixie Browning. Silhouette Romances, 1981.
EAST OF TODAY, Dixie Browning. Silhouette Romances, 1981.
WINTER BLOSSOM, Dixie Browning. Silhouette Romances, 1981.
RENEGADE PLAYER, Dixie Browning. Silhouette Romances, 1982.
ISLAND ON THE HILL, Dixie Browning. Silhouette Romances, 1982.
LOGIC OF THE HEART, Dixie Browning. Silhouette Romances, 1982.
FINDERS KEEPERS, Dixie Browning. Silhouette Special Edition, 1982.
THE LOVING RESCUE, Dixie Browning, Silhouette Romances, 1982.

Note: Dixie Burrus Browning is currently under contract with Silhouette.

MEREDITH BABEAUX BRUCKER
Pseudonyms: Meredith Lindley, Meredith Kingston B. Meredith Lindley Babeaux, Los Angeles, California, married Walter Tuley Brucker, 4/24/65. *Children*: Carson. *Education*: B.A. 1957, Stanford University, speech and drama. *Professional associations*: Pasedena Junior Philharmonic Committee. *Genres*: Category contemporary. *Agent*: Donald MacCampbell, 12 East 41 Street, N.Y., N.Y. *Current residence*: San Marino, Ca.

Favorite authors and books: My favorite books recently were ORDINARY PEOPLE and A WOMAN OF INDEPENDENT MEANS, not, strictly speaking, romances. I also love to read Hollywood biographies, Salinger, Updike, and almost any humor book. But while writing a romance, I do my leisure reading only in the romance category. My mother receives six Harlequins a month, marks five of them "Good!"and passes them on to me. They've been an education and I particularly enjoy Mary Burchell, Charlotte Lamb, Janet Dailey and Anne Mather.

Thoughts on writing: I always counsel beginning writers not to tamper with a proven formula, or deviate from the rules just to prove their originality. Contemporary romances have an established place in fiction because they coincide with the fantasies of a large number of readers. Authors must strive to produce fresh and imaginative stories and characters while strictly following the rules. I enjoy the discipline and the challenge of genre writing. To do otherwise would, for me, be like "playing tennis without a net."

Becoming published/finding an agent: I had worked for many years in the TV news business in Los Angeles, and wanted to tell about it in novel form. When my son was born and I quit work I took a fiction class at a local college, where I turned in each chapter for critique. When it was done I bundled it off to a New York agent I had once heard on a radio interview during one of his California visits. He found a publisher for my book, and also taught me the realities of the publishing world, and soon I was selling romances to Dell, Jove and Silhouette.

Bibliography:

Category contemporary:
ONE LOVE FOREVER, Dell Candlelight,.1978.
CLOSE TO THE STARS, Dell Candlelight, 1978.
AGAINST THE WIND, Meredith Lindley, Silhouette, 1981.
WINTER LOVE SONG, Meredith Kingston, Jove Second Chance at Love, 1981.
ALOHA YESTERDAY, Meredith Kingston, Jove Second Chance at Love, 1981.
PASSION'S GAMES, Meredith Kingston, Jove Second Chance at Love, 1982.
MIXED DOUBLES, Meredith Kingston, Jove Second Chance at Love, 1982.

Non-romance:
ON THE MONITOR, Manor Books, 1978.
Note: Several of the above titles have been translated into German, Swedish or Norwegian for foreign release.

LINDA BURAK
Pseudonym: Alicia Meadowes (Pseudonym shared with co-author Joan Zieg). *B.* Cleveland, OH., married to Dr. Joseph M. Burak. *Education*: B.S. Edinboro College, education; M.A. Villanova University, theatre. *Professional associations*: Author's Guild. *Genres*: Contemporary, historical romance, Regency.

Agent: Denise Marcil, 316 W. 82nd Street, New York, NY. *Current residence*: Bensalem, PA.

Favorite authors and books: Georgette Heyer. I enjoyed any number of her books, but especially THE DEVIL'S CUB. After reading that book, I began looking for romances with a terrific hero. At that time, there weren't as many on the bookshelves, so I decided to try my hand at writing my own romantic novel.

Thoughts on writing: Since the movies are no longer wonderfully romantic like CASABLANCA, I think romance novels are filling that fantasy very nicely.

Becoming published/finding an agent: My sister and I collaborated on a delightful experiment that turned out to be our first published book. After two books, we sought an agent through the Author's Guild, and selected Denise Marcil because she specialized in romance.

Bibliography:
Regency:
    SWEET BRAVADO, Warner Books, 1978.
    TENDER TORMENT, Warner Books, 1979.
Note: Linda Burak currently has two books under contract, one with the Banbury/Dell series, "Woman of Destiny," the other with Avon's series, "Finding Mr. Right."

SHIRLEE BUSBEE
B. Shirlee Elaine Egan, San Jose, CA., married Howard Leon Busbee, 1963. *Education*: Burbank Business College. *Genres*: Historical romance. *Agent*: Jay Acton, 825 Third Avenue, New York, NY. *Current residence*: Fairfield, CA.

Favorite authors and books: Georgette Heyer (the very best!), Mary Stewart (simply marvelous!), Jan Wescott (great!), and, of course, Frank Yerby (particularly his early books).

Thoughts on writing: I can't give my philosophy on writing because I don't have one, but I will say that I do write pure escapism. One might learn a little history in the process of reading one of my books, but the main thrust is the story. I want to entertain people, and I feel I am essentially a teller of tales. Hopefully tales that other people find interesting.

Becoming published/finding an agent: As I'm certain most people are aware, Rosemary Rogers and I are great friends. We worked together for the Solano County Parks department, and it was Rosemary who first suggested that I write. She was the one who put a bug in her agent's ear about reading my manuscript. I guess her editor liked what she saw because Avon bought the manuscript and has bought every book I've written so far.

Bibliography:

Historical romance:
GYPSY LADY, Avon, 1977.
LADY VIXEN, Avon, 1980.
WHILE PASSION SLEEPS, Avon, 1983.

GWENDOLINE BUTLER
Pseudonym: Jennie Melville. *B*. Gwendoline Williams, London, England, married Lionel Butler, 1949. *Children*: Lucilla. *Education*: Lady Margaret Hall, Oxford, History. *Professional associations*: Crime Writers Association, the Detective Club, Romance Novelists Association. *Awards*: Silver Dagger Award, 1975; Romantic Novelists Award for the best romantic novel of the year, 1980. *Genres*: Contemporary, historical. *Agent*: George Greenfield, John Farquaharson, London. *Current residence*: Englefield Green, Surrey, England.

Favorite authors and books: Dorothy Eden, Georgette Heyer, Elizabeth Gundry. I read a lot of crime fiction and a lot of historical memoirs. Picking them up on bookstalls and in second-hand shops is a hobby.

Thoughts on writing: I came into romance through crime-writing.

A great number of my crime novels were published until, writing as Gwendoline Butler, I wrote a book about a girl in Victorian Oxford which won a Silver Dagger from the Crime Writers' Association. I used romantic elements which I developed in later books, until in 1980 THE RED STAIRCASE won a prize for the Best Romantic Novel of the year. Jennie Melville has followed a similar pattern.

Becoming published/finding an agent: I wrote my first novel, my husband introduced me to an agent, and he got my first book published; it was as easy as that. Sticking at it, finding different markets, and building up a reasonably high income has been the hard thing. I am a very professional writer whose backgrounds are accurate; I was, after all, an historian. I never venture back much beyond 1860 and I am now moving forward into contemporary affairs. I am passionately interested in the history of costume, and couture, and they figure in my books. I don't mind a touch of the occult to make the flesh creep a bit, but I will always be at pause to explain it rationally. I like to amuse: I am an entertainer, not a teacher. But I like every sentence, every word, to be as fresh-minted as I can make it.

Bibliography:
(As Gwendoline Butler, beginning in 1956 and coming at almost yearly intervals):
RECEIPT FOR MURDER
COFFIN IN OXFORD
THE DULL DEAD
THE MURDERING KIND
THE INTERLOPER
A COFFIN FOR BABY
COFFIN WAITING
A NAMELESS COFFIN
COFFIN IN MALTA
COFFIN FOLLOWING
COFFIN'S DARK NUMBER
A COFFIN FROM THE PAST
A COFFIN FOR PANDORA
A COFFIN FOR THE CANARY
THE VESEY INHERITANCE

THE BRIDES OF FRIEDBURG, 1977.
THE RED STAIRCASE, 1980.

(As Jennie Melville, starting in 1962):
COME HOME AND BE KILLED
BURNING IS A SUBSTITUTE FOR LOVING
THE HUNTER IN THE SHADOWS
NUN'S CASTLE
IRONWOOD
RAVEN'S FORGE
DRAGON'S EYE
AXWATER, 1970.
MURDER HAS A PRETTY FACE, 1981.

JO CALLOWAY

B. Jo Homan, 6/14/40, Tupelo, Miss. *Children:* Denise. Education: Hinds School of Nursing, Registered Nurse. *Professional associations:* Romance Writers of America. *Genres:* Category contemporary, historical. *Agent:* Denise Marcil, 316 West 82nd Street, New York, N.Y. *Current residence:* Tupelo, Miss.

Favorite authors and books: Violet Winspear is my favorite category romance author, and the late Helen Van Slyke was my favorite contemporary writer. I read and enjoy both Cynthia Freeman and Danielle Steel. My single favorite book is GONE WITH THE WIND. Always has been. Always will be.

Thoughts on writing: To me, writing is just one way of expressing the creative force that dwells within us all. As a child, I loved building sandcastles; as an adult, I love writing. I find the underlying force in both to be much the same: to build a castle from a handful of sand, to fill many pages from a single thought. It's simply a way of satisfying my creative force. I write with two goals in mind: That both the reader and the writer be satisfied with the outcome. I have never considered writing to be a means of escape, nor have I ever considered reading to be one either. To me, reading is one form of action and writing is another. So what if the romance is considered to be the stepchild of publishing? So what if the critics aren't kind to either the romance or the writer?

It has, after all, proven its strength. It doesn't need to be considered on the same level established by other genres. It has established its own level on which I, as a romance writer, take pride. It has always been my belief that romance existed long before heralded literature, and my belief is that when romance dies, so does mankind. Therefore, I am pledged to doing my part in keeping the romance genre alive and well and thriving.

Becoming published/finding an agent: My first sale was made to a "tax shelter" publishing firm, and it was not a warmly memorable experience, nor will it ever be. However, it was a learning experience. The sale was made by my first agent who didn't know the basis of the firm, and, of course, I didn't know. The sale I consider to be my first real one was to Dell in October of 1978, a Candlelight Romance.

My history with agents has not been an ideal one. The fact that I am presently working with my fourth bears this out. It cannot be emphasized enough how very important an agent is to a writer's professional career.

Finding an agent to represent me was not at all difficult. Finding the right agent was extremely difficult, but not impossible—I found her.

There is more to an agent/author relationship than writing and selling. The relationship must be structured on a foundation of trust and the expectations of each must be met. I have found this with my fourth agent. I depend on my agent, and, in return, she can depend on me. To have an agent I trust, respect, and depend on removes the worry cloud away from my head, and I can concentrate on my writing.

The point is that it took four attempts to find an agent I am completely secure with. But then I have never succeeded at anything on my first try.

Bibliography:
Category contemporary:
SPECIAL SPARROW, Manor, 1978.
TO SEIZE THE RAINBOW, Dell, 1980.
TO CATCH THE WILD WIND , Dell, 1982.

DANCE THE SKIES, Dell, 1982.
WHERE THE RIVER BENDS, Dell, 1982.
Historical:
ASHES OF HONOR, Manor, 1978.
Note: Jo Calloway has six books on contract to the "Ecstasy" series of Dell, as well as one book under contract to Avon's "Finding Mr. Right" series.

CANDACE P. CAMP

Pseudonyms: Lisa Gregory, Kristin James, Sharon Stephens. *B.* Candace Pauline Camp, 5/23/49, Amarillo, Tx., married Pete Hopcus, 8/11/79. *Children*: Anastasia (Stacy). *Education*: B.A. West Texas State University, English; J.D. University of North Carolina. *Professional associations*: Romance Writers of America. *Genres*: Category contemporary, historical romance. *Agent*: Cherry Weiner, 1734 Church St., Rahway, N.J. *Current residence*: Temple, Tx.

Favorite authors and books: As far as I'm concerned the best romance of all time was GONE WITH THE WIND. I probably read it fifteen times when I was a teenager. Of the current crop, I particularly like LaVyrle Spencer Roberta Gellis, Janet Dailey, and Dorothy Garlock. And I love romantic suspense a la Mary Stewart. My favorites there are Barbara Michaels, Elizabeth Peters, Anne Stevenson, and Isabelle Holland.

Thoughts on writing: My opinion is that a good book must be, before all else, enjoyable. If it's boring, no matter how fine the thoughts or how beautifully they're expressed, it won't be read, and a novel that isn't read hardly exists. In the literary world of critics, college professors, etc., it seems as though popularity automatically disqualifies a book from being considered good literature. But the authors of the past who are now considered "great"and worthy of teaching in courses, such as Dickens, Hemingway, even Shakespeare were, at the time they wrote, very popular. I'm not saying that all romance is great literature, because that's a rare quality in any kind of literature. What I am saying is that romance is not "bad" because it's popular. Rather it has passed the first major criteria of good writing. I believe that much of the criticism levelled at romance literature has a sexist origin because romance literature is primarily written by and for women, which to many puts it in a lesser category of literature.

I could probably go on for far too many pages about my theory that romance literature (at least the recent boom) is a product of women's liberation. However that's really off the subject of my philosophy of writing. I believe that the first essential thing to do in writing is to tell a good story. Everything else—characterization, style, theme—builds on that, and if you do all of them well, you've probably got an excellent story. Romance is escapism. It's fantasy. It's not real. But then so is all fiction. I think escapism is extremely important to everyone, and such fiction serves a basic human need. I've always loved to read and daydream, and writing is an extension of that. I love to dream up a story and make things come out just exactly like I'd like them to.

Becoming published/finding an agent: I simply mailed in my first manuscript, BONDS OF LOVE, first to Avon, who sent it back saying they had too many romances and then to Jove, who bought it. I sold two books to them before I got an agent. I knew less about getting an agent than finding a publisher. I just sort of stumbled into getting one. She had worked for Jove and liked BONDS OF LOVE, and contacted me after she left Jove.

Bibliography:

Contemporary: (All as Kristin James)
GOLDEN SKY, Gallen/Pocket, 1981.
SAPPHIRE SKY, Gallen/Pocket, 1981.
SUMMER SKY, Gallen/Pocket, 1982.

Historical romance:
BONDS OF LOVE, as Lisa Gregory, Jove, 1978.
RAINBOW SEASON, as Lisa Gregory, Jove, 1979.
ANALISE, as Lisa Gregory, Jove, 1981.
CRYSTAL HEART, as Lisa Gregory, Jove, 1982.
THE BLACK EARL, as Sharon Stephens, Pocket Tapestry, 1982.

BITTERLEAF, as Lisa Gregory, Jove, 1983.

DEBORAH CAMP
Pseudonyms: Elaine Camp, Delaine Tucker, Deborah Benet. *B.* Deborah Elaine Camp, 1/4/52, Hayti, MO. *Education*: B.S. University of Tulsa, journalism. *Professional associations*: Romance Writers of America, Tulsa Night Writers, Northeastern Oklahoma Romance Authors, Sigma Delta Chi, Society of Professional Journalists, Oklahoma Writers Federation. *Awards*: Night Writer of the Year, 1980; and numerous awards for reporting. *Genres*: Category contemporary. *Agent*: Eileen Fallon, Barbara Lowenstein Associates, 250 West 57th Street, New York, NY. *Current residence*: Tulsa, Oklahoma.

Favorite authors and books: Anne Mather, Rachel Ryan, Jayne Castle, Mary Stewart, Phyllis Whitney; and I love Stephen King and Peter Straub too—although they don't write romance. I'm also a fan of Harold Robbins, Peter Benchley, and Robin Cook. I cut my teeth on Emilie Loring, a romance/suspense writer.

Thoughts on writing: I began reading romance suspense and gothic novels when I was about sixteen. Reading for me has always been a means of escaping, of slipping into someone else's skin for a few hours. It's the next best thing to acting and getting paid for it. I don't think there are any stepchildren in publishing. Anyone who writes a book and gets it published has my highest regards. There are no professors in this field; we are all students.

Becoming published/finding an agent: I sent my first three romances to a secondary publisher and got ripped off. But at least I was published. I sent my fourth romance to Silhouette and it was accepted. I found my agent through an editor at NAL. I don't think it's necessary to have an agent as a romance writer, but it is a luxury that I feel is worth the price paid. Any professional who believes in you and what you do is a worthy friend to foster.

Bibliography:

Category contemporarary:
GATEWAY TO THE HEART, Manor, 1980.
TANDEM, Manor, 1980.
TO HAVE, TO HOLD, Silhouette, 1981.
DEVIL'S BARGAIN, Silhouette, 1982.
Note: Deborah Camp has two books currently under contract to Rapture, both to appear under the pseudonym, Deborah Benet; she also has one book under contract to Silhouette under the pseudonym, Elaine Camp.

JASMINE CRESSWELL CANDLISH
Pseudonyms: Jasmine Cresswell, Jasmine Craig B. Jasmine Rosemary Cresswell-Steger, 1/14/41, Dollgelly, Wales, U.K., married Malcolm Candlish, 4/15/63. *Children*: Fiona Jane Candlish, Vanessa Cresswell Candlish, Sarah Sibohan Candlish, John Malcolm Candlish. *Education*: Streatham Hill High School, London, England. Diploma, Lycee Francais, Commercial French and German, London, England,1959. B.A. Melbourne University, Australia, 1970, philosophy and history joint major. B.A. Honours Degree, Macquarie University, Australia, 1971, history. Dissertation on British Poor Law administration in the nineteenth century. M.A. history and archival administration, Case Western Reserve University, Ohio, 1975. *Professional associations*: Romantic Novelists Association (England); Barrington Writers' Workshop; Romance Writers of America, Illinois Chapter; The Authors' Guild, New York. *Genres*: Regencies, Victorian, category contemporary. *Agent*: Maureen Walters, Curtis Brown, Inc., 575 Madison Avenue, New York. Elizabeth Stevens, Curtis Brown, Ltd. 1 Craven Hill, London W2 3EP, England. *Current residence*: Barrington Hills, Illinois.

Favorite authors and books: Jane Austen, whom I have loved since I was twelve, especially PRIDE AND PREJUDICE and PERSUASION. Georgette Heyer, whom I've enjoyed almost as long as Jane Austen. Mary Stewart, who always adds such a satisfying touch of mystery to her novels of romantic suspense. Isabelle

Holland, whose self-doubting heroines are always endearing. I think Anne Mather, Sally Wentworth and Daphne Clair/Laurey Bright all write good category contemporaries. I admire Kristin James' talent for creating compelling, sensuous relationships between her hero and heroine. I think Jayne Castle/Stephanie James is getting better and better.

Thoughts on writing: Writing a tightly constructed, satisfying novel is always difficult, and writing a good romance is every bit as difficult as writing any other good category novel. For some reason, critics have decided that it's acceptable to write James Bond-type stories in order to satisfy male fantasies. Romances, which satisfy equally valid female fantasies, are invariably laughed at. There is urgent need for more informed criticism of all romantic writing, so that the reader and the public at large can learn that in the romance genre—as in any other category—there are good and bad books.

Becoming published/finding an agent: My husband was transferred to Canada when I was in the middle of working for a Ph.D. in history. (This was the third time my attempts at a doctorate had been frustrated by a transfer.) I decided to start writing because that was the only career I could think of which could be taken with me anywhere in the world. When I'd finished writing my romance (it took about six months), I tied it up in fancy ribbon and sent to off to Harlequin and to Robert Hale in London. I chose those two companies because the Toronto library shelves were filled with romances published by those two publishing houses. Harlequin rejected the manuscript but Hale accepted it. That was in 1976.

Bibliography:

Category contemporary: (all as Jasmine Craig)
STORMY REUNION, Second Chance at Love, Oct. 1982.
RUNAWAY LOVE, Second Chance at Love, May 1982.
TENDER TRIUMPH, Second Chance at Love, February 1982.

Regency and Victorian: (all as Jasmine Cresswell)
FORGOTTEN MARRIAGE, Hale, 1977.
THE SUBSTITUTE BRIDE, Hale, 1977, IPC Magazines (paperback) 1980.

THE ABDUCTED HEIRESS, Hale, 1978, Masquerade 1979, Harlequin, 1980.
THE ROSSITER ARRANGEMENT, Hale, 1979, IPC Magazines, 1981.
TARRISBROKE HALL, Hale, 1979, Masquerade, 1980.
THE BLACKWOOD BRIDE, Hale, 1980, Masquerade, 1981, Harlequin, 1982.
CAROLINE, Hale, 1980, Masquerade 1982, Fawcett Coventry, 1982 (retitled: LORD CARRISFORD'S MISTRESS).
THE DANEWOOD LEGACY, Hale, 1981, Masquerade, 1983, Fawcett Coventry, 1982.
THE RELUCTANT VISCOUNTESS, Hale, 1981, Masquerade 1983, Fawcett Coventry, 1982.
THE PRINCESS, Hale, 1982, Masquerade, unscheduled.
Note: Jasmine Cresswell Candlish has one more novel under contract with Second Chance at Love. Her Regencies and Victorians have been published in several European countries, as well as in Australia.

ANNE CARSLEY
B. Anne Carsley, 4/11/35. *Education*: M.A. University of Mississippi, English and philosophy. *Awards*: Mississippi Arts Festival, first prize, 1970-3; essay third prize Mississippi educational television 1971. *Genres*: Historical romance. *Agent*: Donald MacCampbell, 12 East 41 Street, N.Y., N.Y. *Current address*: Jackson, Mississippi.

Favorite authors and books: Victoria Holt, Jocelyn Carew, Norah Lofts, Rosemary Rogers, Laurie McBain, Jennifer Blake, Anya Seton, Kathleen Woodiwiss.

Thoughts on writing: I do not consider romantic novels (especially my own genre of historicals) to be any more escapism than much of the fiction always produced. (Non-fiction can be escapism also—it depends on the individual reader.) They reflect history in a manner that lures many people who otherwise might never read of these times and may lead them on into other paths. They can put themselves into these periods and thereby gain knowledge of a specific period. In having our interest in history stirred, we come to understand ourselves better as both readers and writers. The genre is valuable and useful and I love it! I always loved romance. ROBIN HOOD in my youth and FOREVER AMBER and all in between and beyond. Philosophy of writing? Plato would have thrown us out of his Republic for telling heroic tales.

I am glad this one encourages such tales for we are entertainers, commentators, artists, readers, and creators of kingdoms. I write because I breathe and that is the best of all possible reasons.

Becoming published/finding an agent: I tried to market short stories and essays for years with very little appreciable success. I had always wanted to write novels but felt intimidated by their length. Yet my stories were always considered too long. Finally I wrote two novels and sent them out several times with no success. In the meantime I read a book written by my current agent. I was fearful of writing to him and tore up many copies of my query letter before I finally sent it. He asked that I send my material and, after some revisions, the book which became RAVISHED ROSE was sold. From my own experience I find that working with an agent is best and I would have it no other way. Write letters to them and to publishers—something is bound to give.

Bibliography:

Historical romances:
    THIS RAVISHED ROSE, Gallen/Pocket Books, 1980.
    THE WINGED LION, Dell, 1981.
    THIS TRIUMPHANT FIRE, Avon, 1982.
Note: DEFIANT DESIRES, Dell, will be published in December 1982. Two others are currently in progress and will deal with the period leading up to and during the Civil War.

JUNE CASEY
Pseudonynms: Constance Ravenlock, Casey Douglas. *B.* June Triglia, 10/29/49, McKeesport, Pa., married Douglas Casey, 12/71. *Education*: B.A. California State University at Fullerton, communication. *Professional associations*: Romance Writers of America. *Awards*: Golden Medallion Award, 1982, from the Romance Writers of America for best published historical category novel. *Genres*: Category contemporary, Regency. *Agent*: Pat Teal, Teal and Watt, 2036 Vista del Rosa, Fullerton, Ca. *Current residence*: Cypress, Ca.

Favorite authors and books: My reading preferences in the romantic genre are decidedly biased in favor of English authors. Jane

Austen is my nineteenth century favorite. Those of our own century whom I admire are Daphne du Maurier and Norah Lofts. I love the latter two not only for their wonderful story-telling abilities, but for the incomparable beauty of their prose.

Thoughts on writing: I was a journalist before I became a full-time romance novelist, so I have a very workman-like attitude towards my craft: it's my livelihood. My novels are a product, but a carefully nurtured product whose purpose is to bring the utmost satisfaction to a reader. In some books I succeed more fully than in others, but that aim is always uppermost. I think romance novels (whether they be the female brand of romance a la Harlequin or the male brand a la The Executioner series) are an essential antidote to modern life. Most of us live such tense, routinized 9-to-5 lives that we need an escape valve; we need the vicarious thrill of being swept away by uncontrollable passions and finding ourselves in a lush, exotic part of the world that somehow magically comes alive in our minds. And I think we are enriched a little by the experience. That's why I like to set my novels in little known locales. The challenge to me is to create a believable, richly detailed setting that will touch the reader in a very real way. It's nice too to be able to create witty strong proud, gutsy heroines who are willing to fight for what they want. Perhaps that's also a form of enrichment for the reader in that it provides entertaining yet very positive guidelines in becoming more the type of person she might like to be.

Becoming published/finding an agent: I'd received the usual shoebox full of impersonal, mimeographed rejections which has to be the most depressing part of this writing business. One letter, however, changed all that for me. Though still a rejection, it was a two page typed letter that praised my writing style and encouraged me to try something else for Dell's Candlelight Intrigue line. Bouyed up by that praise, I spent about a year on my next effort. Within a month of its submission, RENDEZVOUS AT GRAMERCY was sold. The sheer serendipity of this story is that the Intrigue line folded; however, by chance, my novel took place in the Regency time period so the company bought on that basis. At this stage in my career I had no agent and had never heard of writer's guidelines, so I floundered around doing two more novels (one historical gothic and one romantic suspense) which haven't sold yet. It was at this point that my husband's mother gave me a magazine article that featured local writers and their agents, Teal and Watt. I wrote to Pat Teal and thus our professional relationship started. She told me that the contemporary romance market was booming, supplied me with a few publishers' tipsheets, and four months later she sold my first Superromance.

Bibliography:

Category contemporary: (all as Casey Douglas)
INFIDEL OF LOVE, Harlequin/Wordwide, 1982.

Regency:
RENDEZVOUS AT GRAMERCY, Constance Ravenlock, Dell, 1981.
Note: June Casey has three books under contract with Harlequin/Worldwide, one with Bantam, and one with Silhouette.

LAURA ANN CASTORO
Pseudonyms: Laura Parker, Terry Nelsen Bonner. *B.* Laura Ann Parker, 9/18/48, Fort Worth, TX., married Christopher Castoro, 1968. *Children*: Theresa, Anthony, Christopher. *Education*: Howard University and Texas A&I, microbiology. *Genres*: Contemporary, historical romance, historical saga. *Agent*: Denise Marcil, Denise Marcil Literary Agency, 316 W. 82nd Street, New York, NY. *Current residence*: Plano, TX.

Favorite authors and books: There are so many. I love to reread anything by Daphne du Maurier, Mary Stewart, Marilyn Harris, Roberta Gellis, John Fowles, Paula Allardyce. And, of course, my favorite romance writer is Kathleen Woodiwiss. Reading THE FLAME AND THE FLOWER prompted me to write my first book, SILK AND SABERS.

Thoughts on writing: Writing, in whatever form, is as poor or as good as the author's skill and interest. A good writer will write good stories; the genre is secondary. I began writing romance from a desire that grew out of my enjoyment of reading romances and from what I felt to be at the time a lack of self-sufficient heroines. I had been reading Raphael Sabatini just before beginning work on SILKS AND SABERS, and I decided it would be fun to write about a heroine with the spirit of a cavalier, one who could handle a sword as well as Scaramouche.

Since then I have written novels which are not strictly romances, but I have found the strong current of emotion—which is the heart of any good romance—to be a valuable tool in creating compelling characters in any novel.

I write what pleases me; I feel that as a reader as well as creator I cannot please anyone else if I am not pleasing myself.

Bibliography:

Historical romance:
SILKS AND SABERS Laura Parker, Dell, 1980.

Historical romance:
JIM BRIDGER: MOUNTAIN MAN, Laura Parker. Dell. 1981.
Note: Laura Ann Castoro has two books currently under contract with Dell: One is to be published under the pseudonym Laura Parker, the other under the pseudonym Terry Nelsen Bonner.

GINGER CHAMBERS
B. Virginia Anne Smith, 1/1/45, Lampasas, TX., married Steve Chambers, 1966. *Children*: Beverly, Chris. *Education*: Secretarial school. *Professional associations*: Romance Writers of America. *Genres*: category contemporary. *Current residence*: Kingwood, Texas.

Favorite authors and books: My all-time favorite is Kathleen Woodiwiss. I have read her book, THE WOLF AND THE DOVE, so many times the pages are becoming worn. Also Anne Mather is a favorite of mine. Marion Chesney is delightful in Regencies and Edwardians.

Thoughts on writing: I write because I enjoy writing. To be published was a dream of mine after many years of being a fan. But it is much more than that. It is the wish to entertain, to touch a soul, and to bring a moment of happiness into someone's life.

Becoming published/finding an agent: I was one of the lucky people who have their first manuscript published. And that came about as a direct result of meeting Vivian Stephens, an editor at Dell, at a writer's conference sponsored by a local university. She liked what she saw of my partial manuscript and asked to see the rest. Of course I gave it to her. Two months later she called to buy it for Dell's Candlelight Romance line. Because of my experience at writer's conferences I strongly advise unpublished writers to attend one if they can. Usually they are the only way to meet editors outside of New York, and there is always that possibility that you will hear those magic words, "I like it! Could you send it to me?"

Bibliography:

Category contemporary:
THE KINDRED SPIRIT, Dell Candlelight, 4/81.
CALL IT LOVE, Dell Candlelight, 2/82.
A FIRE OF THE SOUL, Dell Candlelight, 9/82.
Note: Ginger Chambers has a book currently under contract with Harlequin, and one with Dell Ecstasy.

ELAINE RACO CHASE
B. Elaine Rose Raco, 8/31/49, Schenectady, N.Y., married Gary D. Chase, 9/26/69. *Children*: Marlayna and Marc. *Education*: A.A. in computer programming, Albany Business College. Attended Union College Evening Division. Journalism at SUNY at Albany, Evening Division. *Professional associations*: Romance Writers of America, Mystery Writers of America, Authors Guild, International Women's Writing Guild, Poets & Writers (registered lecturer). *Genres*: Category contemporary, romantic suspense, mystery. *Agent*: Denise Marcil, 316 W. 82nd St., N.Y., N.Y. 10024. *Current address*: Ormond Beach, Fl.

Favorite authors and books: I gobble up anything Elizabeth Peters writes, especially: SUMMER OF THE DRAGON, LEGEND IN GREEN VELVET; I like Georgette Heyer's VENETIA; Dorothy Gillman and the "old" Mary Stewarts.

Thoughts on writing: I love writing contemporary romances. Humor is my most important product. Day to day life is filled with stress, problems, routine and boredom—I enjoy sparking my books with sharp dialogue, battles of wills, sensuous love and glamorous heroines who are often other authors' "bad girls." I also create a dual character theme— getting into the thoughts of the hero as well as the heroine. The books are very well rounded and readers get to know the heroes who keep the heroines on edge. I do a lot of research, read lots of magazines and when my heroes "speak" they reflect all that I've gleaned about what the American male currently wants. I also enjoy and respond to the many women who take the time and trouble to write to me in care of my publisher. These fan letters show that most readers are interested in entertainment, fun and love.

Becoming published/finding an agent: My renewed interest in writing (after a stint as a school editor and a television copywriter) began in October of 1977. I enrolled in a journalism course at the College of General Studies at SUNY in Albany. The course was one night a week, cheap, and, after being home for six years with two children under the age of five, my brain needed to be reactivated!

My journalism teacher, Jane Alderdice, was terrific. She thought my writing was good enough to send my class assignments out to newspapers for sales—unfortunately, that is an impossible market to try to sell to. Undaunted, I began work on a contemporary romance and bundled it to Harlequin Ltd. in Canada, and waited impatiently for them to beat down my door. They didn't. They never said it was bad—never said it was good—what they did say was they had only one North American writer and all others were English or Australian. That was my first rejection and it took its toll. Here I had the greatest thing since chocolate milk and what was I to do with it?

Winter turned into spring and with it came the May issue of THE WRITER, listing 123 summer workshops and writers' conferences.

Saratoga Springs, July 28-30
International Women's Writing Guild, write to Hannelore Hahn

Here was help just six exits up the Northway! I eagerly wrote and was pleased at the immediate response. I joined IWWG and, although couldn't attend every day, settled on Saturday, July 29, as my day to attend. Now all I had to do was get there.

Now, let me tell you that part was tougher than writing WAR AND PEACE! My husband, Gary, works the third shift at the NBC-TV affiliate WRGB, he leaves for work at 4 p.m. and never has weekends off during the summer. We have only one car and two small children and a new puppy. I had a conference and no way to get there.

Well, it took four weeks of fighting, many cold meals and stony silences (plus running away to the A & P) before Gary relented on a car—if I could find one for under $1000, and low car insurance—an almost impossible task. He never dreamed I would find an aging green Toyota with 98,000 miles on it that purred like a kitten (well, almost). The next step was getting a babysitter to come in after 4 p.m., leave breakfast, lunch and dinner clearly marked, extra clothes for the kids, make the beds and tidy the house and make it to Skidmore for breakfast at 8 a.m.

I was there with bells on at 7:30 wondering where to park my beloved little car to keep it safe and sound. I think I was more worried about what to wear and how to talk to a group of creative women. I threw my lot in with Darcy Gottlieb and Audrey Borenstein during breakfast and began to relax and enjoy the talk around me. I decided to join Judith McDaniel's "Starting to Write" workshop for the morning and Jean Rikhoff after lunch.

"Starting to Write " was filled with the most creative, intelligent and determined group of women I had ever met. We all began to talk about our writing and had to tell what we wrote. It became terribly apparent that I was the odd bodkin of the lot. Here was a group of journal keepers, poetesses and autobiographical writers and here I was—writing contemporary romances and detective thrillers! These women were determined to become published by a certain time or (as many of them said) they would feel as if their lives were completely worthless and empty. Many of them were depressed and were writing depressed poems. When it came my turn, I felt very intimidated and found myself apologizing for writing pulp fiction. I explained that while I read a depression piece every so often (i.e. Betty Rollins) I needed two Erma Bombeck's to perk me up. (I use Erma the way other people use Excedrin.) I have been a student of light pulp and hard-boiled detective thrillers since I was ten. My parents were greatly relieved when I read CATCHER IN THE RYE because the language was milder than my you-stab-em we-slab-en detective novels!

Little did I know that an agent was standing in the back of the classroom and listening to my little speech. Later that night during the evening presentation, Denise Marcil asked me to talk with her after the Agenting presentation. She asked me to go into a little more depth on what I was writing and if I had any samples. She took the three chapters and the outline of my manuscript with her and later sent me a contract so she could officially represent me.

On November 20, 1978, just three months after the IWWG conference, I got final approval of the sale to Dell of RULES OF THE GAME.

Bibliography (all category contemporary):
RULES OF THE GAME, Dell Ecstasy, May 1980.
TENDER YEARNINGS , Dell Ecstasy, Aug. 1981.
A DREAM COME TRUE, Dell Ecstasy, March 1982.
DOUBLE OCCUPANCY, Dell Ecstasy, May 1982.
DESIGNING WOMAN, Dell Ecstasy, Aug. 1982.
NO EASY WAY OUT, Dell Ecstasy, Dec. 1982.
Note: Elaine Raco Chase has three books under contract with Dell Ecstasy, one with Avon, and one with Silhouette Desire.

DEBORAH CHESTER
B. Deborah A. Chester, 4/25/57, Chicago, Illinois. *Education:* B.A. in journalism from University of Oklahoma, May 1978; majored in professional writing. *Awards:* Dwight V. Swain award for outstanding professional writing senior at University of Oklahoma. *Genres:* Historical romance and Regency. *Agent:* Charles Schlessiger of Brandt & Brandt, Inc., N.Y., N.Y. *Current residence:* Tulsa, Oklahoma.

Favorite authors and books: Georgette Heyer is tops on my list, followed by Dorothy Sayers. But I also like Jane Austen, Mary Stewart, M.M. Kaye, and Sylvia Thorpe, Dawn Lindsey, and

Patricia Veryan. Oh, and THE SCARLET PIMPERNEL by Baroness Orczy is a must for any Regency fan.

Thoughts on writing: I read for escapism and pleasure, and so when I write I try to provide these elements in my books for others. Real life is always with us, but books are our special passport to somewhere else, some place that's magical, exotic, filled with romance and excitement. I admire those writers who can make contemporary settings and situations exciting and romantic, but for me, historical settings are much more fun.

Becoming published/finding an agent: I had been reading Heyers for a couple of years, but had never attempted a romance until one of my novel-writing classes in college. One of my professors, Robert L. Duncan, who writes espionage books, recommended me to his agent, who looked at my work and took me on as a client. A few months later, a publisher bought my first romance, and so I've been writing them ever since.

Bibliograghy: (all as Deborah Chester)

Historical romance:
A LOVE SO WILD, Ballantine, 1981.

Regency:
FRENCH SLIPPERS, Dell, 1982.
ROYAL INTRIGUE, Dell, 1982.

Non-Romance books:
THE SIGN OF THE OWL, Four Winds Press, 1981; winner of the ALA best books for young adults 1981 award.

MARGARET CHITTENDEN
Pseudonym: Rosalind Carson *B.* Margaret Rosalind Barrass, 1/31/33, London, Eng., married James Carson Chittenden, 10/58. *Children:* Steve, Sharon. *Professional associations:* Romance Writers of America, Pacific Northwest Writers Conference. *Genres:* Category contemporary , occult suspense, romantic suspense, children's books. *Agent:* Curtis Brown Ltd., 575 Madison Avenue, N.Y., N.Y. *Current residence:* Tacoma, Washington.

Favorite authors and books: Mary Stewart; CALIFORNIA and RAMONA'S DAUGHTER by Virginia Myers; Irma Walker; Alla Crone; Willa Lambert.

Thoughts on writing: I feel the writing of romance is an art form and should be treated as such by the writer and the reader. I don't see my own books as pure escapism, rather as optimistic fiction. (They *could* happen.) I read more romantic suspense than romance before writing—I try to read more romance now. However, I'm also addicted to espionage novels—which are another form of romance. My philosophy is to entertain, to provide a good read with interesting characters in an interesting place.

Becoming published/finding an agent: I sold articles to Sunday supplements, then short stories to children's magazines, then finally I sold a children's book. I took the contract to my agent and asked her to represent me. She sold short stories to women's magazines for me, including GOOD HOUSEKEEPING and LADIES HOME JOURNAL, and, eventually, she sold two more children's books and one novel. When she died, I sold three books and some short pieces myself, then asked another agent to represent me on the basis of my credits.

Bibliography:

Category contemporary: (all as Rosalind Carson)
THIS DARK ENCHANTMENT, Harlequin Superromance, 1982.
SONG OF DESIRE, Harlequin Superromance, 1982.

Occult suspense:
THE OTHER CHILD, Pinnacle, 1979.

Romantic suspense:
FINDLAY'S LANDING ACE, Pinnacle, 1975.
SONG OF DARK WATER, Pinnacle, 1978.
HOUSE OF THE TWILIGHT MOON, Pinnacle, 1979.
THE FACE IN THE MIRROR, Pinnacle, 1980.

Non-romance:
WHEN THE WILD DUCKS COME, Follet, 1972.
MERRYMAKING IN GREAT BRITAIN, Garrard, 1974.
MYSTERY OF THE MISSING PONY, Garrard, 1980.

PATRICIA CLARK
Pseudonyms: Claire Lorrimer, Patricia Robbins, Susan Patrick. B. Patricia Denise Robins, 2/1/21, Hove, Sussex, England. *Children*: Iain, Nicola, Graeme. *Education*: University training in Munich. *Genres*: Gothic, historical romance, family saga. *Agent*: Desmond Elliot, 72 East 55th Street, New York, NY. *Current residence*: Edenbridge, Kent, England.

Favorite authors and books: Daphne du Maurier, Penelope Mortimer, Jeffrey Archer, and Frederick Forsyth.

Thoughts on writing: Primarily I think books should entertain and to some extent be thought provoking, as well as being an escape into another world. I try to place my characters in strongly emotional situations that they must solve in a totally believable manner. In my opinion, a good book is one that keeps the reader on tenterhooks from start to finish. And the kind of review that pleases me most is one that will include words like "unputdownable," "gripping,"and "more please."

Becoming published/finding an agent: I found my first literary agent from THE WRITERS AND ARTISTS YEARBOOK that I obtained from the library. My first novel was serialized in a woman's magazine with which I had earlier worked as an editor. Obviously aware of the type of light romantic fiction they required for publication, my first acceptance probably came more quickly for me than for other beginners. I continued writing light romances until 1970 when I changed my name and style.

Bibliography:

Family saga: (all as Claire Lorrimer).
THE CHATELAINE, Arlington, 1981. (New York publisher-Ballantine).
THE WILDERLING, Arlington, 1982.

Gothic: (all as Claire Lorrimer).
A VOICE IN THE DARK, Souvenir Press, 1967 (New York publishers—Bantam, Corgi).
RELENTLESS STORM, Arlington, 1979 (New York publishers-Bantam, Corgi).

Historical romance: (all as Claire Lorrimer)
MAVREEN, Arlington, 1976 (New York publishers—Bantam, Corgi).

TAMARISK, Arlington, 1978 (New York publishers—Bantam, Corgi). CHANTAL, Arlington, 1980 (New York publishers—Bantam, Corgi). Note: Patricia Clark has also published some sixty light romances, as well as many children's stories; neither category is still in print.

MARGARET ANN CLEAVES

Pseudonym: Ann Major. *B.* Margaret Ann Major, 2/13/46, Corpus Christi, Texas., married Ted Cleaves, 6/14/69. *Children*: David, Kim, Tad. *Education*: B.A., University of Texas, English and Spanish; M.A., University of Texas, English and Spanish. *Professional associations*: Romance Writers of America. Genres: Category contemporary, historical romance. *Agent*: Anita Diamant, N.Y., N.Y. *Current residence*: Corpus Christi, Texas.

Favorite authors and books: Catherine Gaskins, Victoria Holt, Nora Lofts, Margaret Mitchell, Kathleen Woodiwiss.

Thoughts on writing: I have always loved romance. I think people should read for enjoyment and part of enjoyment is escape and I write because I want to give pleasure to others who enjoy reading as much as I always have.

Becoming published/finding an agent: I sent my first manuscript over the transom to Dell and it was published by Vivian Stephens.

Bibliography:

Category contemporary: (All as Ann Major)
WILD LADY, Silhouette Romance, 1981.
TOUCH OF FIRE, Silhouette Romance, 1982.
DREAM COME TRUE, Silhouette Romance, 1982.

Historical romance:
MIDNIGHT SURRENDER, Dell, 1980.
Note: Margaret Ann Cleaves has two books under contract with Silhouette.

HELEN CONRAD

Pseudonyms: Jena Hunt, Raye Morgan. *B.* Helen Manak, 4/11/44, Pasadena, California, married Rae Conrad, 2/67. *Children*: Nicholas, Morgan, Jonathan, Kent. *Education*: B.A. California

State University at Los Angeles, English. *Professional associations*: Romance Writers of America. *Genres*: Category contemporary. *Current residence*: California.

Favorite authors and books: Contemporary: Jayne Castle, Marie Charles, Janet Dailey, Jane Donelley, Charlotte Lamb. Mysteries: Ross MacDonald, Dorothy Sayèr. Regencies: Georgette Heyer. Romantic suspense: Mary Stewart, Victoria Holt. Sagas: Anthony Trollope, John Galsworthy.

Thoughts on writing: I started writing to assuage my sense of guilt. Instead of "wasting" my time reading, I would write, thereby enjoying the same stories but hiding behind the excuse that I was actually "working"! I started out writing romantic suspense and historicals but quickly fell in love with category contemporaries. Now I can even claim to be working when I'm reading—research! It's a wonderful life.

Becoming published/finding an agent: I wandered in the unpublished wilderness for years before I found my wonderful agent, who—like a fairy godmother-waved her magic wand and made it all happen for me.

Bibliography:

Category contemporary:
> SWEET VICTORY, as Jena Hunt, Jove Second Chance, 1982.
> SWEETER THAN WINE, as Jena Hunt, Jove Second Chance, 1982.
> JADE TIDE, as Jena Hunt, Jove Second Chance, 1982.
> HOME FOR CHRISTMAS, Bantam, 1982.

Note: Helen Conrad currently has a book under contract with Sihouette's "Desire" line.

THERESA CONWAY

B. Theresa Ann Whitcomb, 6/8/51, St. Louis, MO., married Ron Conway, 1971. *Children*: Amy, Kate. *Education*: Memramec Junior College, St. Louis. *Genres*: Historical romance. *Agent*: Robert Gottleib, William Morris Agency, New York, NY. *Current residence*: St. Louis, MO.

Favorite authors and books: I generally enjoy Rosemary Rogers' historical romances. I also enjoy Patricia Phillips, the Angelique series by Sergeann Golon, and the Catherine series by Juliette Benzoni. Patricia Hagan is also enjoyable.

Thoughts on writing: The first book I ever read in the historical romance genre was THE FLAME AND THE FLOWER by Kathleen Woodiwiss. I did read GONE WITH THE WIND in eighth grade, and always wanted to write a book exactly like it. I do think that romance reading is escape from the sameness of being an "everyday housewife," but I also feel that I put a lot of good historical research into my books and people have told me they've learned a lot of history from my books. So maybe I can consider myself something of a teacher too.

Becoming published/finding an agent: I used to write the beginnings of books, but never finished one until I got married; my husband asked to see what would happen if I finally finished a story. My first manuscript, GABRIELLE, was taken by the third publisher I sent it to. After its publication, I decided to get an agent, and was helped in my decision by other writer friends who already had agents.

Bibliography:

Historical romance:
  GABRIELLE, Fawcett, 1977.
  CRIMSON GLORY, Fawcett, 1979.
  HONOR BOUND, Fawcett, 1980.
  PALOMA, Ballantine, 1981.
  WINE OF PARADISE, Fawcett, 1982.
Note: Theresa Conway has an historical romance under contract with Pocket's Tapestry line.

CATHERINE COOKSON
Pseudonym: Catherine Marchant *B*. Catherine Davies, 6/20/06, Tynedock, England, married Thomas Cookson, 6/1/40. *Education*: LIFE (see autobiography OUR KATE). *Awards*: Royal Society of Literature, Winifred Holoby Award for Best Regional Novel

of the Year (1968), THE ROUND TOWER. *Genres*: I am a novelist, not a romantic novelist in the accepted sense. *Agent*: Wallace, Sheil, New York. *Current residence*: Northumberland, England.

Favorite authors and books: I don't read the work of other fiction writers: I prefer biographies, autobiographies: My stand-bys are Lord Chesterfield's letters to his son; Laurens Van Der Post, and research (e.g. Fehrenback THE COMANCHES & LONE STAR).

Thoughts on writing: I see that which is termed romance as pure escapism and often very misleading in preparing the young to face life as it really is. I feel that the only romance in my books is the love between man and woman, which occurs in all levels of society. I am a realist, but I always endeavour to leave the readers with hope.

Becoming published/finding an agent: After an apprenticeship of twenty years learning my trade writing short stories and plays, I sent my first attempt at the novel (KATE HANNIGAN) to an agent, and it was accepted by the first publisher to whom it was sent.

Bibliography:
(As Catherine Cookson, published by MacDonald, starting in 1950):
> KATE HANNIGAN
> THE FIFTEEN STREETS
> COLOUR BLIND
> MAGGIE ROWAN
> ROONEY
> THE MENAGERIE
> SLINKY JANE
> FANNY McBRIDE
> FENWICK HOUSES
> THE GARMENT
> THE BLIND MILLER
> HANNAH MASSEY
> THE LONG CORRIDOR
> OUR KATE—autobiography
> THE UNBAITED TRAP
> DATIE MULHOLLAND

THE ROUND TOWER
THE NICE BLOKE
THE GLASS VIRGIN
THE INVITATION
THE DWELLING PLACE
FEATHERS IN THE FIRE
PURE AS THE LILY

(published by Heinemann):
THE MALLEN STREAK
THE MALLEN GIRL
THE MALLEN LITTER
THE INVISIBLE CORD
THE GAMBLING MAN
THE TIDE OF LIFE
THE GIRL
THE CINDER PATH
THE MAN WHO CRIED
TILLY

(The "Mary Ann" series, published by MacDonald):
A GRAND MAN
THE LORD AND MARY ANN
THE DEVIL AND MARY ANN
LOVE AND MARY ANN
LIFE AND MARY ANN
MARRIAGE AND MARY ANN
MARY ANN'S ANGELS
MARY ANN AND BILL

(As Catherine Marchant):
HERITAGE OF FOLLY
HOUSE OF MEN
THE FEN TIGER
MISS MARTHA MARY CRAWFORD
THE SLOW AWAKENING
THE IRON FACADE
Note: Several of Catherine Cookson's novels have been adapted into films, and she has written juvenile as well as adult novels.

BARBARA CORCORAN
B. Barbara Corcoran, Hamilton, Ma., 1911. *Education*: B.A. Wellesley College, 1933; M.A. University of Montana, 1955. *Professional associations*: Authors League, Society of Children's Book

Writers. *Genres*: Historical romance, children's books, young adult. *Agent*: Mitch Douglas, ICM, 40 West 57th St., N.Y., N.Y. 10019. *Current residence*: Missoula, Montana.

Favorite authors and books: Joan Aiken.

Thoughts on writing: Romances seem to fill a need in people's lives that the dangers and hardships of modern life exact.

Becoming published/finding and agent: It was so long ago, I don't remember.

Bibliography:

Historical romance (all from Ballantine):
ABIGAIL
ABBIE IN LOVE
A HUSBAND FOR GAIL
BELOVED ENEMY
CALL OF THE HEART
SONG FOR TWO VOICES
LOVE IS NOT ENOUGH
BY THE SILVERY MOON

*Young adul*t:
MAY I CROSS YOUR GOLDEN RIVER? as Paige Dixon, Atheneum and
    Scholastic, 1975.
ASK FOR LOVE AND YOU GET RICE PUDDING, Houghton Mifflin, 1977.
MAKING IT, Atlantic, Little, Brown, 1981.
CHILD OF THE MORNING, Atheneum, 1982.
Note: Barbara Corcoran has also published about thirty other children's and young adult books with Atheneum.

CHRISTINE HELLA COTT
B. Christine Hella Cott, 6/7/54, Winnipeg, Canada. *Genres*: Category contemporary. *Agent*: Anita Diamant, 21 East 42nd Street, New York, N.Y. *Current residence*: Vancouver, Canada.

Favorite authors and books: My taste in literature is eclectic, both in terms of period and style.

Thoughts on writing: Writing is an extension of myself; I do it because there is nothing I want to do more. It also allows me to delve into other professions, as well as allowing me freedom of space and time. I see romances as pure light-hearted and revitalizing entertainment.

Becoming published/finding an agent: I kept trying until someone took me on.

Bibliography:

Category contemporary:
MIDNIGHT MAGIC, Harlequin, July, 1982.
A TENDER WILDERNESS, Harlequin, September, 1982.
Note: Christine Cott has a new book which will be published under the Harlequin label.

TOM and SHARON CURTIS
Pseudonyms: Laura London, Robin James. *B*. Thomas Dale Curtis, 11/11/52, Antigo, Wis., Sharon Lee Blakslee, 3/6/51, Dahran, Saudi Arabia, married 11/70. *Children*: Lanny, Summer. *Education*: University of Wisconsin. *Genres*: Category contemporary, historical romance, regency. *Current residence*: Greendale, Wisconsin.

Favorite authors and books: We don't have any special favorites. There are so many we like, some of which are Mary Renault, Dorothy Dunnett, Saul Bellow, and Georgette Heyer.

Thoughts on writing: It is challenging and difficult to write well about falling in love. We feel a responsibility to be fresh and accurate in the depiction of subtle romantic emotions. Romance books have been tagged as escapism. We prefer to think of them as entertainment. Our readers face the real world all of the time, but like romances because of the positive orientation towards emotions that romances portray.

Becoming published/finding an agent: We don't know of any special trick for getting published. It seems to be a matter of submitting your manuscript to an editor who you hope will like it and keeping your fingers crossed. We are lucky to have a friend who reads our material before it's submitted. If she collapses with laughter during a serious part, we know we have some reworking to do.

Bibliography:

Category contemporary:
THE GOLDEN TOUCH, Robin James, Jove Second Chance At Love, 1982.

Regency: (all as Laura London) A HEART TOO PROUD, Dell, 1978.
THE BAD BARON'S DAUGHTER, Dell, 1978.
MOONLIGHT MIST, Dell, 1979.
LOVE'S A STAGE, Dell, 1980.
THE GYPSY HEIRESS, Dell, 1981.
Note: An historical romance, as yet untitled, is to be published by Dell in early 1984 under the Laura London pseudonym.

JANET DAILEY
B. Janet Ann Haradon, 5/21/44, Storm Lake, Iowa, married William A. Dailey. *Children*: Linda, Jimmy. *Professional associations*: Romance Writers of America, Western Writers of America, National Writers Club. *Awards*: Special Golden Heart Award from the Romance Writers of America for contribution to romantic fiction. *Genres*: Category contemporary, contemporary, family saga. *Agent*: William Dailey, Branson, Mo. *Current residence*: Branson, Mo.

Favorite authors and books: Charlotte Lamb, Anne Mather, and Kathleen Woodiwiss, especially her novel, THE WOLF AND THE DOVE.

Thoughts on writing: I have always regarded romance literature as a form of entertainment, both as a reader and a writer. Please note I use the term, romance literature, because I believe there is a place for it in the fictional classsics in the years to come—just as Agatha Christie and John D. MacDonald are regarded as classic detective writers. I've always considered myself to be a story-teller because—for me—the story always comes first. I worry about it and pay little attention to whether it will be a category contemporary, family saga, or other genre. If I have a philosphy of writing, it's to tell the story you want to tell, and forget the money. If the story is good, everything else will follow in its place.

Becoming published/finding an agent: In response to a challenge from my husband to stop talking about writing a book and do it or shut up, I completed my first manuscript and presented it to him. As I recall, he didn't congratulate me. He merely asked what I intended to do with it now? While I stood there with my mouth open trying to think of something to say, he looked up Harlequin's address. Thus a writing partnership was born—me on the creative side, and Bill on the business end.

Bibliography:

Category contemporary:
NO QUARTER ASKED Harlequin, January, 1976.
BOSS MAN FROM OGALLA, Harlequin, March, 1976.
SAVAGE LAND, Harlequin, May, 1976.
FIRE AND ICE, Harlequin, July, 1976.
LAND OF ENCHANTMENT, Harlequin, August, 1976.
THE HOMEPLACE, Harlequin, October, 1976.
AFTER THE STORM, Harlequin, December, 1976.
DANGEROUS MASQUERADE, Harlequin, January, 1977.
NIGHT OF THE COTILLION, Harlequin, March, 1977.
VALLEY OF THE VAPOURS, Harlequin, April, 1977.
FIESTA SAN ANTONIO, Harlequin, June, 1977.
SHOW ME, Harlequin, August, 1977.
BLUE GRASS KING, Harlequin, September, 1977.
A LYON'S SHARE, Harlequin, October, 1977.
THE WIDOW AND THE WASTREL, Harlequin, November, 1977.
THE IVORY CANE, Harlequin, January, 1978.
THE INDY MAN, Harlequin, February, 1978.
DARLING JENNY, Harlequin, March, 1978.
REILLY'S WOMAN, Harlequin, April, 1978.
TO TELL THE TRUTH, Harlequin, May, 1978.
SONORA SUNDOWN, Harlequin, June, 1978.
BIG SKY COUNTRY, Harlequin, July, 1978.
SOMETHING EXTRA, Harlequin, August, 1978
MASTER FIDDLER, Harlequin, September, 1978.
BEWARE OF THE STRANGER, Harlequin, October, 1978
GIANT OF MESABI, Harlequin, November, 1978.
THE MATCHMAKERS, Harlequin, December, 1978.
FOR BITTER OR WORSE, Harlequin, January, 1979.

GREEN MOUNTAIN MAN, Harlequin, February, 1979.
SIX WHITE HORSES, Harlequin, March, 1979.
SUMMER MAHOGANY, Harlequin, April, 1979.
THE BRIDE OF THE DELTA QUEEN, Harlequin, May, 1979.
TIDEWATER LOVER, Harlequin, June, 1979.
STRANGE BEDFELLOW, Harlequin, July, 1979.
LOW COUNTRY LIAR, Harlequin, August, 1979.
SWEET PROMISE, Harlequin, September, 1979.
FOR MIKE'S SAKE, Harlequin, October, 1979.
SENTIMENTAL JOURNEY, Harlequin, November, 1979.
A LAND CALLED DESERET, Harlequin, December, 1979.
KONA WINDS, Harlequin, January, 1980.
THAT BOSTON MAN, Harlequin, February, 1980.
BED OF GRASS, Harlequin, March, 1980.
THE THAWING OF MARA, Harlequin, April, 1980.
THE MATING SEASON, Harlequin, May, 1980.
LORD OF THE HIGH LONESOME, Harlequin, June, 1980.
SOUTHERN LIGHTS, Harlequin, July, 1980.
ENEMY IN CAMP, Harlequin, August, 1980.
DIFFICULT DECISION, Harlequin, September, 1980.
HEART OF STONE, Harlequin, October, 1980.
ONE OF THE BOYS, Harlequin, November, 1980.
WILD AND WONDERFUL, Harlequin, December, 1980.
A TRADITION OF PRIDE, Harlequin, April, 1981.
THE TRAVELLING KIND, Harlequin, May, 1981.
THE HOSTAGE BRIDE, Silhouette, May, 1981.
DAKOTA DREAMIN', Harlequin, June, 1981.
LANCASTER MEN, Silhouette, October, 1981.
FOR THE LOVE OF GOD, Silhouette, December, 1981.
NORTHERN MAGIC, Harlequin, January, 1982.
WITH A LITTLE LUCK, Harlequin, February, 1982.
A WILDCATTER'S WOMAN, Silhouette, May, 1982.
THE SECOND TIME, Silhouette, September, 1982.
MISTLETOE AND HOLLY, Silhouette, December, 1982.
THAT CAROLINA SUMMER, Harlequin, 1982.
FOXFIRE, Silhouette Special Edition, 1982.
TERMS OF SURRENDER, Silhouette Special Edition, 1982.

Contemporary:
TOUCH THE WIND, Pocket Books, May, 1979.
NIGHT WAY, Pocket Books, January, 1981.

Family saga:
THIS CALDER SKY, Pocket Books, August, 1981.
THIS CALDER RANGE, Pocket Books, March, 1982.
STANDS A CALDER MAN, Pocket Books, January, 1983.
CALDER BORN, CALDER BRED, Pocket Books, 1983.

MARGARET DALEY

Pseudonyms: Margaret Ripy, Patti Moore, Kathleen Daley. *B.* Margaret Kathleen Ripy, 4/27/70, Nashville, Tn., married Mike Daley, 8/70. *Children*: Shaun. *Education*: University of Tulsa, special education. *Professional associations*: Romance Writers of America, Oklahoma Federation of Writers, Northeastern Oklahoma Romance Authors. *Genre*: Category contemporary. *Agent*: Carol Masius, Writers and Artists Agency, 162 West 56th, N.Y., N.Y. *Current residence*: Tulsa, Oklahoma.

Favorite authors and books: Janet Dailey, Brooke Hastings, Stephanie James, Fern Michaels, Bertrice Small, Kathleen Woodiwiss.

Thoughts on writing: Writing is so much a part of my life it's hard to imagine living without it. I write every day and think that succeeding as a writer is a lot of determination and a willingness to listen to criticism. But not only am I a writer but a reader as well; I read romances for years before I sat down five years ago to write my first book.

Becoming published/finding an editor: An editor recommended me to Carol Masius and she took me on in the spring of 1980. In the summer of 1980 I sold my first romance to Silhouette.

Bibliography:

Category contemporary:
A SECOND CHANCE ON LOVE, Margaret Ripy, Silhouette, 1981.
A GIFT OF ORCHIDS, Patti Moore, Jove Second Chance, 1982.
THE FLAMING TREE, Margaret Ripy, Silhouette, 1982.
A TREASURE OF LOVE, Margaret Ripy, Silhouette, 1982.
PROMISED PORTRAIT, Kathleen Daley, Wallaby Serenade, 1982.
TOMORROW'S MEMORY, as Margaret Ripy, Silhouette, 1983.
Note: A MATTER OF PRIDE and RAINY DAY DREAMS have been sold to Silhouette Special Edition under the pseudonym, Margaret Ripy.

MONS DAVESON

B. Mons Violet Henson, Rochester, England, married Leonard Joseph. *Children:* Patricia, Rodney, Adrian, Stacey. *Genres:* Contemporary. *Current residence:* Brisbane, Australia.

Favorite authors and books: Georgette Heyer. Most of the conservative Mills and Boon output. Frances Parkinson Keyes' IF EVER I CEASE TO LOVE. M.M. Kaye's SHADOW OF THE MOON.

Thoughts on writing: I was a fan for years. I believe romance is a kind of escapism, but no more than the male-oriented sex novels of Harold Robbins and Richard Condon. It is nice after the affairs of the day and the alarm of the newspaper headlines to lose oneself in a grand love story.

Becoming published/finding an agent: I sent a manuscript to Mills and Boon in London and had it returned. Later, after revision, they accepted it. I find Mills and Boon a wonderful firm to work with.

Bibliography:
  THE HOUSE IN THE FOOTHILLS, Mills and Boon, 1970.
  THIS TOO I'LL REMEMBER, Mills and Boon, 1970.
  LAND OF TOMORROW, Mills and Boon, 1980.
  SUGAR COUNTRY, Mills and Boon, 1981.
  MY LORD KARRUM, Mills and Boon, 1982.

CELESTE N. DE BLASIS
B. Celeste N. De Blasis, 5/8/46, California. *Education:* B.A. Pomona College, English literature. *Professional associations:* The Author's Guild. *Genres:* historical romance, gothic, mystery. *Agent:* Jane Rotrosen, Jane Rotrosen Agency, 318 East 51 St., N.Y., N.Y. *Current Residence:* Victorville, Ca.

Favorite authors and books: Jude Deveraux, Rebecca Brandewyne (FOREVER MY LOVE), Roberta Gellis, Anya Seton.

Thoughts on writing: My goal is to be a good storyteller, to entertain. Outside category judgements don't concern me. My task is to create worlds peopled by vivid, believable characters and to make the historical setting as accurate as possible. And the final requirement is that I write the story in my own prose style.

Becoming published/finding an agent: I wrote verse for most of my teenage years and in my early twenties several of the poems were published. But when my brother was stricken by cancer at the age of twenty-three, my poetry became so dark and death obsessed, I sought an escape, a more controlled world. I discovered that the poetry had been a training ground for prose, and through my first prose efforts—a short story and a mystery—I obtained an agent. A friend in the film industry read what I had written and took the pages to a well-known coast agent. I never met that agent, but I am still thankful to him. He was heading for Europe and was taking no new clients, but he was impressed enough by my writing to give me an introduction to a respected New York agent, Kurt Helmer. Mr. Helmer's assistant, Jane Rotrosen, was the person in the agency who handled my work, so when she formed her own agency, I went with her. My brother died in 1973, when he was twenty-five. THE NIGHT CHILD was finished a week before he died. When I told him the manuscript was complete, he said, "Oh, no, you'll see, it's not a manuscript, it's a book."

Bibliography:

Gothic:
> THE NIGHT CHILD, Coward, McCann and Geoghegan, 1975 (Softcover, Fawcett Crest, 1976).

Historical:
> THE PROUD BREED, Coward, McCann and Geoghegan, 1978 (Softcover, Fawcett Crest, 1979).
> THE TIGER'S WOMAN, Delacorte, 1981 (Softcover, Dell, 1982. Doubleday Book Club main selection, Literary Guild alternate, foreign editions).

Mystery:
> SUFFER A SEA CHANGE, Coward, McCann and Geoghegan, 1976 (Softcover, Fawcett Crest, 1978, foreign editions.)

EDITH G. DELATUSH
Pseudonyms: Edith St. George, Edith dePaul, Alyssa Morgan
B. Edith Grieshammer, 11/21/21, New York City, married George A. Delatush 5/2/43. *Children:* George, Jr., Paul. *Education:* Long Island College School of Nursing, Registered Nurse, 1942.

Professional associations: Romance Writers of America, regional coordinator for Romance Writers of America (Southern Florida). *Genres:* Regency, Category contemporary, Historical romance, contemporary. *Agent:* Robin Kaigh, Mary Yost Associates, 59 E. 54th Street, Suite 52, N.Y., N.Y. 10022. *Current residence:* Tequesta, Florida.

Favorite authors and books: I enjoy individual books by varied authors. In my opinion, the most consistently good ones are produced by Jayne Castle, Elaine Chase and Anne Reisser.

Thoughts on writing: I've always enjoyed relaxing with a romance novel and resent having it thought as a means of escape any more than any other type book. Isn't that why we read—to enter even momentarily, into another world other than our own? My husband is a physician who's very reluctant to prescribe tranquilizers. I consider reading an excellent substitute. And what better one do we have than the romance where one knows the hero and heroine eventually end "happy ever after"? There's hope for us all!

Becoming published/finding an agent: I found my first agent through the National Writers Club which, I think, is an excellent organization especially for the beginner who's floundering around without any signposts for guidance. After receiving two rejects on my first novel, I sent it to an agent. It was bought by Dell Candlelight for their now extinct intrigue label, and she sold my next eight books as fast as I could produce them. Unfortunately she had to retire, and she recommended my present agent who sold the first one I sent her.

Bibliography:

Category contemporaries:
    BECKONING HEART, Alyssa Morgan, Dell Candlelight, 1981.
    WEST OF THE MOON, Edith St. George, Silhouette, 1981.
    MIDNIGHT WINE, Edith St. George, Silhouette, 1981.
    DREAM ONCE MORE, Edith St. George, Silhouette, 1982.
    WHITE WATER LOVE, Alyssa Morgan, Candlelight Ecstasy, 1982.
    THE VISCOUNT'S WITCH, as Edith dePaul, Candlelight, 1982.
Note: In Edith Delatush's own words, she has some "Biggies awaiting their fate."

BARBARA DELINKSY
Pseudonyms: Bonnie Drake, Billie Douglass. *B.* Barbara Ruth Greenberg, 8/9/45, Boston, MA., married Stephen R. Delinsky, 1967. *Children:* Eric, Andrew, Jeremy. *Education:* B.A. Tufts University, psychology; M.A. Boston College, sociology. *Professional associations:* National League of American Pen Women, Romance Writers of America. *Genres:* Category contemporary. *Agent:* Steven J. Axelrod, Sterling Lord Agency, 660 Madison Avenue, New York, NY. *Current residence:* Needham, MA.

Favorite authors and books: Danielle Steel has to be my favorite author. Any one of her books is well worth my time for a second, third, or even fourth reading.

Thoughts on writing: I am an incurable romantic, and have always enjoyed a good love story. To be able to write one—and to be considered and recognized as an author of one—has been a thrill. Each of my books contains grand doses of my heart and my mind. If I can please others in the process, the circle is complete. The creation of real and romantic characters is a joy, the telling of their story a privilege. And no one can tarnish the pride I feel in my work and in the romance field as a whole.

Becoming published/finding an agent: After reading an article about writers of romance, I set out to research category work, then wrote my own romance. The first book was bought six weeks after its completion. I sold my first seven books on my own before realizing that this was a full-time job which very definitely had a future. At that point I acquired an agent, one whom I'd met at a conference several months before. I've never regretted the decision.

Bibliography:

Category contemporaries:
THE PASSIONATE TOUCH, Bonnie Drake, Dell Ecstasy, 1/81.
SURRENDER BY MOONLIGHT, Bonnie Drake, Dell Ecstasy, 4/81.
SWEET EMBER, Bonnie Drake, Dell Ecstasy, 7/81.
SENSUOUS BURGUNDY, Bonnie Drake, Dell Ecstasy, 12/81.
SEARCH FOR A NEW DAWN, Billie Douglass, Silhouette Special Edition, 2/82.
THE ARDENT PROTECTOR, Bonnie Drake, Dell Ecstasy, 3/82.

WHISPERED PROMISE, Bonnie Drake, Dell Ecstasy, 7/82.
A TIME TO LOVE, Billie Douglass, Silhouette Special Edition, 7/82
LILAC AWAKENING, Bonnie Drake, Dell Ecstasy, 10/82.
KNIGHTLY LOVE, Billie Douglass, Silhouette Special Edition, 11/82.
AMBER ENCHANTMENT, Bonnie Drake, Dell Ecstasy, 12/82.
Note: Barbara Delinsky has four books currently under contract to Silhouette, as well as two books under contract to Dell Ecstasy.

GENELL SMITH DELLIN
Pseudonyms: Gena Dalton. B. Billie Genell Smith, 12/13/40, Poteau, Oklahoma, married Arthur David Dellin, 6/27/76. *Children:* David Michael Dellin. *Education:* B.A. Baylor University, 1961, Education and French; M.A., Oklahoma State University, 1969, English. *Professional associations:* Tulsa Tuesday Writers, Oklahoma Writers Federation. *Awards:* IN MY SISTER'S SHADOW, was a B. Dalton bestseller. *Genres:* Young adult, Category contemporary. *Agent:* Merrilee Heffetz, Writers House, 21 West 26 Street, New York 10010. *Current residence:* Tulsa, Oklahoma.

Favorite authors and books: I read GONE WITH THE WIND five times during my junior year in high school (I'd just discovered it). It is still my favorite. I also enjoyed Danielle Steel's ONCE IN A LIFETIME.

Thoughts on writing: I see these books as pure escapism and feel that that is just as legitimate a purpose for writing as any other. It pleases me tremendously when someone tells me she stayed up late to finish my book or that she got so involved that she wants a sequel. Everyone needs to forget reality sometimes!

Becoming published/finding an agent: I joined a local writers group, and one of the members suggested that I send a manuscript to her agent. That agent was too busy to take on new clients, but she gave my work to a colleague who suggested I write romances.

Bibliography:

Young adult romance:
IN MY SISTER'S SHADOW, Genell Dellin. Silhouette - First Love, 1982;

young adult. (B. Dalton Juvenile bestseller list.)
Note: Genell Smith Dellin currently has two books under contract with
Silhouette.

JOAN DIAL
Pseudonyms: Amanda York, Katherine Kent. B. Joan Mavis
Rogers, Liverpool, England, married Paul E. Dial. Children:
Craig, Gary, and Sharon. Professional associations: Romance Writers of America, Mystery Writers of America. Genres: Historical
romances, Contemporary romances, family saga, romantic suspense, mainstream love stories. Agent: Clair M. Smith, Harold
Ober Associates, Inc., 40 E. 49th Street, N.Y., N.Y. 10017. Current residence: Lake Elsinore, California.

Favorite authors and books: Susan Howatch (PENMARRIC,
CASHELMARA, SINS OF FATHERS, etc., I have read everything she has written.) Also Victoria Holt, Daphne du Maurier,
the Brontë sisters—and too many current favorites to list. I read
at least two novels a week. (In addition to the nonfiction books I
read for my research).

Thoughts on writing: A reader recently paid me a compliment and
at the same time summed up my philosophy . . . she told me she
had just finished reading my ROSES IN WINTER (Pocket Books,
Joan Dial, September 1982) and that— "It isn't just a romance—
it's a love story." That's what I aim for . . . .
I've been writing since I was seven years old—reading even
longer than that.
A writer's only function is to entertain—if you want to call it
escapism, I don't see anything derogatory about that.

Becoming published/finding an agent: I sent a proposal (letter, three
chapters and outline) to Fawcett Gold Medal—they responded
that if I'd do some rewriting, they'd buy. The result was
SUSANNA (1978, Joan Dial). Before I signed the contract with
them, I was approached by a New York agent who wished to represent me. I gladly agreed. (I stayed with that agent until he de-
fected to the other side—he's now a publisher!) I should add that
prior to the Fawcett sale I had been unsuccessful in getting publishers to read the complete scripts I was sending out.

Bibliography:

Contemporary:
DEADLY LADY, Joan Dial. Fawcett Gold Medal, 1980.
DREAMTIDE, Katherine Kent. Gallen/Pocket, 1981.
MIDNIGHT TANGO, Katherine Kent. Gallen/Pocket, 1982.

Epic romance:
ROSES IN WINTER, Joan Dial. Pocket Books, 1982.

Family saga:
SOMEWHERE IN THE WHIRLWIND, Amanda York. Pocket Books, 1980.

Historical romance:
SUSANNA, Joan Dial. Fawcett Gold Medal, 1978.
LOVERS AND WARRIORS, Joan Dial. Fawcett Gold Medal, 1978.
BELOVED ENEMY, Amanda York. Pocket Books, 1978.
WATERS OF EDEN, Katherine Kent. Gallen/Pocket, 1981.

Romantic suspense:
DRUID'S RETREAT, Katherine Kent. Pinnacle, 1979.
Note: Joan Dial is currently under contract with Pocket Books.

CLAIRE DELONG
Pseudonyms: Claire Evans, Eva Claire. *B.* Claire Ann Evans 11/12/33 Endicott, N.Y., married Charles Wilfred DeLong 4/71. *Professional associations:* National Writers Club, Romance Writers of America. *Genre:* category contemporary. *Agent:* Eileen Fallon, Barbara Lowenstein Assoc., 250 W. 57th, N.Y., N.Y. *Current residence:* Marietta, Ohio.

Favorite authors and books: Lilian Peake was the first romance author to really capture my attention. Then Anne Mather, Sara Craven and Charlotte Lamb became my idols. My all time favorite though is Charlotte Brontë. (Ever read the books she wrote in addition to JANE EYRE?) And in the newer authors, I lean toward Carole Halston, Amii Lorin and Jayne Castle.

Thoughts on writing: Writing to me is a means of 1) expressing myself and hopefully enriching someone else's life, 2) living out my own fantasies, and 3) fulfilling a lifelong ambition to do "something constructive." In short, it is a compulsion with me, something that drives me insane and gives me great pleasure at the same time. I am a compulsive reader and only got into romance reading within the last three years. Having made numerous attempts at writing in the distant past, romances seemed to open a world of expression to me and I tried my hand—with success. I hope to continue in this venture for years to come. Romance, after all, is an all-encompassing term that includes so many facets. Like a diamond, it can be see in many lights and reveal something new and exciting each time.

Bibliography:

Category contemporary:
LED INTO THE SUNLIGHT, Claire Evans, Jove Second Chance at Love, January, 1982.
APOLLO'S DREAM, Claire Evans, Jove Second Chance at Love, August, 1982.
Note: Claire Evans has a third book contracted with Second Chance at Love, as well as one contracted with Silhouette Special Edition.

CAROLE NELSON DOUGLAS
B. Carole Frances Nelson, 11/5/44, Everett, Wa., married Sam Scott Douglas, 11/25/67. *Education:* B.A. 1966, The College of St. Catherine, Speech and Theatre. *Professional associations*: The Authors Guild, The Newspaper Guild, Romance Writers of America. *Awards*: Silver Medal for FAIR WIND, FIERY STAR in the WEST COAST REVIEW OF BOOKS' Sixth Annual Porgie Awards (given for paperback originals). *Genres*: Gothic, historical romance, fantasy, category contemporary (although all my books are out-of-category in that they don't follow formula). *Agent*: Frances Schwartz, Frances Schwartz Literary Agency, 60 East 42nd St., N.Y., N.Y. 10017. *Current residence*: St. Paul, Minn.

Favorite books and authors: My favorite authors are all "golden oldies"—Daphne du Maurier, Georgette Heyer and the first female "romancers," such as Jane Austen, the sisters Brontë and their literary kin. Also love the swashbuckling writers, Alexandre Dumas and Rafael Sabatini; mystery mistresses Dorothy Sayers and Josephine Tey; horror master H.P.

Lovecraft, fantasists such as Lord Dunsany. But my favorite, living, breathing writer of current romance is John Fowles.

Thoughts on writing: I'm a writer, not a romance writer—nor an adventure or fantasy writer, though my books usually contain one, more or all of these elements. I take writing for today's women's audience very seriously, whether my heroines wear period dress or contemporary clothes. While one of my books' principal goals is entertainment, the best entertainment always has principles. Romance, or any theme, is most effective within the most skillful literary context being enacted by flesh, bone and blood characters, so it's my constant aim to immerse readers in the worlds I've created—whether historical, contemporary realistic or utterly imaginary.

Becoming published/finding an agent: I sent AMBERLEIGH out unsolicited in late 1976, quickly finding it was returned, not only rejected, but apparently unread, partly because it had Gothic elements, then the kiss of death to a manuscript. But in early 1977, Garson Kanin, a most satisfied subject of an interview and article I'd done with him five years before in my job as a newspaper reporter, came back to St. Paul and I was assigned him again. His enthusiasm for that long-ago article resulted in his offering to take AMBERLEIGH back to his New York publisher personally. I simultaneously got an agent for my next, more marketable historical, FAIR WIND, FIERY STAR. Both books were published by Putnam's paperback arm, Berkley, which later merged with another paperback house acquired by MCA/Universal, the corporate parent of both Putnam's and Berkley. After some delay, my books came out from Jove. A whim to try a fantasy novel proved prescient, as the historical market ebbed. I sold my fantasy, and a sequel to Del Rey, and now write non-formula women's fiction for Ballantine's Love & Life list.

My advice to beginning writers is to study the publishing industry assiduously, and to believe in themselves and their writing no matter what happens—rejections, setbacks, insensitive reviews, editors or even readers. The few negatives are eventually washed away by the joy of making contact with the appreciative professionals and the vast reading public.

Bibliography:

Gothic:
AMBERLEIGH, Jove 1980.

Historical romance:
FAIR WIND, FIERY STAR, Jove, 1981.—Silver Medal, 6th annual Porgie Awards.

Category contemporary:
IN HER PRIME, Ballantine's Love & Life, Sept. 1982.
HER OWN PERSON, Ballantine's Love & Life, Dec. 1982.

Other:
SIX OF SWORDS, Fantasy, Del Ray, 1982.
Note: Carole Nelson Douglas has another book under contract with the Love & Life series, as well as an historical, also with Ballantine (to have a Tom Hall cover!)

RITA CLAY ESTRADA
Pseudonyms: Rita Clay, Tira Lacy. *B.* Rita Clay, 7/31/41, Mt. Clemons, Michigan, married James R. Estrada, 8/22/59. *Children:* Rebecca, Rita, Marissa, Clay. *Education:* Two years at San Antonio College. *Professional associations:* Texas Press Women; Romance Writers of America, President 1980-1982. *Genres:* Category contemporary. *Agent:* John Payne, Lenniger Literary Agency, 104 East 40th Street, N.Y., N.Y. 10016. *Current residence:* Houston, Tx.

Favorite authors and books: Dorothy Dunnett, Roberta Gellis, Parris Afton Bonds, Anne Mather, O. Henry, Dean Koontz.

Thoughts on writing: To me it is more difficult to write the smaller, category books because you must tell a very intense story in a very set amount of words. The characters must be full blown, the happenings real, the plot tight and the entire book has to be well written. If it doesn't have these ingredients then the book will never be sold, for the competition is stiff and there's always a better writer growing up just behind you. It's the competition that makes sure the quality remains high.

These books don't need an excuse to be. There is no difference between a woman reading a romance and a man reading a western. The equivalent of a woman reading a historical ro-mance of 350 pages is the same as a man reading a World War II spy thriller.

As for the happy endings: A good mystery isn't good unless you find out who-done-it at the end of the book. A good sci-fi has to have good conquering evil. A romance needs a happy, re-solved ending.

As long as I read others who write well, I'm entertained. I would also be entertained if I watched television or went to the movies. I'm not sure I would call it escapism . . . just good enter-tainment. I've never imagined that I'm the character and put my-self in his or her place. It's more as if I were the character's friend and watching the by-play in her life. I can enjoy her clothing and the places she goes and the things she does, but I don't confuse my own self with her.

Becoming published/finding an agent: I began a book, read an ad in the paper for a writers' conference, and attended. There I met Kit O'Brian Jones, Parris Afton Bonds, and Carolyn Westregren. They supported my efforts and spurred me on to finish. By the time that ms. was rejected I was well into a second one. By the time the second was rejected I was deeply into the third one. The third one sold to Silhouette. Last year the second one sold and became the #3 book in the Desire line. The first one wasn't a wasted effort, though. It taught me how to put a book together and got enough comments from editors that I knew what not to try to do.

Three months after I sold my first book an agent called. He had heard of me through a mutual friend. He was looking for someone to do a series, would I like to try it? YES! I tried, but I didn't make the grade. However, he's been my agent through the past seven books.

Bibliography:

Category contemporaries: (as Rita Clay)
WANDERER'S DREAM, Silhouette, June 1981.
SWEET ETERNITY, Silhouette, Oct. 1982.
WISE FOLLY, Silhouette Desire, June 1982.
YESTERDAY'S DREAM, Silhouette Desire, Dec. 1982.
Note: Rita Estrada currently has three more books under contract to Sil-

houette Desire, and one under contract to Candlelight Ecstasy, as Tira Lacy.

ROSE MARIE FERRIS
Pseudonyms: Valerie Ferris, Michelle Roland. *B.* Rose Marie Ogden, 1/12/38, Ashland, Oregon, married Charles E. Ferris, 7/29/56; widowed. *Children:* Steve, Bill, David. *Education:* B.A. California State University, Humboldt, English. *Professional associations:* Romance Writers of America. *Genre:* category contemporary. *Agent:* Ellen Levine, 370 Lexington Ave., N.Y., N.Y. *Current residence:* Madison, Wi.

Favorite authors and books: My favorite authors are Anya Seton, Janet Louise Roberts/Janette Radcliffe, Kathleen Woodiwiss, and LaVyrle Spencer. My favorite romance novels are THE FLAME AND THE FLOWER, MOONRAKER'S BRIDE, and ISLAND OF DESIRE.

Thoughts on writing romance: I agree with the view that the current popularity of romance novels reflects a fundamental need for romance. Certainly, aside from novels, romance is a commodity which is in short supply today. In real life, as in movies and on television, a man and woman meet and go to bed with each other so quickly that there is precious little time for romance.

Category romances are escapist, and the kind of escape they offer can be a wonderful and healthy thing. At the same time, however, romances concern themselves with some pretty basic stuff. Nowadays, it's easy for people to feel dehumanized. They are reduced to numbers on a punch card, to zip codes, area codes, etc. The divorce rate is staggering, families are scattered, people are alienated from the government, from each other, sometimes even from themselves.

Because the romance novel explores the development of a highly personal relationship between the hero and the heroine, I think they make the reader feel less isolated. And not just for a few hours but in the "afterglow" of the experience. That is what I hope to achieve with my books.

Although I read hundreds (probably thousands) of romances before I started writing in the fall of 1979, the discipline of writing romance, particularly category romance, has not been an easy one for me to learn. My first two books were strictly learning experiences, and while I've completed a total of nine romances since I began, I still haven't mastered the genre.

For me, writing is its own reward. Knowing that others might be entertained by what I've written is the frosting on the cake. If I ever reach the point where I don't feel this way, if I'm not approaching my work with freshness and enthusiasm and honesty, I hope I will have the good sense to recognize it and the grace to go on to something else.

Becoming published/finding an agent: As I mentioned, the first book I had published was actually the third book I'd written. In September of 1980, I submitted the ms. of THE HEART'S AWAKENING to Dell, not knowing that they were planning the Candlelight Ecstasy series. Three weeks to the day after I mailed the ms., Vivian Stephens telephoned to say that she wanted to buy my book. Besides being one of the happiest moments of my life, this experience taught me the importance of a cover letter. Since I didn't know the name of any editors at Dell, the ms. had been addressed to "The Editors." Vivian Stephens told me that my cover letter had come across her desk; she thought the story sounded original and interesting, so she had taken the ms. home and read it that night. I'm sure the ms. would have been read just as carefully if my letter hadn't impressed her but it did help speed things along.

After THE HEART'S AWAKENING was released, Ellen Levine wrote me a letter. By then I had sold two more mss. to Dell Ecstasy, and I realized negotiating contracts was not my strong suit. After corresponding with Ellen and talking on the phone with her, I was impressed by her manner. The advantages of working through an agent were clear, and I agreed to her offer to represent me. I appreciate having someone who is "in the know" advise me and offer guidance.

My advice to aspiring writers is simply to write and to persevere. It also helps to develop a thick skin, at least so far as rejection slips are concerned. A personal letter (as opposed to a form letter) of rejection is a triumph, and a writer should become adept at looking for rays of hope between the lines in such letters. If the message they contain is basically an encouraging one, and if they offer constructive criticism, you are another step ahead.

For the purposes of learning to define and correct problems for a ms., I would recommend studying THE WRITER'S HAND-BOOK (Burack), and THE ELEMENTS OF STYLE (Strunk and White). THE WRITER and WRITER'S DIGEST also offer much useful information on such matters as technique.

Bibliography:

Category contemporary:
    THE HEART'S AWAKENING, as Valerie Ferris, Dell Ecstasy, 1981.
    PROMISES TO KEEP, as Rose Marie Ferris, Dell Ecstasy, 1981.
    AFTER THE FIRE, as Rose Marie Ferris, Dell Ecstasy, 1982.
    VENUS RISING, as Michelle Roland, Jove Second Chance at Love, 1982.
    A WILD AND TENDER MAGIC, as Rose Marie Ferris, Dell Ecstasy, 1982.

SHERYL HINES FLOURNOY
Pseudonyms: Sheryl Dee, Diane Sheryl. *B.* Sheryl Diane Hines, 11/12/51, Mishawaka, IN., married Keith Flournoy, 1970. *Children:* Sharlette. *Professional associations:* Romance Writers of America *Genres*: Category contemporary. *Agent:* Denise Marcil, 316 W. 82nd Street, New York, NY. *Current residence:* Converse, TX.

Favorite authors and books: My introduction to romance reading was when I came across Patricia Gallagher's book, CASTLES IN THE AIR. She has since become my favorite author, along with Shirlee Busbee and Laurie McBain. Although there are many new authors who are very good, my favorite authors of category contemporary are Amii Lorin, Jayne Castle, Ann Hampson, Dixie Browning, and Brooke Hastings. Favorite male authors include Tabor Evans, Ronald Joseph, and Howard Fast. My favorite non-fiction author is John G. Fuller.

Thoughts on writing: I want all my stories to have merit and to be written with depth, therefore, it is extremely difficult to limit them to a short base or to shallowness. It is very important that I portray my hero and heroine with strong emotions and deep passions. It is equally important that they express profound thinking. To confine my writing to one thing is difficult as I wish to explore every corner of the minds of my characters from their tritest thought to their deepest emotion. They are real to me, and I want them to live, not only for me and my story, but for the reader as well. The writing market is ripe for new ideas. I believe that readers want a happy ending and an everlasting love.

Becoming published/finding an agent: I met Denise Marcil through another agent, Richard Hutner. We met at the first Romance Writers of America conference in Houston, where I also met the Silhouette editor, Karen Solem, who took my manuscript of MAKE NO PROMISES. Denise called a few weeks later to say Karen bought the manuscript. To become published requires long hours, hard work, a belief in yourself, and trust in your agent. I've only been writing for two years, but I've learned much—although I have much more to learn. The old saying, "You have to crawl before you can walk" is very true; all new writers should remember this.

Bibliography:

Category contemporary:
MAKE NO PROMISES, as Sherry Dee, Silhouette, 1982.
Note: Sheryl Flournoy has a book currently under contract with Silhouette, as well as a book under contract with Pocket Books.

RITA GALLAGHER
B. Rita Gallagher, Detroit, Mich. *Children:* Rita Clay Estrada, Jefferey S. Abrams, Gregory Abrams. *Education:* University of Michigan. *Professional associations:* Romance Writers of America, Texas Presswomen. *Awards:* Golden Pen Award, University of Michigan. *Genre:* historical romance. *Agent:* Al Zuckerman, Writer's House, 21 W. 26th St., N.Y., N.Y. 10010. *Current residence:* Houston, Tx.

Favorite authors and books: Patricia Gallagher, Patricia Matthews, Anya Seton, Kathleen Woodiwiss.

Thoughts on writing: I believe there is something to be learned from all reading and writing. Romance books have become synonymous with the category books now on the market such as Harlequin and Silhouette. But when I was growing up, I read romance books such as FOREVER AMBER, FRENCHMEN'S CREEK, ANTHONY ADVERSE, and THE SUN IS MY UNDOING. I learned much about life (and loving) as well as history from these well-researched books. I believe a good book is one that offers escape as well as one that educates.

Becoming published/finding an agent: I have been writing for thirty-five years and have published short stories (when it was possible to be published as an unknown) in women's magazines. My first book was sent to Dell to the attention of Kathy Sagan. SHADOWS ON THE WIND won the Golden Pen Award at the Southwest Writers' Conference in 1980 on the basis of one chapter and a synopsis.

Bibliography:

Historical romance:
SHADOWS ON THE WIND, Dell, 1982.
Note: Rita Gallagher is working on a sequel to SHADOWS ON THE WIND, and on a contemporary horror story.

DOROTHY GARLOCK
Pseudonyms: Johanna Phillips, Dorothy Phillips. *B.* Dorothy Johanna Phillips, Grand Saline, Tx., married Herb Garlock. *Children*: Lindy, Herb, Jr. *Grandchildren*: Adam, Amos. *Professional associations*: National Writers Club. *Genres*: category contemporary, historical romance. *Agent*: Steven Axelrod, The Sterling Lord Agency, 660 Madison Avenue, N.Y., N.Y. *Current residence*: Clear Lake, Iowa.

Favorite authors and books: I read everything so it would be impossible for me to name all authors I like. Louis L'Amour is my hero!

Thoughts on writing: I have always read a lot. And writing your own story is so easy, I'm amazed that half the people who read don't take to writing.

Becoming published/finding an agent: I entered a manuscript in the National Writers Club contest for unpublished writers. I didn't win, but an agent picked the book up and sold it. I've sold twelve since.

Bibliography:

Category contemporary: (All as Johanna Phillips)
GENTLE TORMENT, Jove Second Chance at Love, 12/81.
AMBER-EYED MAN, Jove Second Chance at Love, 2/82.
STRANGE POSESSION, Jove Second Chance at Love, 4/82.
SING TOGETHER SOFTLY, Jove Second Chance at Love, 12/82.

Historical romance: (All as Dorothy Garlock)
LOVE AND CHERISH, Zebra, 6/80.
THIS LOVING LAND, Pocket/Gallen, 9/81.
THE SEARCHING HEARTS, Pocket/Gallen, 5/82.
GLORIOUS DAWN, Ballantine/Fawcett, 10/82.
Note: Dorothy Garlock will have two historical romances, ANNIE LASH and FOREVER, VICTORIA, published by Pocket/Gallen. She is also one of the premiere authors in Bantam's new Loveswept series.

ROBERTA GELLIS
Pseudonyms: Priscilla Hamilton, Max Daniels (science fiction). *B.* Roberta Leah Jacobs, 9/27/27, Brooklyn, N.Y., married Charles Gellis, 4/46. *Children:* Mark. *Education:* B.S. Hunter College, 1947; M.S. Brooklyn Polytechnic Institute, 1953; M.S. New York University, 1959. *Professional associations:* Author's League, Pen and Brush Club. *Genre:* Historical romance. *Agent:* Lyle Kenyon Engel, Book Creations, Inc., Canaan, N.Y. *Current residence:* Roslyn Heights, N.Y.

Favorite authors and books: My favorite authors are not modern: Sir Thomas Malory and Jane Austen. Of the modern authors, I enjoy Mary Renault and Georgette Heyer.

Thoughts on writing: I have never really considered myself a writer of romance. I write historical novels, accurate and informative, which happen to have a strong romance line because people are people and events are meaningful to them. Events are most meaningful when a loved one is threatened. Thus, I deal with the problems of marriage and the strains that war and political events create in love relationships.

Becoming published/finding an agent: I found my first agent in the phone book, and I chose the agent, oddly enough, because her name was the same as the chemical consulting company for which I had worked for many years. Stella Snell sold my first two novels, BOND OF BLOOD and KNIGHT'S HONOR, to Doubleday.

Bibliography:

Historical romance:
Medieval:
> BOND OF BLOOD, Doubleday, 1964; Curtis, 1967; Avon, 1976; Berkley/Jove 1982.
> KNIGHT'S HONOR, Doubleday, 1964; Curtis, 1967; Avon, 1976; Berkley/Jove, 1982.
> THE DRAGON AND THE ROSE, Playboy, 1977 and 80.
> THE SWORD AND THE SWAN, Playboy, 1977 and 80.

The Roselynde Chronicles:
> ROSELYNDE, Playboy, 1978 and 80.
> ALINOR, Playboy, 1978.
> JOANNA, Playboy, 1979.
> GILLIANE, Playboy, 1980.
> RHAINNON, Playboy, 1982.
> SYBELLE, Berkley/Jove, 1983.

The Royal Dynasty Series:
> SIREN SONG, Playboy, 1981.
> WINTER SONG, Playboy, 1982.
> FIRE SONG, Berkley/Jove, to appear in 1983.

Napoleonic:
> THE ENGLISH HEIRESS, Dell, 1980.
> THE CORNISH HEIRESS, Dell, 1981.
> THE KENT HEIRESS, Dell, 1982.
> THE INDIAN HEIRESS, Dell, 1983.

Other:
> THE LOVE TOKEN, as Priscilla Hamilton, Playboy, 1979 (a costume drama).
> STAR GUARDIAN, as Max Daniels, Pocket, 1977—science fiction.
> OFFWORLD, as Max Daniels, Pocket, 1978—science fiction.

MARION CHESNEY GIBBONS

Pseudonyms: Ann Fairfax, Helen Crampton, Jennie Tremaine, Marion Chesney. *B*. Marion Chesney, 6/10/36, Glasgow, Scotland, married Harry Scott Gibbons, 1968. *Children*: Charles. *Education*: Royal Academy of Music. *Professional associations*: National Union of Journalists. *Awards*: Robert Burns Society Award, Dickens Society Award, British Booksellers Diploma. *Genres*: Edwardian, family saga, Regency. *Agent*: Barbara Lowenstein, 250 West 57th Street, New York, NY. *Current residence*: Brooklyn, NY.

Favorite authors and books: Fanny Burney, Jane Austen, Somerset Maugham, Arnold Bennet, Charles Dickens, John Galsworthy, Ada Leverson, E.F. Benson, Stella Gibbons, Norah Lofts, Baroness Orczy, Elinor Glynn, Mary Stewart, Catherine Fellows, Georgette Heyer, Victoria Holt, Daphne du Maurier.

Thoughts on writing: I have been a fan of Regency romances for years. Yes, I think romances are an escape, one of the few safe ones around. You have to enjoy reading the sort of books you plan to write. As Aldous Huxley said, there is no such thing as insincere writing, only bad writing. You must be prepared to put your heart and soul into it. Never skip historical research and study the period you mean to write about so that you can describe it from the inside looking out. Don't ask your friends for praise. The worth of your manuscript is between you and your publisher.

Becoming published/finding an agent: My husband encouraged me to take the plunge and submit my first manuscript to an agent, Barbara Lowenstein. Barbara said I had introduced the characters badly, and if I changed that, she could sell it. I did, and she did. Since then she has worked like a beaver to dig up contracts for me.

Bibliography:

Family saga:
THE WESTERBY INHERITANCE, as Marion Chesney, Pinnacle, 1982.

Regency:
HENRIETTA, as Ann Fairfax, Jove, 1979.
MY DEAR DUCHESS, as Ann Fairfax, Jove, 1979.
KITTY, as Jennie Tremaine, Dell, 1979.
DAISY, as Jennie Tremaine, Dell, 1980.
LUCY, as Jennie Tremaine, Dell, 1980.
POLLY, as Jennie Tremaine, Dell, 1980.
MOLLY, as Jennie Tremaine, Dell, 1980.
GINNY, as Jennie Tremaine, Dell, 1980.
REGENCY GOLD, as Marion Chesney, Fawcett/Ballantine, 1980.
LADY MARGERY'S INTRIGUE, as Marion Chesney, Fawcett/Ballatine, 1980.
THE CONSTANT COMPANION, as Marion Chesney, Fawcett/Ballantine, 1980.
ANNABELLE, as Ann Fairfax, Jove, 1980.
TILLY, as Jennie Tremaine, Dell, 1981.
SUSIE, as Jennie Tremaine, Dell, 1981.
THE HIGHLAND COUNTESS, as Helen Crampton, Pocket Books, 1981.
QUADRILLE, as Marion Chesney, Fawcett/Ballantine, 1981
MY LORDS, LADIES, AND MARJORIE, as Marion Chesney, Fawcett/ Ballantine, 1981.
LOVE AND LADY LOVELACE, as Marion Chesney, Fawcett/Ballantine, 1982.
THE GHOST AND LADY ALICE, as Marion Chesney, Fawcett/ Ballantine, 1982.
DUKE'S DIAMONDS, as Marion Chesney, Fawcett/Ballantine, 1982.
POPPY, as Jennie Tremaine, Dell, 1982.
SALLY, as Jennie Tremaine, Dell, 1982.
PENELOPE, as Ann Fairfax, Jove, 1982.
Note: Marion Chesney has recently signed a six-book contract with St. Martins; these novels will be her first to appear in hardcover in the U.S.

CONSTANCE GLUYAS

B. Constance Harris, 3/28/20, London, England, married Donald Gluyas, 6/27/44. *Children:* Diane Carey Henley, *nee* Gluyas. *Education:* Nine years public school, four years college, Epsom College, Surrey, England. *Awards:* My awards are the thousands of fan letters I receive. *Genres:* Category contemporary, historical romance. *Agent:* Jay Garon-Brooke Assoc., 415 Central Park West, N.Y., N.Y. 10025. *Current residence:* Arcadia, Ca.

Favorite authors and books: Jean Plaidy, Georgette Heyer, Victoria

Holt, who is also Jean Plaidy. Norah Lofts is another favorite of mine. In regard to Jean Plaidy, I have read everything she has written with avid eagerness, and hope for more.

Thoughts on writing: My first (and always) love is historical romance. I was a fan of romance before becoming a writer, and even more so now. Books should be pure escapism; that is why I do not care for the contemporaries. Life is grim enough now, and it is my opinion that the reader should be taken far, far away to a time that was gracious, where women were women, and not poor copies of men, and men delighted in it. I try to take my readers by the hand and show them things that were but may never be again. My hope is to take them away from the difficulties of life for a little while, and if I do this for them, I am happy.

Becoming published/finding an agent: I was extremly lucky with my first book THIS KING'S BRAT. Through a friend, I heard of a local agent. I went to see him, he showed interest, and sent the book to Prentice-Hall. It was accepted immediately. I first came to know of my present agent, Jay Garon, through the good offices of an editor at Prentice-Hall, who knew I was badly in need of an agent who got things done, and made things happen. It was Jay Garon who took my career in hand, and I have never looked back since. I consider that I am most fortunate. I derive my greatest pleasure from the letters my readers send. It is wonderful to know that they enjoy one's work and want more. I answer every letter personally, and, consequently, have made a great many friends in all parts of the country.

Bibliography:

Contemporary:
   BRIDGE TO YESTERDAY, Signet. 1981.

Historical romances:
   THE KING'S BRAT, Prentice-Hall. 1972.
   MY LADY BENBROOK, Prentice-Hall. 1974.
   BORN TO BE KING, Prentice-Hall, 1974.
   BRIEF IS THE GLORY, David McKay. 1975.
   THE HOUSE ON TWYFORD ST., David McKay. 1976
   MY LORD FOXE, David McKay. 1976.
   SAVAGE EDEN, Signet. 1976.

ROGUE'S MISTRESS, Signet. 1977.
WOMEN OF FURY, Signet. 1978.
FLAME OF THE SOUTH, Signet. 1979.
MADAM TUDOR, Signet. 1979.
THE PASSIONATE SAVAGE, Signet. 1980
LORD SIN, Signet. 1980
Note: Constance Gluyas currently has a book under contract with Signet.

DEBORAH H. GORDON
Pseudonyms: Brooke Hastings. B. Deborah Brooke Hannes, 5/31/46, New York City, married David W. Gordon, 8/27/67. *Children:* Jenny, Brian. *Education:* B.A. Brandeis University, Waltham, Mass., 1968 (major: politics). *Professional associations:* California Writer's of America. *Awards:* Golden Medallion Award, 1982 (for WINNER TAKE ALL, a category romance, published by Silhouette in September 1981)—given by RWA. *Genres:* Category contemporary. *Agent:* Ruth Cohen, P.O. Box 7626, Menlo Park, California. *Current residence:* Sacramento, California.

Favorite authors and books: I have too many friends in the romance field whose books I enjoy to list specifics, but certainly Janet Dailey is "the mother of us all" —the one who proved that an American author could write and publish books that would win her a large following.

Thoughts on writing: Romances are fun to write and fun to read. I enjoy stories that involve me emotionally with the characters, and perhaps make me laugh a bit, so that's what I try to write. I don't believe that you can create interesting, consistent characters of plots with any complexity by sitting down at the typewriter and banging out a first draft which you then attempt to sell, so I put a lot of effort into writing my stories . . . and then rewriting, and rewriting, and rewriting!

Becoming published/finding an agent: After receiving my fair share of rejections, I read about Silhouette Romances about nine months before the first Silhouette was actually published and I submitted my manuscript to them. The book was accepted quite quickly, but about five contracts later I realized that I absolutely hated the business aspects of writing, and called up my friend's agent, who I felt had helped my friend a good deal. I would advise any new writer to acquire an agent fairly quickly unless she has a liking for negotiating contracts, etc.

Bibliography: (all as Brooke Hastings)

Category contemporary:
PLAYING FOR KEEPS, Silhouette, 1980.
INNOCENT FIRE, Silhouette, 1980.
DESERT FIRE, Silhouette, 1980.
ISLAND CONQUEST, Silhouette, 1981.
WINNER TAKE ALL, Silhouette, 1981; Golden Medallion Award, 1982.
INTIMATE STRANGERS, Silhouette, 1982.
ROUGH DIAMOND, Silhouette, 1982.
A MATTER OF TIME, Silhouette, 1982.
Note: Diane Gordon is currently under contract with Silhouette.

MARILYN GRANBECK
B. Marilyn Ruth Podest, 9/7/27, Brooklyn, New York, married Robert A. Granbeck, 12/31/49; divorced, 10/73. Second marriage: Morrice R. Henderson, 12/27/79. *Children:* Christine, Leslie, Robert, Laurie. *Education:* B.A. Brooklyn College, 1947, major—chemistry. *Professional associations:* Author's Guild, Romance Writers of America, WNBA, PEN. *Genres:* Historical romance, contemporary. *Agent:* Theron Raines, Raines & Raines, 475 Fifth Avenue, N.Y., N.Y. 10017. *Current residence:* Reno, Nevada; Los Angeles, California.

Favorite authors and books: Helen Van Slyke, Nora Lofts, Ceorgette Heyer. So many of the newer romance writers are so good, it's hard to choose favorites. I particularly enjoy those authors who do in depth research and present colorful settings.

Thoughts on writing: Although I began writing romances at the very beginning of the genre's popularity, I had been writing mysteries and straight fiction for ten years. I saw an opportunity for me to gain intimate knowledge of various historical periods and put it to use in entertaining readers. I have never considered romances any kind of a step-child nor pure escapism. Most are good solid stories to which readers can relate. Would they be so popular otherwise?

Becoming published/finding an agent: My first sale, a mystery short story, came through trial and error. My first book, a mystery, came through persistence and hard work and the helping hand of a writer friend. My first romance sale came through the encouragement of a far-sighted agent who predicted the impact romances would make on the market and encouraged me to write my first one. My success since then has been the result of a lot of hard work and invaluable input from the two editors with whom I've had the good fortune to work.

Bibliograghy:

Contemporary:
THE FIFTH JADE OF HEAVEN, Jove, 1982.

Historical romance:
CELIA, Pyramid, 1977.
ELENA, Jove, 1977.
WINDS OF DESIRE, Jove, 1978.
MAURA, Jove, 1979.
LORIELLE, Jove, 1980.

Juveniles:
THE HIDDEN BOX MYSTERY, Scholastic, 1974.
SUMMER AT RAVENSWOOD, Scholastic, 1976.
THE MYSTERY OF THE JADE PRINCESS, Scholastic, 1980.

Non-Romance Books:
ALICE DIES TWICE, Ben Grant, 1975.
MISTRESS OF HARROWGATE, Jessica Laurie, 1981.
ASSIGNMENT INTERCEPT, Nick Carter, 1975.
BLOOD, Alan Morgan, 1976.
THE ZAHARAN PURSUIT, Adam Hamilton, 1973.
THE YASHIR PURSUIT, Adam Hamilton, 1973.
THE XANDER PURSUIT, Adam Hamilton, 1974.
THE WYSS PURSUIT, Adam Hamilton, 1974.
HOLLYWOOD HIT MAN, Van Saxon, 1976.
THE CORRUPTERS, Clayton Moore, 1974.
END OF RECKONING, Clayton Moore, 1973.

SUSAN ELLEN GROSS
Pseudonyms: Susanna Collins, Sue Ellen Cole. *B.* Susan Ellen Gross, 12/12/44, Oakland, CA. *Education:* B.A. University of Southern California, French. *Professional associations:* PEN. *Genres:* Category contemporary, historical romance. *Agent:* Ellen Levine, Ellen Levine Literary Agency, 370 Lexington Avenue, New York, NY. *Current residence:* Southern California.

Favorite authors and books: Jane Austen seems to be at the top of every writer's list, mine included. I reread EMMA once a year. I adore the ANGELIQUE books. Having done a tremendous amount of research into that era, I am thrilled to find them so accurate. My favorite in the current boom is rather obscure: THE SEA HARROWER, by Abigail Clements.

Thoughts on writing: I would be writing romance even if it weren't a genre. What I am really writing are suspenseful stories in which love is the theme. And what brings out more violent, exhilarating, painful, or soaring passions than love? Is romance pure escape? I'd say readers want to learn and be entertained. Writing novels is the ultimate creative effort for an artist since it involves another person directly—much more than films or television. The reader must visualize, become an active participant in the author's fantasy. And in the romance novel, because it is generally written from a woman's point of view, I think a reader identifies with the heroine. Her love story becomes the reader's. It's quite an extraordinary and beautiful transformation that occurs, and the secret, I believe, for the romance novel's phenomenal success.

Becoming published/finding an agent: I simply wrote a novel. A friend told me about an agent. She sent the book around, and eventually it was published. More interesting was the hypnotic regression to a past life in fifteen-century Spain that inspired THE MIDNIGHT FURY.

Bibliography:

Category contemporary: (All as Susanna Collins)
FLAMENCO NIGHTS, Second Chance At Love, 1981.

HARD TO HANDLE, Second Chance At Love, 1981.
DESTINY'S SPELL, Second Chance At Love, 1981.
ON WINGS OF MAGIC, Second Chance At Love, 1982.

Historical romance:
THE MIDNIGHT FURY, Fawcett, 1981.
Note: Susan Ellen Gross has recently signed a four book contract with Second Chance At Love, and a two book contract with Silhouette.

DONNA A. GRUNDMAN

B. Donna A. Round, 7/7/27, Maquoketa, Iowa. *Children:* Debra Grundman, Dan Grundman, Darrell Grundman. *Genre:* historical romance. *Agent:* Andrea Cirillo, Jane Rotrosen Agency, 318 E. 51st Street, N.Y., N.Y. *Current reisdence:* Anchorage, Alaska.

Favorite authors and books: Kathleen Woodiwiss (ASHES IN THE WIND), Danielle Steel, Madelaine Brent, Dorothy Eden, Catherine Cookson. My reading varies, depending on my mood. Sometimes I like historical romance, sometimes current books; with a bit of Gothic for variety.

Thoughts on writing: Yes, I think romantic novels are escapist. I like to read a novel I can be emotionally involved in. Therefore, when I am writing, I try to bring enough life to my characters that my readers will feel that they really know them personally, sharing the feelings, the laughter and the tears.

Becoming published/finding an agent: The people at Dell introduced me to Andrea Cirillo, and it was one of the luckiest things that has happened to me in my writing career. She knows the writing field from both sides of the fence—as an agent and from her experience working with a publisher. I depend on her advice completely.

Bibliography:

Historical romance:
A DISTANT EDEN, Dell, 1982.
DAYS TO REMEMBER, Dell, 1982.
Note: Donna Grundman is presently working on an historical romance entitled TARNISHED GOLD which is set in Alaska. She enjoys the his-

tory of the western frontier and uses it as the setting of her books.

SUZANNE GUNTRUM

Pseudonyms: Suzanne Simms, Suzanne Simmons. *B.* Suzanne Simmons, 8/29/46, Storm Lake, Iowa, married Robert R. Guntrum, 9/9/67. *Children:* Steven. *Education:* B.A., 1967, Penn State University, English. *Professional Associations:* Romance Writers of America. *Genres:* Category contemporary. *Agent:* Maureen Walters, Curtis Brown Ltd., 575 Madison Avenue, N.Y., N.Y. 10022. *Current residence:* New Castle, Indiana.

Favorite authors and books: Everything by Daphne du Maurier, especially REBECCA and FRENCHMAN'S CREEK. Stephanie James, Bonnie Drake, Elaine Raco Chase, Rachel Ryan, Kristin James, just to name a few.

Thoughts on writing: I was a writer of humor first. A friend introduced me to romance novels and I was soon hooked—as writer and as a reader. I try to write the kind of romance I enjoy reading. (although I rarely feel I succeed.) Writing romance is primarily a matter of "attitude." Most novels, of any genre, are escapism.

Becoming published/finding an agent: I submitted and sold my first eight manuscripts on my own. (What an incredible amount of time and effort and hard work are represented by that one sentence.) When my life as a writer became more complicated, I decided I needed an agent. Maureen Walters was recommended. It was one of my best decisions!

Bibliography:

Category contemporary:
SUMMER STORM, Suzanne Simmons. MacFadden, 1979.
WINTER WINE, Suzanne Simmons. MacFadden, 1980.
FROM THIS DAY FORWARD, Suzanne Simmons. MacFadden, 1980.
VELVET MORNING, Suzanne Simmons. MacFadden, 1980.
TOUCH THE WIND, Suzanne Simmons. MacFadden, 1980.
THE TEMPESTUOUS LOVERS, Suzanne Simmons. Dell Ecstasy, 1981.
NEVER AS STRANGERS, Suzanne Simmons. Dell Ecstasy, 1982.
MOMENT IN TIME, Suzanne Simms. Silhouette Desire, 1982.

OF PASSION BORN, Suzanne Simms. Silhouette Desire, 1982.
AS NIGHT FOLLOWS DAY, Suzanne Simmons. Dell Ecstasy, 1982.
Note: Suzanne Guntrum currently has two books under contract for Silhouette Desire.

JACQUELINE HOPE HACSI
Pseudonyms: Jacqueline Hope, Jacqueline Louis. *B.* Jacqueline
Hope Bassler, 4/27/25, first marriage: 2/28/53. Second marriage:
Louis Hacsi, 12/11/59. *Children:* Jonathan, Timothy. Also three step-
sons: Peter, Michael and Anthony Hacsi. *Education:* BB.A. from the
University of California at Berkeley, 1951, English major, Phi Beta
Kappa. *Genres:* Category contemporary. *Agent:* Patricia Teal, Teal &
Watt, Inc. 2036 Vista del Rosa, Fullerton, California. *Current resi-
dence:* Whittier, California.

Favorite authors and books: My favorite authors include Meredith
Brucker, June Casey, and Linda Wisdom.

Thoughts on writing: I grew up with a compulsion to write, but I
had other compulsions also: to have children, to breathe, drink,
eat and sleep. I was a writer for years—confession stories—
before I read my first romance. My first agent suggested I try the
romance field, so I read some Harlequins and tried writing in the
field. Pure escapism? Few things in life are "pure", it seems to
me, but romances are pretty close to 100% escapism, I would say.

Becoming published/finding an agent: As to book publishing, after
completing a nonfiction book, I wrote to eight agents listed in
WRITER'S MARKET. Donald MacCampbell, New York City
agent, responded, agreeing to allow me to submit my book. He
wasn't interested in my nonfiction—I sold it on my own a few
months later—but he liked the way I wrote and offered to guide
me into the field of women's romantic fiction. I read a few, wrote
three outlines; MacCampbell chose one, I wrote the first two
chapters, Dell bought it.

Bibliography:

Category contemporary:
LOVE'S OWN DREAM, Jacqueline Hacsi. Dell Candlelights, August 1978.

WINTER'S LOVING TOUCH, Jacqueline Hacsi. Dell Candlelights, July 1979.
EAST TO PARADISE, Jacqueline Hacsi. Dell Candlelights, September 1980.
PARADISE ISLE, Jacqueline Hacsi. Dell Candlelights, March 1981.
TOO RICH FOR HER PRIDE, Jacqueline Hacsi. Dell Candlelights, June 1981.
LOVE CAPTIVE, Jacqueline Hope. Silhouette, April 1982.
Note: Jacqueline Hope Hacsi currently has a book under contract with Harlequin.

PATRICIA HAGAN

B. Mary Patricia Hagan, Atlanta, Ga., 8/19/39, married Jerry Howell, 7/20/72. *Children:* Don. *Education:* B.S. 1961, University of Alabama, English. *Professional associations:* ABWA, National Motorsports Press, Assoc., Civitans. *Genres:* Historical romance. *Current residence:* Goldsboro, North Carolina.

Favorite authors and books: The only romance authors I read are Danielle Steel and Rosemary Rogers. When I have time to read, I endeavor to remove myself from my own genre of writing, so I devour mysteries and suspense. My favorite author is Stephen King.

Thoughts on writing: I feel women are basically romantics. I feel all of us survive the harsh reality of life by giving way to the fantasy within us. Romance novels appeal to women, for they allow them to enjoy the fantasy world created by someone else . . . to experience in their hearts the dreams they subconsciously know will never be encountered in their real worlds.

Becoming published/finding an agent: I began writing confession stories in 1961 and had probably written over 2,500 before moving on to books. In 1970, an editor liked a story so much that she showed it to an agent, who felt it could be expanded into a book. It was—and my career an an author began.

Bibliography:

Contemporary:
INVITATION TO THE WEDDING, Bantam Red Rose Romance, 1971.

Gothics:
DARK JOURNEY HOME, Avon, 1972.
WINDS OF TERROR, Avon, 1973.

Historical romances:
LOVE AND WAR, Avon, 1978.
THE RAGING HEARTS, Avon, 1979.
SOULS AFLAME, Avon, 1980.
PASSIONS FURY, Avon, 1981.
LOVE AND GLORY, Avon, 1982.
Note: Patricia Hagan currently has one book under contract to Avon, tentatively scheduled for 1983.

JEAN HAGER
Pseudonyms: Amanda McAllister, Sara North, Marlaine Kyle, Jeanne Stephens. *B.* Wilma Jean Luna, Maywood, Illinois, married Kenneth G. Hager, 1/23/53. *Children:* Kenneth Mark Hager, Elaine Anne Hager Clark, Kyle John Hager. *Education:* Pawnee high school, Pawnee, OK (graduated 1950); attended Oklahoma State University, University of Tulsa, University of Oklahoma, and Central State University, Edmond, OK. Bachelor's Degree in English, 1969, Central State University. *Professional associations:* Oklahoma Writers Federation, Mystery Writers of America, Romance Writers of America. *Awards:* 1978 Teepee Award (given annually by Oklahoma Writers Federation for best novel by an OK author); 1980 Teepee Award; 1982 Oklahoma Write of the year (given annually by the University of Oklahoma). *Genres:* Romantic-suspense, juvenile mysteries, Category contemporary, Regency romances, Gothics. *Agent:* Amy Berkower, Writers House, Inc., 21 W. 26th Street, N.Y., N.Y. 10010. *Current residence:* Pawnee County, Oklahoma (I live on a ranch).

Favorite authors and books: Among my favorite authors are Georgette Heyer, Clare Darcy, Danielle Steel, Kathleen Woodiwiss, Janet Dailey.

Thoughts on writing: Since I am a romantic at heart, I enjoy writing romance novels. I enjoy writing Regencies because of the wit and the great leeway in plot situations. But I think I like doing the contemporary romances better because situations and characters are all around me in everyday life. I also love to travel, and I can use the places I visit as settings for novels. I am fully aware that romance novels are "light reading" with a strong element of fantasy in them. I make no apology for providing a few hours of escape for my readers

Becoming published/finding an agent: I sold my first two books (which were children's mysteries) on my own. I just sent them out again and again until somebody bought them. I've had an agent with all my adult novels (I've sold more than twenty now). I got my agent by asking two editors I'd had contact with to recommend someone. Both the editors gave me several names and I contacted three or four of them and finally settled on my present agent because she sounded enthusiastic about what I was writing and acted as if she wanted me as a client. She's always up-to-date on the markets that I'm trying to sell to, which is important, particularly in the romance market which changes quickly. I would advise beginning writers not to sign up with just anyone simply to get an agent. You can probably market your own stuff better than an agent who is incompetent or not up on the markets you're trying to hit or simply not enthusiastic about your work.

Bibliography:

Category contemporary:
MEXICAN NIGHTS, Jeanne Stephens. Silhouette Books, 1980.
PORTRAIT OF LOVE, Jean Hager. Dell, 1981.
CAPTURED BY LOVE, Jean Hager. Dell, 1981.
WONDER AND WILD DESIRE, Jeanne Stephens. Silhouette, 1981.
WEB OF DESIRE, Jean Hager. Dell, 1981.
BRIDE IN BARBADOS, Jeanne Stephens. Silhouette, 1982.
PRIDE'S POSSESSION, Jeanne Stephens,. Silhouette, 1982.
SWEET JASMINE, Jeanne Stephens. Silhouette, 1982.

Contemporary romance:
YELLOW FLOWER MOON, Jean Hager. Doubleday, 1981.

Regency:
A SUITABLE MARRIAGE, Marlaine Kyle. Dell, 1982.
A GAME OF HEARTS, Marlaine Kyle. Dell, 1982.

Romantic-suspense:
TERROR IN THE SUNLIGHT, Amanda McAllister. Playboy Press, 1977; winner of Teepee Award given annually by the Oklahoma Writers Federation for best novel by an Oklahoma writer.
EVIL SIDE OF EDEN, Sara North. Playboy Press, 1978.
SHADOW OF THE TAMARACKS, Sara North. Playboy Press, 1979; winner of Teepee Award.

Non-Romance Books:
THE SECRET OF RIVERSIDE FARM, Jean Hager. Steck-Vaughn, 1970. (juvenile mystery book).
THE WHISPERING HOUSE, Jean Hager. Steck-Vaughn, 1970. (juvenile mystery book).
Note:Jean Hager currently has two books under contract with Silhouette.

LYNN LOWERY HAHN
Pseudonym: Lynn Lowery B. Mona Lynn Lowery, 7/3/49, Cleveland, Ohio, married James Hahn, 4/17/71. *Education:* B.S.J., Northwestern University. Majored in journalism with an elective major in Russian (language, literature, history, and culture). *Genres:* Historical romance and family saga. *Current residence:* Evanston, Illinois.

Favorite authors and books: I read very widely in all areas of the romance field, and most enjoy historical romance authors who give an authentic historic taste. I like to feel that the author respects her heroine, and I like strong heroines with minds of their own. Claire Lorrimer's MAVREEN and TAMARISK are two of my favorites. As a junior high reader, I was first drawn to history and romance by GONE WITH THE WIND and Kenneth Robert's LYDIA BAILEY—still favorites of mine. Among classics, I enjoyed Tolstoy's WAR AND PEACE (Natasha's thwarted elopement rivals a current-day "hot historical") and the tragic romance of ANNA KARENINA.

Thoughts on writing: I think I was always a romance, and particularly an historical romance, fan. Even as an elementary school student, devouring Laura Ingalls Wilder's books, I loved the last books in the series, such as THESE HAPPY GOLDEN YEARS, in which Laura describes her contentment with Almanzo Wilder. I know that many critics or people who consider themselves "connoisseurs of fine literature" look down on the romantic genre, but I am not concerned with pleasing those people. I know that romances, including mine, bring joy to millions of readers, and that is my major reward in writing them. I truly enjoy reseraching and writing my books, giving my readers stories I would enjoy reading, about people I would enjoy knowing. I always try to write clearly and smoothly, since I don't think someone who reads for relaxation wants to struggle with difficult constructions. Romances definitely provide an escape for readers. But, they also deal with problems that people face every day. Love, romance, and relationships with other people are important parts of most people's lives. A well-written love story, with strong, believable characters, can help a reader see his or her own problems more clearly, and could help to enhance a relationship. However, I don't approach writing as an amateur psychologist. My primary purpose is to entertain. I don't think any writer needs to apologize for writing a romantic story that entertains hundreds of thousands, or even millions. Shakespeare and Tolstoy, whom many consider the greatest writers of our past, never apologized!

Becoming published/finding an agent: In the summer of 1976, when romances were becoming some of the most popular books in the country, it suddenly occurred to me that no one had yet published an historical set in Russia and that I had all the background necessary from my college Russian major and a college study trip to the Soviet Union. Before that, I had written free-lance articles and several non-fiction books for children, in collaboration with my husband, but now I was anxious to begin a novel. I wrote the first fifty pages, and sent them to some editors, who liked them, but weren't willing to publish the book. In the meantime I finished writing the novel, SWEET RUSH OF PASSION, set in the Russian Empire in the 1820's. I wrote a detailed letter about the manuscript to Bantam Books and received a reply from editor Linda Price, asking to see the manuscript. About two months later, she wrote to say Bantam was interested in the book, if I could make a few revisions. Six weeks after that Bantam bought

SWEET RUSH OF PASSION. I immediately started work in another book also with a Russian background. I've continued writing for Bantam and enjoying the help and encouragement of Linda Price ever since.

Bibliography: (all as Lynn Lowery)
SWEET RUSH OF PASSION, Bantam, January 1978.
LOVESWEPT, Bantam, December 1978.
LARISSA, Bantam, November 1979.
LORELEI, Bantam, June 1981.
Note: Lynn Lowery currently has two books under contract with Bantam.

EMILY WATSON HALLIN
Pseudonym: Elaine Harper. *B.* Emily Watson, 10/4/29, Fort Smith, Arkansas, married Clark O. Hallin, 1962. Widowed. *Chlidren:* Dan, Diane, Brian. *Education:* B.A. University of Missouri, English. *Professional associations:* California Writers Club, Romance Writers of America. *Genre:* young adult. *Agent:* Ruth Cohen, P.O. Box 7626, Menlo Park, California. *Current residence:* Los Altos Hills, California.

Favorite authors and books: Jane Austen, Daphne du Maurier, M.M. Kaye, Danielle Steel. I recently enjoyed reading Robin James' THE GOLDEN TOUCH.

Thoughts on writing: My principal aim in writing young adult romances is to entertain, and to induce young people to delight in reading. I also hope I provide my readers with insights on life and people which may then minimize the often painful tensions assailing adolescents. I hope the readers will get more fun out of those wonderful years.

Becoming published/finding an agent: When I heard that Silhouette was starting its First Love line, I wrote three chapters of LOVE AT FIRST SIGHT, which they immediately accepted. I met my agent on a bus. We were both going to the airport after being panelists at a Romance Writers of America conference, and we subsequently struck up a deal.

Bibliography:

Non-romance:
WILD WHITE WINGS, David McKay, 1965.
FOLLOW THE HONEY BIRD, David McKay, 1967.
MOYA AND THE FLAMINGOES, David McKay, 1967.

Young adult: (all as Elaine Harper)
LOVE AT FIRST SIGHT, Silhouette Love at First Sight, 1981.
WE BELONG TOGETHER, Silhouette Love at First Sight, 1982.
BE MY VALENTINE, Silhouette Love at First Sight, 1983.
LIGHT OF MY LIFE, Silhouette Love at First Sight, 1983.

OLIVIA HARPER
Pseudonyms: Jolene Adams, JoAnna Brandon. *B.* Olivia Longoria,
8/9/42, Los Indios, Texas, married Kenneth M. Harper, 6/16/62.
Children: Kevin M. Harper and Michelle L. Harper. *Education*:
high school, three credits short of an accounting degree (hope to
complete these within the next year at California State). *Genres*:
Contemporary (eventually, I hope to have several in the historical genre . . . family saga type, plus a few Regency, Edwardian
and Victorian). *Current residence*: San Ramon, California.

Favorite authors and books: I have no one particular favorite,
though I do frequently go toward Roberta Gellis and Laurie
McBain in the historicals; Laura London, Catherine Coulter and
Elizabeth Neff Walker in the shorter historicals; Jayne Castle,
Anne Reisser, Rachel Ryan and Elaine Raco Chase in contempo-
rary.

Thoughts on writing: I love writing, and whether it's considered
pure escapism it is fulfilling a need. If it brings even a brief respite
for the reader, then let it be called escapism. At times, when I had
spent four to five hours pouring through an assignment in Business Law, it was simple pleasure to pick up a book that had nothing to do with my two heavy subjects. Not that I ever escaped
those debits and credits . . . they were always hovering just at
the edge even while I was immersed in a novel. From childhood,
I knew I had to write. I wasn't patient enough to sit down to do it,
so I talked my stories out loud, to the delight of my two brothers

and one sister who took pleasure in teasing me about this. (Now, however, they seem to be proud of their "baby sister".) I would advise aspiring writers to research the genre and market trends and enjoy what they are doing. If the novel is not one that brings a smile to the author, then chances are it won't cause the editor to smile either.

Becoming published/finding an agent: I went into a creative writing class to fulfill a college requirement and became friends with the teacher who saw my potential and introduced me to Helen McGrath of the McGrath Agency in Concord, California. It was through Mrs. McGrath that I sold my first few books.

Bibliography:

Category contemporary:
FROM THIS DAY FORWARD, Jolene Adams. Jove Second Chance at Love, Mar. 1982.
THE DEVIL'S PLAYGROUND, JoAnna Brandon. Dell Ecstasy, July, 1982.
SING TO ME OF LOVE, JoAnna Brandon. Dell Ecstasy, Jan. 1983.
Note: Olivia Harper currently has a book under contract with Second Chance at Love.

SHANNON HARPER
Pseudonyms: Anna James, Elizabeth Habersham (Both pseudonyms are shared with co-author, Madeline Porter.) *B.* Elizabeth Shannon Harper, Winston-Salem, NC. *Education:* B.A. University of South Carolina; M.A. New York University, English; M.S.W. Tulane University. *Professional associations:* Romance Writers of America, Southeastern Writers Association. *Awards:* Romance Writers of America Golden Heart medallion for THE DAY BEYOND DESTINY (Best historical romance, 1981.) *Genres:* Contemporary, family saga, gothic, historical romance. *Agent:* Sarah Freymann, 59 W. 71st Street, New York, NY. *Current residence:* Atlanta, GA.

Favorite authors and books: Jane Austen is my literary godmother, and D.H. Lawrence is the most sensual writer I know. My current favorites include Phyllis Whitney, Victoria Holt, Anne

Maybury, Mary Stewart, and Helen McInnes. I really enjoy gothics and romantic suspense. The late Helen Van Slyke gave us mature writing, with complex characters and plots.

Thoughts on writing: Very selfishly, I like to write the kind of books I like to read. Some of the elements most appealing are articulate and intelligent characters who have interesting professions, who are strong and resilient, and, *most important*, are not afraid of change. Madeline and I write longer books, trying for fully-rounded characters and a hint of mystery, exciting locales and a deep thread of romance. But most of all, the joy of writing is to tell a good, page-turning story that entertains.

Becoming published/finding an agent: Our first book was a gothic romance, begun when I was travelling as a social worker for the state of Georgia. Bored in small towns at night, I roughed out ISLAND OF DECEIT, which my partner later rewrote and polished. We tried vainly to sell it ourselves for a year. Then when Madeline was in New York, she met our agent through friends, an accident of fate. Within six months, Sara sold ISLAND OF DECEIT, and told us to start on our next book. I never had a doubt that ISLAND OF DECEIT would sell. Never.

Bibliography:

Contemporary:
A WORLD OF HER OWN, Anna James, Gallen/Pocket, 1982.
THE HEART VICTORIOUS, Anna James, Gallen/Pocket, 1982.

Gothic:
ISLAND OF DECEIT, Elizabeth Habersham, Pinnacle, 1977.

Historical romance:
SWEET LOVE, BITTER LOVE, Anna James, Jove, 1978.
THE DARKER SIDE OF LOVE, Anna James, Jove, 1979.
THE DAY BEYOND DESTINY, Anna James, Jove, 1981.

CLAIRE HARRISON
Pseudonyms: Laura Eden, Claire St. John B. Ellen Wisoff, 2/12/46, Brooklyn, NY., married John Edward Harrison, 1965. *Children*: Lisa, Rebecca. *Education*: B.A. Carleton University, La-

tin and Greek, *Professional associations:* Romance Writers of America, Washington Romance Writers, Authors Guild, Washington Independent Writers. *Genres:* Category contemporary. *Agent:* Steve Axelrod, The Sterling Lord Agency, 660 Madison Avenue, New York, NY. *Current residence:* Chevy Chase, MD.

Favorite authors and books: I always like to go back and read the classics, those books by Jane Austen, the Brontës, and Georgette Heyer. I've read PRIDE AND PREJUDICE at least ten times. I admire the historicals, and Susan Howatch, particularly PENMARRIC and CASHELMARA, and LaVyrle Spencer's THE FULFILLMENT and THE ENDEARMENT. I read category contemporary authors for their style and I particularly enjoy Elaine Chase, Charlotte Lamb, Sally Wentworth, Violet Winspear, and Karen Van Der Zee. Some authors who are not "romance" authors but those I love reading are Colette (for sensuality) and John Fowles (for the masculine romantic viewpoint).

Thoughts on writing: I've been a reader since age four and a writer since I was eight; I really believe romance authors are born, not made. The stories appeal to the dramatist within me and that's why I write them. I'm particularly interested in developing characters in my novels who are real, and all my heroes and heroines have past histories that affect the way they act towards one another. I also believe that the category romance is slowly inching its way towards mainstream fiction because the readers want to read about women like themselves who are caught up in contemporary situations. While I will agree that the romance is escapist literature, I think it also satisfies some fundamental needs for its readers, the need to believe in love, in man's commitment to a woman, and, ultimately, that we will all have happy endings.

Becoming published/finding an agent: My first romance novel was written in the backyard on my old Smith Corona while my two children tricycled up and down the driveway. This novel was eventually relegated to the circular file where it deserved to go. But my second book was purchased by Dell for its Candlelight line in 1979, and will probably never see the light of day—it got squeezed out by the emerging Ecstasy line. I have since sold seven more novels—two with an agent I am no longer under contract with, and three with my present agent, Steven Axelrod, whom I signed with after calling and interviewing several other agents.

Bibliography:

Category contemporary:
MISTAKEN IDENTITY, as Laura Eden, Silhouette, 1981.
SUMMER MAGIC, as Laura Eden, Silhouette Special Edition, 1982.
Note: Claire Harrison has currently four books under contract to Harlequin—under the pseudonym, Claire St. John, one book to Silhouette—under the pseudonym, Laura Eden, and one book to Dell Candlelight—under the pseudonym, Ellen Harris.

CONSTANCE HEAVEN
Pseudonyms: Constance Fecher, Christina Merlin. *B.* Constance Fecher, 8/6/11, Enfield, Middlesex, England, married William Heaven, 5/11/39. *Education:* King's College, London University, Honours degree in English, 1928-31. *Professional associations:* Chairman of Romantic Novelists' Association, 1981. *Awards:* Major award for best romantic novel of the year,1973, given by Romantic Novelists' Association. *Genres:* Historical romance, romantic suspense, Victorian family saga. *Agent:* Mr. Carl Routledge, 22 Knoll House, Carlton Hill, St. John's Wood, London, N.W.8, England. *Current residence:* Teddington, Middlesex, England.

Favorite authors and books: Past: Margaret Irwin, Georgette Heyer, Alexander Dumas, Victor Hugo (at school). Present: Catherine Gaskin, Mary Stewart, Rosemary Sutcliff, Edith Pargeter, Hilda Lewis, Victoria Holt,(including a passion for writers of the sea, i.e., Patrick O'Brien, C.S. Forester, Alexander Kent).

Thoughts on writing: One of my passions is history and so when after a career in the theatre I turned to writing a novel, it was a biographical story of Sir Walter Raleigh. Romance came later after six not very profitable books and some children's tales. My first attempt, THE HOUSE OF KURAGIN, set in Russia, hit the jackpot and determined my future career as author. I don't write to a formula and find it difficult to confine myself to pure romance. I need a historical background to give bite to it, e.g., evolution in France or Vienna, industrial unrest in nineteenth-century England, the Crimea, etc. As for escapism—what is wrong with it? Love takes many forms and is a prime mover in human affairs—all kinds of love—and therefore to my way of thinking romance can cover a very wide range from Homer's *Odyssey* to a Regency tale. I think it depends on character presentation and the truth of background and plot whether it is modern or set in the past. I aim to write stories that entertain and have some validity and historical interest for the ordinary reader and am delighted when people write to tell me of their enjoyment.

Becoming published/finding an agent: My first book, QUEEN'S DELIGHT (in the US THE QUEEN'S FAVORITE) was rejected by many publishers. Through the agency of a writing friend I was introduced to Carl Routledge who obtained the interest of publisher Robert Hale. The book was rewritten three times but was finally accepted and published. My first romantic novel was accepted by Heinemann in 1972 and subsequently was translated into seventeen languages.

Bibliography:
(All historicals by Constance Heaven, pub. by Heinemann in Britain, Coward, McCann in the USA):
THE HOUSE OF KURAGIN, 1972.
THE ASTROV INHERITANCE, 1973.
CASTLE OF EAGLES, 1974.
THE PLACE OF STONES, 1975.
THE FIRES OF GLENLOCHY, 1976.
THE QUEEN AND THE GYPSY, 1977.
LORD OF RAVENSLEY, 1978.
HEIR TO KURAGIN, 1979.
THE WILDCLIFFE BIRD, 1981.
THE RAVENSLEY TOUCH, 1982.

Historicals written as Constance Fecher, all Robert Hale in Britain, Dell in USA:
QUEEN'S DELIGHT (THE QUEEN'S FAVORITE in US), 1966.

TRAITOR'S SON, 1967.
KING'S LEGACY, 1967.
PLAYER QUEEN (THE LOVELY WANTON in US), 1968.
LION OF TREVARROCK, 1969.
NIGHT OF THE WOLF, 1972.

Romantic suspense (both as Christina Merlin, published by Robert
Hale):
THE SPY CONCERTO, 1981.
SWORD OF MITHRAS, 1982.

Note: Constance Heaven has also written several children's novels, and
two works of biography under the pseudonym of Constance Fecher,
one a life of Sir Walter Raleigh, the other of Ellen Terry.

VICTORIA J. HELAND

Pseudonyms: Josephine James, Victoria Vaughn. *B.* Victoria J.
Richardson, 2/15/47, Salisbury, MD., married Kenneth V.
Heland, 1970. *Education:* B.A. College of New Rochelle, econom-
ics. *Professional associations:* Author's Guild, Romance Writers of
America, International Women's Writing Guild. *Genres:* Catego-
ry contemporary, Regency. *Agent:* Denise Marcil, 316 W. 82nd
Street, New York, NY. *Current residence:* Salisbury, MD.

Favorite authors and books: Georgette Heyer, Jane Austen, Zabrina
Faire, Amalia James.

Thoughts on writing: As I see it, the point of writing anything is to
engage the reader's attention. If you can't do that, then the
chances of informing, persuading, or entertaining her are slim.
For that reason I have never understood why some critics pooh-
pooh the genre as "unintellectual." Since when was love an intellectual experience? Admittedly, romances portray love in somewhat idealized terms. They leave out some of the flotsam and jet-
sam of everyday life. But all fiction does that. It filters; it does not
in any way purport to present literal reality. But every romance is
grounded in the emotional realities of what happens when people are attracted to each other.

It is highly unlikely that the scores of mystery readers will
ever encounter a dead body, much less solve a crime. And I have
never heard it charged that mysteries as a genre encourage such

fantasies. Likewise, it is highly unlikely that most of us will find ourselves caught up in an international intrigue. We don't read Robert Ludlum as a way of preparing ourselves—just in case. We read for the action and the interaction, to be engaged a while, and thus diverted from our everyday concerns. Therefore, I have never quite understood exactly what it was romance writers (and readers) were supposed to apologize for. Is love any less worthy a subject than murder or politics?

My guess is that romances more closely correspond to reality than many other genres because most everyone has had some experience with love. It may not have lasted; worse, it may have been unrequited. But romances offer an opportunity to relive (and perhaps reawaken) the marvelous feeling of new love— with all its tensions, trepidations, and complications. That is not to say that romance readers and writers are secretly longing to run off with dashing pirates or even their modern-day counterparts in three-piece suits. On the contrary, I think most would blanch at the thought, the same as many mystery readers would if they ever did find a corpse on their doorsteps.

I also find it compelling that in romances women are always the central characters. With few exceptions, the heroines are strong, independent individuals who retain their individuality even in the throes of love. That is, I think, an idea worth having out and around.

Becoming published/finding an agent: I met Denise at an IWWG conference in 1976. After several other projects, she suggested I try a Regency in late 1979. On the basis of that first submission, Jove signed me to a three book contract.

Before turning to romance, I had written articles, short stories, and light verse for a range of publications.

Bibliography:

Regency:
> LONDON FROLIC, as Josephine James, Jove Second Chance At Love, 1982.
> THE ARTFUL COUSIN, Jove, 1982.
> MAYFAIR WAGER, Jove, 1982.
> Note: Victoria Heland also has two books currently under contract: a Regency for Jove's Second Chance at Love line, and a category contemporary for Avon's "Finding Mr. Right" series.

MONIQUE RAPHEL HIGH

B. Monique Raphel, 5/3/49, N.Y., N.Y., married Robert D. High, 6/69; divorced. *Children:* Nathalie. *Education:* B.A. Barnard College, Comparative Literature. *Awards:* Outstanding Young Women of America, 1980; The World's Who's Who of Women; The World's Who's Who of Intellectuals. *Genres:* Contemporary, historical novel, family saga. *Agent:* Roberta Pryor, International Creative Management, 40 W. 57th St., N.Y., N.Y. *Current address:* Beverly Hills, California.

Favorite authors and books: THE THORN BIRDS by Colleen McCullough, TANT QUE LA TERRE TOURNERA by Henri Troyat, WAR AND PEACE by Tolstoi, EVERGREEN by Belva Plain.

Thoughts on writing: I was an only child who began to tell stories to escape from loneliness. Later I felt the need to explore the private lives of all whom I met. I wrote FOUR WINDS because my Russian Jewish Baroness grandmother left me shelves of fascinating diaries. The genre hooked me. ENCORE helped to supply the emotional dimension my failing marriage was not fulfilling. I am a voracious reader. A writer must write in order to keep alive—for us it is a life support *need*—we have no choice. But discipline is essential.

Becoming published/finding an agent: I am French. My neighbor in 1977 turned out to be French. Through her I met her best friend, Dorris Halsey, an independent agent. She circulated the beginning of FOUR WINDS. Dell optioned it and threw in the deal you can't refuse: hardcover! Later, relations cooled between me and Miss Halsey, and the editor-in-chief at Delacorte, Ross Claiborne, suggested I see Roberta Pryor. It has been a wonderful association since 1980.

Bibliography:

Family saga:
   THE FOUR WINDS OF HEAVEN, Delacorte Press, 1980 (also a Dell paperback, published in 1981).

Historical romance:
ENCORE, Delacorte Press, 1981 (also a Dell paperback published in 1982).
THE ELEVENTH HOUR, Delacorte Press, 1983 (also a Dell paperback published in 1981).
Note: Monique High is currently working on a contemporary entitled HARD AS NAILS. Her previous books have been published by Granada, Ltd. in Great Britain; by Editions de Trevise in France; by Hestia Verlag in Germany; by Distribuidora in Portugal; by Schocken in Israel; by Lasser Press in Mexico; and Arnoldo Mondadori, and Sperling and Kupfer in Italy.

BRENDA HIMROD

Pseudonyms: Brenda Trent, Megan Lane. *B.* Brenda Lee Eanes, 4/10/45, Danville, Virginia, married Robert L. Himrod 12/74. *Education*: A.A. Riverside City College, liberal arts. *Professional associations*: Romance Writers of America. *Genres*: category contemporary. *Agent*: Pat Teal and Sandy Watt, Teal and Watt Literary Agency, 2036 Vista Del Rosa, Fullerton, California. *Current residence*: Sunny Mead, California.

Favorite authors and books: Charlotte Lamb, Danielle Steel.

Thoughts on writing: Thank heavens romance books are finally earning respect as good literature. Fiction's primary function is to entertain, and romance books achieve this end beautifully, as proven by their popularity. In today's hectic world, we all need that respite that a good romance book can provide. I'm always thrilled when readers write to say how entertaining my books are. I think it's the greatest compliment a reader can give.

Becoming published/finding an agent: I had written confession stories for years, finally selling a total of twenty-eight. I decided I wanted to try a book and I studied the market to determine what kind of book I wanted to write. Since I enjoyed contemporary romance books, that's what I decided to write. I wrote my first book in less than a year, then submitted it to the Teal and Watt Literary Agency. I had requested a list of agents from the National Writers Club, and I chose Teal and Watt because they were local.

Bibliography:

Category contemporary:
RISING STAR, as Brenda Trent, Silhouette, 1981.
WINTER DREAMS, as Brenda Trent, Silhouette, 1981.
A STRANGER'S WIFE, as Brenda Trent, Silhouette, 1981.
BITTER VINES, as Megan Lane, Dell Candlelight Ecstasy, 1982.
RUN FROM HEARTACHE, as Brenda Trent, Silhouette, 1982.
STORMY AFFAIR, as Brenda Trent, Silhouette, 1982.

MICHAEL THOMAS HINKEMEYER
Pseudonym: Vanessa Royal. *B.* Michael Thomas Hinkemeyer, 10/18/40, St. Cloud, Minnesota, married Arlene Rose Dingilian, 8/5/67. *Children:* Ellen, Jonathan. *Education:* B.S. St. John's University; M.A.T. and Ph.D. Northwestern University. *Professional associations:* Author's Guild, Mystery Writers of America, Romance Writers of America. *Awards:* doctoral fellowship, Northwestern; Special Education Prize, Harvard. *Genres:* historical romances, mysteries, suspense novels. *Agent:* Writer's House 21 W 26 St., N.Y., N.Y. *Current residence:* Manhasset, N.Y.

Favorite authors and books: Kathleen Windsor, Anya Seton, Daphne du Maurier, Thomas B. Costain.

Thoughts on writing: There are two types of literature, the serious kind which seeks to place an author's perspective on life and the entertaining kind, the purpose of which is self-explanatory. Neither is intrinsically better than the other, although both categories have their many bad books and their few good books.

Becoming published/finding an agent: My first book was an occult suspense novel, THE DARK BELOW. I sent it unsolicited to Fawcett, and they published it. After this, I acquired an agent for subsequent books. I cannot stress too strongly the advantages of having an agent—if he or she is good, which mine is. Beware of charlatans who charge too much or give snow jobs.

Bibliography:

Historical romance: (all as Vanessa Royal)
FLAMES OF DESIRE, Dell, 1978.

COME FAITH, COME FIRE, Dell, 1979.
FIREBRAND'S WOMAN, Dell, 1980.
WILD WIND WESTWARD, Dell, 1982.

Suspense:
THE DARK BELOW, Fawcett, 1974.
SUMMER SOLSTICE, Putnam, 1976.
THE FIELDS OF EDEN, Putnam, 1977.
THE CREATOR, Pinnacle, 1978.
SEA CLIFF, Pocket, 1980.
THE HARBINGER, Pocket, 1981.
LILAC NIGHT, Crown, 1981.

JANE AIKEN HODGE

B. Jane Aiken, 12/4/17, Boston, Mass., married Alan Hodge 1/3/48, (deceased). *Children:* Jessica Orebi Gann, Joanna Hodge. *Education:* Somerville College, Oxford, B.A. Honors, English, 1938/ Harvard, 1939. *Professional associations:* Society of Authors, Authors Guild. *Genres:* Historical romance, Regency, modern suspense, biography. *Agent:* Harold Ober Associates, 40 East 49th Street, N.Y., N.Y. 10017. *Current residence:* Lewes, E. Sussex, England.

Favorite authors and books: Jane Austen, Charlotte Brontë, Trollope, Ivy Compton Burnett, Mary Stewart, Helen MacInnes, Sarah Gainham, Mary Renault, Georgette Heyer, Edith Pargeter/Ellis Peters, Barbara Pym, Elizabeth Jane Howard, Lynne Reid Banks, E.H. Young, Margery Sharp, Nevil Shute, and C.S. Forester.

Thoughts on writing: I see absolutely no reason for being apologetic about romance, so long as it is respectable romance. By this I mean a story with a plot, real characters, a moral issue of some kind and some style in the writing. And if that sounds like a recipe for a novel, it is, for the good, solid kind they wrote in the nineteenth century. For me, romance also implies a happy ending, so perhaps it can be described as escapist, but isn't all art to an extent? And mine is a form of escapism that will do no one any harm, which is more than you can say for the porn and violence that passes for so much of modern fiction, and the soft porn that sells as romance.

Becoming published/finding an agent: Through my sister, Joan Aiken, who was already established as a writer and introduced me to her agent. It then took some time; my first three historical romances were universally turned down, but have since been published.

Bibliography: (all as Jane Aiken Hodge)

Historical romance:
    MAULEVER HALL, Doubleday, 1964.
    THE ADVENTURERS, Doubleday, 1965.
    WATCH THE WALL, MY DARLING, Doubleday, 1966.
    HERE COMES A CANDLE, Doubleday, 1967.
    THE WINDING STAIR, Doubleday, 1968.
    MARRY IN HASTE, Doubleday, 1970.
    GREEK WEDDING, Doubleday, 1970.
    SAVANNAH PURCHASE, Doubleday, 1971.
    SHADOW OF A LADY, Coward McCann, 1973.
    REBEL HEIRESS, Coward McCann, 1975.
    RUNAWAY BRIDE, Fawcett Books, 1975.
    JUDAS FLOWERING, Coward McCann, 1977.
    RED SKY AT NIGHT, Coward McCann, 1978.
    WIDE IS THE WATER, Coward McCann, 1981.
    THE LOST GARDEN, Coward McCann, 1982.

SUSPENSE:
    STRANGERS IN COMPANY, Coward McCann, 1973.
    ONE WAY TO VENICE, Coward McCann, 1974.
    LAST ACT, Coward McCann, 1979.

Non-Romance Books:
    THE DOUBLE LIFE OF JANE AUSTEN, Coward McCann, 1972; (Biography).

ELEANOR HODGSON
Pseudonym: Eleanor Howard. *B.* Eleanor Parker, 12/9/31, Winnipeg, Manitoba, married Glen S. Hodgson, 2/54. *Children:* William, Susan, Roy. *Education:* University of Manitoba. *Genre:* historical romance. *Agent:* Meredith Bernstein, 33 Riverside Dr. New York, New York. *Current residence:* 291 Queenston St., Winnipeg, Manitoba.

Favorite authors and books: Rosemary Rogers, Laurie McBain, Victoria Holt, Georgette Heyer.

Thoughts on writing: I have always taken a keen interest in history—particularly British history—so it was only natural that I should lean toward writing historical romances with an English background. Pure escapism they may be, but my books contain historical facts that are as accurate as possible.

Becoming published/finding an agent: I received the names of two New York agencies from Dan Ross, a Canadian writer, and submitted the manuscript of my first historical romance to one of them. I could hardly believe it when I was informed they had sold it!

Bibliography:

Historical romance: (all as Eleanor Howard)
 FORTUNE'S CHOICE, Gallen, 1981.
 CLOAK OF FATE, Pocket Books, 1982.

JOAN M. HOHL
Pseudonyms: Amii Lorin, Paula Roberts. *B.* Joan Maire Reitenauer, 12/31/35, Reading, PA., married Marvin N. Hohl, 1953. *Children:* Lori, Amy. *Professional associations:* Romance Writers of America. *Genres.* Category contemporary. *Current residence:* Reading, PA.

Favorite authors and books: Most everything by Janet Dailey, Jayne Castle, Rachel Ryan, Elaine Chase, Bonnie Drake.

Thoughts on writing: I have read an average of seven books a week since I was eleven. My urge to write began as early as eleven also. When I reached forty, I decided, "Why not?" And I write romances because I enjoy them.

Becoming published/finding an agent: After several rejections, I submitted a manuscript to Dell Candlelight. The editor, Vivian Stephens, read it, liked it, bought it. Thank heavens for editors like Vivian Stephens!

Bibliography:

Category contemporary:
 COME HOME TO LOVE, as Paula Roberts, Tower, 1980.

MORNING ROSE, EVENING SAVAGE, as Amii Lorin, Dell, 1980.
THE TAWNY GOLD MAN, as Amii Lorin, Dell, 1980.
THE GAME IS PLAYED, as Amii Lorin, Dell, 1981.
MORGAN WADE'S WOMAN, as Amii Lorin, Dell, 1981.
BREEZE OFF THE OCEAN, as Amii Lorin, Dell, 1981.
SNOWBOUND WEEKEND, as Amii Lorin, Dell, 1982.
THORNE'S WAY, Silhouette, 1982.
GAMBLER'S LOVE, as Amii Lorin, Dell, 1982.

KAY HOOPER

Pseudonyms: Kay Robbins. *B.* Glenda Kay Hooper, 10/30/57, Atwater, California. *Education:* Isothermal Community College, Liberal Arts major. *Professsional Associations*: Romance Writers of America. *Genres*: Regency, Category contemporary. *Current residence*: Bostic, North Carolina.

Favorite authors and books: My favorite romantic authors include Georgette Heyer, Kathleen Woodiwiss, Jayne Castle, Charlotte Lamb, and Anne Mather. It was Heyer's Regencies which sparked my interest in writing, and I love her humor. In contemporaries, Jayne Castle is by far my favorite. Her characters are strong and believable, and her plots always original and entertaining.

Thoughts on writing: Regencies appealed to me first, mainly because of the sheer romance of that age, but I've since discovered that contemporaries possess their own special brand of magic. In contemporaries I've discovered an opportunity to show that heroes don't have to be macho and brooding, and heroines don't have to be meek and weepy. Modern-day problems and conflicts make fascinating reading! I was a fan of romance for years before trying my hand at writing them, and never believed that romantic novels were simply escapist reading. They're escapist reading only so far as any fiction is escapist reading. Writing—to me—is as close to creation as a single human being can ever come. I've been awed more than once when a character I've created suddenly veers off from a course I've set for him or her, or stubbornly refuses to act in a way I'd planned. They become living beings, in a sense, developing their own little personality quirks.

Becoming published/finding an agent: After years of scribbling poetry and weaving stories in my head, I more or less fell into my first novel. Complaining to a friend that I could write a better romance than the one I happened to be reading at the time, I found myself dared to try it. Knowing absolutely no writers, I had to depend on trial and error, learning as I went along and making more mistakes than I like to think about. If I'd never sold that first manuscript though, I still wouldn't regret it, because I did learn from it. I bought a copy of the WRITER'S MARKET and started sending out sample chapters and query letters before my manuscript was even finished. Several rejection letters later, a positive response to one of my letters arrived from Dell, and I sent them the manuscript. About a month later, an editor from Dell contacted me and offered a contract—revisional, since I had to lengthen the manuscript by about thirty pages. I decided to handle everything myself rather than find an agent, and so far have had no problems. Seeing the trend turning toward contemporaries, I tried my hand at a contemporary text and have concentrated on them ever since. I believe that the romance market is wide-open to new writers and would encourage them to write editors of individual lines for guidelines . . . and learn *patience*!

Bibliography:

Category contemporary:
MASK OF PASSION, Kay Hooper. Dell Ecstasy, August, 1982.
RETURN ENGAGEMENT, Kay Robbins, Jove Second Chance, September, 1982.
BREATHLESS SURRENDER, Kay Hooper. Dell Ecstasy, November, 1982.

Regency:
LADY THIEF, Kay Hooper. Dell Candlelight Regency, July, 1981.

LYN HOWARD
Pseudonyms: Lynsey Stevens, Lynde Howard. *B.* Lynette Desley Howard, 9/28/47, Sherwood, Queensland, Australia. *Education:* Corinda High. *Genres:* Category contemporary. *Current residence:* Bellbird Park, Queensland, Australia.

Favorite authors and books Evelyn Anthony, Catherine Cookson

(UNBAITED TRAP), Dorothy Eden (VINES OF YARABEE), Georgette Heyer, Janet Dailey (MATCHMAKERS), Charlotte Lamb, Anne Mather, Barbara Michaels, Mary Stewart (IVY TREE), Phyllis Whitney.

Thoughts on writing: I see romantic fiction as an entertainment— much the same as a Western, a private detective novel, etc.—and I try to keep that in mind when I'm writing my books. I guess it is a form of escapism, but if romance fiction can make a reader relax, forget troubles and worries for a short time, then surely it can only be therapeutic escape. I get a lot of enjoyment out of writing, and if I can entertain and give pleasure with my books then I am doing what I set out to do. I also try to use authentic Australian settings to give readers a small insight into our "romantic country."

Becoming published/finding an agent: I was introduced to romantic fiction practically from the time I first learned to read. My mother subscribed to the ENGLISH WOMEN'S WEEKLY. I graduated from the serials in the magazines to Mills and Boon hardcovers from the local library. At twenty I tried my hand at writing romantic fiction, but couldn't seem to get it right. (What did a very naive twenty-year-old know about life?)

Four years ago, a little less naive, I decided to have my own house built, and wanted to supplement my income doing something I enjoyed. As a schoolgirl, I had always wanted to be a writer. Writers lead such interesting lives and become very rich—pre my knowledge of typist's backache, lost words, and the taxman!

I finished my first manuscript and dispatched it to London to Mills and Boon; much to my surprise it was rejected. Shocked to the core, I very nearly gave up, but finished my second romance and, not quite as confidently, I sent it to Mills and Boon. At the same time, I sent the rejected manuscript to another firm, Robert Hale, Ltd. I ended up getting both books accepted.

In all honesty, I feel I owe a lot to my editor from Mills and Boon who took the time to set me on the right track, who had the faith in me to sit through a rewrite of my third, and who is always available with help and encouragement.

Bibliography:

Contemporary:
ALL I EVER WANTED, as Lynde Howard, Robert Hale, 1981.
RYAN'S RETURN, as Lynsey Stevens, Mills and Boon, 1981. (New York publisher—Harlequin).
TEREBORI's GOLD, as Lynsey Stevens, Mills and Boon, 1981.
RACE FOR REVENGE, as Lynsey Stevens, Mills and Boon, 1981. New York publisher—Harlequin).
PLAY OUR SONG AGAIN, as Lynsey Stevens, Mills and Boon, 1981. (New York publisher—Harlequin).
TROPICAL KNIGHT, as Lynsey Stevens , Mills and Boon, 1982. (New York publisher—Harlequin).
STARTING OVER, as Lynsey Stevens, Mills and Boon, 1982.
MAN OF VENGEANCE, as Lynsey Stevens, Mills and Boon, 1982.
Note: Lyn Howard has two books currently under contract with Mills and Boon, both scheduled for publication in 1983 under the pseudonym, Lynsey Stevens. Lyn Howard's books have been translated into the German, Spanish, Portugese, Dutch, and Greek.

SUSANNA HOWE
B. 11/19/45, Santa Monica, Ca., married Hal Howe 12/8/69. *Children:* Amy Constance Howe. *Education:* Valley Junior College, North Hollywood, Ca. Major—sociology. *Genre:* Historical romance. *Agent:* Martha Millard, 357 West l9th St., N.Y., N.Y. 10011. *Current residence:* Lake Gregory, Ca.

Favorite authors and books: Kathleen Woodiwiss, THE WOLF AND THE DOVE (my all-time favorite). Fern Michaels, CAPTIVE PASSIONS.

Thoughts on writing: Any form of reading, romance novels no more so than others, is a form of escapism. Writing such a novel is even more so. That someone actually buys the book and enjoys the months I've spent reseraching, getting to know my characters, writing and re-writing is a bonus to the excitement and sense of satisfaction I've already known.

Becoming published/finding an agent: After reading Rosemary Rogers' SWEET SAVAGE LOVE, I told a friend that anyone could write such a book. She challenged me to do so and I quickly found it wasn't as simple as I had thought. I wrote the major love scene first and the rest followed. I was fortunate enough to have the ms. purchased and published without any revisions by Jove in 1978.

Bibliography:
FEVER MOON, Jove 1978.
SNOW FLAME, Jove, 1981.

FLORENCE HURD
Pseudonyms: Fiona Harrowe, Flora Hiller, Felicia Harper. *B.* Florence Schnitzer, Chicago, Ill. *Children*: Susanne Powell, Steve Hurd. *Education*: B.S. University of Chicago, political science. *Genres*: contemporary, Gothic, historical romance. *Agent*: Donald MacCampbell, 12 E. 41st St., N.Y., N.Y. *Current residence*: Encinitas, California.

Favorite authors and books: Though not "category," Norah Lofts is my favorite historical writer; I find THE LUTE PLAYER one of the top historical novels. Lofts' characters are flesh and blood, not caricatures. Above all, she is a superb storyteller who writes with a beautiful command of the English language, never sinking into a quagmire of cliches as so many of our popular romance writers do. Gimone Hall I'd choose for category history romance. FURY'S SUN and PASSION'S MOON contain excellent description and clever, witty dialogue.

Thoughts on writing: Category romance is escapism—how pure depends on the reader. The run-of-the-mill romance is boring, but there are notable exceptions such as Anne Mather (WHISPER OF DARKNESS) who breaks rules and manages to rise above the medium. My personal philosophy is to do the very best I can within the framework of the formula; to have my characters behave consistently and be human; and to involve the reader in a good story.

Becoming published/finding an agent: When I decided to earn my living as a writer, I quit fooling around with short stories and creative writing classes. I sat down and *wrote*. Fortunately my first book, SECRET OF CANFIELD HOUSE, was sold through an agent I was introduced to by a writing friend.

Bibliography:

Contemporary:
TOMORROW, as Felicia Harper, Ballantine Love and Life, 1983.

Gothic:
THE SECRET OF CANFIELD HOUSE, Fawcett, 1966.
WADE HOUSE, NAL, 1966.
THE POSSESSED, Belmont, 1969.
THE GORGON'S HEAD, McFadden, 1971.
THE HOUSE ON TREVOR STREET, Manor, 1972.
WITCHES POND, Manor, 1972.
SEANCE FOR THE DEAD, Manor, 1972.
MOORSEND MANOR, Manor, 1973.
STORM HOUSE, Manor, 1973.
HOUSE OF SHADOWS, Fawcett, 1973.
NIGHTMARE AT MOUNTAIN AERIE, Manor, 1974.
SECRET OF AWEN CASTLE, Avon, 1974.
CURSE OF THE MOORS, Manor, 1975.
THE VOYAGE OF THE SECRET DUCHESS, Avon, 1975.
THE SECRET OF HAYWORTH HALL, Avon, 1975.
TERROR AT SEACLIFF PINES, Manor, 1976.
ROMMANY, Avon, 1976.
THE HOUSE ON RUSSIAN HILL, NAL, 1976.
LEGACY, Avon, 1977.
NIGHT WIND AT NORTHRIDING, NAL, 1977.
SHADOWS OF THE HEART, Avon, 1980.

Historical romance:
LOVE'S FIERY DAGGER, as Flora Hiller, 1971.
LOVE'S SCARLET BANNER, as Fiona Harrowe, 1977.
FOUNTAINS OF GLORY, as Fiona Harrowe, Fawcett, 1979.
FORBIDDEN WINE, as Fiona Harrowe, Fawcett, 1981.
Note: PASSION'S CHILD and PRIDE'S FOLLY, under the pseudonym, Fiona Harrowe, will be published by Fawcett/Ballantine.

AUDREY GRACE HUTTON
Pseudonyms: Barbara Whitnell, Ann Hutton. *B.* Audrey Grace Wilson, 3/30/29, Watford, England, married William West Hutton, 1950. *Children*: Lindsay, Judith, Christopher, Timothy. *Education*: St. Mary's College, Cheltenham, Certificate of Educa-

tion. *Professional associations*: Society of Authors, Romantic Novelists Association. *Genres*: Contemporary, family saga. *Agent*: David Higham Associates, 5-8 Lower John Street, London, Eng. *Current residence*: Epsom, Surrey, England.

Favorite authors and books: Norah Lofts, Anya Seton, Susan Howatch, Mary Stewart.

Becoming published/finding an agent: My first manuscript was published by Robert Hale. I had submitted it to three publishers before that time. He published my second book, and then I asked the Society of Authors to recommend an agent.

Bibliography:

Contemporary:
PASSPORT TO PERIL, Ann Hutton, Robert Hale, 1975.
EDGE OF THE DEEP, Ann Hutton, Robert Hale, 1977.
IVORY SLAVE, Ann Hutton, Robert Hale, 1981.
SEARCH FOR SIMON, Ann Hutton, Robert Hale, 1982.

Family saga:
RING OF BELLS, Barbara Whitnell, Coward McCann, 1982.

JACKIE DIAMOND HYMAN
Pseudonyms: Jacqueline Diamond. *B.* Jackie Diamond Hyman, 4/3/49, Menard, Texas, married Kurt Wilson, 10/8/78. *Education*: Brandeis University, B.A. 1971 in sociology. *Professional associations*: American Theater Critics Association, American Society of Composers, Authors and Publishers. *Awards*: Thomas Watson Foundation Fellowship. *Genres*: Regency, also, currently working on contemporary. *Current residence*: La Habra, California.

Favorite authors and books: My favorite romance authors and books include: PRIDE AND PREJUDICE BY Jane Austen, JANE EYRE by Charlotte Brontë, A REASON FOR RIVALRY by Helen Tucker, REGENCY GOLD by Marion Chesney, and REBECCA by Daphne du Maurier.

Thoughts on writing: I've been a writer since I was a child. Although I prefer fiction, I've earned my living as a journalist for the past ten years, currently as a reporter for the Associated Press. I became interested in writing romance after seeing the PBS version of PRIDE AND PREJUDICE, and then reading Regency romances. Since unfortunately this genre seems to be waning, I've been reading contemporary romance and I am currently working on one. I also write fantasy-science fiction with a romantic twist and I am working on a murder mystery. I think it's unfortunate that due to the romance boom publishers sometimes accept works that lack character development and romantic tension. Even though romances are light, escapist reading, every reader deserves a book that is written in a truly professional, well-thought-out manner.

Becoming published/finding an agent: I sold my first book, LADY IN DISGUISE, by myself after an agent told me she couldn't place it because the market for Regencies was weak. I queried a number of publishers with a letter and then sent it to three publishers, selling it to Walker and Co. the third time out.

Bibliography:
Jacqueline Diamond currently has one book under contract with Walker and Co.

SUSAN JAMISON
Pseudonym: Susan Ross. *B.* Susan Rau, 1/21/46, Bathlehem, Pa., married David Jamison 6/24/67; divorced 2/82. *Children*: Andrew, Edward, Nicholas. *Education*: B.A. 1967, Muskingum College, New Concord, Ohio, Speech; M.A. 1976, University of Akron, Rhetoric. *Genres*: Contemporary romance. *Agent*: Margie Belman, 1176 Sunsetview, Akron, Ohio 44313. *Current residence*: Akron, Ohio.

Favorite authors and books: Trevanian, especially THE LOO SANCTION and THE MAIN, but anything; Helen Van Slyke; Danielle Steel; Mary Gordon; Frederick Forsythe; Leon Uris; James Michner, FIRES OF SPRING, THE SOURCE, THE BOOK OF RUTH; Maxine Hong Kingston.

Thoughts on writing: I spent ten years reading about ten books a week— almost exclusively romance. For me the reading was escapism. The writing I consider a cross between therapy and self-flagelation. But the writing is definitely not escapism. To write a book takes great self-discipline and perseverance. My philosophy of writing is to write about people I know in places I have been to, eating food I've eaten, and doing things that normal, ordinary people do. Realism is important to me.

Becoming published/finding an agent: I took a non-credit writing course that Margie Belman was teaching. She liked a short story I had written—asked me to make it into a novel.

Bibliography:

Contemporary:
HEART, Susan Ross, Bantam, April 1982.
Note: Jamison's second romance is due to be published by Bantam in 1983.

FRANKIE-LEE JANAS
Pseudonyms: Saliee O'Brien, Francesca Greer. *B.* Frances Leroy Griggs, Appleton City, Mo., 11/19/08, married Eugene Janas, January 1960. *Children:* Thurlow Benjamin Weed. *Education:* Junior College in Kansas; University of Texas, English literature. *Genres:* contemporary, family saga, historical romance, Victorian. *Agent:* Jay Garon, 415 Central Park West, N.Y., N.Y. *Current residence:* Hollywood, Florida.

Favorite authors and books: I read all the romance authors and have no favorites.

Thoughts on writing: I write because I must . . . started in early childhood, began romances because there was a demand for them, fell in love with them and believe they are a solace to many readers and I personally take pleasure in helping to provide that solace.

Becoming published/finding an agent: I first became published by magazines, pulps, action western and slicks, including *Post* and *Collier's*. I acquired an agent when I began to write romance novels.

Bibliography:
BAYOU, Bantam.
FIRST FIRE, Warner.
Note: Frankie-Lee Janas has, over the years, published a total of more than thirty novels.

BARBARA FERRY JOHNSON
B. Barbara B. Ferry, Grosse Pointe, Michigan, married William David Johnson, 9/27/47. *Children*: William Green Johnson, Starr Johnson Kellett, Charlotte Johnson Rowland. *Education*: Northwestern University, B.S. in journalism, 1945; Clemson University, M.A. in English, 1964. Graduate study: Oxford University, England; University of South Carolina, University of North Carolina, Greensboro, Western Carolina University. At present, I am Associate Professor of English, Columbia College, Columbia, S.C. *Awards*: Palmetto Writers Fiction Award, 1977, for DELTA BLOOD. *Genres*: Historical romance, family saga. *Agent*: Al Zuckerman, Writers House, 21 West 26th St., N.Y., N.Y. 10010. *Current residence*: Columbia, S.C.

Favorite authors and books: Daphne DuMaurier, Elizabeth Goudge, Anya Seyton, Somerset Maugham.

Thoughts on writing: I write primarily to afford a few hours of pleasureable entertainment for my readers. I do not write to preach a moral, teach a lesson, or proclaim a message, although some of my readers have said they have discovered important messages in my novels. As important to me as a well-wrought plot and well-defined characters in an historical novel is historical accuracy, even with the most minute points. Therefore, I spend weeks doing research before I begin writing, and I continue the research while writing. I've also found that research will lead to interesting additions to the original plot line: for example, research into Viking life for TARA'S SONG led me to researching Constantinople which in turn led to expanding the plot considerably. While I would like to see historical and romantic paperbacks receive better review coverage, I think that the obvious fact of their vast readership indicates how important they are in the literary field. The hundreds of letters I receive from my readers mean a great deal more to me than any formal review. They are telling me that what I write is being read and enjoyed. And that is why I write.

Becoming published/finding an agent: After completing LIONORS, I sent short letters to ten publishers telling them what I had written, enclosing same; all ten responded, Avon first. I sent the ms. and it was accepted. They also accepted DELTA BLOOD a year later. Al Zuckerman then contacted me and asked to become my agent. The best information for new writers is, I think, found in *WRITERS MARKET*. I recommend it to all who ask me how to get published.

Bibliography:
    LIONORS, Avon, 1975.
    DELTA BLOOD, Avon, 1977.
    TARA'S SONG, Avon, 1978.
    HOMEWARD WINDS THE RIVER, Avon, 1979.
    THE HEIRS OF LOVE, Avon, 1980.
    ECHOES FROM THE HILLS, Warner Books, 1982.
Note: Barbara Ferry Johnson's novels have also been published by Sphere Books, England; les Presses de la Cité, Paris; as well in Holland, Germany and Greece; the last four in translation.

SUSAN M. JOHNSON

B. Susan Maria Aho, 7/7/39, Hibbing, MN., married Craig W. Johnson, 1966. *Children:* Taryn, Shawn, Shane. *Education:* B.A. University of Minnesota, art; M.A. University of Minnesota, art. *Professional associations*: Romance Writers of America. *Genres*: Historical romance, young adult. *Agent*: Lisa Collier, 875 Avenue of the Americas, New York, N.Y. *Current residence*: North Branch, Minnesota.

Favorite authors and books: Dorothy Dunnett gives one something to aspire to. She's marvelous. Georgette Heyer is equally good. I also very much enjoy Elinor Glyn, E.M. Hull, Lolah Burford, Jane Morgan, Christianna Brand, Ira Morris, Elizabeth Villars, Edith Wharton, Winston Graham, Elizabeth Harris, Jan Cox Spears, Araby Scott, and of course many others. THE FLAME AND THE FLOWER and SWEET SAVAGE LOVE started this boom, and deserve their reputation: they're great!

Thoughts on writing: Romances are escapism, but then so are detective thrillers, murder mysteries, bestseller "jet set" novels; fiction in general is escapist. I've been a romance reader since my teenage years, but read everything else as well. History fascinates me: the study of manners and morals, the inclination of man to adapt to the world's changes while remaining essentially unchanged on a personal level. Whether one reads accounts of Sumerian or Eygptian civilization, medieval chronicles, Renaissance treatises, eighteenth century diaries or Victorian memoirs, one is struck by the day to day "humaness" of man—the minutiae of life which goes on below, above, around the major upheavals of war, industrial change, diplomacy and manipulation. *That* is what I like to depict, along with the subtle nuances specific to the era I'm writing about. And love, of course, along with money and power has made—and always will make—the world go 'round.

Becoming published/finding an agent: I sent a manuscript of SEIZED BY LOVE to Playboy after a query letter and sample chapter elicited interest. They bought the book and its sequel, LOVESTORM. After two unagented books I asked my editor if she would suggest some agents. Lisa was interested, and I like working with a woman, especially since the romance field is predominately a market for women.

Bibliography:

Historical romance:
    SEIZED BY LOVE, Playboy Press, 1979.
    LOVESTORM, Playboy Press, 1980.
Note: Susan Johnson has a young adult novel currently under contract with Fawcett/Ballantine, and a historical romance under contract to Berkley/Jove.

MARCIA KAMIEN

Pseudonyms: Marcia Rose (in collaboration with Rose Novak) *B.* Marcia Silverman, Mechanicville, NY. *Children*: Sara, Julia. *Education*: B.A. Syracuse University, journalism. *Professional associations*: ASJA. *Genres*: Contemporary. *Agent*: Goodman Associates, 250 West End Avenue, New York, NY. *Current residence*: Brooklyn Heights, NY.

Favorite authors and books: My all-time favorites are: anything by Jane Austen, most of Thomas B. Costain, and GONE WITH THE WIND.

Thoughts on writing: Marcia Rose feels that today's woman with all her new options (and accompanying problems) is at *least* as fascinating as any Regency beauty. Also, very much the *same*. "Romance" novels really deal with human relationships and deserve to be considered mainstream.

Becoming published/finding an agent: Rose Novak and I worked on a manuscript, and it was bought. We were extraordinarily lucky. On the other hand, we read dozens before we began, worked carefully, and rewrote dozens of times—so we were pretty sure we had a saleable book.

Bibliography

Contemporary: (All as Marcia Rose)
    PRINCE OF ICE, Avon, 9/79.
    MUSIC OF LOVE, Ballantine, 9/80.
    SECOND CHANCES, Ballantine, 9/81.
    CHOICES, Ballatine, 9/82.
NOTE: Marcia Kamien currently has a book under contract with Ballantine.

ANNE KOLACZYK

Pseudonyms: Anne Hillary, Anne Benson, Andrea Edwards. *B.* Anne Mikita, 10/7/49, Chicago, IL., married Edward Kolaczyk, 1972. *Children*: Eric, Brian, Kari, Megan. *Education*: B.A. Elmhurst College, elementary education. *Genres*: Category contemporary,

contemporary, Regency. *Agent:* Carol Mann, 168 Pacific St., Brooklyn, NY. *Current residence:* Kildeer, IL.

Favorite authors and books: Regencies: Fiona Hill, Alice Chetwood Ley. Contemporaries: Anybody who ever wrote with originality—Brooke Hastings is good.

Thoughts on writing: I would much rather write a romance than read one because they are so much fun to live. I feel every kind of fiction is really a romance, and hope to write many different kinds. The real challenge is to show the problems today's woman has combining her desire for a career and her need for love.

Becoming published/finding an agent: I enjoyed reading Fiona Hill's SWEET FOLLY so much that I decided to write a Regency myself. I did, sent it to an agent, and it was sold as THE BARTERED BRIDE to Dell.

Bibliography:

Regency:
> THE BARTERED BRIDE, Anne Hillary, Dell Regency, 6/79.
> MISMATCHED LOVERS, Anne Hillary, Dell Regency, 6/80.
> COMPROMISED LOVE, Anne Hillary, Dell Regency, 6/81.
> TANGLED WEB, Anne Benson, Dell Regency, 8/81.
> ESCAPE TO LOVE, Anne Benson, Dell Regency, 10/81.
> LOVE'S GENTLE SMILE, Anne Benson, Dell Regency, 3/82.
> DIAMONDS AND THE ARROGANT RAKE, Anne Hillary, Dell Regency, 3/82.
> HEARTS IN HIDING, Anne Hillary, Dell Regency, 11/82.

Note: Anne Kolaczyk currently has two books under contract with Dell, one in Dell's "Mainstream" line—under the pseudonym, Kathryn Jessup, and another in the "Contemporary"line—under the pseudonym, Andrea Jessup.

JAYNE ANN KRENTZ

Pseudonyms: Stephanie James, Jayne Castle. *B.* Jayne Ann Castle, 3/28/49, San Diego, CA., married Frank A. Krentz, 1971. *Education:* B.A. University of California, Santa Cruz, history; M.L.S. San Jose University. *Genres:* Category contemporary. *Agent:* Steven J. Axelrod, Sterling Lord Agency, New York, NY. *Current residence:* Pasedena, California.

Favorite authors and books: In category contemporary I read anything by Suzanne Simms, Bonnie Drake, Billie Douglass, and Elaine Raco Chase. Outside of romance, I read Dick Francis (suspense), and Andre Norton (science fiction).

Thoughts on writing: Romance writing needs no apology. It is written for pleasure and to escape. It is in the tradition of the ancient and honorable craft of storytelling, and makes no pretensions to being anything else. People who critique it from the perspective of other kinds of literature have missed the point entirely. That's their problem. If they don't like it, they shouldn't read it.

Becoming published/finding an agent: I became published through the diligent use of WRITER'S MARKET. It took six years of trying before I finally sold a manuscript. I was a fan for some time before I started trying to write a romance, and I still feel that the most successful writers in this field are the ones who come to it with a built-in love for the genre. They are the writers who best convey the special mood and attitude needed in these books.

Bibliography

Category contemporary:
>GENTLE PIRATE, Jayne Castle, Dell Ecstasy, 1980.
>WAGERED WEEKEND, Jayne Castle, Dell Ecstasy, 1981.
>RIGHT OF POSSESSION, Jayne Castle, Dell Ecstasy, 1981.
>BARGAIN WITH THE DEVIL, Jayne Castle, Dell Ecstasy, 1981.
>A MAN'S PROTECTION, Jayne Castle, Dell Ecstasy, 1982.
>RELENTLESS ADVERSARY, Jayne Castle, Dell Ecstasy, 1982.
>AFFAIR OF RISK, Jayne Castle, Dell Ecstasy, 1982.
>CORPORATE AFFAIR, Stephanie James, Silhouette Desire, 1982.
>STORMY CHALLENGE, Stephanie James, Silhouette Desire, 1982.
>VELVET TOUCH, Stephanie James, Silhouette Desire, 1982.
>POWER PLAY, Jayne Castle, Dell Ecstasy, 1982.
>RENAISSANCE MAN, Stephanie James, Silhouette Desire, 1982.
>SPELLBOUND, Jayne Castle, Dell Ecstasy, 1982.

Note: Jayne Krentz has two books currently under contract with Silhouette Desire and one book with Dell Ecstasy.

SUSAN KYLE
Pseudonyms: Diana Palmer, Diana Blayne. *B.* Susan Eloise Spaeth, 12/12/46, Cuthbert, Ga., married 10/72. *Children*: Blayne. *Genre*: category contemporary. *Agent*: Steven J. Axelrod, The Sterling Lord Agency, 660 Madison Avenue, N.Y., N.Y. *Current residence*: Cornelia, Georgia.

Favorite authors and books: Magaret Way, RED CLIFFS OF MALPARA; Charlotte Lamb, FRUSTRATION; Dorothy Cork, RELUCTANT DECEIVER; Daphne Clair, A WILDER SHORE; Violet Winspear, THE SIN OF CYNARA; Yvonne Whittal, THE SPOTTED PLUME; Betty Neals, AN APPLE FROM EVE; Jane Donelly, COLLISION COURSE; Robyn Donald, BRIDE AT WHANGATAPU; Frank Yerby, FOXES OF HARROW; Jayne Castle, GENTLE PIRATE, Amii Lorin, MORGAN WADE'S WOMAN.

Thoughts on writing: I think romances are the most delicious escapism available, especially when reality closes in on us. They are dreams that we share with their authors, and for a little while we can be glittering, glamorous, and greatly loved. My philosophy of writing is simply this—never give up until you make a sale. Perseverance will get you published. It worked for me!

Becoming published/finding an agent: One of my good friends coaxed me into sending off one of the manuscripts I'd hidden in my closet, and Anne Gisonny at MacFadden Romances thought I had enough potential to develop. She polished my very rough edges, and encouraged me to send a manuscript to Silhouette. No one was more astounded than I was when they bought it and wanted more. From that day it's been rainbows all the way. The most wonderful fringe benefit is the many readers I've been privileged to meet through correspondence. I found my agent by sending a letter to a literary agency I admired. Steven Axelrod answered the letter and took me under his wing. I think he is the finest agent in the world; no one could prop up my sagging spirits or slumping confidence better.

Bibliography:

Category contemporary: (all as Diana Palmer)
NOW AND FOREVER, MacFadden Romances, 1979.
STORM OVER THE LAKE, MacFadden Romances, 1979.
TO HAVE AND TO HOLD, MacFadden Romances, 1979.
SWEET ENEMY, MacFadden Romances, 1979.
LOVE ON TRIAL, MacFadden Romances, 1979.
BOUND BY A PROMISE, MacFadden Romances, 1979.
DREAM'S END, MacFadden Romances, 1979.
TO LOVE AND TO CHERISH, MacFadden Romances, 1979.
IF WINTER COMES, MacFadden Romances, 1979.
HEATHER'S SONG, Silhouette, 1982.
THE LADY AND THE COWBOY, Silhouette, 1982.

Science-fiction:
THE MORCAI BATTALION, Manor, 1980.
Note: Susan Kyle has a contract with Dell Ecstasy, under the pseudonym Diana Blayne.

ELIZABETH LANE
B. Elizabeth Young, 9/25/41, Pueblo, Colorado (raised in Utah), married Guy Lane, 12/21/62. *Children:* Scott, Tanya, Teresa. *Education*: B.A. University of Utah, 1963, major: biology-education, minors: art, Spanish. *Professional associations*: League of Utah Writers, National League of American Penwomen. *Genres*: Biographical novels, family sagas, historical romance, with a strong emphasis on history. *Agent*: Lea C. Braff, Jarvis, Braff, Ltd, 90 Seventh Avenue, Brooklyn, N.Y. 11217. *Current residence*: Provo, Utah.

Favorite authors and books: Anya Seton, Taylor Caldwell, Norah Lofts, Phyllis Whitney. Outside of the romance category my literary idol is Nikos Kazantzakis—my favorite book, ZORBA THE GREEK.

Thoughts on writing: Although romance is an important element in my writing, I have never categorized myself as a romance writer in the pure sense. I like my readers to come away with the satisfaction of having gained something lasting—a sense of history, a knowledge of personalities, places and events, a glimpse of other times and other lives.

Escapism? Maybe. But an escape from the realities of the present can be an enriching experience. We can enjoy our vicarious romantic experiences and learn from them.

Becoming published/finding an agent: MISTRESS OF THE MORNING STAR was the book I had wanted to write for years before I finally was able to do it. For several months I tried marketing the manuscript on my own, receiving many favorable comments but no acceptances. Following the advice of an article in THE WRITERS' DIGEST, I sent it to Playboy Press. They didn't take it either—their schedule was full—but the editor did recommend an agent she knew, Lea Braff. I sent the ms. to her, she accepted it and sold it the second time out to Richard Gallen Books, a packager. Gallen eventually auctioned the book to Jove, who also took my second novel, DRUMS OF DARKNESS. Subsequently, Gallen asked me to write a series of family saga novels set in China.

Bibliography:

Historical/biographical romance:
   MISTRESS OF THE MORNING STAR, Jove, 1980.

Historical romance:
   DRUMS OF DARKNESS, Jove, 1981.
Note: Elizabeth Lane currently has two family saga novels set in China under contract to Dell Books.

ROCHELLE LARKIN
Pseudonyms: R.T. Larkin, Darrell Fairfield. *B.* Rochelle Richter, 5/6/35, Brooklyn, N.Y. *Children*: Julie, Kim, Teddy. *Genres*: Historical romance, contemporary romance. *Agent*: Roslyn Targ Literary Agency, Inc., 250 W. 57th St., N.Y., N.Y. 10019. *Current residence*: N.Y., N.Y.

Favorite authors and books: The writer whose work I have most enjoyed and most learned from is the English novelist Anthony Trollope.

Thoughts on writing: I believe that contemporary romance is an especially valid genre today. The books we are all writing in this category take into account all of the changes that have occured in women's lives during the past decade. Thus our heroines especially offer role models as well as romance to the reader, although our primary purpose is still storytelling. Perhaps this is why the genre is so popular.

Becoming published/finding an agent: I was first approached to write a non-fiction by by a publisher because of my magazine writing in the entertainment field. I knew the agent I wanted when my market for books expanded, and we've worked together ever since.

Bibliograghy:

Contemporary:
GOLDEN DAYS, SILVER NIGHTS, Dell, 1982.

Historical romance:
HARVEST OF DESIRE, NAL, 1977.
MISTRESS OF DESIRE, NAL, 1978.
TORCHES OF DESIRE, NAL, 1979.
Note: Rochelle Larkin has another contemporary romance currently under contract with Dell. She has also written or co-written over twenty-five other books, both non-fiction and general fiction.

SHIRLEY COX LARSON
Pseudonym: Shirley Hart. *B*. Shirley Roberta Cox, 4/1/37, Ayrshire, Iowa, married Donald E. Larson, 6/6/59. *Children*: Kris, Kara, Keith. *Education*: 1958 degree in music education (BME), Morningside College Sioux City, Iowa, major in music. *Professional associations*: National Writer's Club, Romance Writers of America. *Genres*: Category contemporary. *Agent*: None. *Current residence*: Rochester, N.Y.

Favorite authors and books: My favorites are women in the contemporary field. Janet Dailey, of course—I feel a special affinity for Janet because she is also from Iowa. I absolutely adored the big, sexy novels that she wrote for Pocket. Sara Craven—for her characterization and well-crafted plots. Mary Burchell—she is a marvelous story-teller who has her strong heroines solve their own problems and she uses lots of dialogue. Abra Taylor—she is not afraid to tell a dramatic, forceful story. Charlotte Lamb—has it all, all the characteristics mentioned above. Jayne Castle—has the unique ability to get the hero and the heroine together on the first page and keep them together for the rest of the book.

Thoughts on writing: I take it seriously. I spent six months researching and rewriting my first published novel. I always read more research material than I use. I write one sketchy outline before I start the book, an outline which always turns out to be worthless, but I can't begin without it, and one very useful outline when I get to about page 60. I don't tie myself to an outline but I find you have to have a direction. I write complete (37 questions) character charts for my hero and heroine and the "other woman" or the "other man" or any other characters I feel it necessary to know well. I use the character chart outlined in WRITER'S DIGEST, Nov. 1981 by Colleen L. Reece. I won't start a book without my character sketches because the people in my books are far more important than the plot outlines. I am particularly delighted when I can endow a character with some trait that complicates the book and provides the crisis or turning point in the book. My writing "bible" is Dwight V. Swain's TRICKS AND TECHNIQUES FOR THE $ELLING WRITER.

Writing is a lot of work—and I have come very late to the art. I took creative writing classes in college—and was told in a subtle way that I really had no talent for it. I didn't have the confidence to start writing again until I was thirty-nine, but I can truthfully say it has been one of the most satisfying and exciting things I have ever done.

As for romantic novels being escapist, I find it difficult to understand why romance is criticized for this when most of the other genres are forms of escapism and wish fulfillment, e.g., Westerns, suspense (think of James Bond) and detective stories. One of the problems is that there are really two kinds of romances—at least in the contemporary category—books that are pure froth and books that are realistic. More and more publishers are, I think, turning toward the realistically written romance. Realism is harder to write—but easier to read. But as a romance writer, I applaud the new march toward realism. I believe this will be a turning point for the genre, and that romance will mature and come into its own.

I read my first romance about six years ago, which is really strange since I had been an avid reader all my life. But when I did discover romance—it was like a wonderful new addition to my life. Here was the kind of book I had always wanted to read. A few months and a thousand books later, I decided I wanted to write them as well.

My philosophy? I believe passionately in my reader. I want to bring her every enjoyment I can, with all the skill I have. I want to entertain, enthrall, enlighten and most of all, take her back to that marvelous time of her life when she was being courted by that one special man. Or if the reader is younger, I want to give her hope that somewhere out there is a man who will understand and love her. I work constantly to improve my writing and strive to write the most exciting, engrossing love story that I possibly can—and one that will not insult my reader's intelligence.

Becoming published/finding an agent: I sent my manuscript "over the transom" to Dell. I knew no one in the editorial office and I didn't have an agent. I remember it well because I went to the post office with my manuscript in a scruffy box—I didn't even have an envelope. I had to buy a mailer there and borrow some tape to seal it shut. I walked out—absolutely sure that Dell would sent it back by return mail. It wasn't good enough, sophisticated enough, romantic enough. I was very shocked to get a call from an associate editor—Vivian Stephens had gone to Harlequin and Anne Gisonny had not yet been hired—offering me an advance for my book! I couldn't believe it. Since then, I've enjoyed a marvelous relationship with Anne, who has nurtured and encouraged me and made the books that followed my first one possible.

Bibliography:

Category contemporary:
   A FATAL ATTRACTION, Shirley Hart, Dell Ecstasy, Sept, 1982.
Note: Shirley Larson has four books under contract to Ecstasy, to appear in 1983.

JANE LeCOMPTE
Pseudonyms: Jane Ashford. *B.* Jane LeCompte, Troy, Ohio, 8/20/48. *Education:* Ph.D. English, Miami University, Oxford, Ohio 1976, M.A. English, University of Virginia, Charlottesville 1971. *Genres:* Regency romances. *Agent:* Jean V. Naggar, 336 East 73 Street, N.Y., N.Y. 10021. *Current residence:* New York City and Kent, Connecticut.

Favorite authors and books: Among my favorite authors are Jane Austen and Georgette Heyer.

Thoughts on writing: I was not a romance fan before I began writing Regencies. Though I read Heyer, Victoria Holt, and Mary Stewart in high school, I was probably more a "fan" of science fiction. But I consider romances as a legitimate entertainment across the broad spectrum of types, in the same way that science fiction, westerns, spy adventures etc. are entertainment. This kind of book fills a useful niche between literary classics, which can be difficult and taxing to read, and other forms of entertainment such as television, which are often wholly passive. When well written—and I do my best to write well—the romance is no more a stepchild of publishing than a good mystery or thriller. I have heard concern expressed about their anti-feminism, claiming that romantic novels reinforce limiting stereotypes. For the Regency romance, I would disagree. In the universe of social comedy, the Regency universe heroines are as strong, and have as much power, as heroes. Indeed, they are often more skilled with the medium and weapon of society—language. As in the novels that inspired the genre, Jane Austen's, both the hero and the heroine have strong convictions, and they must come to understand the other's terms, and modify their own, before they can be united. The fact that this process is so much fun does not lessen its significance.

Becoming published/finding an agent: I wrote my first Regency and showed it to Jean Naggar, who agreed to represent me. She sold it to Warner a few months later. When Warner decided to discontinue its Regency line, I moved to Signet (New American Library).

Bibliography: (all as Jane Ashford)

Regency:
GWENDELINE, Warner, 1980.
BLUESTOCKING, Warner, 1980.
MAN OF HONOUR, Warner, 1981.
RIVAL OF FORTUNE, Warner, 1981.
THE THREE GRACES, Signet, 1982.
THE MARCHINGTON SCANDAL, Signet, 1982.
Note: Jane LeCompte currently has two books under contract for Signet.

ALICE CHETWYND LEY

B. Alice Chetwynd Humphrey, Halifax, Yorkshire, England, married Kenneth James Ley, 1945. *Children:* Richard James Humphrey Ley, Graham Kenneth Hugh Ley. *Education:* King Edward VI Grammar School, Birmingham (Matriculation); London University Diploma in Sociology, 1962. Gilchrist Award. *Professional associations:* Romantic Novelists' Assoc. (past Chairman), Society of Women Writers & Journalists. *Genres:* Historical— Georgian and Regency. *Agent:* Curtis Brown, Ltd., 1 Graven Hill, London, W2 3EP. *Current residence:* Middlesex, England.

Favorite authors and books: Everything of Georgette Heyer; older writers such as Jeffrey Farnol (though his style is a little irritating to a modern reader); Robert Neill. Don't like fictionalised biography or "bodice rippers."

Thoughts on writing: I was a fan from my teens, when I started with THE SCARLET PIMPERNEL. I think the historical romance should give the reader as authentic a background as possible without being too boring, but it must be a pleasant read, not sordid. There's enough of that in the world—I can't think why women in particular should want to read it. It's not just pure escapism, because it offers an insight into the social life of the past. I enjoy my writing.

Becoming published/finding an agent: I found an agent through my husband, who was a journalist, now retired. Curtis Brown sold my book right away. In the last ten years, all my books have been paperbacked by Ballantine, USA, and I have recently completed a three-book contract with this firm for original longer paperbacks.

Bibliography:

Historical romances:
> THE JEWELLED SNUFF BOX, Hale, 1959.
> THE GEORGIAN RAKE, Hale, 1960.
> THE GUINEA STAMP, Hale, 1961. (THE COURTING OF JOANNA in US)
> MASTER OF LIVERSEDGE, Hale, 1966. (THE MASTER AND THE MAIDEN in US)
> THE CLANDESTINE BETROTHAL, Hale, 1967.
> TOAST OF THE TOWN, Hale, 1968.
> LETTERS FOR A SPY, Hale, 1970.
> A SEASON AT BRIGHTON, Hale, 1971.
> TENANT OF CHESDENE MANOR, Hale, 1974.
> BEAU AND BLUESTOCKING, Hale, 1975.
> AT DARK OF THE MOON, Hale, 1977.
> AN ADVANTAGEOUS MARRIAGE, Hale, 1977.
> (all of the above paperbacked in the US by Ballantine)
> A REGENCY SCANDAL, Ballantine, 1979.
> A CONFORMABLE WIFE, Ballantine, 1981.

Note: Fawcett is due to publish Alice Chetwynd Ley's THE INTREPID MISS HAYDON in 1983.

PRUDENCE BINGHAM LICHTE

Pseudonyms: Prudence Martin, Henrietta Houston. *B.* Prudence Jane Bingham, 3/3/49, Fort Defiance, AZ., married Martin E. Lichte, Jr., 8/73. *Education*: B.S. Northern State College, history and secondary education. *Genres*: category contemporary, Regency. *Current residence*: Kansas City, Missouri.

Favorite authors and books: Dorothy Dunnett, Roberta Gellis, Georgette Heyer, P.G. Wodehouse, George MacDonald Fraser. In category, I particularly like Charlotte Lamb and Robin James.

Becoming published/finding an agent: A friend encouraged me to write, then to sell the book I'd written. To my surprise, Dell bought COUNTERFEIT COURTSHIP, then purchased another manuscript I'd started in the meantime. When they bought a contemporary proposal, I began reading the genre and have since sold several Ecstasies. In essence, I was a writer before I realized I even wanted to be one. I have no agent, but do believe in the value of them for others.

Bibliography:

Category contemporary: (all as Prudence Martin)
A STRANGE ELATION, Dell Ecstasy, 1982.
HEART'S SHADOW, Dell Ecstasy, 1983.
LOVE SONG, Dell Ecstasy, 1983.
RIVER OF RAPTURE, Dell Ecstasy, 1983.
CHAMPAGNE FLIGHT, Dell Ecstasy, 1983.

Regency:
COUNTERFEIT COURTSHIP, as Prudence Martin, Dell Candlelight, 1982.
AN IMPROPER BETROTHMENT, as Henrietta Houston, Second Chance at Love, 1982.

SUSAN L. LOWE
Pseudonyms: Elise Randolph, Andrea Davidson. *B.* Susan Claire Leach, 3/27/51, Duncan, OK., married James F. Lowe, 1971. *Children:* David, Andrea. *Education:* B.A. University of Missouri, English. *Professional associations:* Romance Writers of America, Women In Communications. *Genres:* Category contemporary. *Current residences:* Houston, TX.

Favorite authors and books: Esther Sager, Kathleen Woodiwiss. LaVyrle Spencer.

Thoughts on writing: I enjoy writing the contemporaries because, through them, I can depict problems that affect so many male-female relationships today. I like to create characters who are trying to find a balance in their lives, women who want both a career and a family, self-sufficient men who have reached the stage where they want and need a woman with whom to share their lives. I like heroes and heroines who opt for a partnership, who work as a team. By all means, the romance and the chemistry must be there. But there must be more; they should also become best friends.

Becoming published/finding an agent: I had never read romances until I met some authors of romance fiction. After reading some of the books on their suggested reading list, I plotted out my own book, worked on the manuscript every day, and sold it to Dell Ecstasy. My first sale was probably due to about ten percent luck, twenty percent skill, and seventy percent hard work. My advice for aspiring writers is to join professional writer's organizations, meet other authors, and by all means read, read, read!

Bibliography:

Category contemporary:
    LOVE, YESTERDAY AND FOREVER, Elise Randolph, Dell Ecstasy, 1982.
    A SPARK OF FIRE IN THE NIGHT, Elise Randolph, Dell Ecstasy, 1982.
Note: Susan Lowe has one book currently under contract to Dell Ecstasy, tentatively scheduled for publication in 1983, and two books currently under contract to Harlequin's "North American Romances" line, also scheduled for 1983.

MARY LYNN
Pseudonym: Angel Milan. *B.* Mary Elizabeth Nelson, 3/17/39, Enid, OK., married Jim Hannan, divorced 5/58. Married Ted Lynn, 11/66. *Children:* Terri, Jon, Kim, Chris. *Grandchildren:* Jake and Marilyn Hart. *Education:* Radiologic Technology (Registered Technician), A.A. degree (Phi Theta Kapps), Okaloosa-Walton Jr. College; Real estate broker, Jones College, Denver; upper level classes at University of Maryland, Far East Division, Tokyo, Japan; upper level classes at Golden Gate University, Ca.; upper level classes, University of Oklahoma; SCUBA certification, Miami, Fl.; private pilot's license, Edwards Air Force Base, Ca. *Professional associations:* Romance Writers of America; Northeastern Oklahoma Romance Authors (NORA), Oklahoma Writer's Federation, Inc. (OWFI); Mid-Oklahoma Writers; Pinocchio Writers of Norman, Okla.; Aircraft Cwners and Pilots Assoc.; National Association of Real Estate Boards; American Registry of Roentgenologic Technologists. *Genres:* Category contemporary. *Agent:* Dixie Lee Davidson, Dixie Lee Davidson Literary Agency, Inc., Omaha, Nebraska. *Current residence:* Albuquerque, N.M.

Favorite authors and books: I've especially enjoyed reading Rachel Ryan, Alice Morgan, Carole Halston, Stephanie James and

Monica Barrie. Janet Dailey is my real-life heroine!

Thoughts on writing: It gives me great pleasure to see the contemporary romances evolving toward maturity through the use of more modern and realistic plots and heroines who are adult, thinking, successful human beings. Our heroines are now (in most cases) women of strength, substance, and vision, their lives enhanced by romance, not dependent upon it as a vehicle for their own happiness. Bravo! Exploring another person's life, even though fictional, is a fine adventure, a relaxing pastime, a mysterious journey that affords great pleasure and easy diversion from the every-every-day. Romance is the finer essence of life, the experiences one should savor and cherish and relive, as often as one wishes through the magic of romantic fiction.

Becoming published/finding an agent: Jack Bickham, professor of professional writing at the University of Oklahoma, is my mentor. Without his guidance and encouragement I doubt I would have become so quickly successful. I began writing in September of 1980 and received my first contract from Simon & Schuster in May of 1981 for the Silhouette Special Edition AUTUMN HARVEST. He also introduced me to Dixie Lee Davidson, my agent and now my close friend. My family is not to be slighted here; they have supported me through the worst of times and rejoiced with me through the best! Advice? Read! Read everything in the category you wish to write, study it. Choose a good teacher, listen. Then work, work very hard at the craft of writing. There are so many rewards for your accomplishments, not the least of which is self-esteem.

Bibliography:

Category contemporary:
   AUTUMN HARVEST, Angel Milan, Silhouette Special Edition, August 1982. Mary Lynn has two books under contract to the "Desire" series of Silhouette, both to appear under the pseudonym of Angel Milan.

PATRICIA ANNE MATTHEWS
Pseudonyms: P.A. Brisco, Patty Brisco, Laura Wylie. *B.* Patricia Anne Ernst, 7/1/27, San Fernando, CA., married Clay-

ton Hartly Matthews, 1971. *Children:* Michael, David. *Professional associations:* PEN (Advisory Board member), Romance Writers of America, Writers Guild, Authors League. *Awards:* Silver Medal of the West Coast Review of Books for NIGHT VISITOR. *Genres:* Gothic, historical romance, occult. *Agent:* Jay Garon, 415 Central Park West, New York, NY. *Current residence:* Los Angeles, CA.

Favorite authors and books: Daphne du Maurier (REBECCA is one of my all time favorites.), Mary Stewart, Margaret Mitchell, Jean Auel—CLAN OF THE CAVE BEAR.

Thoughts on writing: I believe that the requirements for a good book are the same no matter what genre the writer is working in. A good plot and subplot, well-conceived and fully rounded characters, and a professional writing style are, in my opinion, just as necessary to a romance as they are to any other kind of book. In my own books, I try to tell an interesting story involving people the reader can care about and get involved with. I try to make the love scenes romantic, but as real as possible. I believe that writers should give their best to any book they write; and I see no reason why popular fiction cannot be good fiction as well. As far as the complaint that romances are only escape fiction, well, if that were true, there still would be nothing wrong with that. However, an accurately researched historical novel offers considerable historical data, painlessly packaged.

Becoming published/finding an agent: My first published works were poetry, which I submitted directly over the transom. My first sales in short stories were submitted and sold the same way, as was my first book, a science fiction entitled THE OTHER PEOPLE. I did not get an agent until I married Matt (Clayton Matthews) and began to share his agent, Jay Garon. It was Jay who suggested that I try a historical romance. I did and LOVE'S AWAKENING HEART immediately hit the best seller list, starting a lucky string of best sellers.

Bibliography:

Gothic: (all as Patty Brisco)
   HORROR AT GULL HOUSE, Belmont Tower, 1969.

HOUSE OF CANDLES, Manor, 1972.
THE CRYSTAL WINDOW, Avon, 1976.
MIST OF EVIL, Manor, 1976.

Historical romance:
LOVE'S AVENGING HEART, Pinnacle, 1/77.
LOVE'S WILDEST PROMISE, Pinnacle, 6/77.
LOVE, FOREVER MORE, Pinnacle, 12/77.
LOVE'S DARING DREAM, Pinnacle, 5/78.
LOVE'S PAGAN HEART, Pinnacle, 11/78.
LOVE'S MAGIC MOMENT, Pinnacle, 1979.
LOVE'S GOLDEN DESTINY, Pinnacle, 9/79.
LOVE'S RAGING TIDE, Pinnacle, 1/80.
LOVE'S SWEET AGONY, Pinnacle, 5/80.
LOVE'S BOLD JOURNEY, Pinnacle, 10/80.
TIDES OF LOVE, Bantam, 6/81.

Occult:
THE NIGHT VISITOR, as Laura Wylie, Bantam, 3/79.
Note: Patricia Matthews has also published poetry, plays, juvenile books, mysteries, and short stories, as well as having written and sold a property for television. Matthews has two books currently under contract to Bantam, one co-authored by her husband, Clayton Matthews.

LAURIE McBAIN
B. Laurie Lee McBain, 10/15/49, Riverside, California. *Education*: San Bernadino State College. *Professional associations*: Authors Guild, The Authors League of America. *Genres*: Regency, Georgian, Victorian. *Current residence*: Carmel, California.

Favorite authors and books: The novels of Daphne du Maurier, Georgette Heyer, Mary Stewart, and Kathleen Woodiwiss have been very influential in my career and remain favorites of mine.

Thoughts on writing: I have always loved history. I also have always enjoyed reading fiction. Having a deep desire to write, the perfect combination for me was to write a historical novel. I think of myself as a story teller. I want to bring the past vividly alive for the reader. The romance in historical novels is more than the romance between the hero and heroine; it is the romance of the period of history. I strive to recreate this with a blend of romance, adventure, mystery, historical atmosphere, and well-developed characters. Secondary characters are very important to me, as well as including humorous situations. I always hope that the reader will feel a sense of satisfaction when finishing one of my novels, and that is why I believe in happy endings. I don't ever want anyone to feel despondent when turning that last page. My main purpose is to entertain.

Becoming published/finding an agent: After completing my first novel, DEVIL'S DESIRE, I consulted THE WRITER'S HANDBOOK and THE WRITER'S MARKET. These books listed the names of editors, and the names and addresses of the different publishing houses, as well as the types of books they were publishing, and if they wanted an outline and sample chapter, or the whole manuscript. I knew that Avon was publishing historical novels, and were accepting unsolicited manuscripts. I learned this from THE WRITER'S HANDBOOK, as well as how to prepare the manuscript for consideration. Fortunately my novel was accepted, and thus began my career.

Bibliography:

Georgian:
    MOONSTRUCK MADNESS, Avon Books, 1977.
    CHANCE THE WINDS OF FORTUNE, Avon, 1980.
    DARK BEFORE THE RISING SUN, Avon, 1982.

Regency:
    DEVIL'S DESIRE, Avon, 1975.

Victorian:
    TEARS OF GOLD, Avon, 1977.

LORENA McCOURTNEY

Pseudonyms: Rena McKay, Jocelyn Day, Lisa McConnell. *B.* Lorena Knoll, 7/19, Wellpinit, Washington, married Jim McCourtney, 1973. *Children*: Bill. *Education*: B.S. in Agriculture, 1954, Washington State college. *Professional associations*: Romance Writers of America. *Genres*: Category contemporary. *Agent*: Donald MacCampbell, 12 East 41st Street, N.Y., N.Y. 10017. *Current residence*: Grants Pass, Oregon.

Favorite authors and books: I've always loved the old Zane Grey western romances.

Thoughts on writing: I like to write "escapism" —glamorizing settings and characters a bit, but grounding them in reality so the reader feels this could happen.

Becoming published/finding an agent: I started out scribbling horse stories when I was at the horse crazy stage as a girl, went on to a little nonfiction writing, then to juvenile and teenage short stories and romance short stories. About three years ago I turned to book length romances, and this is the field in which I most enjoy writing.

Bibliography:

Category contemgorary:
    PROMISE IN PARADISE, Lorena McCourtney. Candlelight, 1979.
    LEGACY OF THE HEART, Lorena McCourtney. Candlelight, 1980.
    SHADOWS OF THE HEART, Lorena McCourtney. Candlelight, 1980.
    BRIDAL TRAP, Rena McKay. Silhouette, 1980.
    DESERT DEVIL, Rena McKay. Silhouette, 1981.
    GLITTER GIRL, Jocelyn Day. Second Chance at Love, 1981.
    TENDER CONQUEST, Jocelyn Day. Second Chance at Love, 1981.
    STEELE HEART, Jocelyn Day. Second Chance at Love, 1982.
    TARNISHED RAINBOW, Jocelyn Day, Second Chance at Love, 1982.

MARGIE McDONNELL
Pseudonyms: Margie Michaels. *B.* Margie Pritchard, 3/25/54, Corona, California, married Michael McDonnell, 12/16/72. *Children:* Christopher, Shaun, Thomas. *Education:* Graduated Magna Cum Laude from United States International University in 1976, degree in psychology/human behavior. *Genres:* Category contemporary. *Agent:* Donald MacCampbell, Inc., 12 East 41st Street, N.Y., N.Y. 10017. *Current residence:* Vista, California.

Favorite authors and books: Janet Dailey is my favorite romance author, but several other authors influenced both my desire to write and probably my style as well. Among them: Pearl Buck, James Michner, and science-fiction author C.J. Cherryh.

Thoughts on writing: First of all, we all need to be able to put our problems aside for a time, to revitalize our energies and to help us deal with our day-to-day problems objectively; whether we "get away from it all" with a walk in the woods, or my listening to music, running a mile or reading a good book, "escapism" is a very necessary part of our lives. A good romance can provide this. But it does something more. A good romance can serve to remind women how wonderful it feels to be a woman and be in love. Whether a woman works outside or inside the home, we often forget our womanhood, sacrifice it to our careers and our families. Romances can be a touchstone to remind us of our femininity and all that it means to each of us.

Becoming published/finding an agent: I had an intense desire to write, some talent, an agent who believed in me enough to help me along and be supportive during the rough times, and an editor and publisher who were willing to work with me to create what I believe to be two excellent romances.

I had always wanted to be published, but never had the nerve to try. My husband brought a copy of the 1979 WRITER'S MARKET home and told me that I should try. I called Maureen Moran at Donald MacCampbell, Inc., told her that I had a story. She expressed an interest in seeing it. Our association began at that point, as did my writing success.

Bibliography:

Category contemporary:
> BELOVED PIRATE, Margie Michaels. Jove-Second Chance at Love, October 1981.
> MIRAGE, Margie Michaels. Jove-Second Chance at Love, July 1982.

DOROTHY MC KITTRICK
Pseudonyms: Dorothy Mack. *B.* Dorothy Frances Alexander, 6/14/37, Cranston, RI., married Harold V. McKittrick, 1960. *Children:* Neil, Paul, Terry. *Education:* A.B. Brown University, psychology. Ed. M. Harvard University, guidance. *Professional associations:* Romance Writers of America, Washington Romance Writers. *Genres:* Regency. *Current residence:* Oakton, VA.

Favorite authors and books: I was weaned on Emilie Loring and Faith Baldwin, then discovered Georgette Heyer the lucky day I pulled FREDERIKA off a library shelf. It remains one of my all time favorite books. I like Clare Darcy's Regencies, especially GEORGIANNA, and those by Alice Chetwynd Ley. I've read everything I could find by Iris Bromige, Lucy Walker, and Elsie Lee, and I enjoy the humor of Glenna Finley and the wit, style, and pacing of Jacqueline Gilbert. If Mary Stewart and Jane Aiken Hodge are regarded as romance writers, they must be added to my list.

Thoughts on writing: The years my children were small my reading was heavily weighted on the romance side, probably as pure escapism. Poor writing and sudden happy endings that didn't evolve naturally from the progress of the story annoyed me mightily, and I started to rework such endings in my head. At the same time, Georgette Heyer's books led me to a real interest in the late eighteenth century and the Regency period. At first I dabbled in research, then, subsequently invented characters and conceived a plot in my head for a Regency novel—all this before I put a word on paper. When I finally did dirty a page it was to begin the last chapter because I figured there was no point in attempting a romance if I couldn't write a love scene. The rest of the story flowed from beginning to end except for the first chapter which came last because it was the most crucial and the most difficult for me. Since then my novels have been set down in the correct order with the rare exception of a scene that demands to be recorded lest I forget some details. I regard psychological realism as crucial; I dislike any novel where the characters act "out of character" for the convenience of the author. I firmly believe good writing and realism can exist within the romance framework.

Becoming published/finding an agent: The first novel, written in secret, was shown to a friend, a rabid romance reader, who corrected my spelling and suggested I send the manuscript to a publisher. I chose Dell because their Regency writers were so bad I thought they might be more willing than other publishers to read a first novel. By the time I received a very encouraging rejection letter, I was well launched on a second book and enjoying myself too much to stop. The second story earned me an even nicer rejection letter—to the effect that Dell was not acquiring Regencies at that time. A year later, the editor, Beverly Lewis, wrote to me requesting another look at both manuscripts if I hadn't achieved publication elsewhere. Dell bought these books and the next three I wrote. I was never asked to make any revisions in my stories, nor was one word changed for publication.

If this sounds too easy, let me hasten to add that now the the Regency market has contracted, I find myself in the same boat as any novice writer in trying to locate a publisher. I am going to take my own advice and try to find an agent.

Bibliography:

Regency: (all as Dorothy Mack)
THE SUBSTITUTE BRIDE, Dell, 1977.
THE RAVEN SISTERS, Dell, 1977.
THE IMPOSSIBLE WARD, Dell, 1978.
A COMPANION IN JOY, Dell, 1980.
THE BELLE OF BATH, Dell, 1981.

BARBARA METZGER

B. Barbara Metzger, New Rochelle, New York, 1944. *Education:* B.A. Connecticut College, 1966; philosophy. *Genres:* Regency. *Agent:* Myra Gross & Associates, 6930 NW 83 Street, Tamarac, Florida. *Current residence:* Montauk, New York.

Favorite authors and books: Georgette Heyer of course. Claire D'Arcy and Laura London.

Thoughts on writing: I am only concerned with Regencies, and above all, I think they should be fun without taking themselves seriously. I worked as an editor, copy editor, proof-reader, etc, and was introduced to Georgette Heyer over fifteen years ago— instant fascination!

Becoming published/finding an agent: After three or four very nice rejections (we're over contracted; get some experience) my friend started sending the story out to "contacts," then Regency publishers.

Bibliography:

Regency:
BETHING'S FOLLY, Barbara Metzger. Walker & Co., 1981.
THE EARL AND THE HEIRESS, Barbara Metzger. Walker & Co., 1982.

HELEN M. MITTERMEYER

Pseudonyms: Hayton Monteith, Ann Cristy. *B.* Helen Hayton Monteith, 4/30/30, Rochester, N.Y., married W. B. Mittermeyer, 6/21/52. *Children:* Paul Frances, Ann Mary, Daniel Joseph, Cristine Mary. *Education:* two years at the University of Rochester—Nazareth College, two years at Miss McCarthy's School. *Professional associations:* Genessee Valley Writers, Alqonquin West. *Awards:* Made eighth on Walden book list, 4/24/82; made thirteenth on Dalton book list, 4/24/82. *Genres:* Category contemporary. *Agent:* Ellen Levine Literary Agency, Suite 906, 200 Madison Avenue, N.Y., N.Y. *Current residence:* Irondequoit, New York.

Favorite authors and books: William Shakespeare, TAMING OF THE SHREW Also—Shaw, Heyer and among modern romance—Charlotte Lamb, Anne Mather.

Thoughts on writing: Romances are and can be a morality message, and the best way to teach love, travel, understanding and empathy. Escapism is the cheapest way there is to stay on mental keel. I became a fan after deciding to crack the market. To delineate characters in an elusively provocative way, to bury a message that the reader recalls again and again.

Becoming published/finding an agent: I submitted my work to Ecstasy at the urging of a friend. Vivian Stephens bought my book and encouraged me. At the first annual Romance Conference in Houston in 1981 I was approached by a representative from Ellen Levine's literary agency. Ellen called me when I returned home—that was it.

Bibliography:

Category contemporary:
FROM THE TORRID PAST, Ann Cristy. Jove-Second Chance at Love, May 1982.

TO LOVE A STRANGER, Hayton Monteith. Dell Ecstasy, June 1982.
TORN ASUNDER, Ann Cristy. Jove-Second Chance at Love, July 1982.
RELENTLESS LOVE, Hayton Monteith. Dell Ecstasy, August 1982.
Note: Helen M. Mittermeyer currently has a book under contract both
with Second Chance at Love and Dell Ecstasy. She also has four books
contracted to Bantam, to appear under her own name.

ALICE MORGAN
B. Alice Anne Heckler, 7/6/33, Long Beach, CA., married William
G. Morgan, 1950. *Children:* Michael, Nanci. *Professional associatins:*
Romance Writers of America, National Writer's Club. *Awards:* The
Pearl Award for most sensuous novel. *Genres:* Category contempo-
rary. *Current address:* Fort Bragg, CA.

Favorite authors and books: Margaret Way—I adore her heroes and
her descriptions of the Australian countryside. Anne Mather—
because she creates tension beautifully. Violet Winspear—her
older books have terrific foreign heroes.

Thoughts on writing: Category romances are my favorite reading,
though I have only been a fan for the past five years. I like books
that are within the realm of reality. My desire to write comes out
of a dissatisfaction with meek heroines and mild-mannered heroes. I wanted a hero who pursued the heroine from the moment
of first contact, one who didn't vacillate in his determination to
make her his wife. My fan mail has proven there are many readers who are also seeking a more sensuous novel with implicit
scenes and tender, virile heroes.

Becoming published/finding an agent: I submitted a manuscript to
Dell. Direct phone contact with editor Vivian Stephens resulted
in her pulling my manuscript from their slush pile. Revisions followed, a sale, and discussion of ideas for other books. I sold two
additional books within a short period of time to her new, more
sensuous line, "Candlelight Ecstasy." I have now sold two books
to Harlequin's "North American Romances," scheduled to debut
in 1983.

When I was notified that my first book had won an award, it
was one of the most thrilling events of my life. Flying to New
York to receive the award and getting to meet many of the read-

ers who enjoyed my book was the ultimate ego trip for a novice author. I'll never forget it.

Bibliography:

Category contemporary:
MASQUERADE OF LOVE, Candlelight Ecstasy, 4/82.
SANDS OF MALIBU, Candlelight Ecstasy, 5/82.
IMPETUOUS SURROGATE, Candlelight Ecstasy, 7/82.
Note: Alice Morgan has two books currently on contract with Harlequin's new line, "North American Romances."

NANCY MORSE
B. Nancy Lupo, 12/18/46, Brooklyn, N.Y., married Talley Morse, 4/8/67. *Professional associations:* Romance Writers of America. *Awards:* 1978 and 1979 placed within the top one hundred winning entries in the Writers Digest Creative Writing Competition, short story category. *Genres:* Historical romance, Contemporary romance. *Agent:* Irene Goodman Literary Agency, 134 West 81 Street, N.Y., N.Y. 10024. *Current residence:* Bayside, New York.

Favorite authors and books: I adore the kind of sexy historicals that Rosemary Rogers writes, and, of course, the contemporary romances of Janet Dailey. And while Ayn Rand may not be quite in this mode, she wrote some of the most incredible love stories. Can't you just feel the passion raging between John Galt and Dagny Taggart in ATLAS SHRUGGED? Whew! it leaves me limp each time I read it.

Thoughts on writing: Writing romance is fun, if you can call being hunched over a typewriter for twelve hour stretches fun. I write it for the same reason most people read it—escapism. I try to imbue my heroines with a strong sense of self and purpose, so that not only will my books afford a few hours of pleasurable escapism but also provide the impetus for a reader to look into herself and discover her own strengths. To me, writing is demonic possession. My advice to aspiring writers is to ignore rejection slips, develop a thick skin, persevere, and perhaps most important of all if you intend to write for money, learn to live with fear, but don't let it stop you.

Becoming published/finding an agent: At the risk of sounding trite, I was in the right place at the right time. A new romance line was opening up and there I was with not one, but two, manuscripts. My interest in American Indian history and culture led to the inevitable writing of SILVER LADY. After my first two books were published, I didn't exactly find an agent; rather, she found me. Since then I have sold another manuscript, a contemporary romance which, as of this writing, is not yet published. While I was lucky to sell my first three books, I would not advise anyone to underestimate the amount of work that went into it. I have learned that things change constantly, and it pays to keep on top of who's buying what. Aspiring writers should read, read, read the kind of books they're planning on writing before plunging in head first as I did.

Bibliography:

Historical romance:
SILVER LADY, Pocket Books, 1980.
THIS TENDER PRIZE, Pocket Books, 1980.

CARLA A. NEGGERS
Pseudonym: Amalia James. *B.* Carla Amalia Neggers, 8/9/55, Belchertown, Ma., married Joe B. Jewell, 7/23/77. *Children*: Kate. *Education*: B.S., magna cum laude, Boston University, journalism. *Professional associations*: Romance Writers of America, International Women's Writing Guild. *Genres*: Category contemporary, contemporary, historical romance, romantic suspense. *Agent*: Denise Marcil, 316 W. 82nd St., N.Y., N.Y. 10024. *Current residence*: Arlington, Ma.

Favorite authors and books: I enjoy Robin James, Bonnie Drake/Billie Douglas, Elaine Raco Chase, and many others. I also adore Mary Stewart and read lots of other types of fiction: Robert Parker, Gregory MacDonald, Charlotte MacLeod, James Carroll.

Thoughts on writing: I enjoy romances that are a mix of fun and passion, and I have a great time writing them. I work very hard to make everything I write as excellent as I can, and I take my writing very seriously, which isn't to say my writing is at all serious! I respect the intelligence of my readers and believe they don't want to read "junk" any more than I want to write it. A good romance is a good romance is a good romance . . . which is why I read them and why I write them.

Becoming published/finding an agent: I was referred to my agent, Denise Marcil, by the International Women's Writing Guild, of which I am a member. Denise read my first novel—a romantic suspense tale—and loved it, but that genre was not selling, so she suggested I write a romance. I did, and my first romance, MIDSUMMER DREAMS, was sold to Bantam Books.

Bibliography:

Category romance:
MIDSUMMER DREAMS, Amalia James, Bantam Circle of Love, May 1982.
TANGLED PROMISES, Amalia James, Bantam Circle of Love, July 1982.
Note: Carla Neggers currently has two category romances under contract with Bantam's new Loveswept line, an historical romance with Gallen, a longer contemporary with Avon's Finding Mr. Right series, and a romantic suspense with Avon's new romantic suspense line. All of these books will appear under the author's real name.

JESSIE OSBORNE
Pseudonym: Jessie Ford. *B.* Jessie Huggins, 1944, San Diego, Ca., married Ted Osborne, 7/66. *Education:* B.A., San Diego State College, social science. *Professional associations:* Romance Writers of America. *Genres:* Category contemporary, historical romance. *Agent:* Diane Cleaver, Sanford J. Greenburger Agency, 825 Third Ave., N.Y., N.Y. *Current residence:* San Diego, Ca.

Favorite authors and books: Charles Dickens, Charlotte Brontë, Anya Seton, Kathleen Woodiwiss.

Thoughts on writing: I'm encouraged by publisher and reader interest in better quality stories and more richly developed and realistic heroes and heroines. I imagine many readers escape with romantic novels—but I also think the primary emphasis on the male/female relationship in romance novels reflects the readers' basic interest in and need to understand basic human relationships. The rule of a happy ending in romance novels is the wish for the same in real life.

Becoming published/finding an agent: I read three or four historical romances while recovering from a minor auto accident and thought I could write one. I had always wanted to write a novel and when the right time came, I decided to try writing an historical. A year later, LOVE, REMEMBER ME, was finished. My agent was recommended by another agent.

Bibliography:

Category contemporary:
SEARCHING, Jessie Ford, Ballantine Love and Life, Oct. 1982.

Historical romance:
LOVE, REMEMBER ME, Jessie Ford, Ballantine, Oct. 1980.

ELAINE FOWLER PALENCIA
Pseudonyms: Laurel Blake. *B.* Elaine Fowler 3/19/46, Lexington, Kentucky, married Michael Palencia-Roth, 6/1/68. *Children:* Rachel Glenith, Andrew Michael. *Education*: B.A. Magna Cum Romance Writers of America (A.A.U.W., Phi Beta Kappa). *Genres:* Category contemporary. *Agent:* Arthur P. Schwartz, 435 Riverside Drive, N.Y. 10025. *Current residence:* Champaign, Illinois.

Favorite authors and books: For my money, JANE EYRE and MIDDLEMARCH are still the ones to beat.

Thoughts on writing: I do not generally read romances, unless the great 19th century romantics count. The authors who have influenced me the most are Faulkner, Joyce, and the poet Wallace Stevens, with Dashiell Hammett also a big help on technique. Significant writing is writing that changes the way that we look at the world. I will be happy if I can just get someone to change or even think about the way he/she looks at the way men and women relate to each other. Even the category romance can perform this function if the writer takes her job seriously.

Becoming published/finding an agent: I had published short fiction in "little"reviews before coming to romance writing. I outlined a Harlequin, wrote an outline of my own, and started in. I submitted three chapters to Harlequin and was encouraged to finish, but the complete ms. was rejected. I next submitted it to Dell's Candlelight line and it was accepted. With contract pending, I picked an agent out of Literary Market Place and have had him ever since.

Bibliography:

Category contemporary:
   HEART ON HOLIDAY, Elaine Fowler Palencia. Dell Candlelight, 1980.
   STORMY PASSAGE, Laurel Blake. Jove Second Chance at Love, 1982.
Note: Elaine Fowler Palencia currently has two books under contract with Second Chance at Love.

CORNELIA M. PARKINSON
Pseudonym: Day Taylor (shared with co-author Sharon Salvato). *B.* Cornelia M. McNary, Casey, Il., married Richard W. Parkinson, 3/44. *Children:* Cassandra, Claudia, Cornelia. *Professional associations*: Authors League, National League of American Pen Women. *Genres*: category contemporary, historical romance. *Agent*: David S. Hull, Peter Lampack Agency, Inc. , 551 Fifth Ave., Suite 2015, N.Y., N.Y. 10017. *Current residence*: Reynoldsburg, Ohio.

Favorite authors and books. Constance Heaven, THE FIRES OF GLENLOCHY; Belinda Grey, SWEET WIND OF MORNING and LOOM OF LOVE; Sara Seale, TO CATCH A UNICORN; Mary Burchell; Patti Beckman, ANGRY LOVER; Betty Neels, LAST APRIL FAIR; Dixie Browning, WINTER BLOSSOM; Rachel Lindsay, MAN OF ICE and FORBIDDEN LOVE. Old favorites include Christopher Morley, KITTY FOYLE; Marya Mannes, MESSAGE FROM A STRANGER; everything by Norah Lofts and Pamela Frankau; and some of the books of Myrtle Reed and Gene Stratton-Porter.

Thoughts on writing: Yes, these books are pure escapism—and I defend them with my last breath. To me the most satisfying scene to be found in a book is a love scene involving two people who are growing to love each other. The category romance offers fulfillment for our dreams of the perfect lover—exciting, in charge, and yet infinitely patient and tender. I've been an avid reader all my life, but only began category romance reading about a year ago. I like their simplicity and their quality of fantasy, as well as the assurance that everything is going to turn out well. As for writing this kind of book, I love it. I have a happy romantic life, as well as my own fantasies, and it's fun putting this on paper for others to enjoy too. My philosophy of writing is that reading ought to be enjoyable, heart lifting, and painlessly educational.

Becoming published/finding an agent: I first become published as a free-lancer writing articles, short stories, humor, fillers, city brochures and Chamber of Commerce material. I did not then use an agent. Instead, I studied the markets, keeping a lot of queries and written materials in the mails until they sold. For over three years I was the Columbus area stringer for NATIONAL ENQUIRER. After years of professional writing, I turned to writing books. My first published book I wrote with Sharon Salvato and we used her agent, David Stewart Hull.

Bibliography:

Historical romance:
   THE BLACK SWAN, as Day Taylor (with Sharon Salvato), Dell, 1978.
   MOSSROSE, as Day Taylor, Dell, 1980.

RACHEL COSGROVE PAYES
Pseudonyms: E.L. Arch, Joanne Kaye. *B.* Rachel Ruth Cosgrove, 12/11/22, Westernport, MD., married Norman M. Payes, 1954. *Children:* Robert, Ruth. *Education:* B.S. West Virginia Wesleyan College, speech and biology. *Genres:* Gothics, science fiction, mysteries. *Current residence:* Shrub Oak, NY.

Favorite authors and books: I like Georgette Heyer. Other than her books, I find most romances unreadable. For pleasure, I read mysteries, spy and adventure novels, and science-fiction.

Thoughts on writing: Of course romances are pure escape reading—there's nothing wrong with that. Anything that relieves the pressures of modern living is good. Reading anything beats watching the boob tube or playing video games. I write because I must—I'm a writer. I write whatever is going in the mass market, or try to! I write for "fun, fame, and fortune," not necessarily in that order. I like to do historicals because the research is so interesting. It's my excuse for traveling to exotic places, and then I use those locales for background material in my books— which pay for more travel, etc.

Becoming published/finding an agent: I first became published by sending in an Oz manuscript cold and having it accepted. I finally acquired a German agent recently because he sold a story of mine and presented me with a *fait accompli*. I have never felt the need of a US agent. I do my own marketing, bargaining, and contracts. Why should I pay someone else to have all the fun?

Bibliography:

Gothic:
    O CHARITABLE DEATH, Curtis Books, 1969.
    THE SILENT PLACE, Ace Books, 1970.
    MALVERNE HALL, Ace Books, 1970.
    FORBIDDEN ISLAND, Berkley, 1973.
    DEVIL'S COURT, Berkley, 1974.
    THE HOUSE OF TAROT, Berkley, 1975.
    THE BLACK SWAN, Berkley, 1975.
    THE SAPPHIRE LEGACY, Berkley, 1976.
Note: Rachel Payes has published teenage career books, science fiction, and mystery novels since 1960.

CARLA PELTONEN
Pseudonyms: Lynn Erickson (Pseudonym shared by co-author, Molly Swanton). *B*. Carla Friedenberg, 1/22/43, Norwalk, CT., married Erik Peltonen, 1967. *Children*: Lucas, Erika. *Education*: B.S. University of Rochester, English education. *Professional associatins*: Romance Writers of America. *Genres*: Contemporary, historical romance. *Agent*: Writer's House, 21 W. 26th Street, New York, NY. *Current residence*: Aspen, CO.

Favorite authors and books: Susan Howatch, Roberta Gellis, Janet Daily, Rosemary Rogers, Kathleen Woodiwiss.

Thoughts on writing: Reading for pleasure is both an avenue of escape and a tool for broadening horizons. My co-writer and I have been fans of literature—romance included—for many years. Writing is a joy, a way of fulfill ourselves, and also a lot of hard work. It's satisfying to receive a fan letter and know that you have shared your work with others, and brought a little knowledge and entertainment to their lives.

Becoming published/finding an agent: Molly and I wrote two books and tried to sell the manuscripts ourselves but had no luck. We were directed to Writer's House by a friend; the agency sold our two books to Richard Gallen within two weeks.

Bibliography:

Contemporary:
GENTLE BETRAYER, Lynn Erickson, Gallen/Pocket, 1982.

Historical romance: (All as Lynn Erickson)
THIS RAGING FLOWER, Gallen/Pocket, 1979.
SWEET NEMESIS, Gallen/Pocket, 1979.
THE SILVER KISS, Gallen/Pocket, 1981.
WOMAN OF SAN FRANCISCO, Dell, 1982.
HIGH COUNTRY PRIDE, Pocket, 1982.
Note: Carla Peltonen has one book currently under contract with Pocket, under the pseudonym, Lynn Erickson.

PATRICIA SONIA PHILLIPS
Pseudonyms: Patricia Phillips, Pat Phillips, Sonia Phillips. *B.* Patricia Sonia Powell, 1/1/39, St. Helens, England, married Charles Robert Phillips, 5/11/55. *Children:* Catherine Marie, Charles Eugene, John Robert. *Education:* Educated in England and at Rhyl Grammar School, Flintshire, N. Wales. *Professional associations:* Author's Guild. *Genres:* Historical romance. *Agent:* Donald MacCampbell inc, 12 East 41st Street, N.Y., N.Y. *Current residence:* Tulsa, Oklahoma.

Favorite authors and books: Included in my favorite authors and books are: Catherine Cookson, Norah Lofts, Pamela Hill, Velda Johnston, Jan Cox Speas, Frances Murray, Dorothy Eden, Sylvia Sark, Janet Dailey, Frank Yerby. THE YOUNG LIONS, by Irwin Shaw, KATHERINE by Anya Seton.

Thoughts on writing: I have always been a fan of historical romances. When I was a teenager this category was big business. I never read anything else. The historical romance combines escapism with solid information of times past which I find fascinating. For a lighter read modern romances can be a satisfying escape to another world.

Becoming published/finding an agent: After bushels of rejects on my initial efforts I turned to a romantic suspense novel which was accepted by Bouregy. In enquiring about the handling of foreign submissions for that firm, they told me about Donald MacCampbell who was their agent for European sales. I decided to submit one of my historicals to him while I was at it. This resulted in my first sale to Jove (then Pyramid).

Bibliography:

Historical romance:
ROYAL CAPTIVE, Patricia Phillips. Pyramid, 1977.
MY SOUL WITH THINE, Patricia Phillips. Pyramid, 1977.
LOVE'S DEFIANT PRISONER, Patricia Phillips. Jove, 1978.
ANISE, Patricia Phillips. Jove, 1978.
CAPTIVE FLAME, Patricia Phillips. Jove, 1980.
JENNY, Patricia Phillips. Jove, 1981.
TOUCH ME WITH FIRE, Patricia Phillips. Jove, 1982.

Romantic suspense:
LADY OF THE MOOR, Pat Phillips. Avalon, 1973.
MEDITERRANEAN ADVENTURE, Pat Phillips. Avalon, 1974.
LOVE WAITS AT PENRHYN, Pat Phillips. Avalon, 1975.
INVITATION TO DANGER, Pat Phillips. Avalon, 1976.

PHYLLIS TAYLOR PIANKA
Pseudonyms: Winter Ames. *B.* Phyllis Fay Taylor, Rice Lake, Wisconsin 11/12/28, married Edwin Ralph Pianka, 2/21/47. *Children:* Jerry Lynn Pianka. *Professional associations:* Foun-

der, Cupertino Writers 1973; California Writer's club, Romance Writers of America, Chairm. local chapter. *Awards*: Second place, short story contest. Nat'l assoc. of American Pen Women. *Genres*: Regency, Category contemporary, non-fiction self-help. *Agent*: Ann Elmo 60 East 42nd Street, N.Y., N.Y. 10165. *Current residence*: Cupertino, California.

Favorite authors and books: Included in my favorite romance authors are: Danielle Steel, Janet Dailey, Glenna Finley, Phyllis Whitney, Catherine Gaskin, Sidney Sheldon, Helen Van Slyke, Rona Jaffe, Norah Lofts, Taylor Caldwell, Daphne du Maurier, Rachel Carson, dozens of others.

Thoughts on writing: I see fiction as a great healer. With the conviction that stress causes most of our ills, both physical and mental, time alone with a good book is the best medicine I know. I've always loved to read romance novels. To be able to share by writing for others is God's special blessing to me. I hope to give as much pleasure as I receive. Since my husband shares my writing career by both editorial and moral support, my cup runneth over.

Becoming published/finding an agent: I sold my first two novels on my own by submitting a synopsis. Then I called an agent and he agreed to take me on. My very first sale was for $11.00 to a religious magazine. I started writing at age forty. Before that was a professional artist with murals still displayed in several public and private buildings. Was a newspaper reporter for two years and wrote many articles for religious and gardening magazines.

Bibliography:

Category contemporary:
NURSE OF THE ISLAND, Bouregy, 1976.
SHARON GARRISON, CLINIC NURSE, Bouregy, 1977.
THE GOLDEN PIRATE, Dell Candlelight, 1979.
EMERALD BAY, Winter Ames, Second Chance at Love, 1981.
BIRD OF PARADISE, Winter Ames, Second Chance at Love, 1981.

Regency:
THE SLEEPING HEIRESS, Dell Candlelight, 1980.

THE PAISLEY BUTTERFLY, Dell Candlelight, 1980.
HEATHER WILD, Dell Candlelight, 1982.
Note: Phyllis Taylor Pianka currently has a book under contract with Harlequin.

MADELINE PORTER
Pseudonyms: Elizabeth Habersham, Anna James (Both pseudonyms are shared with co-author, Shannon Harper). *B.* Madeline Habersham King, Atlanta, GA. *Children:* Walden, Alec. *Education:* B.A. University of South Carolina, journalism and English. *Awards:* Romance Writers of America Golden Heart medallion for THE DAY BEYOND DESTINY (Best historical romance, 1981). *Genres:* Contemporary, family saga, historical romance. *Agent:* Sarah Jane Freymann-Schwartz, Stepping Stone Literary Agency, 59 W. 71st Street, New York, NY. *Current residence:* Newport Beach, CA.

Favorite authors and books: Actually, I don't read romance. For light reading, I still prefer suspense novels. Otherwise, I have a long list of favorite authors whom I read and read again (when I can find time) that includes Hemingway, Fowles, Nabokov, Didion, and on and on! I love spy novels (e.g., Follet and LeCarre) and my favorite suspense writer is Mary Stewart (Isn't she everyone's?). I also love detective writers such as Hammet and MacDonald. In short, I adore writing romance, so maybe that's why the galleys are read. But I want to relax with something else.

Thoughts on writing: There was no such animal as "modern" or "historical" or any other kind of romance when I first started writing. The escapist novels in the early seventies—and before— were gothic and suspense, both of which are still my favorites. I think that most novels are escapist, unless we include James Joyce, Malcolm Lowry, etc. Of course, real romance writing goes as far back as novels go back, but I do not think such novels as PAMELA qualify as romance today. Perhaps in previous times when, frankly, only the more intelligent read at all. Now practically everyone reads, and the categories are unlimited, the field wide open—thank heavens!

Becoming published/finding an agent: After trying for months to find a publisher on our own, Shannon and I finally realized that an agent was essential. I stumbled upon our agent accidentally, on a visit to New York, and a chance meeting with a friend of a friend who was also a writer, who gave me the name of her agent.

Bibliography:

Contemporary:
A WORLD OF HER OWN, Anna James, Gallen/Pocket, 1982.
THE HEART VICTORIOUS, Anna James, Gallen/Pocket, 1982.

Gothic:
ISLAND OF DECEIT, Elizabeth Habersham, Pinnacle, 1977.

Historical romance:
SWEET LOVE, BITTER LOVE, Anna James, Jove, 1978.
THE DARKER SIDE OF LOVE, Anna James, Jove, 1979.
THE DAY BEYOND DESTINY, Anna James, Jove, 1981.

NINA COOMBS PYKARE
Pseudonyms: Ann Coombs, Nina Coombs, Nan Pemberton, Nora Powers, Nina Pykare, Regina Towers B. Nina Ann Coombs, 12/27/32, Alliance, OH., married Rodney H. Pykare. 1950; divorced 1971. *Children*: Rodney, Michael, Johnathan, David, Rebecca. *Education*: B.A., Youngstown State, 1969; Ph.D. Kent State, 1975—English. *Professional associations*: Romance Writers of America. *Genres*: Category contemporary, historical romance, Regency. *Agent*: Donald MacCampbell, 12 East 41st Street, N.Y., N.Y. 10017. *Current residence*: Cleveland Heights, Ohio.

Favorite authors and books: Georgette Heyer's Regencies—nobody does it better! Raphael Sabatini—THE SEA HAWK, etc.

Thoughts on writing: People who put down romances have probably never read a Regency. No genre takes more talent. Personally, I feel there's enough gloom in the world already. I prefer to add to the world's happiness and I believe that romances do that. My mother is my biggest fan. When I asked her why she likes romances, she said they make her feel good. *That's* what I want to do for my readers.

Becoming published/finding an agent: My first published writing was for children (Sunday School papers, etc.), then I moved to confessions. After writing an historical I saw my agent's name in a publishing autobiography. Because of my previous credits, he read my novel. He steered me into Regencies and category con-temporaries.

Bibliography:

Category contemporaries:
LOVE'S PROMISE, Dell Candelight, 1979.
AFFAIRS OF THE HEART, Nora Powers, Silhouette, 1980.
DESIGN FOR LOVE, Nora Powers, Silhouette, 1980.
HERITAGE OF THE HEART, Dell Candlelight, 1982.
PROMISE ME TOMORROW, Nora Powers, Silhouette Desire, 1982.

Historical romances:
THE FIRE WITHIN, Ann Coombs, Manor, 1979.

Regencies:
SCANDALOUS SEASON, Dell Candlelight, 1979.
A MAN OF HER CHOOSING, Dell Candlelight, 1980.
LOVE IN DISGUISE, Dell Candlelight, 1980.
LADY INCOGNITA, Dell Candlelight, 1980.
THE DAZZLED HEART, Dell Candlelight, 1980.
THE INNOCENT HEART, Dell Candlelight, 1981.
THE RAKE'S COMPANION, Regina Towers, Dell Candlelight, 1980.
LOVE'S DELUSION, Nan Pemberton, Pocket Books, 1980.
LOVE'S FOLLY, Dell Candlelight, 1980.
LOVE PLAYS A PART, Dell Candlelight, 1981.
A MATTER OF HONOR, Dell Candlelight, 1982.
Note: Nina Pykare has two books under contract to Silhouette Desire, as Nora Powers, and two under contract to NAL Rapture, as Nina Coombs.

DEBORAH ARLENE RATHER
Pseudonyms: Arlene James. *B.* Deborah Arlene Roper, 5/14/52, Duncan, Oklahoma, married James E. Rather, 4/16/76. *Children:* Ross Edward Kelly Rather, Joseph Colin Rather. *Education:* High School diploma. *Professional associations:* Romance Writers of America. *Genres:* Category contemporary. *Agent:* Charles Stern, 319 Coronet, San Antonio, Texas. *Current residence:* Lewisville, Texas.

Favorite authors and books: Included in among my favorite authors are Dixie Browning and Kathleen Woodiwiss.

Thoughts on writing: I was not a fan until a college professor gave me a book with the comment, "study—it's a good place to start." Was he ever right! I thoroughly enjoy romance writing and I would very much like to be able to present attitudes which would enhance the quality of romance shared between mature, loving adults. It grieves me that some women have bought the theory that romance is somehow demeaning. Romance is essential to good marriage, and it is just as important to men whether they realize it or even admit it (thank God that mine does). Romance is not escapism only, but the fact that it is entertaining is certainly something of which we romance authors can be proud.

Also there is good romantic fiction and lousy romantic fiction (as in all other types of literature). Readers should be more discerning and more vocal (publishers do read their mail). I certainly want the input of readers. After all, my job is to produce the best written piece that I possibly can, and to entertain my reader while injecting something of value.

Becoming published/finding an agent: After finishing the first manuscript, I fortunately came into contact with other writers who urged me to submit to Silhouette. An extraordinary editor took interest in me, made some suggestions, which I needed, and then bought the book on the second submission.

Bibliography:
CITY GIRL, Arlene James. Silhouette, March 1982.
Note: Arlene James currently has three books under contract with Silhouette.

BARBARA RODDICK
Pseudonym: Hilary Mason. *B.* Barbara Roddick, 5/11/29, London, England, married Ian Roddick, 8/49. *Children:* Jennifer and Andrew. *Education:* Studied education at Homerton College, Cambridge, England, 1947-49; London University Diploma in Theology. *Professional associations*: Society of Authors. *Genres*: Historical romances, family sagas. *Agent*: Michael

Sissons, A. D. Peters & Co., U.K., and Literistic, N.Y. *Current residence*: Leeds, England.

Favorite authors and books: What is meant by "romance?" The definition I prefer is "A spirit of or inclination for adventure, excitement or mystery." I've enjoyed Robert Louis Stevenson, Charles Dickens, Tolstoy and Naomi Mitchison.

Thoughts on writing: Writing is a form of communication which comes naturally to some people. You do it if you have something to say which is best expressed in the form of a story than in any other way. The main purpose of both reading and writing would seem to be enjoyment, in the fullest sense of the word. Escapism, that is freedom and refreshment of the spirit, is part of this. Good romantic writing caters to this need.

Becoming published/finding an agent: I began without using an agent, submitting different scripts to various British publishers. After I had four books published I applied to Michael Sissons of A. D. Peters & Co., who sold MORISCO to Atheneum through the Matson Agency.

Bibliograghy:
THIEVES OF MERCY, Robert Hale, 1976.
THE SHADOW OF HONOUR, Robert Hale, 1977.
ALL THE PROUD REBELS, Robert Hale, 1977.
THE GOLD AND THE FEVER, Robert Hale, 1977.
THE TREASON BIRD, Robert Hale, 1978.
MORISCO, Collins and Pan, 1979; Atheneum, 1979; Ballantine, 1980.
Note: Barbara Roddick's most recent novel, BLOOD ROYAL, was published in Britain by Hodder & Stoughton in a Coronet paperback edition. It has not yet found a U.S. publisher.

ROSEMARY ROGERS
B. Panadura, Ceylon, 12/7/32, married Summa Navaratnam, divorced; married Leroy Rogers, divorced. *Children*: Rosanne, Sharon, Michael, Adam. *Education*: University of Ceylon, B.A. *Genres*: Contemporary, historical romance. *Current residence*: New York and California.

Bibliograghy: (All published by Avon Books)

Historical romance:
SWEET SAVAGE LOVE, January 1974.
THE WILDEST HEART, October 1974.
DARK FIRES, August 1975.
WICKED LOVING LIES, October 1976.
LOST LOVE LAST LOVE, November 1980.
SURRENDER TO LOVE, July 1982.

Contemporary:
THE CROWD PLEASERS, September 1978 (trade paperback); April 1980 (mass-market)
THE INSIDERS, January 1979.
LOVE PLAY, September 1981 (trade paperback); December 1982 (mass-market)

ELIZABETH ROTTER

Pseudonyms: Laura Matthews, Elizabeth Walker, Elizabeth Neff Walker. *B.* Elizabeth Neff Walker, 8/12/41, Pittsburgh, Pa., married Paul Rotter, 6/66. *Children:* Laura, Matthew. *Education:* B.A., Brown University, English. *Professional associations:* Romance Writers of America. *Genres:* contemporary, Regency. *Agent:* Denise Marcil, 316 W. 82nd Street, N.Y., N.Y. *Current residence:* San Francisco, California.

Favorite authors and books: My favorite Regency authors are Georgette Heyer and Joan Smith because they both write such delightfully humorous books with a wonderful flavor of the early nineteenth century. I'm new to reading contemporary romances, which have the kind of wit and strong heroines I particularly enjoy.

Thoughts on writing: The most fascinating thing about life to me is human interaction; and nothing is as satisfying as writing about the love that develops between men and women. I find myself tossing bits of my philosophy into books I write, whether they're Regencies or contemporaries. In order to stay within the time frame, Regency heroines have some limitations to their behavior which need not occur in a contemporary romance. The more sophisticated heroine appeals to me, one who moves in a realistic world and who confronts problems and makes decisions in a modern context. I would rather concoct a modern love story than an erotic fantasy. More intriguing than plot to me are the elements of character and dialogue.

Formula books have never fared well with critics, but they are popular with a wide audience of readers who finds the kind of escapism it wants. Romance writers should stop worrying about criticism and acknowledge the appreciation they receive from their readers who are, after all, the only ones they should worry about.

Becoming an author/finding an agent: After writing my first Regency, I sent it to a publisher and heard nothing. So I wrote another one and sent it to the same publisher, but there was still no response. Deciding that they were lost under an enormous slush pile, I got an agent's name from the LITERARY MARKET PLACE. My letter of query was passed along to Denise Marcil, who asked to see my books; she took me on as a client. Denise had me do some revision, and within a few months sold two books on the same day to two different publishers. Several months later, I finally heard back from the original publisher I'd sent to who wanted to buy the book they'd read.

Bibliography:

Regency:
> THE SEVENTH SUITOR, Laura Matthews, Warner, 1979.
> THE AIM OF A LADY, Laura Matthews, Warner, 1980.
> THE NOMAD HARP, Elizabeth Neff Walker, Fawcett, 1980.
> ALICIA, Elizabeth Walker, Dell, 1980.
> A CURIOUS COURTING, Elizabeth Neff Walker, Fawcett, 1980.
> LORD CLAYBORNE'S WIFE, Laura Matthews, Warner, 1980.
> A BARONET'S WIFE, Laura Matthews, Warner, 1981.
> HOLIDAY IN BATH, Laura Matthews, Warner, 1981.
> THE LADY NEXT DOOR, Elizabeth Neff Walker, Fawcett, 1981.
> IN MY LADY'S CHAMBER, Elizabeth Neff Walker, Fawcett, 1981.
> A PROPER WIDOW, Laura Matthews, Signet, 1982.

Note: Elizabeth Rotter has sold two books, PAPER TIGER (Avon) and SEASONS OF LOVE (Dell) which will be published in the summer of 1983.

MARIE RYDZYNSKI
Pseudonyms: Marie Charles, Marie Michael. *B.* Marie Rydzynski,

3/28/48, W. Germany, married Charles Ferrarella, 10/27/73. *Children:* Jessica. *Education:* B.A. Queens College, 6/69; M.A. Queens College, 6/72, English/Math. *Genres:* Historical romance (unpublished), category contemporary. *Agent:* Pat Teal, 2036 Vista Del Sol, Fullerton, Ca. *Current residence:* Irvine, Ca.

Favorite authors and books: Anything by Katherine Woodiwiss, but especially SHANNA; Margaret Mitchell's GONE WITH THE WIND (all-time favorite book); Jena Hunt's SWEET VICTORY.

Thoughts on writing: I love to write and to me it's a way of sharing pleasure. I hope to be able to contribute to people's "well-being" by entertaining them. I've been writing (and collecting rejection slips) since I was eleven years old and I've written everything— poetry, screenplays, short stories, musical comedies, etc. As far as romance goes, I've always been in love with it in general. To me, what it does, what the category contemporaries do, is recapture what once was when you first met the man you fell in love with—before the routine set in. It's revitalizing.

Becoming published/finding an agent: I had an agent for five years and was going nowhere. My husband (bless him) found Pat's name in an article in the paper. Since she was a local agent (the other was in New York), I gave it a try. She suggested I write a category comtemporary (I was doing historical romances at the time) and four months later, I sold my first book to Second Chance at Love.

Bibliography:

Category contemporary:
    SMOLDERING EMBERS, Marie Charles, Second Chance at Love, 1982.
Note: Marie Rydzynski currently has two more books under contract with Second Chance at Love.

SHARON SALVATO
Pseudonym: Day Taylor (shared with co-author Cornelia M. Parkinson). *B.* Sharon Anne Zetler, Columbus, OH., married Guido J. Salvato, 1961. *Children:* Christopher, Gregory, Stephen, Daniel, Patrice. *Education:* B.S. University of Cincinnati, education. *Professional associations:* NLAPW. *Genres:* Historical ro-

mance. *Agent:* David Stewart Hull, 551 Fifth Ave., Suite 2015, New York, NY *Current residence:* Columbus, OH.

Favorite authors and books: Anya Seton, Taylor Caldwell— ANSWER AS A MAN, Norah Lofts—SILVER NUTMEG.

Thoughts on writing: Because romance is a part of every life, it is difficult to conceive of it as a stepchild of anything in life. Romance has its place in literature, just as it has in the private and public lives of people. Fiction writing to me is merely a translation of the events and happening of different periods of history. Many historical trends are difficult to see or understand in a larger view, but are very understandable when seen in their effect on individual's lives. Historical romance has the advantage of playing out men's and women's private hopes, dreams, and desires against the unalterable movement of their times. When it is well done and well researched, historical romance has value as entertainment and as a means of understanding the world and its people as they were—and most likely still are.

Becoming published/finding an agent: I won second place in a contest Lancer Books offered. After the contest, I sent the book to James Brown Associates, and David Stewart Hull became my agent. He sold the book to Stein and Day; later the book came out as a Dell paperback.

Bibliography:

Gothic:
>   BRIARCLIFF MANOR, Stein and Day, 1973.
>   THE MEREDITH LEGACY, Stein and Day, 1974.
>   SCARBOROUGH HOUSE, Stein and Day, 1975.
>   THE BLACK SWAN, Day Taylor, Dell, 1976.
>   BITTER EDEN, Dell, 1979.
>   MOSS ROSE, Day Taylor, Dell, 1980.

Note: Sharon Salvato has a book currently under contract with Dell.

ANNETTE SANFORD
Pseudonyms: Anne Shore, Mary Carroll, Anne Starr. *B.* Annette Schorre, 8/3/29, Cuero, Texas, married Lucius Sanford,

3/17/53. *Education:* B.A. degree in English from the University of Texas, 1950. *Professional associations:* Romance Writers of America. *Awards:* Under my own name I write short stories and have received a grant from the National Endowment for the Arts, and a story of mine was included in BEST AMERICAN SHORT STORIES OF 1979. I have also won awards from WRITERS DIGEST, Indiana University Writers Conference, The Catholic Press Association. In 1981 I was awarded a Texas Commission on the Arts Writer Recognition Award. All of these awards are for short stories. *Genres:* Category contemporary. *Agent:* Donald MacCampbell, Inc. 12 E. 41st Street, N.Y.,N.Y. 10017. *Current residence:* Ganado, Texas.

Favorite authors and books: I like Harlequin's Charlotte Lamb and I enjoy Danielle Steel's books—I especially admired THE RING.

Thoughts on writing: I think of romances as entertainment fiction which, at its best can release the reader from everyday tensions and also offer insights into life's problems. My goal when I begin a book is to create interesting, believable characters that my readers will trust and care about and to create a world for these characters that will enchant the reader and broaden her horizons.

Becoming published/finding an agent: I first began publishing short stories, but when I decided to give up teaching high school English in order to write full time, I looked around for a genre that would support me. I like to travel and I love happy endings, so I settled on the romance category. I wrote two. A friend introduced me to her agent who sold those two and every one I've written since.

Bibliography:

Category contemporary:
> THE HEART'S HORIZONS, Anne Shore. Dell Candlelight, 1978.
> WHISPERS OF THE HEART, Anne Shore, Dell Candlelight, 1978.
> WINTER KISSES SUMMER LOVE, Anne Shore. Dell Candlelight, 1978.
> PROMISE BY MOONLIGHT, Anne Shore. Dell Candlelight, 1979.
> TENDER IS THE TOUCH, Anne Shore. Dell Candlelight, 1980.
> SHADOW AND SUN, Mary Carroll. Silhouette, 1980.
> THE SEARCHING HEART, Anne Shore. Dell Candlelight, 1980.

TOO SWIFT THE MORNING, Mary Carroll. Silhouette, 1980.
DIVIDE THE WIND, Mary Carroll. Silhouette, 1981.
VALLEY OF THE BUTTERFLIES, Anne Shore. Dell Candlelight, 1981.
HOLD BACK TOMORROW, Anne Shore. Signet, 1981.
TAKE THIS LOVE, Mary Carroll. Silhouette, 1981.
THE FARAWAY LAND, Anne Shore. Dell Candlelight, 1982.
COME KISS A STRANGER, Anne Starr. Signet, 1982.
A TIME FOR LOVING, Anne Starr. Signet, 1982.

Short fiction written under the name of Annette Sanford has appeared in:
BEST AMERICAN SHORT STORIES OF 1979.
REDBOOK, December 1977.
YANKEE, September 1980.
PRAIRIE SCHOONER, Summer 1982.
Note: Annette Sanford currently has three books under contract with Silhouette.

PAULA SCHWARTZ
Pseudonyms: Elizabeth Mansfield, Libby Mansfield. *B*. Paula Reibel, New York, NY., married Ira A. Schwartz, 1956. *Children*: Wendy, David. *Education*: B.A. Hunter College, M.S. City University of New York, English education. *Professional associations*: Author's Guild, Dramatist's Guild. *Awards*: Irene Leach Memorial Award, The Pauline Eaton Oak Award, DRAMATICS One-Act Play Contest. *Genre*: Regency. *Agent*: Victoria Pryor, Literistic, 32 West 40th Street, New York, NY. *Current residence*: Annandale, VA.

Favorite authors and books: Jane Austen—for her sense of the real life of the period, and for her sharp, incisive humor. Georgette Heyer—for entertaining bathtub reading, for pure escapism, and for charming dialogue.

Thoughts on writing: Yes, romances are escapism, but to be truly entertaining, they must be of high quality. Each reader finds her/his own level of entertainment; some like sci-fi, some murder mysteries, some espionage, etc. I've enjoyed love stories since childhood, but I only enjoy those with wit, sense, and literary quality. I'm not interested in the bodice rippers or the soft porn. It's the leading up, not the consummation, that has variety and charm for me. The act of love is the same—it's the nature of the lovers, what they see in each other and how they discover themselves and each other—that interests me.

Becoming published/finding an agent: I wrote a literary analysis of Georgette Heyer, comparing her "entertainments"with Jane Austen's authenticity, which won a prize. An editor who saw the article suggested that I "write the sort of books you're writing about." I did and found it terrifically enjoyable. I still enjoy writing them sixteen years later.

Finding an agent is not the essential factor in writing. I would advise aspiring writers to write the book they love, and try to sell it themselves. Then, when they can pick and choose, they can find the right agent whose personality suits their own. I dearly love my agent, but it took me a long while to find her.

Bibliography:

Regency:
> UNEXPECTED HOLIDAY, Libby Mansfield, Dell, 1978.
> MY LORD MURDERER, Elizabeth Mansfield, Dell, 1978.
> THE PHANTOM LOVER, Elizabeth Mansfield, Dell, 1979.
> A VERY DUTIFUL DAUGHTER, Elizabeth Mansfield, Berkley, 1979.
> REGENCY STING, Elizabeth Mansfield, Berkley, 1980.
> A REGENCY MATCH, Elizabeth Mansfield, Berkley, 1980.
> HER MAN OF AFFAIRS, Elizabeth Mansfield, Berkley, 1980.
> DUEL OF HEARTS, Elizabeth Mansfield, Berkley, 1980.
> A REGENCY CHARADE, Elizabeth Mansfield, Berkley, 1981.
> THE FIFTH KISS, Elizabeth Mansfield, Berkley, 1981.
> THE RELUCTANT FLIRT, Elizabeth Mansfield, Berkley, 1981.
> THE FROST FAIR, Elizabeth Mansfield, Berkley, 1982.
> THE COUNTERFEIT HUSBAND, Elizabeth Mansfield, Berkley, 1982
> HER HEART'S CAPTAIN, Elizabeth Mansfield, Berkley, 1982.

Note: Paula Schwartz has currently under contract two books with Berkley under the pseudonym Elizabeth Mansfield.

MARY FANNING SEDERQUEST

Pseudonyms: Katherine Granger, Katherine Ransom. *B*. Mary Frances Fanning, 8/19/45, Attleboro, Mass., married Edward L. Sederquest III., 11/21/70, divorced 9/14/81. *Education*: B.A. 1968, University of Connecticut, Sociology. *Professional associations*: Romance Writers of America; currently president of the Connecticut chapter of the RWA. *Genres*: Category contemporary. *Agent*: Eileen Fallon, Barbara Lowenstein Assoc., Inc. 250 W. 57th St., N.Y., N.Y. 10016. *Current residence*: South Windsor, Ct.

Favorite books and writers: Catherine Gaskin, Mary Stewart, Helen MacInnis, Dorothy Eden, Daphne du Maurier, Evelyn Anthony, Kathleen Woodiwiss, Janet Dailey. JANE EYRE, REBECCA, GONE WITH THE WIND, THE FRENCH LIEUTENANT'S WOMAN.

Thoughts on writing: It bothers me to hear romance called "publishing's step-child." Where is it written that a romance can't be well written, can't involve real, believable characters, can't move the reader? Those certainly are my goals in writing romance: to write well, and write a story with real, believable characters that move the reader. I think romances right now are probably in about the same spot that the mystery/detective story was in the days of the "pulps" And then it was good writing which rescued the mystery/ detective story—Raymond Chandler and Dashiell Hammett particularly. I believe good writing which can only develop over time, will ultimately do for the romance what it did for the detective story.

Before I began reading category romances, I was reading Mary Stewart and Helen MacInnis, Phyllis Whitney and Victoria Holt. I read all the Gothics and most of the Regencies. Then a friend introduced me to Harlequins and I was hooked. After I'd been reading them about three years, I began to think I'd like to write one, but it was two more years before I really sat down to write my first novel (which never sold).

I believe these category romances are mostly escape fiction— but good heavens!—what's inherently wrong with that? When you get right down to it, some of the best books on earth are escape fiction so we're in pretty good company! To me, it is precisely a book's ability to help us escape that makes it worthwhile. When I pick up a book, I *want* to escape—into its pages, into a new world, with new people, new sights and new sounds. If at the end of the book I can also say I cared about these people, or was moved, or grew as a person, then I have truly had a wonderful journey. It is my goal to be able one day to do that for my readers.

Becoming published/finding an agent: I sent three chapters and a synopsis of what was to become A MAN'S PERSUASION to Jove's Second Chance at Love and they asked me to write fifty more pages. I did and was then awarded a contract. My agent contacted me because she had known of me when she worked for Jove.

Bibliography:

Category contemporary:
A MAN'S PERSUASION, Katherine Granger, Second Chance at Love, December 1982.
Note: Mary Sederquest also has three books under contract with NAL's Rapture series, to appear under the pseudonym Katherine Ransom.

ALEXANDRA SELLERS
B. Alexandra Sellers. *Professional associations*: Romance Writers of America. *Genres*: category contemporary, contemporary. *Agent*: Nancy Colbert, 303 Davenport Road, Toronto, Ontario.

Favorite authors and books: Jane Austen (especially PRIDE AND PREJUDICE), D.H. Lawrence (LADY CHATTERLEY'S LOVE, of course), Jane Donnelly, Mary Burchell.

Thoughts on writing: I think romance, like science, spy and detective fiction, is escapist. But that doesn't mean one can be contemptuous of its audience or its subject matter. To write good romance you must take it seriously. The need for escapism is a valid need.

Becoming published/finding an agent. Oh hell—I just wrote a book, you know, and sent it to a publisher. A friend recommended an agent. Don't worry about "finding a publisher." Worry about writing a good book. Romance, at least, is a seller's market now.

Bibliography:

Category contemporary:
　　THE INDIFFERENT HEART, Dell Candlelight, 1981.

LINDA SHAW

B. Linda Louise McCullough 11/28/38 El Dorado, Arkansas, married Bennett Shaw, 6/20/57. *Children:* Randy, Shelley, Tim. *Education:* Bachelor of Music, North Texas State University, 1977. *Professional associations*: Phi Kappa Lambda. *Genres:* Historical romance, contemporary, Category contemporary. *Current residence*: Keene, Texas.

Favorite authors and books: I read Susan Howatch, Mary Stewart and Jan Westcott. Of the current romance authors I read the early Woodiwiss because it influenced me to begin writing. Shirlee Busbee's GYPSY LADY helped me get some of my first historical down on paper.

Thoughts on writing: Yes, I do it for escapism. Just as television programs are escapism. To pretend it's anything else, to me, is a fallacy. I do, however, like my escapism to be of high quality and done with skill. There is a certain beauty, even in lesser literary works, that is worth noting and even learning from, if they're done with excellence and taste.

Becoming published/finding an agent: I went over the transom and just kept submitting. No, I didn't have an agent. I used two books—A WRITER'S GUIDE TO BOOK PUBLISHING by Balkin and the WRITER'S MARKET.

Bibliography:

Contemporary:
　　AN INNOCENT DECEPTION. Gallen, 1981.

Category contemporary:
　　DECEMBER'S WINE. Silhouette Special Edition, 1982.
　　ALL SHE EVER WANTED. Silhouette Special Edition, 1982.

Historical romance:
　　BALLAD IN BLUE. Ballantine, 1979.
　　THE SATIN VIXEN. Gallen, 1981.

Note: Linda Shaw currently has three books under contract, two with Silhouette Special Edition and one with Pocket Books.

NOREEN SIEGEL

Pseudonyms: Noreen Nash. *B.* Norabelle Roth, 4/4/24, Wenatchee, Wa., married Lee Siegel, 12/42. *Children:* Lee A. Siegel, Robert James Siegel. *Education:* UCLA major—history and French. *Professional association:* Formerly an actress in films and television. *Genres:* Historical romances *Agent:* Irving Paul Lazaf So. Beverly Drive, Beverly Hills, CA. *Current residence:* Beverly Hills, CA.

Favorite authors and books: I am not an avid reader of these books although I have great admiration for those authors who have mastered the genre. I read mostly histories, biographies. My favorite writers are Herman Wouk, James Clavell, Irving Stone, and Colleen McCullough, especially THE THORN BIRDS, and I am a great reader and admirer of Taylor Caldwell and Norah Lofts.

Thoughts on writing: Basically I am an historian, my expertise being in French history and history of medicine. By writing in the romantic style I hope to make history come alive and acquaint my readers with some fascinating history. Most historical novels are well researched and offer their readers more than escapism, however, I do not underestimate the value of escape, sheer pleasure, and I admire any writer than can give their reader just that.

Becoming published/finding an agent: I had known Irving Lazar when I was an actress. I took the book to him and he sent it to Warners.

Bibliograghy:

Historical romance:
   BY LOVE FULFILLED, Noreen Nash. Warner Books, November 1980.

BERTRICE SMALL

B. Bertrice Williams, 12/9/37, Manhattan, married George

Sumner Small IV. *Children:* Thomas. *Education:* graduate St. Mary's school, attended Western College, Oxford, Ohio. *Professional associations:* Author's Guild/Author's League. *Genres:* Historical romance. *Agent:* Eli Schoenfield, Fulop & Hardee, One Hammerskjold Plaza, NYC 10017. *Current residence:* I can be reached through either my publisher or my lawyer.

Favorite authors and books: Anya Seton, KATHERINE; Sergeanne Golon, ANGELIQUE books; Shirlee Busbee, GYPSY LADY, LADY VIXEN; Jennifer Wilde LOVE'S TENDER FURY; Cynthia Wright, CAROLINE; Rosemary Rogers, SWEET SAVAGE LOVE; Pat Gallagher, CASTLES IN THE AIR; Mary Canon, THE O'HARA DYNASTY; Lucia St. Clair Robson, RIDE THE WIND; Roberta Gellis, ROSLYN CHRONICLES.

Thoughts on writing: My philosophy is quite simple. Write a well written, well researched, swashbuckling romance with a happy ending. Get your manuscript in on time (barring a nuclear holocaust. I did galleys in the hospital last year). Do your own editing when necessary, fight for what is necessary to the plot, and don't believe your own publicity. Answer all fan mail, and even when feeling rotten and faced with an eager fan, SMILE and be NICE!

Bibliography:

Historical romances:
> THE KADIN, Avon Books, February 1978.
> LOVE WILD AND FAIR, Avon Books, December 1978.
> ADORA, Ballantine Books, May 1980.
> SKYE O'MALLEY, Ballantine, Books October 1980.
> UNCONQUERED, Ballantine Books, January 1982.
> Note: Bertrice Small is currently under contract with Ballantine Books.

LaVYRLE SPENCER
B. LaVyrle Joy Kulick, 8/17/43, Long Prairie, Minn., married Daniel F. Spencer, 2/10/62. *Children:* Amy Elizabeth, Beth Adair. *Education:* High school graduate, Staples (Minnesota) High School. *Professional associations:* Romance Writers of America (regional advisor). *Genres:* Historical romance, category contemporary, contemporary romance. *Agent:* Neil Meyer, 1814

First Bank Place West, Minneapolis, Minn. 55402. *Current residence*: Minneapolis, Minn.

Favorite authors and books: Kathleen Woodiwiss was my idol, and remains so. She was my inspiration to begin writing, and when my first book was only partially done, she read the ms., liked it, and sent it to her editor, Nancy Coffey, and thereby got me published. Other favorites: Esther Sager, Rachel Ryan, Lisa Gregory, Kristin James (both of which are pseudonyms for Candace Camp).

Thoughts on writing: For a romance to grip its reader, it must expand the reader's senses, all five of them! The writer must consciously search for vehicles which can bring the reader's five senses alive (i.e., soap upon skin has scent, taste, feel, sound— the sucking sound of a palm upon slick flesh), and, of course, sight, which is too often the only sense employed by writers. The most important element in a love story is sexual tension. Once that tension is released, the book loses impetus. The fastest way to ruin a good plot is to put too many love scenes in a book. Build to them, savor them when they arrive, and give the reader as sensual a scene as it is possible to give. Tongues do not taste like honey unless their owners have been eating it, so it is always my goal to provide a vehicle to have given the mouth a flavor (strawberry soda, mint gum) which the readers know. The best love scenes too I feel are those in which the characters speak to each other. A third person description which is all done in vague terms delineating a trip down a water slide just doesn't cut it any more! The modern day reader of romance wants realism within a framework of a believable plot.

I was born in Long Prairie, Minnesota (the setting of THE ENDEARMENT) and lived nine years in Browerville (setting of THE FULFILLMENT), my second and first books, respectively. I was weaned on movies, and the strongly romantic movies of the 50's and 60's greatly influence my writing yet. I often cull long remembered scenes and interject them into my books. I did not attend college, but married a boy from Staples high school, which I graduated from in 1961. We have lived in Minneapolis for twenty years, have two daughters, a cat and dog. Dan and I enjoy music more than any other pastime. We both play guitar and sing, and

I also play piano and arrange music for it, and dabble in piano composition. We love to travel, and I've used vacation spots as settings in some of my books. I never had a thing published before writing my first book, had written no more than effusive letters and diaries. I enjoy most creative things: cooking, gardening, interior decorating, sewing, calligraphy.

Becoming published/finding an agent: (Refer to question one.) After the publication of my first book, my next two manuscripts were rejected. I nearly gave up writing at that point in my career, but was encouraged by many friends and supporters, thus trudged on. Both of those books were subsequently bought, and one is on the market already.

Bibliography: (all as LaVyrle Spencer)

Contemporary:
  SEPARATE BEDS

Historical romance:
  THE FULFILLMENT, Avon, 1979.
  THE ENDEARMENT, Richard Gallen Books, 1982.
  HUMMINGBIRD, Richard Gallen Books, 1982.
Note: LaVyrle Spencer currently has two books under contract with Second Chance at Love.

SONDRA STANFORD
B. Sondra Williams, 3/20/42, El Campo, Tx., married Huey Stanford, 9/2/61. *Children:* Rhonda, Denise. *Education: University of Southwestern Louisiana, commercial art. Professional associations:* Romance Writers of America. *Awards:* Golden Pen Award (short story), Southwest Writers Conference, 1978. *Genre:* category contemporary. *Agent:* Anita Diamant, 51 E. 42nd St., New York, New York. *Current residence:* Corpus Christi, Texas.

Favorite authors and books: Georgette Heyer, Phyllis Whitney, Victoria Holt, Kathleen Woodiwiss.

Thoughts on writing: Sure, they're escapism, and what's wrong with that? It's the same principle involved as watching television, going to the movies, or reading any other fiction: It allows us to daydream a while. When a man watches a football game or a John Wayne movie, he's "escaping" every bit as much as a woman who enjoys reading a romance. Yet society never puts men down for their little pleasures. I've always been a fan of romantic fiction. I was fifteen when I first met Rhett Butler in GONE WITH THE WIND, although I had already seen the movie. And since then I have reread the book about every ten years. Reading a good romance gives me great pleasure and writing them brings me even more. My philosophy for writing? To give the best story, to entertain, to give pleasure to others. I like characters with dimension, multi-faceted, good and bad, warts and all, and I do my utmost to give depth to mine so that they reflect real people as much as possible. The rewards: the satisfaction of creating something to the best of my ability. And when I receive fan mail that tells me that I succeeded in giving pleasure to someone else, I'm on a high for days.

Becoming published/finding an agent: I wrote a Harlequin, which sold, then a second. Then someone told the Silhouette editor about me when they were looking for authors. She called and asked to look at something. I sent GOLDEN TIDE and she offered me a contract for several books. An editor at another company told me I should get an agent and recommended me to Anita Diamant.

Bibliography:

Category contemporary:
    A STRANGER'S KISS, Harlequin, 1978.
    GOLDEN TIDE, Silhouette, 1980.
    SHADOWS OF LOVE, Silhouette, 1980.
    BELLEFLEUR, Harlequin, 1980.
    STORM'S END, Silhouette, 1980.
    NO TRESPASSING, Silhouette, 1980.
    LONG WINTER'S NIGHT, Silhouette, 1981
    AND THEN CAME DAWN, Silhouette, 1981.
    YESTERDAY'S SHADOW, Silhouette, 1981.
    WHISPER WIND, Silhouette, 1981.
    TARNISHED VOWS, Silhouette, 1982.
    SILVER MIST, Silhouette Special Edition, 1982.

MAGNOLIA MOOD, Silhouette Special Edition, 1982.
SUN LOVER, Silhouette Special Edition, 1982.
LOVE'S GENTLE CHANGE, Silhouette Special Edition, 1982.

REGINALD THOMAS STAPLES

Pseudonyms: Robert Tyler Stevens, James Sinclair. *B.* Reginald Thomas Staples, 11/26/11, London, England, married Jo Anne Hume, 6/12/37. *Children:* Jeffery Charles. *Education:* Grammar school, 1923-1928 (West Square, Westminster). *Genres:* Historical romance. *Agent:* Patsy Brougham, WOMAN magazine, King's Reach Tower, Stamford Street, London, England. *Current residence:* Caterham, Surrey, England.

Favorite authors and books: R.D. Delderfield—A HORSEMAN RIDING BY (trilogy).

Thoughts on writing: Historical romance is pure escapism, of course. Escapism in literature, cinema and theatre is thoroughly enjoyable. I dislike all authors and playwrights who insist I am in need of social messages.

Becoming published/finding an agent: I went to a bookshop to buy some paperbacks for holiday reading. They all seemed to be written by people with frantic sex problems. So on my return from holiday I wrote THE SUMMER DAY IS DONE, a novel about the last Tsar of Russia and his family, with a special emphasis on his eldest daughter, Olga. No sex, no four-letter words, simply a story of a very charming Grand Duchess. It was accepted for serialization by a magazine and subsequently issued in hardbook. Six other novels followed.

Bibliography:

Historical romance:
> THE SUMMER DAY IS DONE, Robert Tyler Stevens. Souvenir Press, 1976, (New York publisher—Doubleday, 1977).
> FLIGHT FROM BUCHAREST, Robert Tyler Stevens. Souvenir Press, 1977. (New York publisher—Doubleday).
> APPOINTMENT IN SARAJEVO, Robert Tyler Stevens. Souvenir Press, 1978. American title MY ENEMY, MY LOVE, (New York publisher-Doubleday).

WOMAN OF CORDOVA, Robert Tyler Stevens, Souvenir Press, 1979. American title WOMAN OF TEXAS, (New York publisher-Doubleday). THE FIELDS OF YESTERDAY, Robert Tyler Stevens. Hamlyns, 1982. WARRIOR QUEEN, James Sinclair. Souvenir Press, 1977. (New York publisher-St. Martins Press, 1977). CANIS THE WARRIOR, James Sinclair. Souvenir Press, 1979. (New York publisher-St. Martins Press, 1979).

DANIELLE STEEL
B. New York, N.Y., 8/48. *Education*: Educated in France and at New York University. *Genres*: Contemporary; novels set in the 1930s and 1940s. *Current residence*: New York and California.

Bibliography:
GOING HOME, Pocket, 1973.
PASSION'S PROMISE, Dell, January 1977.
NOW AND FOREVER, Dell, February 1978.
THE PROMISE, Dell, August 1978 (based on a screenplay by Garry Michael White).
SEASON OF PASSION, Dell, February 1979.
SUMMER'S END, Dell, August 1979.
TO LOVE AGAIN, Dell, January 1980.
LOVING, Dell, September 1980.
THE RING, Delacorte, October 1980; Dell, September 1981.
LOVE: POEMS BY DANIELLE STEEL, Dell, January 1981.
PALOMINO, Dell Trade, April 1981; Dell, December 1982.
REMEMBRANCE, Delacorte, October 1981.
A PERFECT STRANGER, Dell, February 1982.
ONCE IN A LIFETIME, Dell Trade, April 1982.
CROSSING, Delacorte, September 1982.

ANN E. STEINKE
Pseudonyms: Elizabeth Reynolds, Anne Williams, Anne Reynolds. *B.* Ann Elizabeth Reynolds, 11/5/46, River Falls, Wisconsin, married William Steinke, 10/28/67. *Children:* Christopher, Elizabeth. *Education:* one year at State University college at Buffalo, New York. Art major. *Professional associations:* Romance Writers of America, charter member. *Genres*: Category contemporary, both adult and young adult. *Agent:* Denise Marcil, 316 W. 82 Street, N.Y., N.Y. 10024. *Current residence:* New York state.

Favorite authors and books: Janet Dailey,but read anything that sounds interesting. Love the Scholastic YAs and especially Emilie Loring and Cynthia Freeman.

Thoughts on writing: I write romances because I enjoy reading them. I feel the readers like romance because it is woefully lacking in everyday life for the majority of them. I personally enjoy humor and interesting locations and occupations, and when I write I try to make sure my books measure up. I don't feel romances should be considered the "step-children" of publishing's other genres; I feel authors should write as well as they would any other type they chose and therefore not shortchange the reading public.

Becoming published/finding an agent: Three years ago I was put in touch via some mutual friends with another friend who was also pursuing a writing career. She had attended the Skidmore conference and had jotted down Denise Marcil's address. I asked her for it and after trying to get published on my own with a Canadian firm decided to write her. I sent her some short stories and asked her if, based on my abilities illustrated by the stories, she would represent me. She replied that generally she didn't deal with short fiction but should I develop some book length fiction she would "take a look" at it. A year later after my second rejection from the Canadian firm I sent Denise a romance/intrigue. Based upon that book (which still awaits purchase) she decided to take me on, particularly after reading a book I had recently gotten back from Mills and Boon—a romance which she sold to Silhouette. Denise and I have just recently entered our third year of working together.

Bibliograghy:

Category contemporary:
AN OCEAN OF LOVE, Elizabeth Reynolds. Silhouette, 1982.
Note: Ann Steinke currently has three books under contract, a category romance with Bantam to appear under the pseudonym Anne Williams, one with Avon, and a young adult with NAL.

SERITA MENDELSON GLASSENBERG STEVENS
Pseudonyms: Serita Stevens, Megan MacDonnell. *B.* Serita

Mendelson, 1/20/49, Chicago, Il., married Raymond Glassenberg, M.D. 8/29/71; Divorced 7/1/80. *Children:* None, but two cats, Alexander the Great and Miss Francis. *Education:* B.S. in nursing, 1971, University of Illinois; a variety of classes at night schools, and then a Masters in literature, 1977, Antioch University British Center. Student taught at Oxford's Platter College. *Professional associations:* Romance Writers of America, Society of Romance Novelists, Romance Novelists of U.K., Society of Children's Writers, Midwestern Travel Writers Assoc., Chicago Press Club. *Awards:* Cape Cod Writer's Conference, 1979 award for best unpublished work—it later became the basis for THIS BITTER ECSTASY. *Genres:* Historical romance, young adult, travel articles. *Agent:* Denise Marcil, 310 W. 82nd St., N.Y., N.Y. 10016. *Current residence:* Evanston, Il.

Favorite authors and books: Victoria Holt, Norah Lofts, Mary Stewart and Phyllis Whitney were the folks that I grew up with and devoured! While still enjoying them I also like Janet Dailey, Rebecca Brandewyne, Roberta Gellis, Georgette Heyer and so many others that I couldn't list them all here! I respect and like the authors who can teach historical fact and make it entertaining and have their facts straight!

Thoughts on writing: I was a fan for years before I wrote, reading the gothic, the romantic suspense and the Harlequin romance from my junior years up. My nickname is "Ritie" because I always had a book in my hand. I believe that there is romance everywhere and that in all the major books, there is romance, too; it's just a matter of how much emphasis you want to put on it. These books are escapism but they're also an education. I believe, especially with the historicals, that they should teach and enlighten the reader as well as give her some fun.

Becoming published/finding an agent: I was living in London at the time and I crashed a party because I had heard that Rosemary Gould (a well-known romance agent in London) was going to be there. At the party, I cornered her and asked that she see my work. She did and liked it. When I returned to the States, she hooked me up with one American agent. That didn't work out. At the RWA conference in June 1981 I met Denise Marcil. When Fawcett accepted my young adult romance I asked her to represent me and we've been together since.

I first became published through persistent pounding at the doors (via mail) of publishing houses, writing and rewriting, taking classes, talking to people, and listening! No, I did not have an agent for my first book.

Bibliography:

Historical romance:
> THIS BITTER ECSTASY, Serita Stevens, Gallen, May 1981.—Won 1979 award at Cape Code Writer's Conference, best unpublished work; was also featured on a special CBS program as one of the romance novelists.

Note: Serita Stevens has a young adult romance under contract with Fawcett. It will appear under the pseudonym of Megan MacDonnell.

FLORENCE STEVENSON
Pseudonyms: Zandra Colt, Lucia Curzon, Zabrina Faire. *B.* Florence Stevenson, Los Angeles, Ca. *Education*: B.A., M.A. 1950, University of Southern California. *Professional associations*: Authors' League, Dramatists' Guild. *Awards*: Theater Americana Award for Best Play of 1951—"Child's Play" *Genres*: Category contemporary, Gothic, historical romance, occult, Regency. *Agent*: Phyllis Westberg, Harold Ober Assoc., 40 E. 49th St., N.Y., N.Y. 10017. *Current residence*: New York, N.Y.

Favorite authors and books: The total output of Georgette Heyer, Jeffrey Farnol and Lady Eleanor Smith.

Thoughts on writing: I became a writer because I love to write. I have been writing poems, short stories and essays since I was old enough to hold a pencil. I started as a playwright—I still have productions and it is still my favorite medium of expression. However, I also like to write novels, with emphasis upon romance and the occult.

Becoming published/finding an agent: I wrote a book called OPHELIA about a cat that fell into a wishing well and became a woman. Then my friends told me it had publishing possibilities, so I took it to Simon & Schuster, where it was turned down. I tried Roger

Straus because I'd met him at a party, and he said he hoped OPHELIA would find a home, since she wouldn't with him. Finally, Katherine Kidde, then at NAL, liked it and bought it. It was serialized in "Cosmo," and later in French "Cosmo," and published in Italy and Germany. As for agents, someone recommended Blanche Gregory, and I was her client for ten years. I later moved to Phyllis Westberg at Harold Ober Associates (writers often get dissatisfied with their agents, through no one's fault, and move on), and I'm happy with our relationship. I was fortunate that I'd written plays before getting into novel writing, so I had connections who could refer me to people in book publishing.

Bibliography:

Category contemporary: (all as Zandra Colt)
    CACTUS ROSE, Second Chance at Love, 1982.
    SPLENDID SAVAGE, Second Chance at Love, 1982.

Gothic/occult romance:
    THE WITCHING HOUR, Award Books, 1971.
    WHERE SATAN DWELLS, Award Books, 1971.
    KILMENY IN THE DARK WOOD, NAL, 1973.
    ALTAR OF EVIL, Award Books, 1973
    THE SORCERER OF THE CASTLE, Award Books, 1974.
    DARK ODYSSEY, NAL, 1974.
    THE IDES OF NOVEMBER, NAL, 1975.
    A SHADOW ON THE HOUSE, NAL, 1975.
    WITCH'S CROSSING, NAL, 1975.
    THE SILENT WATCHER, Award Books, 1975.
    A DARKNESS ON THE STAIRS, NAL, 1976.
    THE HOUSE AT LUXOR, NAL, 1976.
    DARK ENCOUNTER, NAL, 1977.
    THE HORROR FROM THE TOMBS, Award Books, 1977.
    MOONLIGHT VARIATIONS, Jove, 1980.
    JULIE, NAL, 1978.
    THE GOLDEN GALATEA, Jove, 1979.

Regency:
    LADY BLUE, Zabrina Faire, Warner, 1979.
    MIDNIGHT MATCH, Zabrina Faire, Warner, 1979.
    ROMANY REBEL, Zabrina Faire, Warner, 1979.
    ENCHANTING JENNY, Zabrina Faire, Warner, 1979.
    THE WICKED COUSIN, Zabrina Faire, Warner, 1980.
    ATHENA'S AIRS, Zabrina Faire, Warner, 1980.

MAD PURSUIT, Zabrina Faire, Warner, 1981.
KITTY AND THE CAPTAIN, Zabrina Faire, Warner, 1981.
THE CHADBOURNE LUCK, Lucia Curzon, Second Chance at Love, 1981.
AN ADVERSE ALLIANCE, Lucia Curzon, Second Chance at Love, 1982.
THE MOURNING BRIDE, Lucia Curzon, Second Chance at Love, 1982.
QUEEN OF HEARTS, Lucia Curzon, Second Chance at Love, 1982.
Florence Stevenson is the co-author of two other books, the author of a Gothic satire called THE CURSE OF THE CONCULLENS, and her two earliest novels were not romances—OPHELIA and FEAST OF EGG-SHELLS. Several of her novels have been published abroad, and three of her NAL Regencies have been reprinted by large-print houses.

PAT WALLACE STROTHER
Pseudonyms: Vivian Lord, Patricia Cloud, Pat Wallace. *B.* Patricia Wallace, 3/11/29, Birmingham, Alabama, married (1) Lee Levitt, 1951; (2) David G. Latner, 1958; (3) Robert A. Strother, 1980. *Children*: (stepchildren) Andrea Strother, Douglas Strother, Robert Strother, Jr.; (grandchild) Cassandra Rose Strother. *Education*: Attended University of Tennessee, Knoxville, Tennessee, major—English. *Professional associations:* Authors Guild. *Awards*: WHO'S WHO OF AMERICAN WOMEN—1979-1980, Pat Wallace: 1981-1982, 1983-1984, Pat Wallace Strother. *Genres:* Historical romance, family saga, fantasy-gothic, Category contemporary. *Agent:* Jane Rotrosen Agency, 318 East 51st Street, N.Y.,N.Y. 10022. *Current residence*: New York, New York.

Favorite authors and books: Among my favorite authors are Daphne du Maurier and Victoria Holt. I have come so recently to the Contemporary romance scene I haven't had time to develop favorites, but I've enjoyed a number of fine Silhouette writers, including the excellent Judith Baker.

Thoughts on writing: Because my first published book was sheer fantasy, I incline towards writing for the reader's pure entertainment and escapism. But it's a little deeper than that — I was originally a poet and was born a Pisces, therefore I naturally see the glory and splendor below ordinary things and events. As an optimist I believe that with hope and effort one can win almost any goal. My basic philosophy on writing is to give others hope, pleasure and joy.

Becoming published/finding an agent: I bombarded New York publishers with manuscripts for three years until Bob Wyatt at Avon wrote me he "had a feeling" they'd publish me someday. We had lunch and I combined my six short "Astrological Gothics" — I was the inventor of Astrological fiction in its purest form— into a massive one thousand page manuscript published as HOUSE OF SCORPIO in 1975. I then hired an agent (not my present one, who is top notch and with whom I've been associated since 1978.)

Bibliography:

Family saga:
> THE VOYAGERS, Vivian Lord. Fawcett GM, 1980. Sphere Books, England, 1981; Doubleday Book Club Alternate, November 1980.
> ONCE MORE THE SUN, Vivian Lord. Fawcett GM, 1982. (accepted for publication, Sphere Books, England.)

Historical romance:
> THIS WILLING PASSION, Patricia Cloud. Putnam, 1978; Berkeley, 1980; Robert Hale, England, 1979.
> TRAITOR IN MY ARMS, Vivian Lord. Fawcett Gold Medal, 1979.

Non-Romance books:
> HOUSE OF SCORPIO, Pat Wallace. Avon, 1975. (Astrological Gothic.)
> THE WAND AND THE STAR, Pat Wallace. Pocket Books, 1978. (Astrological Fantasy.)

Note: Pat Wallace Strother currently has a book under contract with Silhouette.

MOLLY SWANTON

Pseudonyms: Lynn Erickson (Pseudonym shared by co-author, Carla Peltonen). *B.* Molly Butler, 9/12/46, Bryn Mawr, PA., married Terry Swanton, 1968. *Children*: Megan. *Education*: George Washington University, foreign affairs. *Genres*: Contemporary, historical romance. *Agent*: Merrilee Heifitz, (Writer's House, 21 W. 26th Street, New York, NY. *Current residence*: Aspen, CO.

Favorite authors and books: Susan Howatch, Roberta Gellis, Janet Dailey, Rosemary Rogers, Kathleen Woodiwiss.

Thoughts on writing: Reading for pleasure is both an avenue of escape and a tool for broadening horizons. My co-author and I have been fans of literature—romance included—for many years. Writing is a joy, a way to fulfill ourselves, and also a lot of hard work. It's satisfying to receive a fan letter and know that you have shared your work with others, and brought a little knowledge and entertainment to their lives.

Becoming published/finding an agent: Molly and I wrote two books and tried to sell the manuscripts ourselves, but had no luck. We were directed to Writer's House by a friend; the agency sold our two books to Richard Gallen within two weeks.

Bibliography:

Contemporary:
GENTLE BETRAYER, Lynn Erickson, Gallen/Pocket, 1982.

Historical romance: (all as Lynn Erickson)
THIS RAGING FLOWER, Gallen/Pocket, 1979.
SWEET NEMESIS, Gallen/Pocket, 1979.
THE SILVER KISS, Gallen/Pocket, 1981.
WOMAN OF SAN FRANCISCO, Dell, 1982.
HIGH COUNTRY PRIDE, Pocket, 1982.
Note: Molly Swanton has one book currently under contract with Pocket Books, under the pseudonym, Lynn Erickson.

ANGELA TALIAS
Pseudonyms: Angela Alexie. *B*. Angela Dunton, 11/14/48, Atlanta, GA., married Nicholas Talias, 1970. *Children*: Alicia, Christina. *Education: Professional associations*: National League of American Pen Women, Atlanta Writers. *Genres*: Contemporary, historical romance. *Agent*: Denise Marcil, 316 W. 82nd St., New York, NY. *Current residence*: Marietta, GA.

Favorite authors and books: Kathleen Woodiwiss (THE WOLF AND THE DOVE, THE FLAME AND THE FLOWER), Laurie McBain (MOONSTRUCK MADNESS); both authors were my inspiration to attempt a writing career.

Thoughts on writing: Many times you hear that an author was an avid reader—such is the case with me. I found well-written and well researched historicals addictive. I don't know that romances are escapism as much as they are entertaining and enjoyable. The same can be said of contemporary romances if the plot is realistic.

Becoming published/finding an agent: Through a business associate, my husband, Nicky, was introduced to Denise Marcil. He mentioned I had begun a novel, she asked to look at it, and voila! That first book didn't sell, but the next one did.

Bibliography:

Contemporary:
SOMETIMES A STRANGER, Angela Alexie, Gallen/Pocket, 1981.

Historical: (All as Angela Alexie)
THE TREACHEROUS HEART, Fawcett, 1g80.
THE VELVET THORN, Fawcett, 1982.

KATHRYN GORSHA THIELS
B. Kathryn Maxine Gorsha, 3/18/49, Morgan City, LA., married Francis L. Thiels 12/74. *Professional associations:* Louisiana Press Women's Association. *Awards:* Margaret McDonald Press Award (Fiction), 1981; Citizen of the Year, Alexandria, Louisiana, 1981; Honorary Colonel on the staff of David Treen, Governor of Louisiana. *Genres:* category contemporary, historical romance. *Current residence:* Alexandria, Louisiana.

Favorite authors and books: Edgar Rice Burroughs, Edgar Cayce, Janet Dailey, Raymond Giles, Wilbur Smith, Harold Robbins.

Thoughts on writing: Contemporary romance is fun to write, but my real love is historical romance. Yes, they're total escapism in that the reader is given the opportunity to actually become the characters as she reads the books. Yes, I read for years and still do read everything I can find, no matter what type work it is. Philosophy: Through creating, we express. Through expression, we entertain. Happiness follows.

Becoming published/finding an agent: A romantic by nature, it wasn't difficult to devise an intricate plot and begin writing. My greatest trial was in finding an agent, because they're as elusive as publishers. Once I found an agent, SAVAGE FANCY was immediately accepted. Although my education was in medicine, totally opposite to journalism, I've proven that a true talent can make it. I encourage others to do the same.

Bibliography:

Category contemporary:
SAVAGE FANCY, Pocket Books, 1980.
TEXAS ROSE, Silhouette Special Edition, 1982.

JOYCE THIES
Pseudonyms: Janet Joyce (shared with co-writer Janet Bieber). *B.* Joyce Ann Scott, 4/2/48, Minneapolis, Minnesota, married Arnold L. Thies, 8/30/68. *Children:* Paul, Melissa. *Education:* University of Minnesota, major English, minor journalism. *Genres:* Contemporary romance, Historical romance. *Agent:* Irene Goodman, 134 West 81 Street, N.Y., N.Y. 10024. *Current residence*: Columbus, Ohio.

Favorite authors and books: Past: Glenna Finley, Victoria Holt, Mary Stewart. Present: Laverle Spencer, THE ENDEARMENT. Anything by Kathleen Woodiwiss, and Jayne Castle/Stephanie James.

Thoughts on writing: Writing romance means more to me than escaping the humdrum, everyday things of life. Always a fan, I have noted that there is generally a sense of tragedy in most love stories when in real life most people find many things to laugh about. I try to incorporate real life humor into my stories and write about strong men who never lose their ability to be romantic.

Becoming published/finding an agent: My collaborator and I sent our first manuscript to Gallen and it was accepted. We caught their attention with a tongue-in-cheek query and an outrageous marketing idea. Our editor than suggested several agents and we chose Irene Goodman.

Bibligraphy:

Historical romance:
CONQUER THE MEMORIES, Janet Joyce. Richard Gallen Books, 1982.
Note: Joyce Thies is currently under contract to Pocket Books — Tapestry series, and to Silhouette—Desire series.

JOAN THOMPSON
B. Joan Russell Phillipps, 2/26/43, Boston, Ma., married Stephen William Abbot Thompson, 12/20/63. *Children:* Christopher Phillipps and Andrew Abbott. *Education:* Melrose, Ma. public schools, B.A. 1964, Colby College, French Lit. *Professional associations:* Authors Guild. *Genres:* Historical romance, general fiction, mysteries. *Agent:* Charles D. Taylor, Books and Productions East, 23 Elm St., Manchester, Ma. *Current residence:* Marblehead, Ma.

Favorite authors and books: Gustave Flaubert, MADAME BOVARY; Leo Tolstoy, ANNA KARENINA; Shirley Hazzard, THE TRANSIT OF VENUS; all of Thomas Hardy.

Thoughts on writing: I don't consider myself a "romance" writer. My field is general fiction, although my first two books, MARBLEHEAD and PARKER'S ISLAND were marketed as romances. My third book was a family saga (with romance) centering around World War I. My fourth is a mystery. All my work has an element of romance in it.

Becoming published/finding an agent: I became published through my good friend Charles D. Taylor who expressed interest in my work. Thomas Dunne at St. Martin's Press first published me and was encouraging.

Bibliograghy:

Family saga:
INTERESTING TIMES, St. Martin's, 1981.

Historical romance:
MARBLEHEAD, St. Martin's, 1978. Reprinted as HARBOR OF THE HEART, Ballantine, 1981.
PARKER'S ISLAND, St. Martin's, 1979, Ballantine, 1981.

CAROLYN STROMEYER THORTON

Pseudonym: Carolyn Thorton. *B.* Carolyn Stromeyer, 6/30/51, Hattiesburg, Mississippi. *Education*: B.A. University of Southern Mississippi, journalism. *Professional associations*: Romance Writers of America. *Genre*: category contemporary. *Agent*: Emilie Jacobson, Curtis Brown Agency, N.Y., N.Y. Current residence: Hattiesburg, Mississippi.

Favorite authors and books: Mary Stewart.

Thoughts on writing: A lot of interviews I've done—on everything from beer can collecting to muscadine wine making in Mississippi—are beginning to appear in my novels. I like to give my books a sense of reality by slipping in some facts every now and then, humorously done, if at all possible.

Through my writing I can be anybody. I can go anywhere. I can do anything. And I want to take my readers with me. I want to touch their hearts and make them feel the same emotions I do when I'm writing—sadness, joy, love. I never know when I'll see the germ of a new story idea, and so I walk around with an open eye for things happening around me.

Becoming published/finding an agent: I think the thing is—once you start a book—not to keep hashing up the first few chapters but to finish it. Don't always keep the objective that: Hey, it's going to sell. The first one may not, but it's going to answer a lot of questions that will prepare you for writing the next one and the next one. You're going to get better, the more you write. Persist, and DON'T give up! Because giving up is SO easy, and that separates the professional from the amateur.

Bibliography:
    THE HEART NEVER FORGETS, Silhouette romance, July 1980.
    LOVE IS SURRENDER, Silhouette Special Edition, March 1982.
    PRIDE'S RECKONING, Silhouette Special Edition, November 1982.
Note: Carolyn Thorton has five more books under contract with Silhouette. She also writes magazine articles, including travel, interviews, and features, under the names Carolyn Stromeyer and Carolyn Stromeyer Thorton.

AIMEE THURLO
Pseudonyms: Aimee Martel, Aimee Duva. B. Aimee Salcedo, 6/1/51, Havana, Cuba, married David Thurlo, 7/31/70. *Genres*: Category contemporary. *Agent*: Cherry Weiner, 1734 Church St. Rahway, N.J. *Current residence*: Albuquerque, New Mexico.

Favorite authors and books: Janet Dailey, the CALDER series, Jude Deveraux, HIGHLAND VELVET.

Thoughts on writing: I read all fiction—especially romances, for entertainment and escapism. To relive old memories and feelings—happy and sad—and experience new events and sensations through the characters I create or read about—makes me a fan as well as a writer. I write for two people—myself and the reader. It turns out we have a lot to share.

Becoming published/finding an agent: I tried publisher after publisher. The sixtieth one finally said yes. After that, I contacted Cherry Weiner, an agent for a writer friend, and she agreed to represent me. Since then I've written four books for the Second Chance line.

Bibliography:

Category contemporary:
    SECRETS NOT SHARED, Aimee Martel. Leisure Books, 1981.
    TOO NEAR THE SUN, Aimee Duvall. Jove-Second Chance, 1982.
    HALFWAY THERE, Aimee Duvall. Jove-Second Chance, 1982.
    LOVER IN BLUE, Aimee Duvall. Jove-Second Chance, 1982.

LINDA TRIEGEL
Pseudonyms: Elisabeth Kidd B. Linda Jeanette Triegel, 8/9/42, New York City. *Education*: B.A. (Spanish), Mills College, Oakland, California, 1964, M.A. (Spanish), Middlebury College, Vermont, 1965. *Professional associations*: Romance Writers of America. *Genres*: Regency. *Agent*: Anita Diamant, 51 East 42nd Street, N.Y., N.Y. 10017. *Current residence*: New Fairfield, Connecticut.

Favorite authors and books: Georgette Heyer, far ahead of anyone else, but also: (current favorites) Elizabeth Mansfield, Elsie Lee, Joan Smith, Clare Darcy: (perennials) L.M. Montgomery, Edna Ferber, Marcia Davenport, Daphne du Maurier, Jessamyn West, Gwen Bristow, Anya Seton, and of course—Jane Austen.

Thoughts on writing: I am convinced there will always be a market for the well written Regency romance. Georgette Heyer is still selling well, after all, because of her wit, her care for language and accurate period detail, and her wonderfully ALIVE characters. These are the qualities I strive for in my work. This is not to say I don't enjoy some of the contemporary romances and wouldn't like to try my hand at them, but the Regency genre is unique and should continue to be practiced and polished, like the gem it is.

Becoming published/finding an agent: When MY LORD GUARDI-AN, my first published novel, was almost finished, I began sending out an outline and sample chapters. They made the rounds for about a year until Walker made an offer for the book. Like most authors, I had other manuscripts in various stages of completion in my desk drawer, but MY LORD GUARDIAN was the first I was particularly confident of. After it was accepted, I contacted agent Anita Diamant, whom I had heard speak at a writers panel, who agreed to represent me on my next effort (another Regency).

Bibliography:

Regency:
  MY LORD GUARDIAN, Elisabeth Kidd. Walker and Company, 1982.

DONNA KIMEL VITEK
Pseudonym: Donna Alexander. *B.* Donna Jean Kimel, 11/10/47, Winston-Salem, NC., married Richard John Vitek, 1969. *Children*: Susan, Thomas. *Education*: Appalachian State University, English. *Professional associations*: Author's Guild, Romance Writers of America. *Genres*: Category contemporary. *Current address*: Winston-Salem, NC.

Favorite authors and books: Anne Mather, Roberta Leigh, Rebecca Stratton (almost all their books are well-written and highly enjoyable); Anne Reisser's FACE OF LOVE and Laurie McBain's TEARS OF GOLD.

Thoughts on writing: There are of course well-written romances and there are poorly writen romances. All romantic novels, therefore, cannot be judged en masse. Perhaps in the past, when most romances *were* ridiculously sugary and totally unrealistic, this genre did become publishing's stepchild, but present romantic novels deserve more respect. Although romantic novels do provide escape reading, today's trend is towards exploring realistic problems between men and women who are falling in love. Thus a good romance can often give a reader a new perspective on the dilemmas in her or *his* own love life.

When my children were very young, I read many romances, preferring the works of those authors who presented believable characters, storylines, and dialogue. Now, as a writer of romances, I feel an obligation to provide my readers with realistic stories and characters with whom they can identify. In other words, good writing is good writing.

Becoming published/finding an agent: During my children's younger years, I read romances for relaxation. Then, in late 1978, I decided to write a romantic novel. I sold my first manuscript to MacFadden in mid-1979. MacFadden's editor-in-chief, Anne Gisonny, provided me with so much encouragement and support that writing was truly a delight. When Simon and Schuster began seeking manuscripts for their Silhouette line, I submitted a partial that was accepted. After writing ten books for Silhouette, I began to feel the desire to write more and more serious and more realistic stories. Because Anne Gisonny, who had since been named editor-in-chief for Dell Ecstasy, was seeking only strong, believable, and truly contemporary stories for her line, I was extremely pleased to sign with Dell and have the opportunity to work again with Anne.

Bibliography:

Category contemporary:
A LOVER'S QUESTION, Donna Alexander, MacFadden, 10/79.

RED ROSES, WHITE LILIES, Donna Alexander, MacFadden, 10/79.
NO TURNING BACK, Donna Alexander, MacFadden, 11/79.
IN FROM THE STORM, Donna Alexander, MacFadden, 12/79.
A DIFFERENT DREAM, Silhouette, 9/80.
SHOWERS OF SUNLIGHT, Silhouette, 12/80.
PROMISES FROM THE PAST, Silhouette, 3/81.
VEIL OF GOLD, Silhouette, 6/81.
WHERE THE HEART IS, Silhouette, 9/81.
A VALESQUEZ BRIDE, Silhouette Special Edition, 2/82.
GARDEN OF THE MOONGATE, Silhouette, 3/82.
GAME OF CHANCE, Silhouette, 6/82.
Note: Donna Vitck currently has under contract two books to Silhouette, three books to Dell Ecstasy, and one book to Bantam.

DOROTHY LILLEY WAKELEY
Pseudonyms: Jane Lockwood, Lucy Lilley. *B.* Dorothy Lilley Wells, 1/22/13, Neaton, Warwicks, Eng., married Ronald Francis Wakeley, 1940. *Children*: Jane. *Education*: Swindon College of Art. *Professional associations*: Romantic Novelists Association. *Awards*: Federation of Business and Professional Women. *Genres*: Contemporary, Regency, Victorian. *Agent*: Laurence Pollinger Ltd., 18 Maddox Street, Mayfair, London, England. *Current residence*: Burbage, England.

Favorite authors and books: Jane Austen, the Brontës, Mary Renault for Greek mythology, Doris Leslie for historical, Colleen McCullough, Dorothy Eden, Evelyn Anthony, Winston Graham, Thomas Armstrong, Jean Alexandre.

Thoughts on writing: Since I was a child I was a great reader, and, as a girl, I dabbled in short stories to entertain my sisters. Historical novels are my favorite, and are, to my way of thinking, not escapism—although I adore a little embroidery! I find one often learns much about factual history from such books as GONE WITH THE WIND. I knew nothing about American history until reading Margaret Mitchell's book.

Becoming published/finding an agent: The Victorian period has always fascinated me. I did some research before starting my first novel. I was lucky to find Robert Hale to publish it so quickly. I then contacted Pollingers, and although I heard conflicting reports about agents, I have been most grateful for their help and guidance and for the fact that they accepted me so willingly.

Bibliography:

Regency:
> REMEMBER CAROLINE MARY, Hale, 1982. (New York publisher-Berkley/Jove)

Victorian:
> THE HOUSE IN HOLLY WALK, Hale, 1978. (New York publisher-Berkley/Jove).
> MERCY'S STORY, Hale, 1979. (New York publisher—Berkley/ Jove).

Note: Dorothy Wakeley has a contemporary novel currently under contract with Hale; it is scheduled to be published in 1983 under the pseudonym, Lucy Lilley.

LYNDA CATHERINE WARD

Pseudonyms: Lynda Ward, Julia Jeffries. *B*. Lynda Catherine Miller, 1/24/47, Fort Smith, Arkansas, married Richard Larry Ward, 12/19/65. *Children*: Marshall, Daniel, Gregory. *Education*: A.A. Santa Ana College, English; Cosumnes River College, music. *Professional associations*: California Writers Club, National League of American Penwomen, Romance Writers of America. *Genres*: Category contemporary, Regency. *Agent*: Ruth Cohen, Inc., P.O. Box 7626, Menlo Park, Ca. 94025. *Current residence*: Sacramento, Ca.

Favorite authors and books: Brooke Hastings—INTIMATE STRANGERS; Anne N. Reisser—THE FACE OF LOVE; Dorothy L. Sayers—GAUDY NIGHT; Georgette Heyer—DEVIL'S CUB.

Thoughts on writing: Although I did not become a regular reader of romances until after I was a published writer, I realize now that I had been reading up to writing them all my life. Romance and love stories are part of a long and honorable tradition dating back at least until Biblical times and probably before (e.g., the stories of Ruth and Esther would make great Harlequins). The art of storyteller has to be at least the second oldest profession, and I imagine one of the oldest phrases in any language is the one that means "and they lived happily ever after."

Becoming published/finding an agent: I got my first rejection slip at age thirteen; it took me another eighteen years to sell *anything*. Then I sold confession stories for two years while I tried to market a novel, THE MUSIC OF PASSION, which I finally did sell on my own. I soon realized that life would be a lot easier with an agent, and when I met Ruth Cohen at a writing conference, I liked her and what she had to say. After talking, she agreed to represent me, and I think the relationship has been mutually beneficial ever since. I know I have never regretted it, and I credit her with much of the subsequent success I've enjoyed.

Bibliography:

Category contemporaries: (all as Lynda Ward)
THE MUSIC OF PASSION, Harlequin, 1981.
THE TOUCH OF PASSION, Harlequin, 1982.

Regencies: (all as Julia Jeffries)
THE CHADWICK RING, NAL, 1982.
THE CLERGYMAN'S DAUGHTER, NAL, 1983.

MAUREEN ANN WARTSKI

Pseudonyms: M.A. Crane, Sharon Francis, Francine Shore. *B.* Maureen Ann Crane, 1/25/40, Ashiya, Japan, married Maximilian Wartski, 6/1/62. *Children:* Bert and Mark. *Education:* University of Redlands, B.A. Sophia University, English literature. Also certified as a secondary school teacher in Massachusetts in English and Social Studies. *Professional associations*: Author's Guild. *Awards*: 1980 annual book award of the Child Study Committee at bank Street College (A BOAT TO NO-WHERE); 1980 honor's book award of the Child Study Committee (A LONG WAY FROM HOME); both books listed by the same committee as notable books in the field of social studies, 1980. *Genres*: Category contemporary, mainstream young adult. *Agent*: Eileen Fallon, Barbara Lowenstein Assoc., 250 W. 57th St., N.Y., N.Y. 10107. *Current residence*: Sharon, Mass.

Favorite books and authors: I enjoy the classics, notably the works of

Shakespeare, Tennyson, Malory. I also enjoy Kipling, Hawthorne, Dickens, Scott, Victor Hugo, Tolstoy, Doyle, and the terrific adventures written by Dumas. More currently, I enjoy Steinbeck, Tolkien, Pearl Buck, M.M. Kaye, and have read and re-read Adams' WATERSHIP DOWN. These are a mere sampling. I don't just love books, I need them; I will read a book a day and be completely happy.

Thoughts on writing: I have always and forever wanted to write, and so I enjoy writing. That means, writing *anything*. I find that I am completely lost in the writing of a book, whether this be a young adult novel or a category romance. It is the crafting of the book and the joy of craftsmanship that is important to me; and so I can't empathize with those who "look down on" a particular branch of writing. Romances? *Vive la romance*. They make a lot of readers happy, and, besides, they sell well!

Becoming published/finding an agent: The road to getting published was rocky and paved with stubborn determination. I sent my first YA novel (MY BROTHER IS SPECIAL) to eleven publishers before Barbara Bates at Westminster Press gave it a try. I wrote my current four YA titles without an agent; it's interesting to note that my entree to the category romance field came through contacts with New American Library, who were handling the paperback editions of the YA books. The editor who worked with me at Jove, which handled my first category romance, later became my (indispensible) agent.

Bibliography:

Category contemporary:
GARDEN OF SILVERY DELIGHTS, as Sharon Francis, Second Chance at Love, April, 1982.

Other (all mainstream young adult novels):
MY BROTHER IS SPECIAL, Westminster Press, 1979; NAL, 1981.
A BOAT TO NOWHERE, Westminster, 1980; NAL 1981.
A LONG WAY FROM HOME, Westminster, 1980; NAL 1982.
THE LAKE IS ON FIRE, Westminster, 1981, NAL to publish in paperback.
Note: Maureen Wartski currently has five category contemporary romances under contract with NAL, to appear under the pseudonym of Francine Shore.

NANCY WEBER

Pseudonyms: Jennifer Rose, Olivia Harmston, Lindsay West. *B.* Nancy Weber, 1/22/42, Hartford, Connecticut, married Charles Platt, May 1977; divorced December 1978. *Children*: Rose. *Education*: Sarah Lawrence College, 1964 B.A. *Genres*: Category contemporary. *Agent*: Jane Rotrosen, 318 East 51st Street, N.Y., N.Y. 10022. *Current residence*: Greenwich Village, U.S.A.

Favorite authors and books: Among my favorite authors are Charlotte Brontë, Charlotte Prentiss, and Charlotte Lamb.

Thoughts on writing: I love making chocolate truffles and other confections—and always serve them up a bit guiltily. Writing romances arouses the same measures of delight and guilt. Writing them has helped me become a better storyteller, and I like thinking I've provided readers with a few sighs and laughs; but I do worry that they may spoil readers' appetites for more substantial fare. Someone tell me: Do hardcore romance readers (which I've never been) also buy lots of other fiction? Which isn't to say that serious or hightoned is always good: Give me Charlotte Lamb over John Irving any day! I hope to get more bold and experimental with my romances as I get a surer grasp of the genre; ultimately, maybe, fuse "romance" and "mainstream" —Jane Austen, Scott Fitzgerald, John O'Hara, and Charlotte Brontë did. After all, why not do it in our time? Meanwhile, I'll write the best romances I can, trying to combine real emotions and fantastical situations, being scrupulous about details (if I say there is an 8:48 train from New York to Montreal, there really is one).

Becoming published/finding an agent: I went to work for THE NEW YORK POST after college, as an editorial assistant with an occasional byline; after a year and a half I submitted a piece to COSMOPOLITAN over the transom, sold it, and went free-lance, a precarious but thrilling life made possible because of connections established while on the POST. My first agent was as new at his work as I was at mine; when I wanted to change agents subsequently I picked up the telephone—always with a specific potentially commercial project to talk about. Agents can be life preservers, but a new writer should know that an agent can't sell talent, can only sell work (or maybe ideas for work).

Bibliogragy:

Category romance: (all as Jennifer Rose)
OUT OF A DREAM Second Chance at Love, 1981.
SHAMROCK SEASON, Second Chance at Love, 1982.
TWILIGHT EMBRACE, Second Chance at Love, 1982.

Non-Romance Books:
STAR FEVER, Nancy Weber. Signet, 1971. (rock novel)
THE LIFE SWAP, Nancy Weber. Dial Press, 1974, Dell, 1975. (first person adventure).
THE COEDS PART II, Olivia Harmston. Ace, 1975. (''Modern career girl''fiction—campus story)
$500.,Nancy Weber. Ace 1976. (Paperback original fiction)
EMPIRE OF THE ANTS, Lindsay West. Ace, 1977. (Movie novelization)
LILY, WHERE'S YOUR DADDY?, Nancy Weber. Richard Marek Publishers, 1980. (First person non-fiction)
Note: Nancy Weber currently has a novel under contract with St. Martin's/ Marek.

JUDE GILLIAM WHITE
Pseudonym: Jude Deveraux. *B.* Jude Gilliam, 9/20/47, Louisville, KY., married Claude White, 1970. *Education*: B.S. Murray University, fine arts. *Professional associations*: Costume Society of America. *Genres:* Historical romance. *Current residence:* Santa Fe, NM.

Favorite authors and books: Roberta Gellis, Kathleen Woodiwiss, Anne McCaffrey, Herman Raucher.

Thoughts on writing: I believe the same rules that apply to ''literature'' apply to writing a romance. A romance must be carefully planned, the characters must have personality, the research must be accurate. Before writing, I was frustrated by the fact that my favorite authors seemed to write the same book over and over again. Now I try to write very different books, yet stay within the framework of romance. I rarely ever read romances today because they are too much like a busman's holiday to me.

Becoming published/finding an agent: I wrote my first book, chose a publisher that had pretty covers, mailed it to them, and they wrote back in twenty-eight days, and offered me a contract.

Bibliography: (all as Jude Deveraux)

Historical romance:
THE ENCHANTED LAND, Avon, 1977.
THE BLACK LYON, Avon, 1979.
THE VELVET PROMISE, Gallen, 1980.
HIGHLAND VELVET, Pocket, 1982.
CASA GRANDE, Avon, 1982.

PHYLLIS A. WHITNEY
B. Phyllis A. Whitney, Yokohama, Japan, 9/9/03 (parents were American), married twice, is now a widow. *Children*: Georgia Garner, now Georgia Pearson. *Education:* McKinley High School, Chicago. My parents were both dead, and I went to work in libraries and bookstores. A very good education, while I learned to be a writer. *Professional associations*: Mystery Writers of America, Midland Authors, Children's Reading Round Table, Society of Children's Book Writers, Authors Guild. *Awards*: Two Edgars from Mystery Writers of America for best juvenile mystery: 1960 and 1964 (plus other citations for juveniles); my favorite honor was being president of Mystery Writers of America in 1975. *Genres*: My early books were teen-age novels, then I wrote mysteries for the 10-14 age group. My adult novels are all romantic suspense, and I've written a total of sixty-five books. In terms of romance, I am "borderline," since I consider myself more a mystery writer than a romance writer. Romantic suspense is my field. *Agent*: Mrs. Patricia Myrer, McIntosh & Otis, 475 Fifth Ave., N.Y., N.Y. 10017. *Current residence*: Long Island, N.Y.

Favorite authors and books: My reading is mostly in the mystery and suspense fields. I enjoy Victoria Holt, Joan Aiken, Barbara Michaels, Elizabeth Peters, and many others.

Thoughts on writing: I have enjoyed reading mystery novels since I was a child, and enjoy writing mysteries. I don't follow the straight romance field. Mysteries, too, have been in the stepchild position, and are now becoming "respectable" and respected. When there is good writing and good story telling, the books earn their right to be read. I hope I am still learning and growing as a writer.

Becoming published/finding an agent: That's too long a story. It is told in full in my GUIDE TO FICTION WRITING. My present agent was my first editor in the adult field. I reviewed books, taught writing at universities and conferences, read mss. for publishers, lectured, etc., until I could earn enough to just write!

Bibliograghy: (Adult books only)
RED IS FOR MURDER, Ziff-Davis, 1943.
THE QUICKSILVER POOL, Appleton-Century-Crofts, 1955.
THE TREMBLING HILLS, Appleton-Century-Crofts, 1956.
SKYE CAMERON, Appleton-Century-Crofts, 1957.
THE MOONFLOWER, Appleton-Century-Crofts, 1958.
THUNDER HEIGHTS, Appleton-Century-Crofts, 1960.
BLUE FIRE, Appleton-Century-Crofts, 1961.
WINDOW ON THE SQUARE, Appleton-Century-Crofts, 1962.
SEVEN TEARS FOR APOLLO, Appleton-Century-Crofts, 1963.
BLACK AMBER, Appleton-Century-Crofts, 1964.
SEA JADE, Appleton-Century-Crofts, 1965.
COLUMBELLA, Doubleday, 1966.
SILVERHILL, Doubleday, 1967.
HUNTER'S GREEN, Doubleday, 1968.
THE WINTER PEOPLE, Doubleday, 1969.
LOST ISLAND, Doubleday, 197U.
LISTEN FOR THE WHISPERER, Doubleday, 1972.
SNOWFIRE, Doubleday, 1973.
THE TURQUOISE MASK, Doubleday, 1974.
SPINDRIFT, Doubleday, 1975.
THE GOLDEN UNICORN, Doubleday, 1976.
THE STONE BULL, Doubleday, 1977.
THE GLASS FLAME, Doubleday, 1978.
DOMINO, Doubleday, 1979.
POINCIANA, Doubleday, 1980.
VERMILION, Doubleday, 1981.
EMERALD, Doubleday, 1983.

Note: Phyllis A. Whitney is the author of a number of mysteries for juveniles, several of which have won awards, and the author of two non-fiction books for writers, WRITING JUVENILE STORIES AND NOVELS and the recent GUIDE TO FICTION WRITING. Over twenty-one million copies of her novels are in print in paperback editions (Fawcett) and not one of her adult novels has ever gone out of print.

JEANNE WILLIAMS
Pseudonyms: Megan Castell, Jeanne Crecy, Jeanne Foster, Kristin Michaels, Deirdre Rowan. *B.* Dorothy Jean Kreie, Elkhart, Kansas, 4/10/30, married Gene Williams, 1949; John Creasey (the English mystery writer), 1970; Bob Morse, 1981. *Children:* Michael, born 1949, Kristin, born 1960. *Education:*Public schools in Kansas, Kansas, Missouri, and Oklahoma; University of Oklahoma (didn't graduate). *Professional associations:* Authors Guild; Western Writers of America (past president). *Awards:* Levi Strauss Golden Saddleman, three Golden Spur Awards from Western Writers of America. *Genres:* Family saga, historical romance (accent on historical!), contemporary romance, gothics, historical teen-age novels; mainstream novels. *Agent:* Mrs. Claire Smith, Harold Ober Associates, 40 East 49th Street. *Current residence:* Portal, Arizona.

Favorite books and authors: Anya Seton, Norah Lofts, Victoria Holt, Georgette Heyer.

Thoughts on writing: I like books with romance but not where that is the main and only object. I try to write the kind of books I like, strongly developed characters, plenty of adventure and authentic background, books to be savored and remembered. I research with great care and hope to leave my readers with something nourishing and a frame of values I believe in. I have never let "love" be the total and prime realization of my heroines' womanhood; in fact, some of them deny the men they love over an ideal or duty. In other words, while entertaining, I do not offer some fantastic never-never land. Love of all kinds is terribly important, for friends, family, animals. I don't like to narrow it to the feeling between lovers.

Becoming published/finding an agent: I began publishing short stories when I was twenty-two, eased into books in 1957. I tried five agents without much rapport developing till I was introduced to my present (and dearly beloved) agent in 1970. I sold seventy short stories before I turned to books entirely and marketed most of them myself, which was excellent experience. I think would-be writers are confused about the function of agents and would do better to sell several books before attempting to secure one.

Bibliographies:

Contemporaries: (all as Kristin Michaels)
TO BEGIN WITH LOVE, Signet (NAL), 1975.
ENCHANTED TWILIGHT, Signet (NAL), 1975.
A SPECIAL KIND OF LOVE, Signet (NAL), 1976.
ENCHANTED JOURNEY, Signet (NAL), 1977.
SONG OF THE HEART, Signet (NAL), 1977.
VOYAGE TO LOVE, Signet (NAL), 1977.
MAKE BELIEVE LOVE, Signet (NAL), 1978.
MAGIC SIDE OF THE MOON, Signet (NAL), 1979.

Gothics: (as Jeanne Crecy)
HANDS OF TERROR, Berkley, 1972.
THE LIGHTNING TREE, Berkley, 1973.
THE WINTER KEEPER, Signet (NAL), 1975.
THE NIGHT HUNTERS, Signet (NAL), 1975.
MY FACE BENEATH THE STONE, Signet (NAL), 1975.
THE EVIL AMONG US, Signet (NAL), 1975.

(as Deirdre Rowan)
DRAGON'S MOUNT, Fawcett, 1973.
SILVER WOOD, Fawcett, 1973.

Historical novels: (as Megan Castell)
THE QUEEN OF A LOVELY COUNTRY, Pocket Books, 1980.

(as Jeanne Foster)
DEBORAH LEIGH, Fawcett, Oct. 1981.
EDEN RICHARDS, Fawcett, 1982.

(as Jeanne Williams)
A LADY BOUGHT WITH RIFLES, Coward McCann, 1976, Pocket Books, 1977.
A WOMAN CLOTHED IN SUN, Coward McCann, 1977, Pocket Books 1978.
BRIDE OF THUNDER, Pocket Books, 1978.
DAUGHTER OF THE SWORD, Pocket Books, 1979.

Family saga: (all as Jeanne Williams)
THE VALIANT WOMEN, Pocket Books, 1980.
HARVEST OF FURY, Pocket Books, 1981.
Note: Jeanne Williams currently has one book under contract to Pocket Books, and one under contract to Fawcett, as Jeanne Foster.

FRANCES ENGLE WILSON

Pseudonyms: Fran Wilson. *B*. Frances Engle, 7/31/22, El Reno, Oklahoma, married Thomas Douglas Wilson, 6/20/42. *Children*: Doug, Pamela. *Education*: English and Speech at the University of Oklahoma (freshman and sophomore years) University of Iowa (junior year), World War II began and I left before my senior year to get married. *Professional associations*: Tulsa Tuesday Writers, Romance Writers of America, Oklahoma Writers Federation Inc. *Awards*: Oklahoma TEPEE Award 1981, given by OWFI. *Genres*: Contemporary romance, Category contemporary. *Agent*: Amy Berkower of Writers House Inc. 21 W. 26th Street. N.Y., N.Y. 10010. *Current residence*: Tulsa, Oklahoma.

Favorite authors and books: Danielle Steel's LOVING and PERFECT STRANGER. Helen Van Slyke, MIXED BLESSING, THE HEART LISTENS, and RICH AND THE RIGHTEOUS. Esther Sager, CHASING RAINBOWS and ONLY TIL DAWN. The books of Robert Nathan, Elizabeth Cadell and Coleen McCullough's THORN BIRDS and of course, Margaret Mitchell's GONE WITH THE WIND.

Thoughts on writing: I've always enjoyed reading romance and romantic suspense. I want to write the kind of stories that I myself most like to read, the tender touching love story which moves a reader to laughter and tears. I aim to touch the emotions by creating believeable characters and situations which a reader can identify with. I feel settings are very important. There should be a well drawn sense of place and if the reader can travel to a fascinating and different area in one of my books, all the better. My philosophy of writing is to bring enjoyment and catch the reader up in the story so that he or she really cares what is going to happen to the characters. The best books are those the reader can't put down because he is so involved with the story and the people in it.

Becoming published/finding an agent: Thanks to the encouragement and help of other writers and the support of my engineer husband, I began writing first short stories, personal experience pieces and children's fiction. My early publications were in magazines and one story in a children's anthology. I entered a romantic short story contest of Harlequin Magazine and my story was one of the twelve chosen out of several thousand entries. This gave me heart to try a romantic novel. I attended a novel workshop as well as attending the annual writers conference at the University of Oklahoma. At the latter, I met editors and agents and through one of these editors I sold my first contemporary romance. When I had sold three romances I began seeking an agent in earnest. I feel extremely fortunate because I have received such help and guidance from the editors I've been lucky enough to work with, and instruction and advice from my agent to further my career.

Bibliography:

Category contemporary:
AMBER WINE, Fran Wilson. Silhouette, 1982.

Contemporary romance:
UNTIL SUMMER, Frances Engle Wilson. Bouregy, 1981.

Other:
WHERE MOUNTAINS WAIT, Fran Wilson. Silhouette, 1980. (Young Adult).
Note: Fran Wilson currently has two books under contract with Silhouette.

DAVID M. WIND
Pseudonyms: Monica Barrie, Jennifer Dalton. *B.* David M. Wind, 2/29/44, New York, NY, married Bonnie Marilyn, 1981. *Children:* Lucian. *Education:* Southern Technical Institute, John Marshall University Law School. *Professional associations:* Author's Guild, National Writer's Club, Romance Writers of America. *Genres:* Category contemporary, contemporary, historical romance. *Agent:* Julia Coopersmith Agency, New York, NY. *Current residence:* Pomona, NY.

Favorite authors and books: Jude Deveraux, Kathleen Woodiwiss, Linda Shaw, Jackie Marteen, Barbara Faith.

Thoughts on writing: Writing romance is no different than any type of writing, no matter what the publishing industry thinks. Romance novels serve a purpose: to entertain, to let the readers escape into a different world than they live in. Don't most novels do that? My philosophy of writing is simple: to entertain. To tell a story that the reader can understand, follow, and be a part of.

Becoming published/finding an agent: When I asked an editor friend of mine to critique my first attempt at a novel, she told me she liked my writing style. From there, she gave me a dozen romances to study. I submitted an outline and sold it. From that point my writing career began. With my second novel, I used an agent and found the task of selling a novel easier when an agent handles it.

Bibliography:

Contemporary:
BY INVITATION ONLY Monica Barrie, Gallen, 1982.
WHISPERS OF DESTINY, Jennifer Dalton, Gallen, 1982.
Note: David M. Wind has two books scheduled to be published in the spring of 1983.

LINDA WISDOM
B. Linda Jean Randall, 4/18/50, Santa Monica, California, married Bob, 12/17/71. *Education:* three years college, Golden West College, one year—Journalism major/English minor, one year Fashion Merchandising, one year misc. *Professional associations:* Romance Writers of America, charter member. *Genres*: Category romance. *Agent:* Pat Teal, Teal & Watt Literary Agency, 2036 Vista del Rosa, Fullerton, California 92631. *Current residence*: Fountain Valley, California.

Favorite authors and books: My favorite authors include: Victoria Holt, Janet Dailey, Celeste DeBlasis, Brooke Hastings, Jayne Castle/Stephanie James, Rachel Ryan, Kristin James, June Lund Shiplett.

Thoughts on writing: I've read romance books for as long as I can remember. For me, they're a type of escape. I certainly did that when I read them during my lunch hours! I like to portray my heroes as a little less than perfect; perhaps, a little insecure. I've never known a man I could count as a "10" and I don't know if I'd want one who is! Love and romance are so very important in everyone's life, so why not read about the subject we all enjoy.

Becoming published/finding an agent: I had always enjoyed writing and after getting hooked on Janet Dailey books, I decided to write a romance in early 1978. I wrote it, sent it off to Harlequin and sat down and wrote another. Harlequin sent my book back, but I wasn't going to stop there. This time, both books were sent off to Silhouette which was just getting started. A month later, on my wedding anniversary no less, DANCER IN THE SHADOWS and FOURTEEN KARAT BEAUTY were sold. I met Pat Teal at the Romance Writers of America convention in Houston in 1981 and we had a long, very satisfying talk. She's a great lady to work with. Writing may be harder than many of my other jobs, but it's certainly more satisfying to me. Sometimes, I'm not sure if I'd rather be reading romances or writing them!

Bibliography: (all as Linda Wisdom)

Category contemporary:
DANCERS IN THE SHADOWS, Silhouette, 1980.
FOURTEEN KARAT BEAUTY, Silhouette, 1981.
BRIGHT TOMORROW, Silhouette, 1982.
A MAN WITH DOUBTS, Silhouette, 1982.
DREAMS FROM THE PAST, Silhouette, 1982.
Note: Linda Wisdom currently has two books under contract with Silhouette.

KATHLEEN E. WOODIWISS
B. Alexandria, La., married Ross Woodiwiss. *Children*: Three sons. *Education*: Attended schools in Alexandria, La. *Genres*: Historical romance. *Current residence*: Minnesota.

Bibliography: (All historical romance)
THE FLAME AND THE FLOWER, Avon, 1972.
THE WOLF AND THE DOVE, Avon, 1974.
SHANNA, Avon, 1977.

ASHES IN THE WIND, Avon, 1979.
A ROSE IN WINTER, Avon, 1982.

CYNTHIA WRIGHT

Pseudonyms: Devon Lindsay. *B*. Cynthia Challed, 4/1/53, Cedar Rapids, Iowa, married Richard Allen Wright, 1972. *Children*: Jennifer. *Education*: University of Iowa. *Genres*: Historical romance. *Agent*: Charles Schlessiger, Brandt and Brandt Literary Agency, 1501 Broadway, New York, NY. *Current residence*: East Lyme, CT.

Favorite authors and books: Kathleen Woodiwiss—especially SHANNA and THE WOLF AND THE DOVE; Margaret Mitchell; Alexandra Sellers (CAPTIVE OF DESIRE); Beatrice Small (LOVE WILD AND FAIR), Georgette Heyer—especially BEAUVALLET; Jennifer Wilde; Shirlee Busbee; Jude Deveraux.

Thoughts on writing: I was a fan for years. In fact, I spent months writing a sequel to GONE WITH THE WIND when I was fourteen. (My parents were dubious about this pastime—if we'd only known!) After my daughter's birth in 1973, I discovered Barbara Cartland, Kathleen Woodiwiss, Georgette Heyer, etc., which led to CAROLINE. I agree that romances are predominately for escape, but an author can give a great deal more to her readers. I don't want to sound pretentious, but I do feel that the creation of human, warm characters and situations can lend itself to subtle messages such as the value of women's talents and opinions.

Becoming published/finding an agent: I sold CAROLINE in 1977 without an agent. I had merely followed the instructions in WRITER'S MARKET—query letters to three publishers—until I struck gold at Ballantine. I signed a contract with them for three more books, but now I do have an agent. He contacted me after reading CAROLINE, and we had an instant rapport. I value his advice, support, and friendship . . . and his ability to intercede in touchy situations.

Bibliography:

Historical romance:
CAROLINE, Ballantine, 1977.

TOUCH THE SUN, Ballantine, 1978.
SILVER STORM, Ballantine, 1979.
CRIMSON INTRIGUE, Richard Gallen Books, 1981.
Note: Cynthia Wright currently has two books under contract with Ballantine, one scheduled for publication in 1983, the other in 1984.

PATRICIA WRIGHT
Pseudonyms: Mary Napier. *B.* Mary Patricia Matthews, Warlingham, Surrey, U.K., married Richard Mounsteven Wright, 4/25/59. *Children:* Katherine, Penny. *Education:* Professional associate of the Royal Institution of Chartered Surveyors and Land Agents, 1955. After marriage took a postal degree in history from the University of London, 1st class honours, 1967. *Professional associations:* International PEN. *Genres:* Historial—harder-cored than straight romance. I always take great care with research and background. Thrillers—contemporary and romantic. *Agent:* Carol Smith, 25 Hornton Court, Kensington High Street, London W8. *Current residence:* Frant, Sussex, England.

Favorite authors and books: HORSEMAN RIDING BY, trilogy by R.D. Delderfield; Dorothy Dunnett's "Lymard" books; Anya Seton's KATHERINE as an example of how to make a difficult period live for the modern reader; some of Georgette Heyer, especially THE GRAND SOPHY.

Thoughts on writing: I have always loved history and found it deeply interesting, although before marriage I qualified as a surveyor (realtor). So my first attempts at writing were nonfiction, but I came across the letters of an ancestress who went to Russia as a governess in the 1850s, and they were so fascinating—and Russia a special interest of mine—that I decided to use them as the basis of a novel—A SPACE OF THE HEART, which I was lucky enough to get published in the States as well as England. I followed it with a sequel on twentieth-century Russia, JOURNEY INTO FIRE, which was also successful and have never stopped writing since! Although things have become more difficult of late, I thoroughly enjoy the opportunities to explore contemporary themes in thrillers under the pseudonym of Mary Napier.

Becoming published/finding an agent: I found Carol Smith as my agent through fury with a publisher who refused to make up his mind or answer letters when I switched from non-fiction to fiction. It was before she set up on her own and she was recommended as a hard worker—she is and we clicked!

Bibliography:

Historicals (all as Patricia Wright)
SPACE OF THE HEART, Doubleday,1976.
JOURNEY INTO FIRE, Doubleday, 1977.
SHADOW OF THE ROCK, Doubleday, 1978.
HEART OF THE STORM (STORM HARVEST in U.K.), Doubleday, 1979.
STORMS OF FATE (THIS, MY CITY in U.K.), Doubleday, 1981.
WHILE PARIS DANCED, Doubleday, 1982.

Romantic thrillers: (all as Mary Napier):
THE WATCHING. Bantam, 1980.
FORBIDDEN PLACES, Coward McCann, 1981. (Bantam paperback projected 1982-3).

Non-romance books:
WOMAN'S ESTATE, Mary Napier, Rupert Hart-Davies, pub., 1959—nonfiction on being a woman in the real-estate world.
CONFLICT ON THE NILE, Patricia Wright, Heinemann, pub., 1972—nonfiction on an historical theme.

JOAN ZIEG
Pseudonyms: Alicia Meadowes (Pseudonym shared with co-author, Linda Burak). *Children:* Tracy. *Education:* B.S. Edinboro College, education. M.A. Gannon University, Erie, PA., English literature. *Genres:* Contemporary, historical romance, Regency. *Agent:* Denise Marcil, 316 W. 82nd Street, New York, NY. *Current residence:* Erie, PA.

Favorite authors and books: Georgette Heyer, Jane Austen, and especially Charlotte Bronte. I reread JANE EYRE at least once a year.

Thoughts on writing: I read Regencies for years because I thrive on elegance and gallantry, which are pure escapist pleasures for anyone immersed in the twentieth century—with its blue jean mentality. I regard romances as popular entertainment that has as much validity as television. I have no delusions that I write "literature."

Becoming published/finding an agent: My sister and I collaborated on a delightful experiment that turned out to be published. After two books, we sought an agent through the Author's Guild, and selected Denise Marcil because she specialized in romance.

Bibliography:

Regency:
SWEET BRAVADO, Warner Books, 1978.
TENDER TORMENT, Warner Books, 1979.
Note: Joan Zieg currently has two books under contract, one with the Banbury/Dell series, "Woman of Destiny," the other with Avon's "Finding Mr. Right" series.

Guide To Authors' Pseudonyms

Curzon, Lucia	Stevenson, Florence
Daley, Kathleen	Daley, Margaret
Dalton, Gena	Dellin, Genell Smith
Dalton, Jennifer	Wind, David M.
Daniels, Max	Gellis, Roberta
Davidson, Andrea	Lowe, Susan L.
Dee, Sheryl	Flournoy, Sheryl Hines
DePaul, Edith	Delatush, Edith G.
Deveraux, Jude	White, Jude Gilliam
Diamond, Jacqueline	Hyman, Jackie Diamond
Douglas, Casey	Casey, June
Douglass, Billie	Delinsky, Barbara
Dozier, Zoe	Browning, Dixie Burrus
Drake, Bonnie	Delinsky, Barbara
Duvall, Aimee	Thurlo, Aimee
Eden, Laura	Harrison, Claire
Edwards, Andrea	Kolaczyk, Anne
Erickson, Lynn	Peltonen, Carla and Swanton, Molly
Evans, Claire	DeLong, Claire
Faire, Zabrina	Stevenson, Florence
Fairfax, Ann	Gibbons, Marion Chesney
Fairfield, Darryl	Larkin, Rochelle
Fecher, Constance	Heaven, Constance
Ferris, Valerie	Ferris, Rose Marie
Ford, Jessie	Osborne, Jessie
Foster, Jeanne	Williams, Jeanne
Francis, Sharon	Wartski, Maureen Ann
Granger, Katherine	Sederquest, Mary Fanning
Greer, Francesca	Janas, Frankie-Lee
Gregory, Lisa	Camp, Candace
Guest, Diane	Biondi, Diane Guest
Habersham, Elizabeth	Harper, Shannon and Porter, Madeline
Hamilton, Priscilla	Gellis, Roberta
Harmston, Olivia	Weber, Nancy
Harper, Elaine	Hallin, Emily Watson
Harper, Felicia	Hurd, Florence
Harrowe, Fiona	Hurd, Florence
Hart, Shirley	Larson, Shirley Cox
Hastings, Brooke	Gordon, Deborah H.
Hillary, Anne	Kolaczyk, Anne
Hiller, Flora	Hurd, Florence

Hope, Jacqueline	Hacsi, Jacqueline Hope
Howard, Eleanor	Hodgson, Eleanor
Howard, Lynde	Howard, Lyn
Hunt, Jena	Conrad, Helen
Hutton, Ann	Hutton, Audrey Grace
James, Amalia	Neggers, Carla A.
James, Anna	Harper, Shannon and Porter, Madeline
James, Arlene	Rather, Deborah Arlene
James, Kristin	Camp, Candace
James, Robin	Curtis, Sharon and Tom
James, Stephanie	Krentz, Jayne Ann
Janes, Josephine	Heland, Victoria J.
Jeffries, Julia	Wand, Lynda Catherine
Jewell, Amalia	Neggers, Carla A.
Jordan, Laura	Brown, Sandra
Joyce, Janet	Bieber, Janet and Thies, Joyce
Kavanagh, Ian	Bringle, Mary
Kaye, Joanne	Payes, Rachel Cosgrove
Kent, Katherine	Dial, Joan
Kidd, Elisabeth	Triegel, Linda
Kingston, Meredith	Brucker, Meredith Babeaux
Kyle, Marlaine	Hager, Jean
Lacy, Tira	Estrada, Rita Clay
LaDame, Cathryn	Baldwin, Cathy Jo LaDame
Ladd, Cathryn	Baldwin, Cathy Jo LaDame
Lane, Megan	Himrod, Brenda
Larkin, R.T.	Larkin, Rochelle
Lindley, Meredith	Brucker, Meredith Babeaux
Lindsay, Devon	Wright, Cynthia
London, Laura	Curtis, Sharon and Tom
Lord, Vivian	Strother, Pat Wallace
Loren, Amii	Hohl, Joan M.
Lorrimer, Claire	Clark, Patricia
Louis, Jacqueline	Hacsi, Jacqueline Hope
Lowery, Lynn	Hahn, Lynn Lowery
MacDonnell, Megan	Stevens, Serita
Mack, Dorothy	McKittrick, Dorothy
Major, Ann	Cleaves, Margaret Ann
Mansfield, Elizabeth	Schwartz, Paula
Mansfield, Libby	Schwartz, Paula
March, Jill	Aufdem-Brinke, Eleanor R.

Marchant, Catherine	Cookson, Catherine
Martel, Aimee	Thurlo, Aimee
Martin, Prudence	Lichte, Prudence Bingham
Mason, Hilary	Roddick, Barbara
Matthews, Laura	Rotter, Elizabeth
McAllister, Amanda	Hager, Jean
McConnell, Lisa	McCourtney, Lorena
McDonnell, Megan	Stevens, Serita
McKay, Rena	McCourtney, Lorena
Meadowes, Alice	Burak, Linda and Zieg, Joan
Melville, Jennie	Butler, Gwendolin
Merlin, Christina	Heaven, Constance
Michaels, Kristin	Williams, Jeanne
Michaels, Margie	McDonnell, Margie
Milan, Angel	Lynn, Mary
Monteith, Hayton	Mittermeyer, Helen M.
Moore, Patti	Daley, Margaret
Morgan, Alyssa	Delatush, Edith G.
Morgan, Raye	Conrad, Helen
Morris, Kathleen	Bringle, Mary
Napier, Mary	Wright, Patricia
Nash, Noreen	Siegel, Noreen
North, Sara	Bonham, Barbara
North, Sara	Hager, Jean
O'Brien, Saliee	Janas, Frankie-Lee
Palmer, Diana	Kyle, Susan
Parker, Laura	Castoro, Laura Ann
Patrick, Susan	Clark, Patricia
Pemberton, Nan	Pykare, Nina Coomb
Phillips, Dorothy	Garlock, Dorothy
Phillips, Joanna	Garlock, Dorothy
Phillips, Pat	Phillips, Patricia Sonia
Phillips, Patricia	Phillips, Patricia Sonia
Phillips, Sonia	Phillips, Patricia Sonia
Powers, Nora	Pykare, Nina Coombs
Pykare, Nina	Pykare, Nina Coombs
Randolph, Elise	Lowe, Susan L.
Ransom, Katherine	Sederquest, Mary Fanning
Ravenlock, Constance	Casey, June
Reynolds, Anne	Steinke, Ann E.
Reynolds, Elizabeth	Steinke, Ann E.

Ripy, Margaret	Daley, Margaret
Robbins, Kay	Hooper, Kay
Robbins, Patricia	Clark, Patricia
Roberts, Nora	Aufdem-Brinke, Eleanor R.
Roberts, Paula	Hohl, Joan M.
Roland, Michelle	Ferris, Rose Marie
Rose, Jennifer	Weber, Nancy
Rose, Marcia	Kamien, Marcia and Novak, Rose
Ross, Susan	Jamison, Susan
Rowan, Deirdre	Williams, Jeanne
Royal, Vanessa	Hinkmeyer, Michael Thomas
Ryan, Rachel	Brown, Sandra
St. Claire, Erin	Brown, Sandra
St. George, Edith	Delatush, Edith G.
St. John, Claire	Harrison, Claire
Sheryl, Diane	Flournoy, Sheryl Hines
Shore, Anne	Sanford, Annette
Shore, Francine	Wartski, Maureen Ann
Simmons, Suzanne	Guntrum, Suzanne
Simms, Suzanne	Guntrum, Suzanne
Sinclair, James	Staples, Reginald Thomas
Starr, Anne	Sanford, Annette
Stephens, Jeanne	Hager, Jean
Stevens, Serita	Stevens, Serita M.G.
Stevens, Lynsey	Howard, Lyn
Stevens, Robert Tyler	Staples, Reginald Thomas
Stevens, Sharon	Camp, Candace
Taylor, Day	Parkinson, Cornelia M. and Salvato,
Thorton, Carolyn	Thorton, Carolyn Stromeyer
Towers, Regina	Pykare, Nina Coombs
Tremaine, Jennie	Gibbons, Marion Chesney
Trent, Brenda	Himrod, Brenda
Tucker, Elaine	Camp, Deborah
Vaughn, Victoria	Heland, Victoria J.
Vitek, Donna	Vitek, Donna Kimel
Walker, Elizabeth	Rotter, Elizabeth
Walker, Elizabeth Neff	Rotter, Elizabeth
Wallace, Pat	Strother, Pat Wallace
Ward, Lynda	Ward, Lynda Catherine
West, Lindsay	Weber, Nancy
Whitnell, Barbara	Hutton, Audrey Grace

Williams, Anne	Steinke, Ann E.
Wilson, Fran	Wilson, Frances Engle
York, Amanda	Dial, Joan

Guide To Authors' Sub-genres*

Category contemporary
Andrews, Barbara
Aufdem-Brinke, Eleanor R.
Baldwin, Cathy Jo LaDame
Bieber, Janet
Boeckman, Charles and Patti
Bonds, Parris Afton
Brown, Sandra
Browning, Dixie Burrus
Brucker, Meredith Babeaux
Burak, Linda
Calloway, Jo
Camp, Candace
Camp, Deborah
Candlish, Jasmine Cresswell
Casey, June
Chambers, Ginger
Chase, Elaine Raco
Chittenden, Margaret
Cleaves, Margaret Ann
Conrad, Helen
Christina, Hella Cott
Curtis, Sharon and Tom
Dailey, Janet
Daley, Margaret
Delatush, Edith G.
Delinsky, Barbara
Dellin, Genell Smith
DeLong, Claire
Douglas, Carole Nelson
Estrada, Rita Clay
Ferris, Rose Marie
Flournoy, Sheryl Hines
Garlock, Dorothy

*For definitions of the romance sub-genres, see page 61.

Gluyas, Constance
Gordon, Deborah H.
Gross, Susan Ellen
Guntrum, Suzanne
Hacsi, Jacqueline Hope
Hager, Jean
Hallin, Emily Watson
Harper, Olivia
Harrison, Claire
Heland, Victoria J.
Himrod, Brenda
Hohl, Joan M.
Hooper, Kay
Howard, Lyn
Hurd, Florence
Kolaczyk, Anne
Krentz, Jayne Ann
Kyle, Susan
Larson, Shirley Cox
Lichte, Prudence Bingham
Lowe, Susan L.
Lynn, Mary
McCourtney, Lorena
McDonnell, Margie
Mittermeyer, Helen M.
Morgan, Alice
Neggers, Carla A.
Osborne, Jessie
Palencia, Elaine Fowler
Pianka, Phyllis Taylor
Pykare, Nina Coombs
Rather, Deborah Arlene
Rydzynski, Marie
Sanford, Annette
Sederquest, Mary Fanning
Sellers, Alexandra
Shaw, Linda
Spencer, LaVyrle
Stanford, Sondra
Steinke, Ann E.
Stevenson, Florence
Strother, Pat Wallace
Thiels, Kathryn Gorsha

Thies, Joyce
Thorton, Carolyn Stromeyer
Thurlo, Aimee
Vitek, Donna Kimel
Ward, Linda Catherine
Wartski, Maureen Ann
Weber, Nancy
Wilson, Frances Engle
Wind, David M.
Wisdom, Linda
Zieg, Joan

Contemporary

Bradley, Muriel
Bringle, Mary
Butler, Gwendoline
Camp, Candace
Dailey, Janet
Daveson, Mons
Delatush, Edith G.
Dial, Joan
Granbeck, Marilyn
Harper, Shannon
High, Monique Raphael
Hutton, Audrey Grace
Jamison, Susan
Janas, Frankie-Lee
Kamien, Marcia
Kolaczyk, Anne
Larkin, Rochelle
Peltonen, Carla
Porter, Madeline
Rogers, Rosemary
Rotter, Elizabeth
Shaw, Linda
Spencer, LaVyrle
Steel, Danielle
Swanton, Molly
Talias, Angela
Thies, Joyce
Wakely, Dorothy Lilley
Williams, Jeanne

Wilson, Frances Engle
Wind, David M.

Edwardian

Gibbons, Marion Chesney

Family saga

Clark, Patricia
Dailey, Janet
Dial, Joan
Gibbons, Marion Chesney
Hahn, Lynn Lowery
Harper, Shannon
Heaven, Constance
High, Monique Raphael
Hutton, Audrey Grace
Janas, Frankie-Lee
Johnson, Barbara Ferry
Lane, Elizabeth
Porter, Madeline
Roddick, Barbara
Strother, Pat Wallace
Thompson, Joan
Williams, Jeanne

Georgian

Ley, Alice Chetwynd
McBain, Laurie

Gothic

Alexander, Marsha
Blickle, Katrinka
Clark, Patricia
DeBlasis, Celeste N.
Douglas, Carole Nelson
Harper, Shannon
Hurd, Florence
Matthews, Patricia Anne
Payes, Rachel Cosgrove

Stevenson, Florence
Williams, Jeanne

Historical romance

Aiken, Joan
Bieber, Janet
Blickle, Katrinka
Bonds, Parris Afton
Bonham, Barbara
Bradley, Murial
Brandewyne, Rebecca
Bringle, Mary
Brown, Sandra
Burak, Linda
Busbee, Shirlee
Butler, Gwendoline
Calloway, Jo
Camp, Candace
Carsley, Anne
Castoro, Laura Ann
Chester, Deborah
Clark, Patricia
Cleaves, Margaret Ann
Conway, Theresa
Corcoran, Barbara
Curtis, Sharon and Tom
De Blasis, Celeste N.
Delatush, Edith G.
Dial, Joan
Douglas, Carole Nelson
Gallagher, Rita
Garlock, Dorothy
Gellis, Roberta
Gluyas, Constance
Granbeck, Marilyn
Gross, Susan Ellen
Grundman, Donna A.
Hagan, Patricia
Hahn, Lynn Lowery
Harper, Shannon
Heaven, Constance
High, Monique Raphael

Hinkmeyer, Michael Thomas
Hodge, Jane Aiken
Hodgson, Eleanor
Howe, Susanna
Hurd, Florence
Janas, Frankie-Lee
Johnson, Barbara Ferry
Johnson, Susan M.
Lane, Elizabeth
Larkin, Rochelle
Matthews, Patricia Anne
Morse, Nancy
Neggers, Carla A.
Osborne, Jessie
Parkinson, Cornelia M.
Peltonen, Carla
Phillips, Patricia Sonia
Porter, Madeline
Pykare, Nina Coombs
Roddick, Barbara
Rogers, Rosemary
Salvato, Sharon
Shaw, Linda
Siegel, Noreen
Small, Bertrice
Spencer, LaVyrle
Staples, Reginald Thomas
Stevens, Serita M.G.
Stevenson, Florence
Strother, Pat Wallace
Swanton, Molly
Talias, Angela
Thiels, Kathryn Gorsha
Thies, Joyce
Thompson, Joan
White, Jude Gilliam
Williams, Jeanne
Wind, David M.
Woodiwiss, Kathleen E.
Wright, Cynthia
Wright, Patricia
Zieg, Joan

Regency

Aiken, Joan
Burak, Linda
Candlish, Jasmine Cresswell
Casey, June
Chester, Deborah
Curtis, Sharon and Tom
Delatush, Edith G.
Gibbons, Marion Chesney
Hager, Jean
Heland, Victoria J.
Hodge, Jane Aiken
Hooper, Kay
Hyman, Jackie Diamond
Kolaczyk, Anne
LeCompte, Jane
Ley, Alice Chetwynd
Lichte, Prudence Bingham
McBain, Laurie
McKittrick, Dorothy
Metzger, Barbara
Pianka, Phyllis Taylor
Pykare, Nina Coombs
Rotter Elizabeth
Schwartz, Paula
Stevenson, Florence
Triegel, Linda
Wakeley, Dorothy Lilley
Ward, Lynda Catherine
Zieg, Joan

Romantic suspense

Biondi, Diane Guest
Bonham, Barbara
Chase, Elaine Raco
Chittenden, Margaret
Dial, Joan
Hager, Jean
Heaven, Constance
Hinkmeyer, Michael Thomas

Hodge, Jane Aiken
Whitney, Phyllis

Victorian

Aiken, Joan
Candlish, Jasmine Cresswell
Janas, Jackie-Lee
McBain, Laurie
Wakeley, Dorothy Lilley

Non-romance titles (incl. fantasy, general fiction, mysteries, occult, non-fiction, biography, thrillers, and young adult novels)

Aiken, Joan
Alexander, Marsha
Bringle, Mary
Chase, Elaine Raco
De Blasis, Celeste N.
Dellin, Genell Smith
Douglas, Carole Nelson
Hager, Jean
Hallin, Emily Watson
Hinkmeyer, Michael Thomas
Hodge, Jane Aiken
Johnson, Susan M.
Lane, Elizabeth
Larkin, Rochelle
Matthews, Patricia Anne
Payes, Rachel Cosgrove
Pianka, Phyllis Taylor
Steinke, Ann E.
Stevens, Serita M.G.
Stevenson, Florence
Strother, Pat Wallace
Thompson, Joan
Wartski, Maureen Ann
Weber, Nancy
Whitney, Phyllis
Williams, Jeanne
Wilson, Frances Engle
Wright, Patricia